THE VALLEY OF SILENCE

CONTRIBUTORS:

MARIAN RECHOWICZ

STEFAN CARDINAL WYSZYŃSKI

MIECZYSŁAW GOGACZ

WINCENTY GRANAT

JÓZEF PASTUSZKA

MIECZYSŁAW KRĄPIEC

ZDZISŁAW PAPIERKOWSKI

JERZY KŁOCZOWSKI

ALEKSANDER KOSSOWSKI

JAN TUROWSKI

JERZY OZDOWSKI

JÓZEF MAJKA

STEFAN KUNOWSKI

PRZEMYSŁAW MROCZKOWSKI

STANISŁAW MICHALCZUK

MIECZYSŁAW ŻYWCZYŃSKI

STEFAN SAWICKI

LEOKADIA MAŁUNOWICZ

THE VALLEY OF SILENCE

Catholic Thought in Contemporary Poland

EDITED BY

JAMES J. ZATKO

UNIVERSITY OF NOTRE DAME PRESS

NOTRE DAME AND LONDON

To
MY
PARENTS
PAUL AND MARY ZATKO

EDITOR'S PREFACE

THE REASON FOR PUBLISHING THIS BOOK SHOULD BE FAIRLY OBVIOUS from the title. The very idea of Catholic thought in contemporary Poland seemed intriguing. But the decisive reason is, of course, the intrinsic value of the material. While the anthology is generally restricted to the ubiquitous problem of God, man, and society, these writings reveal the vigor abounding among the Catholic intellectuals in Poland. The writers and thinkers represented in this anthology are certainly not isolated from Poland's contemporary problems; nor are they content with the boring repetition of tired and weary formulas (sometimes the characteristic of Catholic "thought"). They create new viewpoints, wrestle with unexpected and often agonizing problems, and fearlessly attack unexplored areas. It is, indeed, unfortunate that the limitations of space prevented a wider scope of the varied and rich veins of Catholic thought in Poland.

As to the principle of choice, the central theme of society, man, and religion dictated the selection, except that circumstances suggested the inclusion of material that may seem remote from this vital theme. I refer to the historical, literary, and artistic selections. It seemed to me very important to stress emphatically the Catholic past in Poland's history and its cultural contribution, which in so many ways moulded Polish society, its religion, and its people.

It remains for me to thank my many good friends, true and loyal, at the Catholic University of Lublin; they have been kind and generous to me, and throughout they have had the patience of a midwife in the difficult task of editing across thousands of miles of sea. I hope this anthology will reveal the Catholic University's vitality and fix world attention on its important function in Polish society. Unfortunately a more complete presentation of the splendid work done by these scholars is impossible. In originality of subject matter and perfection of method, their creative achievements can certainly serve as an inspiration and model for the many Catholic universities that have lately embarked on the pursuit of excellence.

For me personally the anthology has been a rewarding effort. Through it I have experienced the exhilarating and intimate contact with acute and judicious minds. I recall the penetrating intelligence of my good friend Professor Mieczysław Żywczyński, whose insights raise his work so far above the "dry-as-dust" chronicler of obscure events.

Miss Emily Schossberger, director of the University Press at the University of Notre Dame, must receive special recognition for her interest, kindness, and generosity. The high quality of the Press' publications derives very much from her unfailing inspiration.

And so here, within sound of the Pacific and in the very shadows of the Santa Cruz mountains, I entrust this work of several years to the care and interest of those who will read it.

James J. Zatko

July 16, 1966
Santa Cruz, California

INTRODUCTION

IN AUGUST 1958 THE CATHOLIC UNIVERSITY IN LUBLIN WELCOMED A
delegation from two universities in the United States. The delegation consisted of the then vice-president of the University of
Notre Dame, Father Philip S. Moore, C.S.C., and Professor Nor-
man J. G. Pounds of Indiana University. This small delegation
came to Poland by means of invitation, sponsored by educational
foundations, in order to arrange an exchange for the professors
and students from the Catholic University of Lublin, as well as
from the oldest university in Poland, in Cracow, and those from
American universities. Political difficulties made it impossible to
realize this plan. Nevertheless, in the same year the Catholic
University welcomed a guest, from the University of Notre Dame,
Father James J. Zatko, Ph.D. (presently at Loras College, Dubu-
que, Iowa), who devoted several months to gathering material
on the fortunes and history of the Eastern and Western Churches
in Eastern Europe. Father Zatko used his time to great advantage.
Not only had he taken with him vast amounts of material for
scholarly publication, but also established close friendships and
contacts with many of the professors and lecturers at the Lublin
university, thus having become well acquainted with its educational, scientific, and publishing endeavors.

The Catholic world certainly knows what the Catholic University is in Poland and recognizes it as the only university which
from an ideological viewpoint implements a scientific and educational concept differing from that of the government. Western
Catholicism is also aware that this University not merely exists,
but that after 1956 it had expanded its activity to a significant
degree—in spite of political difficulties. In Poland the University
is subject to the Polish episcopate, headed by Stefan Cardinal
Wyszyński, who is the chairman of the Episcopal Commission for
the Affairs of the Catholic University of Lublin. The University
also depends on the hundreds of thousands of members belonging

Introduction

to the *Towarzystwo Przyjaciół K.U.L.* (association of benefactors). It depends, therefore, on the whole of Catholic society, which sees in the existence of the University and its work a criterion of its own freedom.

Outside of Poland, many circles of the above mentioned Friends of the Catholic University in Poland continue their activity. Such circles, for instance, in Trenton, Toronto, and London, possess charters from their political and ecclesiastical authorities and are completely autonomous and independent of the authorities of the Catholic University in Lublin.

The Catholic University of Lublin is affiliated with the *Association Internationale des Universités* (UNESCO) and *Catholicarum Universitatum Foederatio.*

A particular bond of friendship unites the professors and students of the Catholic University in Lublin with the Catholic University in Washington, with the University of Notre Dame, and with Fordham University in the United States; and in Europe with the Catholic Universities of Louvain and Lille. Close bonds exist between the Catholic University of Lublin and the great youth organization, the *Pax Romana.* Knowledge about the Catholic University of Lublin has been spread in foreign areas by the scholarly travels of its professors and students, perhaps less frequent today. The University publications, exchanged with other centers of learning and publishers in the world, fulfill the same function.

The University publishes a tri-monthly, *Zeszyty Naukowe K. U.L.,* which contains scholarly work and a chronicle. A particularly meritorious publication is the *Annales,* issued in four series: Theological-Canonical, Philosophical, Humanities, and Social Studies. Another of the University's periodicals is *Archiwa, Biblioteki, i Muzea Kościelne,* which contains information on scholarly trends in the field of Church history.

The *Towarzystwo Naukowe K.U.L.* publishes the scholarly monographs of its professors and lecturers. The works of the Catholic University scholars are also being published elsewhere.

Catholics as well as non-Catholics in the West are frequently informed of the existence and activity of the Lublin university. Unfortunately, the University's publications appear in Polish* and reach only a limited number of readers, those who know Slavonic

---

* The publications of the Catholic University of Lublin are printed in Polish; only short summaries are provided in French or in English.

languages. Therefore, the task of composing and publishing in English an anthology of writings by the professors of the Catholic University is particularly valuable for us, and it testifies to the great friendship and unity of ideas manifested by our Catholic universities.

To Father Theodore M. Hesburgh, C.S.C., president of the University of Notre Dame, and to Father Zatko, as well as to all those who contributed in any way to the appearance of this publication, I express heartfelt thanks for their expenditure of mind and heart in the composition of this book.

Marian Rechowicz
Rector
Catholic University
of Lublin

CONTENTS

Contents

I walk down the Valley of Silence—
Down the dim, voiceless valley—alone!
And I hear not the fall of a footstep
Around me, save God's and my own; . . .
                    Abram J. Ryan

CHRISTIAN MORALITY AND

POLISH YOUTH

Stefan Cardinal Wyszyński

I. IS CHRISTIAN MORALITY RELEVANT?

IS CHRISTIAN MORALITY STILL RELEVANT? TIME AND TIME AGAIN, especially in the press, we find discussions on this subject addressed to young people. And we know the intent of the questions. I think it is possible to give an answer, even though it would apply only to the life of one human being, which means that if Christian morality produces full fruit in the life of but one individual, then it is relevant. For it was thus, by the resurrection of one man, that St. Paul believes resurrection is possible. If Christ has not risen from the dead, then vain is our hope, and vain is our faith. But Christ did rise from the dead; hence, how is it possible to say that there is no resurrection? If there is no resurrection, then Christ has not risen from the dead. But he did rise, and so there is a resurrection.

Let us pause then over the question whether Christian morality is relevant. It suffices to consider the life of one human being and here we have an adequate answer. We can even add that this one human being reached the fullness of Christian morality in his youthful years. St. Stanisław Kostka was but eighteen when he died; therefore, it is possible to achieve the fullness of Christian morality in a short time—in this case called holiness—which means that it is truly relevant.

In the life of the Church there are even more eloquent examples. Sometimes even children achieved this fullness of holiness, like Maria Goretti, or the young friend of St. John Bosco, Dominic Savio. God himself cooperates with the will of man, his mind,

1

and his heart. He cooperates through a faith that he himself awakens, through a grace that he alone gives, through a holy love that only he can arouse. It is God himself who is effective in us. There is no need of prolonged time or life in order to achieve the fullness of perfection, although that is often the ideal and desire of human beings.

II. THE CHURCH DOES NOT FEAR YOUTHFUL POLAND

Normally youth is extremely impulsive, with arms uplifted to everything that is noble and good, that is nobler and better, that is noblest and the best. This is a characteristic of youth.

Examples of this drive toward freedom, toward the fullness of life, are found in nature itself. Is youth not charmed by the beauty of plant life awakening in the spring? Who can block the flow of life-energy to the buds that draw it from the earth? Everything rushes upward, expands, is transformed into leaf, into flower, into fruit. In the springtime we admire the abundance and bounty of nature in the blossoming apple trees, cherry trees, and shrubs, which like a bride adorn themselves with a veil of joy.

Thus we find that all of nature is an image and picture of God, who himself is inexhaustible energy, forever young and never ancient. For God is great beyond time. His fathomless energy expresses itself in the created world, operating through the countless phenomena of awakening and developing life.

God does not grow old. As a Father, he is full of energy; he does not fear the young, and through the parents that fulfill his will and commandments he sends the young out into the world. The God of old does not fear the youthful generations, who are sometimes feared by those who have conquered and mastered the earth. Youth always awakens joy. If we develop normally, even when we get old, we do not fear the young; on the contrary, we rejoice in them, smile at them, and have confidence in them.

Who, if not the Church, rejoices in youth and always maintains contact with it? It is not only the young priests who rejoice —as we hear in the Mass: "I shall go to the altar of God, the God who is the joy of my youth"—but also all priests rejoice in them, even the aged ones who with unsteady hands pour water on a small head and say "Receive the salt of wisdom . . . I baptize you. . . ." These aged ones smile at youthful Poland as it comes for the first time to the altar of the Lord. Young Poland comes to receive new life. There is one kind of life received from the mother, but now youth desires to be born again of water and the Holy Spirit. Although the Church is ancient (almost two thousand years), it is always young, constantly becoming youthful. For it always baptizes, always embraces young generations, and blesses them in song: "Come Holy Spirit."

III. HARMONY AND UNITY IN MAN

The Church is courageous in the presence of youth and trusts it. It forms youth effectively, as it formed young Stanisław, Gemma Galgani, Maria Goretti, Aloysius, John Berchmans, and so many, many youthful hearts. However, it expects the formation of youth to be harmonious and interrelated in all things. The formation of man must strive toward the image and likeness of God. God, the Father of man, had so formed man that in him exists an amazing tendency toward unity and harmony.

Although man is composed of body and soul, the body needs the soul and the soul exists and feels its best in the body. Blessed is the man in whom the spirit is bound to the body and the body with the spirit. But woe to him, if there is a dissolution or a division, and each goes its own way—the deeds of the flesh or the deeds of the spirit. Blessed is the man where all this remains united in him. It is, indeed, a marvelous property of man that such elements as matter, body, and soul are diametrically different, and yet exist together in harmonious cooperation—thus forming a true and complete man. This is true of man's psyche. Only the harmonious cooperation of mind, will, and heart give full humanity.

God is one, and his Son prayed for unity: "Father, that they be one." For this reason he called into existence the Church, which works to form and to strengthen unity. Christ himself does all things in unity. *Qui facit utraque unum.* And he left us the ideal of defeating the rampant divergences for the good of the unified psyche of the human personality.

IV. YOUTH STRIVES FOR A SYNTHESIS

Another characteristic of youth is the desire to attempt all things. This is not a tragedy, even though youth as such lacks the

3

virtues of patience, perseverance, and restraint. Youth does not know how to preserve that which it has achieved and which it has found valuable. It is soon sated with it and seeks further values. Youth at times burns its fingers, cools them, and tries something new. Thanks to this, it knows experimentally the world and the meaning of life. The price of such experience is sometimes high, sometimes too high, but the experience is always useful.

Hence, youth will invariably strive for some kind of synthesis. It is here that the Church comes to be of help to the youth. The Book of Wisdom so beautifully demonstrates this point. God himself ennobles us in our labors and completes them. On the road of life he gives man intelligence, will, and heart; and then he cooperates with man by completing the values of nature through supernatural values, namely, revealed faith, sanctifying grace, and supernatural love. It is here that Catholic education begins.

V. COOPERATION OF REASON AND FAITH

It is man's obligation to test the mind in all branches of knowledge. It is good to test the mind; to submit one's self to examination; not to trust our minds too much; to ask continuously: What is this? Why? Why? But man is free to ask; he must ask; it is his obligation to ask.

God so respects the freedom of the mind that he admits it to the very threshold of faith; and even there he permits man to ask, according to the example of the great master of theology, *Utrum Deus sit?* Though we may be strong in faith, intelligence and Catholic education would have us test even that kind of faith; to this degree therefore and in this unique manner, faith must cooperate with our mind. There cannot be any division here, even though a methodological division is made: the foundation of reason and the foundation of supernatural faith. At times this is necessary, as for instance in theology; however, ultimately, we verify the achievements of pure reason in the light of the faith.

In investigations and in our searchings on the way to God through faith, we must use reason: not *only* reason, but *also* reason. Without the use of reason there is no basis for even the most profound faith.

Only a rational being can believe. Often it is the fault of the rational substance that it does not know how to relate reason with faith. God himself, who gives faith to rational beings, demands from us the ability to relate the two. Woe if man does not relate faith and reason. If reason frees itself from faith, we have rationalism; and if faith frees itself from reason, we have fideism. If, on the other hand, we have an intelligent faith, then we have real Christianity—Catholicism.

In the areas of reason and faith God guarantees freedom. This is assured to rational beings. Only when we achieve freedom of rational action and freedom for acts of faith, do we have real development, progress, and education.

The Church longs for the faith of youth, but yet wants them not to believe blindly. The Church desires that insofar as possible youth deepens its faith by rational process. Theological method permits us to go very far in applying the reasoning process to faith—indeed, to the very gates of mystery. As a result of theological study, the mystery of faith, while always remaining a mystery, recedes before the reasoning process, and man comes closer and closer to the depth of mystery. In human life there comes a time when man's eyes are opened, and that which was a mystery will be seen face to face, even as it is.

VI. COOPERATION OF WILL AND GRACE

This same process occurs in the cooperation of the will with grace. Fundamentally, as philosophy teaches, man's will—even after original sin—by its very nature tends to good. However, this tendency is limited. It comes to certain gates which open to man only if man's good will is strengthened by the grace of God. The most powerful and the best will is all too weak if it is not supported by the power of God acting in our souls. Hence God wishes to be in us and to fill us. God the Father, the Son, and the Holy Spirit wish to dwell in man through grace. Only the cooperation of will and grace provides the unity and internal peace which all men so desire. This is not the peace of repose, but the peace of certainty that enables man to go forward.

VII. NATURAL AND SUPERNATURAL LOVE

There is still another great area of human life, though the philosophers themselves, unable to name it properly, wanted to place it under the control of the mind or of the will. There are, however, those who would distinguish it according to its own sphere, its own dimensions. This is the area of love, the sphere of the heart. It is not clear whether the heart of man is more strongly connected with the will or the mind. There are those who uphold a trichotomy of the powers of the soul; others, however, combat this view energetically.

As we pass over theoretical questions, we see a convincing reality in that our life energy is connected to a great degree with the activity of the heart. We see that everything, even the mind, needs the heart, so that we can attain truth in love. The will needs the heart lest it become egotistical, although the will, too, has its own rights. What is important is that that splendid power which is love and the heart of man become a blessing and not a curse. Here we come across a certain danger, for if the power of love becomes too independent in us, man becomes a slave. And after all, what matters is to be free.

What is needed? That supernatural love come to the assistance of natural love. Where these two loves are united, there is harmony and order.

It does not matter whether love is an independent faculty or a derivative one. It is a powerful force. It influences marvelously the whole area of the will wedded to grace, the whole area of reason connected with faith. Then peace and order follow in the life of man.

THE CULTURAL ROLE OF A

CATHOLIC UNIVERSITY

Marian Rechowicz

UNDOUBTEDLY THE ROLE OF A UNIVERSITY, AS WELL AS EVERY SCIEN-
tific institution, is above all in the field of culture. It functions
as a factor that almost officially objectivizes cultural phenomena
arising in the past or the present; in itself, the university is a
group of creators and popularizers.

In the area of creativity and objectivization the university finds
itself in the position of the elite. But creative "elitism" cannot be
confounded with consumptive "elitism." With a certain amount
of satisfaction we declare that today elitism in the sense of consumption is disappearing. The benefits of culture, in its broadest
reaches, both spiritual and material, are shared by the wide social
circles. This phenomenon was expedited by the democratization
of social life, the systematic approximation of the village to the
city and to technology, with their achievements in the press, radio,
television, cinema, the theater, and so on. By every standard this
is a positive phenomenon. It is one of the twentieth century's
recognized titles to pride.

But this is only one side of the problem. The disappearance of
elitism in consumption is accompanied by another. This is a matter of culture not in the sense of consumption but in the sense of
creativity.

During the time of a certain primitivism, creativity in culture,
like consumption, was rather individualized. Such a picture is
particularly clear in material culture. A hundred years ago a
farmer managed to produce the most necessary implements of his
calling. Today, with a mechanized economy, this is impossible.
The same thing can be said of the instruments of every profes-

7

sion, especially in the circumstances that surround our daily lives. With the progress of technology, and expressly with the possibility of using atomic energy, the chances of individual production have almost completely disappeared. The place of the individual has been taken by large associations, scientific and technical, that often employ thousands of trained technicians and highly skilled workers in large combinations. The individual, forced from his position, becomes only one of the links in the institution. The process of technical creativity has thus been basically institutionalized.

Do these same terms find application in the area of spiritual culture? Are the problems of creativity and objectivization on this level also being formed within an institutional structure? It seems that in large measure it is essentially so. If, according to contemporary methodological principles, only social, objectivized facts that are capable of life apart from their creators enter into the treasury of culture, it is certain that the actualization of these facts is conditioned to a high degree by a series of institutions wherein they are born. And even if they are born of individual effort, it is institutionally that they achieve the form of opinion, system, and objectivization. On a lower level of development, institutionalism was not necessary. The majority of philosophical views among the Greeks was objectivized in the market place, and their heroic poems were objectivized by unknown singers as they traveled from castle to castle. But cultures that reached a development corresponding in a measure to the growing spiritual wealth could no longer do without institutions. From antiquity we have examples in the Academy in Athens or the Museum in Alexandria; another typical example, from this viewpoint, would be the universities of the Middle Ages. This in fact occurred because the growing richness of a certain period had become so great, so vast, that an individual could no longer encompass it. Specialization and the development of particular disciplines also contribute to this. Into this world only highly trained minds can move, controlling not only information but also a developed style of creativity in terms of a method of research. The further development of culture in specialized areas demands a deeper and fuller qualification. Because of this, artists must complete their studies in schools of art, physicians in their medical schools, students of humanities in the universities, and engineers in their technical schools. But even this is not enough. In the present flood of literature, *belles-lettres*, as well as specialized, even the intelligent and highly-trained individual feels awed, and he sinks into an ocean of titles and books, into the varied heaps of notes.

To embark on a broader problem, he seeks the support of a group with a stronger or weaker institutional stamp. Hence, there are new institutions of research, there is an increase in bibliographies, bibliographies of bibliographies of bibliographies.

Almost the entire creativity and objectivization of culture (among the few exceptions we must above all reckon art) have in some manner been institutionalized, or at least seek the support of some institution. In this situation the role of the university gains and loses. It gains to the extent that its social function finds a stronger support in the whole social life, and it loses to the extent that the university is no longer alone the highest and universal center of science. Beside it and outside it, other centers develop. What saves the university's situation in this new state of affairs is that it combines science with teaching, that the current of creativity flows together with education and popularization. It must be emphasized that the founders of the Catholic University of Lublin were concerned with its scientific function in a modern age. In a country with a Catholic majority it was perhaps not too necessary to be concerned about educating Catholics—other universities did it as well—but it was necessary to objectivize the vast cultural inheritance on which Christianity had placed its seal in the course of a thousand years. Obviously through Christianity Poland not only entered the political orbit of the West but also rose from her original barbarism. The whole of her spiritual culture—and hence her religion with a concept of man and the world, her morality, her habits, her art, her politics —were transformed in the course of time.

But at the present time we shall not occupy ourselves with history. We are interested in the present form, which is the last link, or rather the latest physiognomy in the dynamic development of the nation. We shall not understand the morphology of that culture, if we do not realize that there are in it objectivized facts, old and new; that the entire multiformed reality of today, in its harmonies and its dissonances, is in some way involved in a constantly transforming current of that very same stream. There flow within it the waters of baptism from a thousand years ago, enforced with new springs down to today. The vast preponderance of believers and churchgoers among us testifies to this. Christianity influenced their religious, philosophical, and social concepts; formed their view of life; influenced the development of language, moral values, educational ideals, and esthetic experiences. In the totality of our culture there are par excellence social religious facts, which must be counted, systematized, objectivized, and directed toward further development. Insofar as they have a general character, all Polish learning is interested in them. But there are some areas of culture, to whose study and to whose further development Catholics are called *ex professo*. They concern such phenomena as the investigation and formulation of the present form of religion; the objectivization of religious creativity in the area of literature; the arts; the investigation of religious usages; the transformation of that which has become deformed; and the harmonization and modernization of elements that conflict with the present age.

With regard to this form of our spiritual treasure, the Catholic University fulfills a twofold function. First of all, it takes part in the program of investigations determined by the cultural policy of the government. In this sense it is not only concerned with the problems of the millennium of Christianity in Poland, but also takes an active part in the preparations for celebrating the millennium. Our scholars share in the work of the Polish Academy of Sciences, the Institute of Literary Research, the Literary Society, and in many national and regional learned societies. The entire humanities program of the Catholic University of Lublin in all its sections implements a scientific and educational program and thus fulfills the cultural plan defined by the proper governmental departments. In its activity the University takes an open position. The existence of the commissions attached to the Learned Society at the Catholic University, the numerous scientific seminars, and the series of public lectures are evidence of this. In organizing seminars our philosophers invited representatives of every tendency. In the public lectures for the academic year 1959–1960 the following subjects were treated: the sociological analysis of the attitudes of the young generation; contemporary art; the political problems of contemporary Poland. Not only were Catholic writers and scholars invited to lecture, but also eminent representatives of other centers. We proceeded from the supposition that Polish reality is one, in spite of ideological conflicts. At the basis of this reality there will be found the common stream of humanistic culture. We know that there will always be ideological conflicts. It is not only the gospels but also the whole history of the world and the history of the church that assure us of this. It must be thus so long as we treat man as a rational and free essence, who in the disturbance of his own existence will seek solutions of the mysteries that surround him. But there is a level without conflict. For us Catholics this is a matter of charity to assure for every man the conditions of a full physical and spiritual development. This attitude requires no explanation at a Catholic institution of learning; it is something natural. Therefore, after due emphasis on the meaning of the ecclesiastical departments, the development of humanistic studies at the Catholic University is most relevant. These studies fulfill not merely an auxiliary role for advanced specialization in history or philology in other departments; nor are they simply necessary for broadening the horizons of general culture and for the creation of a corresponding educational atmosphere; they do, however, guarantee the formation of a humanistic area of cooperation with all people interested in the development and enrichment of Polish culture.

The other function of the University is based on the scientific objectivization of religious culture. From this viewpoint a significant role is played by the faculties of theology, canon law, and philosophy.

During the last academic year the Catholic University published a memorial volume to honor the third of its rectors, Father Jacek Woroniecki. The ideal dominating this eminent scholar and writer was the elevation of the religious culture in our Catholicism. Father Woroniecki accused Polish Catholicism of traditionalism, fideism, sentimentalism, individualism, and so forth. Even though we may not agree with him in everything, we are confronted by the demand for a more scientific handling of historical and present religious problems. From this viewpoint we have been very neglectful. In his time, for instance, the distinguished historian, Władysław Konopczyński, correctly called attention to the fact that in Poland a special journal was being published on the Reformation, but there was not one learned journal devoted to the history of the Catholic Church. The vast veins of religion buried in Polish culture are waiting for scientific statement in the field of faith, morality, customs, sacred art, religious and ascetic literature, specialized religious writing, and so on. And there remain masses of error, falsehood, and misunderstanding of the essential content of Christianity. If, for instance, it is the task of the Academy of Fine Arts to analyze past and contemporary creativity and to distinguish between art and pseudo-creativity, if the higher agricultural schools correct the errors of agriculture, and if medical schools combat incompetence—then the higher ecclesiastical schools face analogous tasks. It is not possible to reproach Polish Catholicism if it does not depend on an institution whose task it is to remove any warping that actually exists. But these are not the only and exclusive tasks. There are others as well. They deal with the popularization of culture that a university is also called upon to perform. These tasks are often related to consumption. However, this assumption is incorrect. Education, teaching, educational activity, a book that popularizes science, the contact of the creator of culture with its consumer—all these form the human being, integrate his spirituality, and belong to the area of most responsible creativity. We must not forget that the externalization of cultural values also depends on those who receive them. The same value can be accepted in different ways. The manner of reception often transforms the value and its final form. These things are not achieved without a dialogue.

ST. ANSELM'S

ONTOLOGICAL ARGUMENT

Mieczysław Gogacz

I. PERSPECTIVES OF INTERPRETATION

AN ADEQUATE INTERPRETATION AND AN UNDERSTANDING OF ANSELM'S thought as he understood it are the purposes of every reading of the texts of the *Proslogion*. Historical evidence shows that every reading of these texts is also an interpretation. It is obviously important that such an interpretation be correlated as much as possible with the times of Anselm and the character of his thought, for only an immanent analysis and criticism can be a justified method of investigation. However, results of analysis and criticism depend on the instrument. A new interpretation has a chance of acceptance only insofar as it uses a more exact investigative apparatus.

If we look at past interpretations negatively, they wandered down erroneous paths. In general, they try to omit everything that disqualifies or disfigures Anselm's thought. If we consider them positively, these interpretations claim that Anselm's argument is a proof of a special kind, but still a rational proof. This conclusion is basic for the interpretation of the whole problem.

I accept the proposition of Gilson that the ontological argument is not theology, or mysticism, and possibly not even philosophy. Anselm's proof has been considered in each of these areas taken separately; there might also be an interesting interpretation that embraces all these areas at once. And there can be an interesting interpretation on the basis of the relationship among theology, mysticism, and philosophy. Evidently, one must consider these groups of problems in their status at Anselm's time, but this does

13

not exclude the application of all the terminological specifications, which are presently actual in science.

Besides this, Gilson examined the proof on the basis of the theory of truth in *De veritate*. And he achieved significant results. There can also be an interesting examination of the argument on the basis of the theories of being which were current in Anselm's time. M. Cruz Hernandez actually distinguished them and called attention to them. Moreover, since Malcolm, in attacking the theory of existence as a perfection, introduced another understanding of existence, namely as act, he examined the argument with the aid of concepts that are current and that violate Kantianism. There can also be an interesting examination of the argument in terms of the theory of the knowledge of existence, insofar as the theory has been made more precise by Maritain, Gilson, and Krąpiec. The basis for this perspective is the problem of causality and the reason of being, in Anselm, so very much inclined to common sense.

P. Evdokimov's article, published in the memorial volume of the Congress at Bec, is much inclined to the investigation and the statement that Anselm was working with the theory of negation in the type of negative theology of a Pseudo-Dionysius. This then leads to the eventual discovery of what, for Anselm, were the specific connections that exist between the content signified by the concept of God and the existence of God. This, then, is not only connected with logic and the theory of knowledge, but also with medieval methodology and the whole metaphysics of Anselm's time.

Malcolm also intends to place a strong accent on the problem of necessity in the relationship existing between the object of the concept of the most perfect being, and most perfect existence, which are both fulfilled in God.

This last perspective in the interpretation of the argument is already a partial indication of the solutions of the new interpretation. A complete answer is given in the article "Le ratio Anselmi en face du problème des relations entre métaphysique et mystique."[1] This was an article for the Anselmian Congress in Bec. But this essay is based on other material and does not consider the relations between metaphysics and mysticism as its main problem.

The point of departure for the above mentioned article was the conflict between Anselm's own theory of knowledge and the theory criticizing him from the position of empiricism and the statement that the *Proslogion* is a rational proof of the existence of an object of faith. Moreover, the article accepted the emphasis raised by Gilson. The search for an answer did not go in the direction suggested by Gilson, an examination of Anselm's theory of knowledge and an examination of the type of thought of Clement of Alexandria. The article arrived at conclusions by an analysis of the theory of the knowledge of existence by the possible intellect, since it assumed that Anselm worked with common sense and with the normal cognitive powers, which Aristotle and then Thomas called the senses, the active and the possible intellect. Anselm proved the existence of concrete things, and he used this common sense knowledge to create the concept "God" from the demonstrated existence of things. The method of Pseudo-Dionysius, revealed in the *Proslogion,* does not permit one to affirm contingent existence of God. Anselm knew perfect and necessary existence either through the method of negation by denying the existence demonstrated with common sense and the possible intellect, or he knew that existence from a mystical experience of his own or other mystics. The article considered the connection between metaphysics and mysticism.

In summary, the proof is placed within the context of the theory of the knowledge of existence and the method of negation, taken from the negative theology of Pseudo-Dionysius. However, this position is obvious: for from the viewpoint of the theory of existence and the method of negation it only glances at the hierarchy of causes and effects established by Gilson in Anselm's texts. That hierarchy shows itself to be not only a thesis in the theory of knowledge close to Neoplatonist metaphysics, but also a method of affirming existence about God by way of negation. Anselm's argument, then, is interpreted in the sense that the knowledge of existence by common sense in things or by mysticism in God is connected by Anselm with the content of the concept "God," indicating the necessary correspondence of the content of the concept and the existence of God.

It must be considered that the article read at Bec on September 9, 1959, presented an interpretation based on connecting the theory of existence with the method of negation and the problem of necessity even before the appearance in *Spicilegium Beccense* of the articles by Cruz Hernandez, Evdokimov, De Lubac, Thonnard, or Bechaert. Their research is used only in the present essay, which poses the problem of a broader interpretation than was possible in the article read at Bec.

II. THE METHOD OF NEGATION

1. Analysis of Anselm's Texts. Reading the *Proslogion,* one cannot deny that Anselm operates with the method of negation in the sense of the negative theology of Pseudo-Dionysius. Briefly, the method consists in that the essence of some thing is observed —a quality proper to that thing and affirmed univocally of it is denied—so that the negation can be affirmed of God, to whom it does not apply in the same sense as it does to the thing in which it is known properly. If, for instance, this thing is finite, finiteness is its property. Only the negation of that quality can be affirmed of God. Similarly, when we say that a thing is good, God is not good in the sense that the good of that thing is in God. God is not good with the goodness of that thing. God is good in another way. He is infinitely good. With negation there is connected the method of affirmation, which is an accentuation of the highest degree of perfection of a given characteristic. And this highest degree we affirm of God.

But first we must analyze the texts.

"If, namely, created life is good, how good is the life that creates! If health is pleasant, how pleasant must be that health which produces all health. If wisdom is lovable in the knowledge of created things, how much more lovable is the wisdom which created all things from nothing! Finally, if there are many great delights in pleasurable things, how great and of what kind must be the delight in him who made all pleasurable things!"[2] "Thou fillest and embracest all things, thou art before and beyond all."[3] "What good then is lacking to the highest good through whom all good exists? Thou art, therefore, just, truthful, blessed, and all that which it is better to be than not to be. For it is better to be just than unjust, blessed than not blessed."[4] "Thou, therefore, art the life by which thou livest, and the wisdom by which thou art wise, and the very goodness by which thou art Good to the good and the evil."[5] "How art thou sensible, since thou art not a body but the highest spirit, which is better than the body."[6] "Although thou art not a body, thou art supremely sensible in the manner in which thou knowest all supremely."[7] "And whatever else there is other than thou alone, can be thought not to exist. Thou alone hast being therefore most truly and most greatly of all things; for whatever else exists does not do so truly, and therefore has a lesser being."[8] "Thou art greater than can be thought."[9] "That which is greater than anything that can be conceived intellectually cannot exist solely in the intellect. For if it is only in the intellect, it can be conceived intellectually as existing in reality, which is greater. If, therefore, that than which no greater can be conceived intellectually exists solely in the intellect, then that than which no greater can be conceived intellectually is something than which a greater can be conceived intellectually. But this certainly cannot be. Therefore, without doubt that than which nothing greater can be conceived intellectually exists in the mind and in reality."[10]

First of all, attention must be called to such expressions as "Thou art beyond things [*Tu es . . . ultra omnia*],"[11] "Thou art, therefore, just, truthful and blessed, and whatever is better to be than not to be [*Tu es itaque iustus, verax, beatus et quidquid melius est esse quam non esse*],"[12] "Thou art, therefore, the life by which thou livest, and wisdom, and goodness [*Tu es igitur ipsa vita qua vivis, et sapientia, et bonitas*]."[13]

These expressions recall the entirely normal way of describing God. They are completed by the considerations that "if created life is good, how much better is the life that creates [*si enim bona est vita creata, quam bona est vita creatrix?*],"[14] "Thou art beyond things [*Tu es ultra omnia*]," "All things can be considered as nonexistent; thou alone dost possess existence in the highest degree [*Quidquid aliud praeter te solum potest cogitari non esse, solus maxime omnium habes esse*],"[15] "Thou art greater than that which can be thought [*Es quidem maius quam cogitari possit*]."[16]

In these texts Anselm describes what God is, but at the same time he adds that God is something more than these names which describe him. He is more than "just, true, and blessed." "He is something which is more than all other things." Moreover, he negates the names applied. "That which is greater than can be thought cannot exist only in the intellect. It is also in reality. And to exist in reality is more than to exist only in the intellect [*Id quo maius cogitari nequit non potest esse in solo intellectu. Si enim vel in solo intellectu est, potest cogitari esse et in re, quod maius est*]."[17]

Anselm negates two things: the existence of God only in the intellect and the definitions of God. He asserts at once that God really exists and that he is not only just, true, and blessed, but that he is something more than just, true, and blessed. He is something more than other things.

Thus, one can study Anselm's argument by treating his reasoning as the application of the method of negation. There is the positive statement first, and then immediately Anselm denies it, and immediately understands it *eminenter*. God is just, but he is not just in the same sense as other things are just; he is more just than anything else. This is a schema of Pseudo-Dionysius' method.

The metaphysics of Pseudo-Dionysius is essential. It is only a systematization of the essence of being. Hence, it is chiefly a method.[18] It investigates whether a given part of known essences is already in God. If it is not, it is denied, in order to seek further the essence of plenitude. The understanding of essence is related to concepts that are univocal. God is not good in the same manner that a thing is good. The goodness of a thing must be negated, if one wishes to transfer it to God. Negation, then, is a normal rational manner of affirming univocal essences of God. It is a consequence of perceiving the absurdity of affirming them of God univocally. And it is a description of that which God is.

Anselm tries to prove something else, namely, that God exists. He speaks first of how he understands God, that is, he analyzes the content of the concept of God and immediately adds that God is something more than we know of him from the concept. For God exists. And this a characteristic that specially distinguishes God, as *summus spiritus, maxime omnium habens esse*. Other things exist, but actually in such a way that it is possible to call them nonexistent (*quidquid aliud praeter te solum potest cogitari non esse*). God exists fully, and possesses existence in the highest degree, *existit*.[19] *Maxime omnium habet esse.*[20]

Anselm actually speaks of God in such a manner that the terms *maxime esse* follow from negating the contingent existence of things in relationship to God. This does not mean that by the method of negation Anselm was discovering the existence of God. But it does mean that Anselm by this method applies to God the properties affirmed of being. I wish only to establish that Anselm applies to God, really existing, as to a subject, the concepts which he knows from faith, and existence which he knew in contingent being. This must be derived from a review of the texts. For in that situation there would be no proof if Anselm applied a concept to God whose existence he was to prove; more precisely one must state that Anselm by way of negation united the acquired concept of existence with the concept of God, as two most perfect moments, signifying a really existing God.

P. Evdokimov would emphasize the application of concepts and known existence to a really existing God. It is thus that he understands the negative theology. It was thus that Pseudo-Dionysius formulated it. In that work what is rather emphasized is that discovery by Anselm of an infinite existence by the method of negation, and the necessary correspondence of that existence and the subject of the concept of God.

2. The Position of P. Evdokimov. Actually Evdokimov has no questions about the negative theology in Anselm's texts. Evdokimov merely draws other conclusions than does the author of the present work.

First of all, Evdokimov renders more precise the concept of the negative method by distinguishing the negative method in logical knowledge and in negative theology. In logical knowledge what matters is the distinction of objects and a choice of one from among them. This type of knowledge does not apply to God, for God is not in the order of objects of our immediate knowledge. Hence, the negative method used in logic does not apply to God. In negative theology what matters is the discovery of a new order, which does not deny the logical order but transcends it. The first degree of negation in this theology leads the human intellect to transintellectual and transcognitive "divine antinomies," that is, the unknowable attributes of God. From here contemplation carries the intellect to the state in which the intellect is actually powerless, and only God himself actuates knowledge of himself, perhaps even by a mystical experience.[21]

Hence, the goal and limit of the method of negation, according to Evdokimov, which characterizes the Fathers and Pseudo-Dionysius, is the entrance of human knowledge into completely different dimensions. This method culminates in a mystical experience. Evidently, great caution must be used in accepting Pseudo-Dionysius Neoplatonist ontological and necessary series of stages in this knowledge.

I do not accept this view presented by Evdokimov. The fact of the method of negation in Anselm's texts, which affirms the denial of contingent existence of God, is quite enough.

Evdokimov adds, and in fact first of all establishes, that Anselm's ontological argument is purely logical, that it shows the absurdity of uniting certain concepts, that is, Anselm eliminates what is not compatible with the concept of the perfection of God. In the proof he does not affirm anything of God positively. Only an immediate perception of the divine essence would justify positive statements. We do not have such a perception, for the essence of God is completely unknowable.[22]

With this position Evdokimov attacks in part the statement of Malcolm, who declares that according to Anselm, if God exists, he exists as a necessary being. Otherwise the concept of God is contradictory. Evdokimov does not see any positive statements in Anselm, and the consistency of the concept of God is for him a theory of Leibniz's. Establishing this consistency proves nothing. God is beyond logical affirmation. God cannot be revealed. The only way to go to God is to begin with God.[23] According to Evdokimov, Anselm accepts the intuitive evidence of God. We know in a completely evident manner that God exists. But we do not know anything about what God is. This is the view, also, as Evdokimov informs us, of Maximus the Confessor. This proposition actually expresses the meaning of the negative method in Anselm's proof.[24]

Evdokimov by the method of negation brings the human intellect to mystical experience and arrives at the cognitive evidence of God. This is possible in the order of mystical experiences. However, we must reply to Evdokimov that this is not possible in the order of natural human knowledge. The existence of God is not evident to the knowing intellect. And it is not evident for Anselm.

From the method of Pseudo-Dionysius Anselm only took what sufficed to establish necessary and infinite being as a possible "property" of being. Anselm seeks that being. It seems that God, whose concept Anselm knew from faith, can be that being.

This conclusion from the considerations on the method of Pseudo-Dionysius, revealed in the texts of Anselm, is closer to the content of the texts than is the view of Evdokimov, that the object of negative theology is not the knowledge of God but a mystical union with God.[25] Certainly Pseudo-Dionysius understood his theology so, but Anselm did not use it to arrive at those conclusions.

III. KNOWLEDGE OF EXISTENCE

The analysis of the proof by applying or rather by discovering in it the method of negation aids in still further explanations.

Anselm took the concept of God from faith.[26] Every concept expresses constituent notes, distinguishing the given being from others. Using reason, Anselm examined a concept received from faith by showing that God is something greater than any existing thing. God is just, true, and blessed. But he also exists. Existence is not included in a concept—not even in the concept of God. Existence is in God. All metaphysics knows this, and Anselm knows it. He tries to demonstrate that God, whose concept we have, also exists in reality.

If Anselm applies the method of negation in his proof, we can admit that he also introduces a personal concept of existence into the concept of God.

This existence Anselm was able to know on the basis of things he met immediately through his cognitive powers, and this known existence he transferred by way of negation to the object of the concept of God, which he had taken from the realm of faith.

If Anselm emphasized the method of negation, which is a method of transferring to God the achieved results of knowledge by denying these results, the problem moves in the direction of the general problem of human knowledge, which is never merely a creation of concepts, but also a cognitive apprehension of existence by the possible intellect.

First of all, the primary problem is the problem of the knowledge of concrete being. Independently of whatever theory of knowledge Anselm made his point of departure, or according to which he constructed his reasoning, he always knew being by human cognitive powers. He had always to be in contact with being and apprehend it as something which exists. It is only this moment that I wish to accept in relationship to Anselm. I am considering this moment obviously from the Aristotelian-Thomistic position. What matters is only this, to show the significance of the method of negation in Anselm, who relates known existence with the concept of God.

1. The area of common sense. Knowledge of existence, later interpreted in various theories of knowledge, occurs, above all, primarily and always in a prescientific knowledge, a common-sense knowledge, that is analyzed and only then established in science. This proposition provides vast opportunities for seeking the sources of the knowledge of existence, which Anselm knew. Anselm, too, operated with common sense and the normal cognitive powers of man, and therefore with the senses and the intellect.

Anselm evidently distinguished things. And in distinguishing things he operated with the principle that being is itself, and with the principle that being cannot at the same time be itself and something else. He worked with the principle of identity and the principle of contradiction. By the same token he took a position in favor of the pluralism of beings. In the *Monologion* he spoke "of the numberless multitude of goods, whose vast variety we experience by our corporal senses and know by our intellect."[27] Anselm then admitted sense-knowledge and sense-experience. And with this experience, aided by the principles of identity and contradiction, he connected the proposition that we can call principle of the reason of being: only being is the cause of being, "in no way does anything exist through nothing." ". . . man exists, and he exists through something else."[28] And Anselm justifies this proposition by a method proper to metaphysics, namely, by showing the absurdity of rejecting the proposition. For then things would exist through nothing. "If that being, because of whom all exist, is nothing, then all those things which depend on it, are also nothing. And the proposition that things do not exist, is false and absurd."[29]

The purpose here is not to use and to interpret the *Proslogion* by means of texts taken from the *Monologion*. This is not using the *Monologion* to explain the ontological proof. The purpose is to supplement the view that Anselm operated with common-sense knowledge, that he accepted sense-experience and reflection, and formulated first principles, among which the reason of being was an instrument to single out the first being. Anselm simply gathers the necessary and always actual elements of a demonstration of God's existence: the experience of things (*innumerabilia bona, quorum diversitatem sensibus corporeis experimur*),[30] and the reason of being (*quidquid est, per aliquid est*).[31] After proper analysis it follows from these two propositions that God exists (*necesse est unum illud esse, per quod sunt cuncta quae sunt;*[32] *non solum certissime existit, sed etiam summe omnium existit*).[33]

The statement that Anselm operated with common sense was necessary to show that, independently of any theory of knowledge, Anselm experienced existing things. Besides, he knew that a concept is something other than existence; having a concept of God, he tried to prove that God exists. The negation of known contingent being Anselm associates with the concept of God.

The experience of existence is something real in the area of common sense. The mechanism of that experience and its course have been interpreted by Maritain, Gilson, and Krąpiec. I shall try to present this in their language and with their concepts.

Being[34] is every concrete object, apprehended cognitively not from the aspect of its concreteness but of its being. The concrete object, existing beyond the knowing subject, strikes man's cognitive powers in such a way that it produces a contact of the cognitive powers with itself. The stimulated cognitive powers of man affirm the existence of something beyond themselves, something that penetrates into the inner world of the knowing subject. The object penetrates to the interior of the sense powers of cognition, received through perceptive contact with the object, from which the active intellect extracts universal elements and transforms them into concepts. In these operations and together with them, by these very perceptions, the existing concrete object meets with the existing knowing subject. And even more exactly, the meeting of the two existences occurs within the scope of the *vis cogitativa*,[35] according to the explanation of A. Krąpiec who developed the ideas of Maritain and Gilson. For existence cannot be apprehended by concepts themselves. Nor can a concept of existence be created. One can only affirm existence. And the intellect affirms it in the existential judgement: something exists. Without the aid of the active intellect the possible intellect knows directly in the *vis cogitativa* the existence of the thing, for it is an act that transcends matter and that does not have to be presented to the possible intellect by the active intellect, in order to aid it in the act of knowing the thing and to prepare from perceptions conceptual elements specifically for their reception by the possible intellect. That reception is the essence of the act of knowledge. What is significant, first of all, is the experience of the thing as existing, hence, the experience of existence. And evidently the active intellect immediately extracts from perceptions essential notes that define the object's group and species. It creates concepts. This is the operation that accompanies the meeting of the two existences.

For the consideration of Anselm's proof, the distinction by contemporary philosophy of two operations in the very act of knowing is important: the apprehension of existence and the apprehension of constituent notes. For this theory of knowledge does not prove true in relationship to God. God is not immediately given. Hence, Anselm properly took the concept of God from faith and was able to apply to the subject of that concept existence apprehended in things, asserting that God exists as do things but not in the same way—rather in a way completely different, as the *maxime habens esse,* whereas every other thing *minus habet esse.*

On the basis of the texts discussed, in which Anselm shows what things are and what God is in relationship to them, it is possible to admit the method of negation. From a comparison of these texts: "Other things are less true and therefore have less

Mieczysław Gogacz

existence; thou art most true of all and therefore dost possess existence in the highest degree [*Quidquid aliud est non sic vere, et idcirco minus habet esse, solus igitur verissime omnium, et ideo maxime omnium habet esse*],"[36] one can conclude that as a consequence of the method of negation Anselm applied to God *eminenter* the *minus esse* perceived in things. God possesses *maxime esse*.

It is possible to establish two facts: Anselm applies the method of negation and Anselm knows contingent being. The combination of these two facts and the texts in the *Proslogion,* that in comparison with other things God *maxime omnium habet esse,* permits us to recognize that Anselm transferred the negation of contingent existence known in things to the object of the concept *God,* taken from faith.

2. The considerations of P. Stolz, E. Gilson, and M. Kiteley. The statements so far about Anselm's knowledge of existence are a conclusion from the fact of the method of negation and the statements of common sense in his texts. Anselm does not speak directly of the knowledge of existence. He says only that God *summe omnium existit, maxime habet esse,* whereas things *minus habent esse.* For Anselm *esse* means what today would be called existential. It is a matter of real existence. Anselm wishes to prove the actual existence of God. Gilson confirms this about Anselm when he objects to Stolz, that according to Stolz Anselm does not prove the existence of God. If he does not prove existence, but only, as Stolz says, explains that God is he than whom nothing greater can be thought, then Anselm uses the term "existence" in a different meaning, and not in the meaning of real existence.[37] Evidently, Stolz thinks that Anselm, following Augustine, emphasizes the immutability in God, that he is not proving existence, but only explaining what God is. It is not possible to agree with Stolz on this interpretation of Anselm. Nor can one agree, as Stolz would have us do, that Anselm accepted *vere esse* literally from Augustine. According to Stolz, it seems that Anselm's *maxime habens esse* means *incommutabiliter esse.* Hence, according to Stolz, in the *Proslogion* Anselm is not speaking of the existence of God, but about his immutability.[38] Stolz says properly that Anselm is concerned with *Gottes Wesen,* but ultimately he equates immutability with *maxime esse.* But in the *Proslogion* this *maxime esse* means the real existence of God.

In another place, namely, in the *Monologion,* Anselm expressly distinguishes existence and essence. He explains that *essentia,*

24

esse and *ens existens* are related as *lux, lucere,* and *lucens.* It is very difficult to give the exact meaning of these terms, explained only by means of one comparison. However, it is clear from this text that for Anselm *esse* is one thing and *existens* is another.[39] Certainly Anselm did not forget this; nor did he reject it in the *Proslogion.* For he would not have been seeking arguments for the existence of God.

That existence is not for Anselm a note or an attribute of God. Even Cappuyns through the concept of God sees God existing and not existence as a characteristic of God. It is not a question of ascribing existence to God, but of asserting that God *in re* exists really, whereas God *in intellectu* exists in thought only. Malcolm strongly emphasizes this and specifies it in discussing the problem of existence, considered as a perfection in the meaning of a real predicate. M. Kiteley also discusses this matter. In his article "Existence and the Ontological Argument,"[40] he calls attention to the fact that the ontological argument in discursive reasoning includes the supposition that the concept of perfection includes the concept of existence. Kiteley explains that the force of the demonstrative argument is not to be sought in resolving these abbreviated assumptions. However, Kiteley does not suggest his own solution.[41]

3. The problem of mystical experience. (a) The position of Audet, Vignaux, and De Lubac. In a monograph on the problem of interpreting the ontological argument one cannot ignore a subject to which so much space has been given by Stolz, Gilson, Audet, Vignaux, Evdokimov, and De Lubac. This is the problem of mysticism. One cannot deny that Buonaiuti and Stolz represent an expressly mystical interpretation of the proof. In fact, in his article, "Sens et nature de l'argument de Saint Anselme," Gilson carefully analyzed Stolz's position and rejected the mystical interpretation. According to Gilson, the argument is not based on mystical experience. Anselm is not speaking of mystical contemplation, but of the intellectual vision of truth. Undoubtedly, Gilson's reasons show that the argument cannot be placed within the framework of only theology, mysticism, or philosophy. However, Evdokimov also has reasons in showing the consequences and perspectives of negative theology, which Anselm used in some degree. That theology leads to mystical experience[42] and actually to some theory of evidence. This could be an intuitive evidence of God, the evidence of revelation, or mystical evidence, and hence a real, even though supernatural, presence of God in man.[43]

I do not agree with Evdokimov in these conclusions. The method of negative theology does not lead automatically to these stages of knowledge. Human knowledge has its limits. Mystical knowledge is a gift of God. Evdokimov cites Neoplatonism, which, however, does not agree with common sense.

What is interesting is Evdokimov's emphasis on the possibility of a mystical experience in Anselm. Even Gilson agrees that Anselm is a religious author of first rank.[44] And an interpretation of the renowned fourteenth chapter of the *Proslogion* expressly approaches the problematic of mysticism. Vignaux and De Lubac are of the same opinion. Truly, De Lubac formulates this more cautiously, and he arrives at other conclusions than does Vignaux on the basis of an analysis of this chapter: in each case he considers the ontological proof from the viewpoint of the prayerful atmosphere of the *Proslogion*.

According to De Lubac, Anselm through the intellect demonstrated and apprehended God. This does not mean that Anselm discovered God. De Lubac expressly contrasts two terms, *prouvé* and *trouvé*. God is not present, even though his existence has been demonstrated, and hence Anselm did not experience ecstasy. This was not the God toward whom his longing tended.[45] De Lubac emphasizes the moment of arrival in Anselm's searchings. This moment is identical with the point of departure. God is not present. Anselm is not united with his God after proving his existence, just as he was not before the proof.[46] According to De Lubac, Anselm by way of mystical contemplation arrives at rational conclusions. Rational conclusions are not the full contact of the soul with God, and hence arises Anselm's yearning. Establishing the transition in Anselm's thought from the way of mystical contemplation to the way of the rational and dialectical characterizes De Lubac's position. This differs from Vignaux's stand, who sees the thought of Anselm as belonging to the realm of contemplation.

The position of Vignaux is an essential supplement to the thought of Audet. Audet expresses the opinion that Anselm's proof from the very beginning touches the existential order, and not the epistemological.[47] With regard to this, Gilson's proposal that the proof should be analyzed in the light of *De Veritate's* theory of knowledge is not correct. Beyond this, Audet considers the *Proslogion* as a prayer; but he does not wish to determine whether the prayer is mystical. He sees in the *Proslogion* an expression of religious emotion, of a power that is sometimes found only in mystical prayer.[48] He adds that in the *Proslogion* there is a very express effort by a believer for cognitive apprehension of that reality in which he believes.[49] This is a personal and living God, known in a vital intellectual experience. And to this Person the believer turns with all his prayer, which is the *Proslogion*. And the statement *non possim non intelligere* would be based on the psychological situation, which allows one to turn to God as *tibi, tu,* which points to an experience *de la foi*.[50]

In speaking of the knowledge of a reality in which one believes, Audet is very close to De Lubac. But in emphasizing the religious experience and the close contact of man with God, he is near the position of Vignaux.

With regard to the *Proslogion* Vignaux establishes his own theology of "spiritual yearning," possible only in a theocentric mysticism. He thinks that the elements of such a mysticism can be found in the *Monologion*. He explains that in the experience undergone by a believer, or in that which is called a *fides viva,* there is included that yearning possible only where love is presupposed.[51] Anselm states that the highest good, which demands love for itself, is also at the same time an object of desire for the one who loves.[52] Love evokes this yearning.[53] Vignaux says that such a conception of the spiritual life facilitates the understanding of the *Proslogion*. For one who lives by the love of a chosen object always strives to behold that object; hence, he always strives for a rational understanding of the faith.[54]

Vignaux also considers the two orders established by De Lubac: the mystical-contemplative and the rational. De Lubac realized that Anselm passed from one order to the other. Vignaux sees the possibility of Anselm's rational analyses in the entire context of mysticism. For actually desire demands to know the object of love.

From this survey it is clear that the extreme views really interpret Anselm less than do the moderate ones. Buonaiuti, Evdokimov, and Stolz—somewhat too strongly exclusive of other interpretations—emphasized the mysticism of the *Proslogion*. Gilson and De Lubac, too, radically denied this undoubted element in Anselm. De Lubac finally did recognize the mystical point of departure, and Evdokimov resolved Anselm's search in mysticism. Audet and Vignaux established the ontological argument on the basis of a mysticism in Anselm confirmed at least partially in the texts.

It is necessary to accept a moderate view. It depends on admitting the possibility that Anselm knew existence eventually either from his own mystical experience or that of others, and not only on the basis of things. And that existence, contingent if known in things, and perfect if known in a mystical experience, he applied to God by negation.

(b) The possibility of Anselm's mystical knowledge of God. Calling attention in contemporary theories of knowledge to the fact of a twofold operation of the intellect in the act of knowledge[55] is very useful for mysticism. The ontological foundation of a mystical experience is love in man; and the foundation of operation, or of executing a mystical experience, is the gift of the Holy Spirit.[56] When God evokes a mystical experience in man, man by his possible intellect experiences the existence of God present in him. He cannot apprehend the essence of God, even though the essence of God is identical with his existence. The knowledge of essence must be executed in man by means of the senses. In mystical experience he knows only the existence of God. The mystics say that the mystical experience of God is unclear, that they sense the presence of God, but they do not know God, they do not see him.[57] This testifies to the fact that in the mystical experience there is an apprehension only of God's existence in a transconceptual manner. Thus understood, mystical experience, as an experience of existence, and not a conceptual contact with the essence of God, is in conformity with the nature of human knowledge. God, present in man by charity, in a mystical experience stands before the human intellect not only as the object of faith, but also as a present object of knowledge. The possible intellect then apprehends the existence of God.[58]

Anselm either knew the experience of the mystics, or he himself experienced the existence of God in a mystical way. And this experienced existence of God he applied to the concept of God, which he had from faith. In order to resolve this in some manner, it is necessary to return to the texts and principally to the *Proslogion,* for there especially he demonstrates that God exists.

Evidently, it is not possible to prove that the *Proslogion* is a tract in mystical theology.[59] In no case do I say that the argument of Anselm is mystical or theological. Obviously Anselm, by way of meditation and contemplation, endeavors to prove the object of faith, to prove by means of a reasoning process that is related with his particular theory of knowledge. Independently of this, Gilson affirms that Anselm is a mystical author,[60] but evidently not in the sense that the *Proslogion* informs us of Anselm's mystical experience. Nor does Stolz have any reason to say that in the

Proslogion we do not find proof as much as the mystical contemplation of the existence of God.[61] I shall not return to the statements so ably criticized by Gilson.[62] In saying that Anselm is a mystic, I wish only to emphasize a new matter: in the *Proslogion* Anselm does not give proof by describing a mystical experience of God; but the existence of God known from such experience in the course of the considerations of the *Proslogion,* he connects with the subject of the concept of God.

Following Gilson's studies we come to the conclusion that the whole theory of knowledge in Anselm's time is the result of seeking a method to connect the existence of a thing with the thing itself signified by the concept. The entire problem of *rectitudo,* the relationship between the thing and the concept, expressed in the thesis that something exists in *intellectu et in re,* is the question of interpreting knowledge as knowledge in a universal manner, but always a knowledge of the existing concrete object: to the concept there corresponds a concrete object, or that concept is taken from that concrete object. This then is a special problem.

In the *Proslogion* the matter of referring the concept of existence to the concept of God by means of the method of negation, and of existence already mystically experienced elsewhere, can be emphasized also from the view which Anselm took of faith. *Credo ut intelligam.* It is from faith that Anselm takes the object of knowledge and research. Not all agree to this.[63] One must add here that over and above the knowledge of faith is mystical knowledge. It is, as Maritain formulates it,[64] the apprehension of the divinity as such in a supernatural manner by the acceptance of the knowledge of God through an act of faith, perfected in its operation by the gifts of the Holy Spirit, especially the gifts of knowledge and wisdom. According to Maritain, mystical knowledge is knowledge perfected through faith. In the *Proslogion* Anselm does not describe knowledge by faith, even as he does not describe a mystical experience. However, if he takes from faith the concept of God, then he can also take from it the existence of God experienced in its higher stage, in order to establish by proof in the *Proslogion* that to the concept of God, which he has from faith, there corresponds the mystically experienced existence of God.

The problem then depends on this—that the existence of God known in an intellectual experience is connected by Anselm with the subject of the concept of God, which is taken from faith. Both the existence and the concept Anselm knew outside the limits of the *Proslogion*. Within the limits of the *Proslogion* by the method of negation he executes the connection of existence with the subject of the concept of God. The problem then is: the general concept designates that concrete thing which exists.

Anselm did not formulate his position in this manner. But an analysis of the texts and a discussion of the literature dealing with the ontological argument lead to this interpretation.

(c) The texts of Anselm. It is difficult to establish that Anselm had a mystical experience of God. He knew that "God dwells in inaccessible light,"[65] and that we are created to see God.[66] However he complains: "Thou art my God and my Lord, but I have never seen thee."[67] "Who will lead me to the light in which thou art, so that I may see thee?"[68] "I have never seen thee, my Lord God, I do not know thy countenance."[69] "I have never seen thee [*Nunquam te vidi*]."

We know that Anselm wished to express the difference between the fate of man on this earth and after death, between the knowledge which man had before the fall of Adam, and which he has after the sin of the first parents. "We are exiles from our fatherland, *a visione Dei in caecitatem nostram.*"[70]

There are texts in the *Proslogion,* which by their admiration of God, their transport, yearning and prayerful strain, and the expression of ecstatic love, qualify as mystical texts. "Does the highest good lack any good?"[71] "What art thou, Lord, since it is not possible to think of anything greater than thou?"[72] "I give thee thanks that thou hast created in me thine image, by which I can remember thee, think of thee, and love thee, O Lord."[73] "Thou art fully present everywhere, and I do not see thee. I move in thee and I am in thee, but I cannot draw close to thee. Thou art in me and about me, and I cannot sense thee."[74] "Why does not my soul sense if I find thee?"[75] "I have never seen thee, and I do not know thy countenance."[76] "My Lord and my God, my hope and the joy of my heart."[77] "Tell my yearning soul, in what thou art different from that which it sees, that I may see purely that which it desires. It seeks to see more, and it sees nothing beyond what it sees except darkness; moreover, it does not see darkness, of which there is none in thee, but it sees that because of darkness it cannot see more."[78]

These texts are prayers, full of admiration of God, transport, and yearning. This yearning expresses the greatest love: "I can know and think of thee . . ."[79] my hope and the joy of my heart."[80] It also expresses a cognitive situation peculiar to mystics:[81] "Thou art everywhere, and I do not see thee,"[82] "I do not see thee because of the darkness which is in me."[83]

In the fourteenth chapter, from which the last text is taken, Anselm explains that the soul knows light and truth "when it sees light and truth," but "it does not see thee as thou art[84] because of the darkness which is in it." Here Anselm is concerned with intellectual knowledge, with the fact that it is not immediate, when God is known—that he does not know God *sicuti est*. But the mystics wish only to say that God, whom they have in themselves, is not known clearly, conceptually, and that they have only an experience of his presence. It is significant that Anselm knows on what mystical experience depends. He knows that God is not known immediately in the usual process of knowledge. Precisely then, when God is present in us and when he makes it possible through his image in us to express love for him, cognitively he always remains distant from our intellect by a certain amount of darkness, which exists in us. In mysticism then man does not come into contact with God as a subject of conceptualization, but only with God as permitting the experience of his existence when he is present in us.[85] Anselm does not define this presence, but neither does he define exactly many other matters in the *Proslogion,* for instance, even the matter of concepts being *in intellectu et in re*. And according to Gilson, there are reasons to consider this matter in the light of the noetics of his time. There are also reasons, it seems, to interpret *vidit tenebras* in the sense of the *via negativa*.[86] In his investigations this produces a particular emphasis, which recalls Augustine, Boethius, Proclus, and Pseudo-Dionysius—but especially Pseudo-Dionysius.

IV. CONCLUSIONS FOR A FORMULA
OF INTERPRETATION

It seems that Anselm's proof, placed in the context of contemporary theory of the knowledge of existence, achieves an interpretation as probable as that theory of knowledge which most exactly explains the considerations in the *Proslogion*. For the solution that Anselm within the sphere of the *Proslogion* connects the essence of a concept with the existence of its subject, it is necessary to accept the method of negation, or rather the negative theology as a method of forming, on the basis of reality, a concept of the most perfect existence. I tried to show that Anselm did use such a method; for otherwise there would remain these bothersome texts: "Whoever sees light and truth sees thee. If he does not see thee, he does not see light and truth. But even if someone sees light and truth, he does not see thee. The reason is that he sees thee otherwise, he does not see thee as thou art."[87] "Thou, O God, art light and truth, but thou art more than light and truth."

The solution of the problem of the negative theology in the *Proslogion* must always somehow be undertaken. The remark of A. Audet, that Anselm's proof touches the existential order, permits the further statement that Anselm by negation connects the experienced existence of things with the concept of the God drawn from the mystically experienced presence of God.

On the basis of all these data, I wish to state that Anselm in the *Proslogion* is working with a particular method of negation, proper to negative theology, by relating existence with the content signified by the concept of God; this existence was known in things themselves, and with the content of the concept signified by God he unites existence as taken from mystical experience. It is not excluded that this was his own experience. From the *Proslogion* only the disposition for such an experience and information about it can be applied to Anselm. And that suffices. It suffices as an argument that the method of negation could have been applied in the *Proslogion,* for Anselm possessed, wherever acquired, an experience of the existence of things or directly of the existence of God. He was able to demonstrate the relationship between existence and the concept signified by the concept of God, known to him from faith. If he applied to God existence as experienced in things, he was applying the method of negation. If he applied to God existence as known to him from other mystics, he applied the method of negation. Even if he applied to God existence which he knew from his own mystical experience, he still applied that method, for he applied to God his own existence, but as experienced by man. God does not exist in that empirical existence, but in his own. God exists *maxime omnium habens esse.*

The whole matter, however, leaves the impression of a somewhat complex problem. In the *Proslogion* by accentuating the manner of ascribing existence to God, one emphasizes the type of existence attributed to God. And then on a further plane there appears the problem: Does the *Proslogion* prove the existence of God? From these considerations it is clear that in the *Proslogion* Anselm rather points to the connection between existence and the content signified by the concept God. This connection is necessary, according to Anselm, on the basis of the statement that the most perfect being must exist, in order to be fully perfect. This proposition can be expressed in the thesis that to every concept there corresponds a reality. That proposition—valid, as Gilson says, in the noetics of Anselm—is not universally true. However, if one says that Anselm knew the imperfect existence of things or knew the most perfect existence in a mystical experience, then he sought for that existence a corresponding subject apprehended in its constituent elements. He searched for a concept whose content could be united with that existence. He recognized that only to the content signified by the concept of God could he attribute the most perfect existence. The most perfect existence and the content signified by the most perfect concept correspond in a necessary manner. Thus does Anselm execute his demonstration.

Concept and existence correspond in a necessary manner, for it follows from the theory of *rectitudo* that, if there is a concept, it exists only if there exists a subject. If the intellect by way of negation formed the concept of the most perfect being by denying experienced contingent existence, at the same time it affirmed in a necessary manner the subject of the most perfect existence. If there is a concept, there exists a subject. Anselm based himself on the idea that the concept exists. Since the concept of God exists, then God exists. In the *Proslogion* Anselm proved that God exists, for the most perfect existence exists as does the most perfect content signified by the concept of God. They are both realized in some object.

V. THE FORMULA OF THE PROPOSED INTERPRETATION

The interpretation of the argument proposed in this essay depends on the statement that Anselm did not deduce the existence of God from a concept, as even his first opponents understood it; nor from the necessity of the existence of God does there follow the proposition of his existence, as E. Gilson interprets the argument; but on the fact that to existence, as something really most perfect, there must correspond the object signified by the concept of God as the most perfect being, known by faith. The difference between the proposed understanding of the argument and the two others is obvious: not from concept to existence, or from existence to concept, but by this means that there is a necessary relationship between existence, as the most perfect property of being, and the content of something most perfect. The most perfect thing can only be one thing: *Solus maxime habens esse*. Existence and the notes defined by the concept are necessarily one thing.

Briefly, Anselm by the method of negation formed a concept of the most perfect existence. Namely, he denied contingent existence, which he knew in things, and acquired the concept of infinite existence. To this concept, by reason of the theory of *rectitudo,* there necessarily corresponds a subject. Seeking that subject, that is, the subject existing most perfectly and apprehended in its constituent notes, Anselm arrived at the concept of God. He realized that only the concept of God identified the subject of the concept of the most perfect existence. The concept of God and the concept of the most perfect existence are the formal sign of the very same subject. They indicate the very same subject.

This interpretation includes also the emphases of the Anselmian texts thus far neglected, namely, the method of negation and mysticism, which do not in any way contradict the statement that the *Proslogion,* as Gilson would have it, is a study of Holy Scripture with the goal of a rational understanding and demonstration of the object of faith. Rather they broaden the interpretation.

CONCLUSION

In the literature dealing with Anselm's proof there is a tendency to show its structure, independence of theology, mysticism, and even philosophy—the independence of the very proof in the *Proslogion* itself, which by its nature is reasoning on a subject of faith. The present essay supplements this by evaluating the hitherto neglected emphases in the *Proslogion* according to the outline of negative theology. The context of the argument from the whole *Proslogion* has been used. Thus the interpretation of the argument has changed. It depends on the statement that between the most perfect known being and the most perfect content signified by the concept of God, there is a necessary relationship that fulfills itself in God. This interpretation is consonant with the method of negation established in the texts, the common-sense judgments of Anselm, and ultimately with mysticism, as related to the problem of the knowledge of existence. It embraces all the material of the *Proslogion* without eliminating anything. It is compatible with any theory of knowledge (except that of Roscelin), especially the Thomistic, in the sense that the reasoning of the *Proslogion* fits splendidly into the Thomistic theory of the knowledge of existence. This interpretation also affirms in Anselm's proof a special kind of *a posteriori* quality. Not from a concept do I infer the existence of God. Hence I do not assert the existence of the concepts, "God exists." I know the most perfect existence by way of negation; I know the content of the most perfect concept taken from faith; and actually, both, the concept of existence and the concept of God, indicate to me their subject, God, on the basis of the necessary relationship between that which is most perfect— that which is most perfect is, and it is one.

Skilled in Neoplatonism, in dialectic, and in medieval method, Anselm[88] proposed an idea, which even today can in its own way, but with all the force of rational proof, teach the human mind that God exists.

FOOTNOTES

1. M. Gogacz, "Le Ratio Anselmi en face du problème des relations entre métaphysique et mystique," *Spicilegium Beccense* II.
2. *Proslogion* 24, 3–9, 118: "Si enim bona est vita creata: quam bona est vita creatrix. Si iucunda est salus facta: quam iucunda est salus quae facit omnem salutem. Si amabilis est sapientia in cognitione rerum conditarum: quam amabilis est sapientia quae omnia condidit ex nihilo. Denique si multae et magnae delectationes sunt in rebus delectabilibus: qualis et quanta delectatio est in illo qui facit ipsa delectabilia."
3. *Ibid.* 20, 18, 115: "Tu ergo imples et complecteris omnia, tu es ante et ultra omnia."
4. *Ibid.* 5, 14–17, 104: "Quod ergo bonum deest summo bono per quod est omne bonum. Tu es itaque iustus, verax, beatus, et quidquid melius est esse quam non esse. Melius namque est esse iustum quam non iustum, beatum quam non beatum."
5. *Ibid.* 12, 6–8, 110: "Tu es igitur ipsa vita qua vivis, et sapientia qua sapis, et bonitas ipsa qua bonis et malis bonus es; et ita de similibus."
6. *Ibid.* 6, 24–25, 104: "Quomodo es sensibilis, cum non sis corpus, sed summus spiritus, qui corpore melior est."
7. *Ibid.* 6, 4–6, 105: "Quamvis non sis corpus, vere tamen eo modo summe sensibilis es, quo summe omnia cognoscis."
8. *Ibid.* 3, 6–9, 103: "Et quidem quidquid est aliud praeter te solum, potest cogitari non esse. Solus igitur verissime omnium, et ideo maxime omnium habes esse; quia quidquid aliud est non sic vere, et idcirco minus habet esse."
9. *Ibid.* 15, 14, 112: "Es quidem maius quam cogitari possit."
10. *Ibid.* 2, 15 nn, 101–102: "Id quo maius cogitari nequit, non potest esse

in solo intellectu. Si enim vel in solo intellectu est, potest cogitari esse et in re, quod maius est. Si ergo id quo maius cogitari non potest est in solo intellectu: id ipsum quo maius cogitari non potest est quo maius cogitari potest. Sed certe hoc esse non potest. Existit ergo procul dubio aliquid quo maius cogitari non valet, et in intellectu et in re."

11. *Ibid.* 20, 18, 115.

12. *Ibid.* 5, 15, 104.

13. *Ibid.* 12, 6–7, 110.

14. *Ibid.* 24, 3–4, 118.

15. *Ibid.* 3, 7–8, 103.

16. *Ibid.* 15, 14, 112.

17. *Ibid.* 2, 15–17, 101.

18. M. D. Chenu, *Le Théologie au douzième siècle* (Paris, 1957) 131: "Denys demeure pleinement fidèle au neoplatonism qui est essentialement une méthode pour accéder a la realité intelligible, non une explication du sensible par cette realité."

19. *Proslogion* 2, 2, 102.

20. *Ibid.* 3, 8, 103.

21. P. Evdokimov, *L' Aspect apophatique* 253: "La négation dans toute connaissance est une méthode de discernement. Nous connaissons tel object en le distinguant de tout ce qui n'est pas lui. Les jugements positifs ou négatifs coordonnés permettent de faire un choix et de procéder à une détermination. Or, au sujet de Dieu, nous ne pouvons faire aucun choix car Dieu ne se trouve pas parmi les réalites de ce monde. . . . La théologie apophatique procède par la voie des négations toutes différentes . . . elle découvre le plan métalogique qui ne détruit pas le logique. . . . Sa première négation s'élève au monde supraintellectuel des 'antinomies divines.' . . . La contemplation sur-élève l'esprit humain et le réssemble dans le bien de Dieu ou il ne peut plus s'ouvrir qu'a une solution venant de Dieu, car ici ce n'est pas l'esprit humain qui saisit Dieu, mais c'est Dieu qui saisit le centre pré-conceptuel du coeur humain. . . . Le dépassement du conceptuel, et dans le sens particulier, 'l'inconnaissance' devient une mode de connaissance intériorisée jusqu'a l'expérience mystique."

22. *Ibid.* 236: "La preuve semble-t-il est purement conceptuelle, elle découvre l'incompatibilité logique des certains prédicats. Elle relève ce qui ne convient pas à la conception de la perfection de Dieu, elle n'affirme aucune attribution positive. Seule la perfection directe pourrait affirmer le positif, et de l'essence de Dieu conclure a son existence nécessaire. Or, toute analyse est interdite, Saint Anselm nie toute possibilité de la Connaissance de l'essence divine absolument inconnaisable."

23. *Ibid.* 239: "Leibniz pensa la trouver dans l'idée de Dieu totalement positive et qui ne peut contenir aucune négation, donc l'idee de Dieu n'a pas de contradiction. On voit bien qu'ici on ne sort point d'une démonstration conceptuelle. Elle ne prouve rien car justement à toute affirmation logique de Dieu s'applique la négation apophatique. Dieu est au-dessus de toute affirmation logique mais toute affirmation vraie à son sujet ne reçoit sa force que de son Être seul. . . . On ne peut jamais inventer Dieu car on ne peut jamais aller vers Dieu qu'en partant de Lui."

24. *Ibid.* 240: "Saint Anselme est un penseur réligieux des plus profonds, en suivant Saint Augustine il fait réposer toute son argumentation sur l'évi-

dence intuitive de Dieu"; 251: "De Dieu nous savons seulement d'une manière absolument évidente qu'il est, c'est précisement la formule même ou l'aspect apophatique de l'argument de Saint Anselme."

25. *Ibid.* 25: "La théologie apophatique a ainsi pur object non pas la connaissance de Dieu, lequel demeure à jamais '1' Inconcevable,' mais l'union mystique avec Dieu."

26. *Proslogion* 2, 5, 101: "Credimus te esse aliquid quo nihil maius cogitari possit."

27. *Monologion* 1, 5–7, 14: "Innumerabilia bona sunt, quorum tam multam diversitatem et sensibus corporeis experimur et ratione mentis discernimus."

28. *Ibid.* 3, 1, 16: "Nullo modo quidquid est per nihil"; *ibid.* 3, 1, 16: "Quidquid est igitur, non nisi per aliquid est."

29. *Ibid.* 6, 21–22, 19: "Quod igitur illa natura sine qua nulla est natura, sit nihil, tam falsum et quam absurdum erit, si dicatur quidquid est nihil esse."

30. *Ibid.* 1, 5–7, 14.

31. *Ibid.* 3, 16–17, 16.

32. *Ibid.* 3, 16–17, 16.

33. *Ibid.* 27, 13–14, 45.

34. M. Gogacz, "Mistyka a poznanie Boga," *Znak* 59 (1959) 597.

35. A. Krąpiec, "Analysis formationis conceptus entis existentialiter considerati," *Divus Thomas* (Piacenza, 1956) III–IV, 320–351; A. Krąpiec, "Próba ustalenia struktury bytu intencjonalnego," *Collectanea Theologica* (1957) 353.

36. *Proslogion* 3, 7–9, 103.

37. E. Gilson, "Sens et nature de l'argument de Saint Anselme," *Archives d'histoire doctrinale et littéraire du moyen âge* 9 (1934) 38: "Si cette phrase ne veut pas dire qu'il a trouvé l'existence d'un souverain bien . . . il faut ôter a 'esse' sa signification existentielle pour ne lui conserver qu'une fonction attributive. C'est ce que fait courageusement le P. Stolz. . . . Le premier résultat des récherches de Saint Anselme aurait été, non pas qu'il existe un souverain bien, dont on ne peut rien concevoir de plus grand, mais que Dieu est ce dont on ne peut rien concevoir de plus grand."

38. P. Stolz, "Vere esse im *Proslogion* des Hl. Anselm," *Scholastik* 9 (1934) 406: "Anselm bewegt sich also in seiner Auffassung von Gottes Wesen ganz in Augustinischen Gedanken: Gott ist also vere, verissime et maxime habens esse. . . Das ist aber das vere esse oder das incommutabiliter esse."

39. *Monologion* 6, 15–19, 20: "Quemadmodum enim sese habent ad invicem lux et lucere et lucens, sic sunt ad se invicem essentia et esse et ens, hoc est existens sive subsistens. . . . Ergo summa essentia et summe esse et summe ens, id est, summe existens sive summe subsistens, non dissimiliter sibi convenient, quam lux et lucere et lucens."

40. M. Kiteley, "Existence and the Ontological Argument," *Philosophy and Phenomenological Research* 18 (1958) 533–535.

41. *Ibid.* 535. The neglect of the conceptual confusion which makes it seem true—viz., either assimilating the joint necessary applicability of the concepts of the divinity, and perfection with the necessary self-applicability of the concept of divinity, or assimilating "Divinity is perfect," with "whatever is divine is perfect"—has been a serious impediment to understanding the irrepressible persuasiveness of the ontological argument. Unraveling the threads of confusion in the argument's "perfection entails existence" premise

is not enough. Defensive maneuvers can be made that avoid these errors. It also needs to be shown that these defensive maneuvers inevitably lead into the "cul de sac" of the homological mistake.

42. P. Evdokimov, *L' Aspect apophatique* 250: "La théologie apophatique introduit ainsi à l'expérience de la Présence et du sentiment mystique de la proximité de Dieu."

43. *Ibid.* 254: "L'argument de Saint Anselm rélève de la philosophie de l'évidence, mais celle-ci est encore entièrment à faire. Si elle se constitue, elle sera certainement 'la philosophie de la révelation.' L'évidence est peut-être le même type de la connaissance apophatique. Elle invite l'esprit à l'extase, à la sortie de ses propres limites, à une transcendance vers une realité cachée qui se rélève. L'évidence est toujours une révelation, et c'est peut-être sa seule définition possible. Elle se pose et s'impose avec son absolute certitude et qui est tout autre dimension qu'une certitude intellectuelle."

44. Gilson, "Sens et nature" 30–31: "Un auteur spirituel de première importance."

45. H. de Lubac, "Sur le Chapitre XIV du *Proslogion*," *Spicilegium Beccense* I, 301: "Il y a donc . . . à distinguer la pensée anselmienne . . . d'une extrême rationalité; d'autre part, une insatisfaction extrême. Dieu est prouvé, il est même en quelque sort compris; mais il n'est pas trouvé par la, il n'est pas devenue présent. . . . Plus Dieu est 'prouvé' . . . moins il est 'trouvé.' "

46. *Ibid.* 300: "On discerne . . . deux sortes 'd'intelligence de la foi' . . . l'une qui s'applique à l'ensemble du mystère chrétien, est plutôt contemplative et mystique; l'autre, dans son application au problème de Dieu, est surtout dialectique et rationelle. . . . Or, dans le climat continue de la première sort d'intelligence de la foi, la pensée anselmienne, en ce qu'elle offre de plus original, en fait, la seconde. Mais tandis que la première pouvait bien être en effet considerée comme une étape sur la voie qui conduit de la foi obscure à la vision . . . la second est orientée dans une direction différente. Anselme, arrive au terme de son premier effort, s'en aperçoit: d'où sa déception."

47. A. Audet, "Un source augustinienne de l'argument de saint Anselme," in E. Gilson, *Philosophie de la Chrétienté* (Paris, 1949) 121. "Je vois bien que l'argument, se meut dès le début dans l'ordre existentiel, mais je ne vois pas que ce soit ou que ce doive être l'ordre épistemologique, tel que l'a défini le dialogue *De Veritate*."

48. Audet, "On source augustinienne" 127: "Le *Proslogion* a été écrit comme une prière, dont je ne me préoccupe pas de savoir si elle est mystique aux termes de notre théologie ou de nos discernements critiques; mais qui est certes une éffusion fervente et progressive, dont l'émotion cherche à s'exprimer en des analogies que ne désavouerait pas l'histoire de la mystique."

49. *Ibid.* 133: "C'est la tendance même de son esprit, de son âme entrainée vers la vision qui éprouve un transport plus fervent dans son élan vers la réalité vivant en qui il croit 'in id in quod credi debet.' "

50. *Ibid.* 135–136: "C'est un être personnel et vivant qu'il reconnait dans l'expérience vive de sa pensée et c'est à cette Personne qu'il s'addresse dans le tutoiement familier et serein d'une présence et d'une prière. Pour moi, dans le texte final du chapitre IV, toute l'autonomie dialectique incluse dans la clause 'non possim non intelligere' ne peut exclure dans son interprétation de la lettre et de l'esprit du traité la valeur psychologique de 'tibi,' de 'te,' la valeur d'une expérience de la foi."

51. P. Vignaux, "Note sur la chapitre LXX du *Monologion*," *Revue du Moyen Âge Latin* 3 (1947) 333: "On pourrait chercher dans le *Monologian* dès éléments de 'théologie mystique.' Ce désir, en effet, se situe dans une expérience de croyant: celle de la 'fides viva.' Definie au chapitre LXXVIII, ou l'adhésion ne va pas sans l'amour qui la suppose."

52. *Monologion* 70, 21–22, 80: "Etenim idem ipsum bonum quod se sic amari exigit, non minus se ab amante desiderari cogit."

53. Vignaux, "Note sur la chapitre LXX" 327: "Ici, dans la dialectique anselmienne, s'insère le désir de Dieu . . . l'acte de désire suivant l'amour en acte."

54. *Ibid.* 429: "Il ne semble pas douteux que, Saint Anselme expliquant Saint Anselme, cette conception de la vie de l'esprit aide à comprendre le *Proslogion:* on conçoit que tende à l'intelligence un foi qui, vivant de l'amour de son object, se trouve impliqué le désir de le voir."

55. J. Maritain, *Distinguer pour unir ou les degrés du savoir* (Paris, 1932) 218; E. Gilson, *L'Être et L'Essence* (Paris, 1948) 286.

56. Maritain, *Distinguer pour unir* 513: "La grâce sanctifiante et l'habitation de Dieu dans l'âme en état de grace: voilà les fondements ontologiques, les principes premiers de l'existence mystique"; *Ibid.* 503: "Dans l'ordre de l'exercice ou de l'opération la manière dont a lieu cette expérience et les moyens qu'elle met en jeu: c'est-à-dire les dons du Saint Esprit et la connaissance par connaturalité due a la charité."

57. Reason, it seems to me, does not think, nor does it lose itself; only as I have said, reason does not operate, being as it were overwhelmed by the magnitude of the things which it sees. St. Teresa, *Życie dzieła św. Teresy* (Cracow, 1939) I, 142–143. This was translated from the Spanish.

58. For the definitions of philosophical contemplation, mystical contemplation, mysticism, mystical experience, asceticism, see M. Gogacz, "Mistyka a poznanie Boga" 593–596.

59. Gilson, "Sens et nature" 42: "On ne trouve rien de tel (contemplation extatique) chez Saint Anselme et vouloir tirer de ses textes, où il n'est question ni de mystique ni de théologie, la preuve que le *Proslogion* est un traité de théologie mystique, c'est une entreprise sans espoir."

60. *Ibid.* 30–31: "Enseignant parallèlement . . . la mystique cistercienne et la doctrine de Saint Anselme, je n'avais pu m'empêcher de faire observer combien son entreprise résssemble à celle des mystiques. Non seulement luimême est un auteur spirituel de première importance . . . mais il est clair que l'effort de l'intelligence poursuit chez lui une fin analogue à celle que l'ascèse des mystiques se propose." E. Gilson, *Etudes sur le rôle de la pensée medievale dans la formation du système cartesien* (Paris, 1930) 218.

61. Gilson, "Sens et nature" 39: "Personne, pas même le P. Stolz, n'ose nier que l'argument de Saint Anselme ne vise en un certain sens l'existence, mais il nous démande d'y voir une contemplation mystique de l'existence divine non sa démonstration."

62. In the article "Sens et nature"; but see also E. Gilson, "Réflexions sur la controverse Saint Thomas-Saint Augustine," *Mélanges Mandonnet* I, 372: "Le preuve de l'existence de Dieu par Saint Anselme dans le *Proslogion* et les preuves de l'existence Dieu par Saint Thomas dans la *Somme théologique* reviennet théologiquement au même, elles restent entièrement différents pour la philosophie ou pour l'historien, parce que, bien qu'elles aillent au même

Mieczysław Gogacz

Dieu, elles n'y vont pas par les mêmes voies rationelles."

63. Gilson, "Sens et nature" 39: "Nous accordons tous que l'argument d'Anselme présuppose la foi."

64. Maritain, *Distinguer pour unir* 502: "La sagesse infusé . . . que consiste a connaître la Deité comme telle . . . il faut que (la foi) soit perfectionnée dans son mode d'opérer par les dons du Saint Esprit, don d'intelligence et surtout don de sagesse. C'est là l'experience mystique."

65. *Proslogion* 1, 4, 98: "Habitas lucem inaccessibilem."

66. *Ibid.* 1, 14, 98: "Ad te videndum factus sum."

67. *Ibid.* 1, 12, 98: "Deus meus es et dominus meus es, et nunquam te vidi."

68. *Ibid.* 1, 5, 98: "Quis me ducet et inducet in illam ut videam te in illa."

69. *Ibid.* 1, 7, 98: "Numquam te vidi, domine deus meus, non novi faciem tuam."

70. *Ibid.* 1, 3–5, 99: "Sumus expulsi . . . a patria in exilium, a visione Dei in caecitatem nostram."

71. *Ibid.* 5, 14, 104: "Quod ergo bonum deest summo bono?"

72. *Ibid.* 5, 11, 104: "Quid igitur es, domine deus, quo nihil maius valet cogitari."

73. *Ibid.* 1, 12–13, 100: "Gratias ago, quia creasti in me hanc imaginem tuam ut tui memor, te cogitem et amem."

74. *Ibid.* 16, 2–4, 113: "Ubique es tota praesens et non te video. In te moveor et in te sum et ad te non possum accedere. Intra me et circa me est, et non te sentio."

75. *Ibid.* 14, 14–15, 111: "Cur non te sentit, domine deus, anima mea, si invenit te."

76. *Ibid.* 1, 7, 98: "Numquam te vidi, domine deus meus, non novi faciem tuam."

77. *Ibid.* 26, 23, 120: "Deus meus et dominus meus, spes mea et gaudium cordis mei."

78. *Ibid.* 14, 22, 111–112: "Domine deus meus . . . dic desideranti animae meae quid aliud es, quam quod vidi, ut pure videat, quod desiderat. Intendit se ut plus videat et nihil videt ultra hoc quod vidit nisi tenebras, immo non videt tenebras, quae nullae sunt in te, sed videt se non plus posse videre propter tenebras suas."

79. *Ibid.* 1, 12, 100: "Ut tui memor te cogitum et amem."

80. *Ibid.* 26, 23, 120: "Spes mea et gaudium cordis mei."

81. St. John of the Cross writes further that he dwells as it were in a dark cloud; one can compare the creator to the dark storm, which he used in revealing his mysteries to Job (St. John of the Cross, *Droga na Górę Karmel* 139). I am citing this according to W. Granat, "Mistyczne poznanie i jego wpływ na etyczną osobowość," *Roczniki Teologiczno-Kanoniczne* 3 (1956) 38.

82. *Proslogion* 16, 2, 113: "Ubique es tota praesens et non te video."

83. *Ibid.* 14, 1, 112: "Non plus posse videre propter tenebras suas."

84. *Ibid.* 14, 18–21, 111: "Si ergo vidit lucem et veritatem vidit te . . . et tamen nondum te vidit . . . non vidit te sicuti es."

85. *Ibid.* 16, 4, 113: "Intra me . . . es."

86. M. D. Chenu, *La Théologie au douxième siècle* (Paris, 1957) 129: "Contemplatio se renforce de l'aura de la 'theoria,' 'nescientia' des ténèbres de la 'via negativa.'"

87. *Proslogion* 14, 18–21, 111: "Si ergo vidit lucem et veritatem vidit te. Si

non vidit te, non vidit lucem nec veritatem. An et veritas et lux est quod vidit, et tamen nondum te vidit, quia vidit te aliquatenus, sed non vidit te sicuti es."

88. J. de Ghellinck, *Le mouvement théologique du XIIe siècle* (Paris, 1948) 78: "Génie, que n'a pas son égal en Occident entre l'époque de Saint Augustin et celle de Saint Thomas."

THE ETHICAL AND

SOCIAL PERSONALITY

Wincenty Granat

I. THE ETHICAL PERSONALITY

MAN IS NOT ONLY A CONSCIOUS SUBJECT THAT INCLUDES PSYCHIC activity, but he also exists on a plain of moral good and evil and can direct himself by the voice of obligation and conscience—this is a new existential structure of human life not met with in other living essences. In a voluntary way man can choose in the sphere of moral values and thus develop and create good for himself and for society.[1] The ability of human nature to create an ideal image of man as an individual and as a social essence is amazing; all the social Utopias—so loved by mankind, and formulated in vast philosophical systems—originate not only in the fact that man has the ability to sketch and paint a beautiful, distant, and ideal world, but also in a firm faith that man can transform the world.

Man's ability to act in a sphere of moral and religious values raises him above the biological necessities of nature, and sometimes propels him toward acts contrary to it (for instance, one's own death to save another's life). These significant characteristics cause one to see in man not only a psychic person, but also an ethical person. This view of man is known in all religious and ethical systems, although the expression "ethical personality" is new. From the time that Kant defined the personality as "freedom and independence from the mechanism of all nature," masses of writings have appeared on this subject. Kant understood freedom as "the power of the essence subject to its own individual right, granted by its own reason." Such a notion of personality caused in great measure the incorporation of the features of freedom and almost absolute autonomy into the given idea.

A contemporary classical example of this is the ethics of Nicholas Hartmann, who so much exaggerates the autonomy of man that he sees in the existence of a suprahuman form of personality, that is God, a contradiction to the ethics of man, or at least an unsolved problem. Hartmann defines person as a subject who "by its transcendental acts is the bearer of value" (*Werte und Unwerte*).[2] He considers this notion of person as central to all ethics, and in the idea of values he sees as a characteristic that they oblige, but they do not force.

Others emphasize the idea of an ethical person as containing internalness, self-transformation, social work. Here Mounier can serve as an example: he builds the definition of the human personality from the elements of internalness, transcendence, action (in the matter of the world's reform, anti-individualism, and freedom).[3]

Besides the idea of transcendence, existentialism sees in the ethical person the concept of guilt, unrest, anguish, and the incessant command to arrive at an internal humanity.

In particular, many educators have defined the ethical personality as the harmonious development of all the powers of man.[4] The Soviet educator Levitov, writing on the psychology of personality, raises psychological and ethical problems of the harmony of the separate structures of man. "Personality, taken psychologically, presents itself as a unity of temperament, talent, inclinations of character, but that unity can be maintained only if it does not exclude the existing unity, for instance, between the mind and character, temperament and character."[5] The definition of personality as the harmonizing agent in man is quite popular and practical in fixing educational goals.

It is worthwhile to pause over the question as to what minimum elements the idea of personality ought to include so as to embrace the greatest number of definitions. Kant, seeing in the person complete autonomy, introduced the idea into the realm of conflict between world views, for many religious systems will certainly not accept such an autonomy of man. Would it be possible for the "minimum" to consider the empirical freedom of man without raising metaphysical debates on the theme of psychological freedom? It seems that from the methodological viewpoint the idea of empirical freedom would be such a minimum, for even the supporters of determinism should be able to agree that man in his external conduct is free. The above view would be a very unstable one—if we take the matter philosophically—for the empirical freedom of human acts raises at once the problem of internal psychological freedom that ultimately is the instrument and center of the ethical personality and the theoretical minimum for confirming its actuality.

Accepting psychological freedom as an indispensable feature of the ethical person, we can further enrich it with the help of formal or essential attributes. In the first instance, the idea of person will grow by adding such features as unity, self-activity, action, persistent striving for goals once chosen, transcendence, involvement, originality. These attributes satisfy the manner of human behavior but are not wholly conclusive about its full value; they can in fact already be the goal of efforts that are individual or collective.

If someone takes as his goal and ideal the conduct of man as harmonized, monolithic, or active and self-determinative—this would be a formal ideal; it is self-evident that such a goal already establishes potential unity, freedom, and the possibility of development.[6]

The consideration of the ethical personality, richer or poorer in attributes, results in two conceptions: the person will be an actual one or an ideal one, the pattern at which the development of the human person aims.[7]

The form of personality says nothing as yet about essential attributes and does not introduce the element of values; for one can be very independent, active, and free, but in a direction that he himself or society condemns; it is difficult to speak here of an ethical personality. The introduction of the factor of value brings into being the idea of the ethical personality with essential features. It is no easy matter to establish who can be called an ethical man; for the ethos of man is usually evaluated from a chosen world view or from certain chosen principles of behavior. If one accepts some principles of the natural law or general human ethics, then it is not very difficult to fix a criterion of the ethical personality and this from the viewpoint of essence, and not just form. Even in religious and philosophical conflicts, it is not difficult to establish who is a good father, mother, or friend.

Besides the ethical personality, it is a natural thing to establish essential and real goals for one's self, such as form the ideal personality; in this sense one speaks often of the ideal Pole, or Frenchman, or Italian, or of the ideal Catholic, or Moslem, or Buddhist. Dependent on the chosen world view, the essential ideal of the ethical person is formed in a diverse manner; besides this, the formation of such an ideal is within the bounds of human possibility, so that every human individual can develop its attributes in it.

What is the relationship of the concept of the ethical personality to the integral personality? As soon as one reviews these four ideas—two notions of the ethical ideal personality (formal and essential) and two notions of the real ethical personality (formal and essential)—it is easy to find their relationship to the integral personality. At once one must point out that the ethical personality has its grounds in the attribute of free will, and hence can exist without biological elements; on the other hand, these are included in the integral human person. The ethical personality is an indispensable element of the integral human person and determines the greatness of man, for it gives meaning to existence, speaks of goals and the means that lead to them, distinguishes us from the world of nature, and is the foundation of social and political organizations specifically human.

The ethical personality establishes the existence of the psychic personality, and the elements of one and the other are found in the full, that is, integral, human person that embraces the totality of man's existential structure. The ethical and psychic personalities are not distinct subjects; this would be contrary to reality and man's behavior. The same subject considered as the center of the data of consciousness is the psychic personality, and the same subject analyzed in its functions of free choice is called the ethical personality. The formulation of new notions in modern philosophy in the area of the human personality is worthwhile from the viewpoint that it opens new channels in the existential layers of man, and further analyzes those that have already been investigated; in this it can err, but ultimately it leads to an understanding of the wealth of human nature.

From St. Thomas Aquinas to twentieth-century psychology, ethics, and metaphysics we have made a long journey into the depth and width of human nature—and we must keep this in mind in studying personalism. Thomas did not give a full and original description of the integral person, but he used the description of Boethius, even though he did introduce many ideas complementary to that definition so often analyzed by medieval philosophy and theology. In a similar manner, Aquinas in his works did not give a description of the ethical personality, even though one can easily find among them scattered details from which one can establish the whole.[8] Only here appear the many things in Thomism that are relevant and are being discovered anew by contemporary thought. The ideal of the ethical personality, formal and essential, as sketched by Aquinas is a synthesis of the morality of Aristotle and that of the gospel proclaimed by the Church. The ethical personality according to Thomistic thinking is an indispensable element of the integral person, for when Aquinas explains the definition given by Boethius he adds immediately that rational substances have control over their actions (*dominium sui actus*), and are not only subject to action but act by themselves (*per se agunt*).[9]

1. The person, according to St. Thomas, is not an instrument, but a cause and principle of action, or an individual subject. Man lives in a world of necessity, but he can enter a world where force does not exist; he is not subject in any degree to biological and psychological necessities; nor is he subject (or can he be subject) to the drive of instincts or social pressure. Freedom, according to Thomas, is not some conscious necessity, but rather self-determination. The person decides and determines his relationship to God, the world, and his neighbor; the person is not determined but guides himself, for he has control over his own actions.

2. The person acts in a world of good. The general idea of good is the motive force in man, who, moved in this manner, can choose this good or that, even though it be disadvantageous. Today we speak of positive or negative values.

3. The structure of the ethical personality. St. Thomas Christianized the morality taught by Aristotle and by the Stoics. Conforming to the *Nichomachean Ethics* he speaks of the virtues, dividing them into groups and analyzing them in detail. Thomas incorporates charity into the harmonious structure of human morality, as well as the theological virtues and the gifts of the Holy Spirit; the opposite of virtues are the vices (*vitia*). The structure of the ethical personality presented in Thomas' writings charms by its compactness; and even though it offends some by the Gothic quality of its form and the lack of concrete solutions, it nevertheless sheds light on many contemporary problems.

4. Autoteleology. In the *Summa Contra Gentiles* St. Thomas writes: "Rational natures were established by Divine Providence for their own sakes; other things exist for their sake."[10] Again he says in the *Summa Theologica*: "Man is by nature free and exists for his own sake."[11] Man, therefore, does not exist in order to become the litter of history; nor can he therefore be subordinated as an instrument to another's pleasure, ambition, absolute power; nor can he finally be the slave of abstract values. Even God does

not wish man to be an instrument of his glory, for beside God man is the secondary goal of creation. All values, even the most noble, are on a lower plane, and therefore exist for man, and not the opposite; culture remains in the service of humanity and its goal; the state is to be an instrument for the development of man, and not the reverse. The slogan "For God and the Nation" (or humanity) must be understood in the sense that it is a mutual relationship with God and with labor by free persons for the welfare of society. In a wonderful manner Thomas establishes the autoteleology of man: if it were possible to use man as a part, then he would be subordinated to someone or something, but man is a whole; for every intellectual substance encloses as it were everything within itself, since with its mind it embraces the totality of being (*totius entis comprehensiva*). From that viewpoint man cannot be treated as an instrument, for "possessing reason he decides what is good or bad for him according to time and place."[12] In this way the rational creature shares in the councils of God, for it directs itself and others.[13]

5. Relationship to society. St. Thomas argues that man as an individual needs many things and is not self-sufficient in life; hence, besides divine aid, he also needs human aid.[14] In his writings Thomas repeats sixty times the aphorism that the common good is better than the particular good of an individual; and twenty times he repeats that man is a social animal. We also find the analogy of society with the human body, and the simile that the individual person is related to the "multitude" as part to a whole.[15]

However, it is not permissible on the basis of these quotations to think that man, according to Thomas, is only a part of the social organism, as is a cell in the body. The particular person—he writes—can be considered as a part of society or as possessing something from God, for he is God's creature and image.[16] From the fact that the person has something from God, Thomas argues about his relation to society: "Man is not subject to political society with all his being and with everything he possesses . . . but everything that man is, what he can do and whatever he has must be directed to God."[17] From the thirteenth to the twentieth century mankind has not thought out anything better for the solution of the eternal problem, that of the individual and society; the human person is a part of society and has obligations to it, but the person possesses his own spheres, in which other human beings cannot interfere, and commands would destroy the vital powers of human persons. Thomas' thought reaches even further. Man cannot be an atom or a wheel in the social mechanism, for he has something from God. It would be worthwhile to pause here and to consider the logic of the following questions: If a man believes that he has nothing from God and is only a product of the cosmos, will he not be inclined to treat human individuals exclusively as part of a ruling organization? Does not faith in God lead to human values? The saying *res sacra homo* (man is a holy thing) finds good support in religious faith and in the intellectual system of Thomism.

6. The dynamics and development of the human person. A man with values is also a creature of culture; in the system of St. Thomas one cannot think of human values rising without technical values as well; he saw in the human mind the ability to form an unlimited number of conceptions, and in human hands the instrument of instruments. That very expression Thomas took from Aristotle, but he added the words that man can prepare instruments in unlimited number, so that he can perform works in increasing number.[18] The dynamics of technical or economic development Thomas connects very closely with man's striving for all truth and goodness. The human mind is basically capable of knowing every truth, and therefore there exists in us according to Thomas "a natural desire to see God, and the human will" is capable of accepting the Highest Good (*capax summi boni*).[19] Strange as it seems, it is true that Thomas was not a dogmatist in the sense we give to that expression today. All dogmatism is alien to the idea of the ethical personality; it would depend on some unreal and impractical limitation on the way to truth, yet the striving after truth is not such a limitation. Dogma in the concept of Thomism depends on the struggle with artificial limitations: the only norm is reality; the paradox of Christian dogmas depends precisely on this: that it fights limitations. Choose every truth, and strive for good—that is the ideal of the ethical personality in Thomas. The activities of the human person and their ethical development are directed to eternity, since rational essences by their very nature desire always to live in a supratemporal manner.[20]

7. The participation of the ethical personality in the life of God. St. Thomas adopted St. Augustine's view about the participation of all creatures in the being of God and connected it with the teaching about the divine image and Divine Providence. Man, being a reflection of the Highest Wisdom, has the natural law inscribed in his soul, according to which he can rule himself, other

human beings, and all things. Thomas writes in the *Summa Contra Gentiles*: "The rational creature shares in Divine Providence not only because he receives directives but also in the sphere of governance—by his activity he directs himself and others."[21]

The idea of an ethical order is for Thomas something essential; he repeats the thought of Aristotle: *rationis est ordinare.* The whole tract on the natural, eternal, and positive law speaks of norms for the ethical personality, norms that are very human, for they are inscribed in human nature.

In the light of Thomas' principles it is consequently possible to describe the real human ethical personality: a conscious and rational subject, which in union with all human society strives in an orderly[22] but unforced manner for all truth and goodness, thus enriching himself and mankind.[23]

In connection with the idea of ethical personality, it is worthwhile to analyze the problem of humanism in Catholic personalism, in which it is a central idea. Perhaps the matter will become clearer on the basis of objections. A Polish writer, L. Kołakowski, establishes six basic questions in the area of morality; the negative or positive reply is to be the criterion of a humanistic (or nonhumanistic) morality.

(a) Does the moral doctrine acknowledge that man is the proper source of values and moral precepts?

(b) Does it acknowledge that man's conduct—understood in this way or otherwise—is the principal criterion of moral values?

(c) Does it recognize that man is the proper and principal object of conduct which can be evaluated morally?

(d) Does it acknowledge that man is capable by his own efforts of reaching moral perfection, or at least of bringing it to a high level?

(e) Does it acknowledge that human dignity and the value man achieves come from man himself?

(f) Does it acknowledge that man is the highest value or, at least, in the words of Kant, that man is an end in himself in the field of morality?[24]

Kołakowski is convinced that a truly humanistic morality must answer all these questions positively; for thus has humanism been understood historically.[25] Catholic teaching should really reply negatively to all the above questions; hence the conclusion that it is antihumanistic. The teaching of the Church is supposed to be that "not man, but God, is the source of the values of moral precepts."[26] The meaning of that statement is not very clear, for it can be understood as though man is not the source of any values and precepts and therefore is not a creator of moral values at all. No Catholic, or in general any religious moralist, would approve of that explanation, for it contradicts the most fundamental truths of human nature possessed of reason and free will; being an image of the Wisdom of God and sharing in God's activity, man judges and decides. Through natural law rational creatures or essences participate in the eternal law; for all beings, according to St. Thomas, have the eternal law impressed on their nature, and thanks to it are directed to actions and goals proper to them.[27] Rational creatures participate in Divine Providence in the more particular manner, for they direct others and themselves.[28] Man, therefore, creates moral values, since there exists in him the light of natural reason, which is a reflection of the Divine Light.

To the question, therefore, whether man is the proper source of moral values, Catholic morality must give an affirmative answer. In a certain sense it must be acknowledged that man is the ultimate source of moral values, because the ultimate subject of appeal in judging what is good or evil is conscience; however, it must base itself on the objective condition of things, that is, the conformity of the act with the existing order, and hence with its own nature. That will be objectively good which is good for human nature, and therefore subjectively and objectively man is the source of moral values—obliged not to surrender to self-will, but to approve reality. In this way we approach the reply to the second question: Is human conduct the principal criterion of moral values?

Kołakowski once again is convinced that human affairs (even eternal salvation) are the chief criteria of moral values in consideration of the "love of God for himself"—(the words "for him" are underlined by L. K.)—and not the "good of man." His proof is a citation from the *Imitation of Christ:* "Seek not what is sweet and useful for yourself, but that which agrees with my will."[29] Actually does a Christian—who believes that the Son of God became man "for us and for our salvation," and who also believes that the commandment of the love of neighbor is similar to the commandment of the love of God—have the obligation to recognize that human conduct is not the chief standard of moral values? It seems not; at the most, he could say that it is one of the principal criteria; but that statement would be inexact. When one says in the objection that the commandment of the love of God for himself is the chief criterion, one would have to indicate at once how Christianity understands it. It is known that disinterested and friendly love of God is at the same time necessarily a love for all his works, that it does good in whatever form, and that it enriches the one who loves and all of humanity generally.

Scripture expresses this connection briefly and clearly: "If anyone says, 'I love God,' and hates his brother, he is a liar. For how can he who does not love his brother, whom he sees, love God, whom he does not see. And this commandment we have from him, that he who loves God should love his brother also (1 Jn 4:20–21). A Christian knows well the gospel's description of the last judgment when the highest and ultimate moral value will be applied: "Come, blessed of my Father, take possession of the kingdom prepared for you from the foundation of the world; for I was hungry and you gave me to eat. . . . 'Lord, when did we see thee hungry'. . . . 'Amen I say to you, as long as you did it for the least of my brethren, you did it for me' " (Mt 25:34–40). The love of Christ, the God-Man, is identified with an active friendship of human beings, and the principal criterion of moral values is precisely human affairs. Kołakowski errs profoundly if he thinks that Catholicism has any other teaching.

Another reproach against Catholicism is that not man but God is the object of moral progress, and that it is a sin to do anything only on behalf of man.[30] Anyone hearing such an opinion might well ask himself: Then perhaps the Son of God committed the greatest sin, having become man for our sake and for our salvation. The Church teaches that man is an end in himself, and that not only is it not a sin to do something only for man's sake but also it is simply a moral obligation. A Christian who would act otherwise and use man as an instrument of anybody's glory, even God's, would sin grievously.[31] Man is, indeed, the secondary goal of all creation, but this does not mean a succession to the primary goal, the glory of God, since it depends really on his conscious and voluntary share in the activity of God, the highest blessedness of rational creatures; the two goals are not then really distinct from one another.

The next question—Can man by his own efforts achieve moral perfection?—is so formulated that from a Christian (who believes that the grace of God is necessary for salvation, and therefore also for an upright life) one would have to expect an exclusively negative answer;[32] but even here certain explanations are indispensable. The grace of God is not something alien to man, but an internal strength uniting with nature as a freely accepted world of the love of friendship.[33] Under the influence of new energy, man, not by alien but by his own effort (although not through the strength of nature alone) can reach moral perfection. Hence the command is intelligible: "You therefore are to be perfect, even as your heavenly Father is perfect (Mt 5:48). The statement of St. Paul has a profound meaning: "But by the grace of God I am what I am, and his grace in me has not been fruitless—in fact I have labored more than any of them, yet not I, but the grace of God with me" (1 Cor 15:10). This is a strange objection to those who assert that the individual human being would never have been humanized without the indispensable aid of society: this aid differs from the grace of God by the fact that it originates in the absolute rights of nature, and not from the highest personal love. It would indeed be contrary to human nature to accept aid that weakens our activity, but not cooperation which increases our strength, develops, and leads us to full humanity.

A truly humanistic morality should demand that the value man achieves and his dignity come from man himself; here it must be asked in what sense is that postulate established. Perhaps here the view (anarchistic in principle) is not accepted that man's value and dignity depend only on his individual efforts and that man in achieving values does not use the resources of matter, the vegetable life, animals, the help of past and present generations? If anyone agrees that it is through necessary forces of development that all values in the intellectual and moral life are created—how can he say that man achieves his own value and dignity? Catholicism expressly teaches that especially human dignity (arising from nature itself) depends on the action of reason and the possibility of free choice; with this dignity there is connected a second—called divine sonship. Man, an intellectual and rational creature, with the dignity of nature and the dignity of a child of God perfects his own values and activates his own attributes.

Catholic morality is seen in a distorted mirror if one says that it does not recognize man as the highest value and end in himself, and believes in God as the absolute value. No theist could call himself a humanist if he does not recognize an absolute in man. It is not today or yesterday or a thousand years ago that we became aware of this compulsion to impress upon man that he is the highest value, but at the moment we shall avoid such reflection and rather turn our attention to the problem that asks in what sense can man be called a value and goal in himself. According to Catholic teaching, man is not a value subordinated to anything else (even the glory of God), and exists beside God—or to use a Christian expression, he is in the family of God, sharing in his nature, fullness of being, and independence. Once again it must be emphasized that the autoteleology of man is inseparable from his rational nature and his call to divine sonship. All earthly nature, all natural societies, and the supernatural organization of the Mystical Body according to the teaching of the Catholic Faith work toward the end that man achieve his goal, that is, an immortal participation in the independence of God. Whence then comes the view of some opponents of Catholic ethics, that the doctrine on the independence of man contradicts it?

Catholic morality is supposed to be antihumanistic because it demands faith in mysteries revealed by God, and this is supposedly the greatest degradation of the human mind.[34] "To the essence of the humanistic view of the world belongs the principle of man's loyalty to his own reason," so that formulas whose meaning cannot be comprehended "are to be treated as something which is neither true nor false, but simply as something irrational." This objection is again a classical example of attributing to Catholic teaching something alien to it.[35] It is indeed irrational and absurd to accept such opinions as oppose the principles of identity, contradiction, and sufficient reason, and hence contradictory formulas, or propositions not based on rational motivation. Catholicism has never held that dogmatic formulas are accepted by reason without sufficient reason and that no one understands their meaning.[36] Indeed, all of Catholic theology tries to explain the meaning of dogmas by pointing to the analogical content of the terms; it endeavors to guard revealed truth against the objection of contradiction and tries to establish the reasonableness of their acceptance. Vatican I teaches that reason is able to achieve a knowledge of mysteries to some degree (intelligentia mysteriorum), except that it cannot demonstrate them scientifically. One can refuse to agree with the Church's efforts to explain given revelations, but to say that the Church orders one to believe in such truths whose very meaning cannot be basically understood, is contrary to reality. In evaluating the above objection it is difficult to oppose the biblical thought; for long ago it was said to man that faith in what God has revealed has no meaning and is a lie.

Objections against Catholicism, as though it were opposed to the intellectual values of man, are also formulated on a basis of prejudices more general than those on the character of dogmas. All religion is supposed to have a "negative influence on the intellectual efforts of man,"[37] and this from various viewpoints; for it gives to an "amazed or frightened man" an explanation of all things, and that in a manner apparently wise, deep, and effective. Science demands hard work in independent thought, and it therefore is "dry and not very romantic," leaving little room for illusions, but Catholicism "provides an easy realization of dreams," and "does not control the metaphysical fantasies of man by reason." Catholicism introduces men "into the wonderful world of metaphysical fairy tales," "responds to the desire for the deepest knowledge, reaching beyond the attainable and visible world."[38] The conclusion from this kind of reflection is that Catholicism "continues to be to this very day one of the great tragedies of intellectual people" and "gives a mystified answer with frankly unheard of harm."[39] Thus Catholicism leads man away from "the road of heavy and arduous, but practically only real effort by human reason," that is, "from the one road on which humanity can reveal itself."[40]

There are among the opponents of Catholicism those who wish that Catholicism would surrender the role of reason in religious truth and base faith on faith alone, "since the more rationalization there is of them, the more doubt and infidelity will there be."[41] Such a position, they say, is forward looking and farsighted and would even have the support of the gospel's Sermon on the Mount ("Blessed are the poor in spirit, for theirs is the kingdom of heaven"); for "if all rationalization of religion were removed from the realm of faith, in all fairness, how shall doubts arise about the truth of the faith?"[42] This excellent notion of the faith the Church has not recognized, but on the contrary sanctioned the teaching of St. Thomas "depending on the rational demonstration of the articles of faith,[43] and of the reality of God himself."[44] The acceptance of Thomism was for the Church a *malum necessarium;* it was important to hinder the development of human thought "by yoking reason to the chariot of the faith."[45]

St. Thomas, unmindful of the "bitter testimony of Scripture," was able to plant "in his theological garden another tree of knowledge,"[46] "realizing that reason and knowledge, which had driven the first parents from paradise, would, owing to Thomas' wisdom, open the gates to paradise for man."[47]

Thomas did not slay reason, but, as the objector asserts, dressed it in a monastic habit, and only its irreligious appearance vanished; even so the Trojan horse was introduced into the sanctuary; doubts began to arise and to deepen the contradictions between reason and faith; he had to proceed against himself, dissimulating his own weakness and the rightness of the articles of faith. Because of the division of faith into two zones, one knowable and the other unknowable, human reason found itself in a confused situation, since it became the "source of knowledge of a goal, which does not fit within the bounds of rational knowledge."[48]

Beyond this, reason directs certain questions against the reasonableness of the faith. "For instance, can God, as the personification of highest wisdom, order man, under the pain of the cruelest eternal punishments, to believe in something whose understanding is impossible for him?" The notion of the goodness of God excludes all despotism, "but do you not say that man is the slave of God, a plaything in his hands, that the involuntary tribute paid to God by his will and command is the holiest obligation of man?" "Can you explain who created evil in the world?" "You say, Satan." "But could Satan do anything against the will of God?" "Perhaps you will be able to explain who created Satan?"[49] It is worthwhile to note that these questions and reflections testify to a deep interest in the problematic of religion and the continuing actuality of the biblical narrative. The very same thoughts that appeared in the minds of the first parents about the reasonableness of faith in the word of God and the thought that God envied man's greatness, so that he alone would receive tribute and rule over man in his abasement—these thoughts are repeated in history, and even today they have the flavor of reality. God, religion, revelation, and the Church are supposed to be the opponents of human intellectual development. Knowledge, by which man conquers himself and the world, is represented as original sin, and hence against the will of God; but this reproach is completely false. This idea of God disagrees with Scripture and the teaching of the Church and has its correspondent in the temptation that attacked the first parents rather than in the positive teaching of revelation.

The personality of man is, according to Catholic teaching, the highest goal of human action; and it is enriched by the privilege of divine sonship. When we tend toward God, then we achieve full humanity and we share in his inner life. We are, therefore, on the way

from limitation—to participation in the fullness of being;
from faith to the vision of God and all reality in him;
from a mortal life to immortality;
from the limitations of full autonomy to the independence of God.

II. THE SOCIAL PERSONALITY

It is easy to see that the human individual from the dawn of his life dwells in social groups which influence him in many various ways.[50] The mutual relationship of the individual and society is the subject of many sciences, especially sociology. Every normal personality not only concentrates its life-experience around itself, and therefore does not wish to play a lonely role, but rather learns also to be a human being within a community, and thus to play some particular instrument in the orchestra.[51] Mutual interaction of human consciousnesses is somehow a primitive datum. According to contemporary personalists, it is possible to observe in human relations a taking and a sharing, variety and yet some kind of identity, and the development of union by the performance of tasks imposed by society. Besides such a bond, mutual interaction of human beings is always limited, for it does not reach the depths of our being.[52]

Society forms individuals from a moral, intellectual, religious, and economic viewpoint, and finally also influences the formulation of the individual's concepts about himself. The circumstances in which anyone lives create a social position for him and create, as it were, a new being in man which is called by many contemporary sociologists "a social personality."[53] According to Znaniecki[54] and J. Chałasiński,[55] the following elements reveal the social personality: a reflected entity; social position; social function; and life meaning.

1. People in the defined social circles do not have the same values. In the hierarchy of values, for instance, intellectual values can appear on the first level; in connection with that a given individual can endeavor to play a role adapted to the demands of opinion and forms himself in that direction; and this is its reflected entity.[56]

2. The next element in social personality is social status, which includes "moral position, economic position, the area of security, and the realm of privacy."[57]

The moral position depends on the specific social rights given an individual in a given group (rights as well as obligations); these are the rights to respect, assistance, defense, and trust.[58] The protection of economic circumstances,[59] in which the individual lives, and, in general, the protection of acknowledged rights belong to the social position of the person and enter as elements into the idea of the social personality. In the social position of the individual the protection of private activity, to which society does not wish to lay claim,[60] must also be included.

3. In the idea of the social personality, according to Znaniecki and Chałasiński, those features must be included which touch the function performed within a given group. "Thus, for instance, the actual task of the physician in the circle of his patients is the performance of professional activity according to existing criteria of science and medical practice." By professional performance and in general by influencing the social group, the individual forms his own personality, wins opinion for himself, and finally appears as a social being or a social person.

4. The last element of the social personality, "its life meaning," depends on the influence which the performance of a given role by an individual exercises on his own life, on the cultural and social life of his environment."

On the basis of all the properties appearing in a given individual, either actually or in the opinion of the social group, we can formulate for ourselves the concept of the social personal (personality). Znaniecki gives this definition: We call a social person the individual human being in a defined personal role, which he actually plays in a defined social circle.[61] S. Baley gives a little different definition: "The sum or result of all the roles, which a given individual fills in society, is based ultimately on his social personality."[62] We distinguish the social person from the legal-moral personality, because in the first case we speak of the sum of relations existing between the individual and a social group, and in the second about the whole of humanity; they are "persons" only in an analogical sense, for a whole is not the subject of action, but the individual, who bears responsibility and is properly and immediately responsible.

What is the relationship between the social personality and the psychic personality, the ethical and the integral human person? In one view, to which Znaniecki inclines,[63] "the social personality would be something engrafted on the psychological personality."[64] Some sociologists take an extreme position, that the subjective "I" is the creation of the influence of the social group; man, ultimately, in it and through it, becomes aware that he is a separate subject, which means that he would perceive the existing relations between "I" and "you," "I" and "we." Prominent exponents of this view are C. H. Cooley[65] and G. H. Mead.[66] Both these authors demonstrate above all that consciousness of one's own self, of one's own "I," as a separate something and equal to the selves of other people, is formed in man in the course of social contact.[67] Individuality is the total of an individual's active relationships with other human beings and with nature, and personality as the consciousness of these relationships.[68] E. Mounier emphasizes strongly the dependence of the psychic subject on the social group, although he somewhat reserves himself against the view according to which the "I" would be exclusively the product of society: "The person only exists thus toward others, it only knows itself in knowing others, and only finds itself in being known by them. The *Thou*, which implies the we is prior to the "I" or at least accompanies it."[69] The expression *at least* indicates that Mounier does not consider the subjective "I" as the creation of society exclusively.

If we wish to define more exactly the influence of society on the formation of the consciousness of the distinct subject called the psychic personality or self, we meet sharp philosophical and sociological conflicts. It is difficult to demonstrate that the consciousness of the "I" is a social product; the alleged proofs from child psychology, according to which the child is supposed to achieve its own awareness of its distinctiveness only by contact with the environment—[70] confuse two distinct ideas: the notion of an occasion or, at the most, a condition, with the idea of a causal influence that is exclusive. The capability of an awareness of a bond of psychic acts with a central point, the subject, results from a general psychic power called reflection; we do not receive it from a social group, but we possess it because of our human nature. The social person presupposes the existence of the psychic personality, which perceives many individuals, distinct subjects, and also the various relations among them. Opinions given by anyone about other persons are based on an analogy with one's own person and on the priority of the knowledge of one's own "I." The social personality would have no bases, if a real subject did not exist. We must indisputably accept the existence of social influence on the formation of the ideal of personality, on enriching the psyche, but a conclusion that the ontological self is but the product of a social group goes beyond the bounds of logical truth, for dependence in particulars is one thing, and the origin of the self by social influence is quite another.[71]

In the idea of the social personality one does not find ethical elements, and therefore it does not encompass the total of man's actions; every human individual evaluates this means and has the capacity to choose between that which it considers morally good and bad for itself, esthetical or unesthetical, economically advantageous or injurious. The existence of an ideal world of values and its transfer to the sphere of reality is the task of man, and therefore he is an ethical person; to some degree he depends on the social personality and is connected with it, but the social and ethical personalities are not conceptually identical. The subject considered in its social relations is the social personality: in its relations to the sphere of values and in its own character of an essence acting freely, it is an ethical personality. Neither the one nor the other is the integral human being, an essence of body and soul, including in itself the potential awareness of itself and the capability of creating values.

FOOTNOTES

1. See the beautiful passage of P. Teilhard de Chardin, quoted by Mounier: "Il n'est pas rien de plus préparé dans l'histoire de l'univers que l'homme et sa liberté." E. Mounier, "Tâches actuelles d'une pensée d'inspiration personnaliste," *Esprit* 11 (1948) 703.

2. N. Hartmann, *Ethik* (Berlin, 1920) 205.

3. See Mounier, note 1.

4. Besides the many meanings of that term (personality) we find it includes the postulate of a harmonious, many-sided development of the psychic structure of man (K. Sośnicki, *Dydaktyka ogólna* [Toruń] 9, 38); see B. Nawroczyński, *Zasady nauczania* (Wrocław, 1957) 14–15, 121.

5. "There are two opposite errors in the concept of the structure of personality. Representatives of one theory emphasize the mutual bond of the particular elements of personality, and finally they cover the properties of the particular components. . . . The opposite error consists in such isolation of one element from another, that the person as a whole dissolves." N. D. Levitov, "Voprosy psychologii lichnosti," *Sovietskaia pedagogika* 6 (1948) 91.

6. More being for one's self implies that one already possesses being. To acquire more personality and freedom, one must already be a person and possess freedom.

7. "The fullness of personal existence is to be acquired with the aid of passing from less being to more. Man is called to personalization, to growth, to maturity; he must pass from anarchy to unity, from flux to stability, from infancy to manhood, from slavery to freedom. With the help of God's grace he is to obtain the perfection of his being. From that particular viewpoint a person is a call to self-conquest." P. Rideau, "Qu'est ce que la personne," *Nouvelle Revue Théologique* 2 (1925) 153.

8. The expression "personal morality" is not found in St. Thomas, but the term "person" is an element in it. See E. Gilson, *Le Thomisme* (Paris, 1944) 420–421. The person promulgates the law, applies it, gives it sanctions in the name of the demands of reason. The person is dependent on God, but this dependence, in the thought of St. Thomas, is a share in an infinitely wise and

free Power, and hence possesses the light of reason and the initiative of freedom. See J. Lenz, "Die Personwürde des Menschen bei Thomas von Aquin," *Philosophisches Jahrbuch der Görres-Gesellschaft* 49 (1938) 1–2.

9. *S. Th.* q. 9, a. 1.

10. *S.C.G.* III, c. 112: "Naturae ergo intellectuales sunt propter se a divina providentia procuratae, alia vero omnia propter ipsas."

11. *S. Th.* II–II, q. 64, a. 2, ad 3: "Propter seipsum existens."

12. *S.C.G.* III, c. 113.

13. *Ibid. c.* 113. Some centuries after the death of St. Thomas, Kant recognized this view as the categorical imperative. The philosopher from Królewice did not give such simple arguments as did St. Thomas. Therefore, it is invalid to object that Catholic personalism sees man's worth as a person not in man himself but in God. Hence, that it does not seek the emancipation of man in the transformation of the world by man and the transformation and humanization of social conditions in which man lives, but above all in a union with God.

14. *S. Th.* II–II, q. 129, ad 6, ad 1.

15. *Ibid.* II–II, q. 64, a. 2; *De Malo* IV, a. 4.

16. *Ibid.* q. 64, a. 2.

17. *Ibid.* I–II, q. 21. a. 4, ad 3.

18. *Ibid.* I, q. 76, a. 5.

19. *Ibid.* I, q. 93, a. 2, ad 3.

20. *Ibid.* q. 75, a. 6.

21. *S.C.G.* III, c. 113: "Participat igitur rationalis creatura divinam providentiam non solum secundum gubernari, sed etiam secundum gubernare."

22. When man does not live in accordance with his reason, he can be called an ethical person only in the formal sense.

23. It would be worthwhile here to quote some fragments from the discourse of Pius XII to the participants of the twelfth Congress of the International Society of Applied Psychology (April 10, 1958). The Pope was paying particular attention to the ethical personality. We give first the definition of personality: "The psychosomatic unity of man, as it is governed and determined by the soul."

"The individual as a unity and undivided whole forms the only and general centrum of being of action called 'I' which possesses itself and rules itself . . . personality can be considered as a fact, and beyond this also in its relations to moral values."

"Metaphysics considers man as a living being, endowed with intelligence and freedom; in him body and soul are united in one nature that possesses independent existence. Using technical terms we speak of an individual substance on a rational nature (*S. Th.* I, q. 29, a. 1). In that sense man is always a person, an individual, distinct from others, he is an 'I' from the first to the last moment of his life, even when he does not possesses consciousness." We see that Pius XII distinguishes the psychic and ethical personality (*la personalité*, that is, the psychic subject of moral values) from the integral person. From the moral and religious viewpoint, personality has these most important features: 1. The entire man is the work of the creator . . . by creation he is the image of God, and by redemption he receives in Christ the divine sonship. . . . The Christian personality is not understandable, if one does not consider these things; particularly applied psychology falls into many misunderstandings and errors if it does not recognize this. 2. Consideration of the goal is equally essential for the personality from the moral and religious viewpoint. Man has the obligation and the power of perfecting his nature according to the plan of God. 3. The property of responsibility and freedom is essential for the personality. In connection with this it is necessary to establish these propositions or theorems: man must be treated as normal, until the opposite is known; normal man not only has freedom in theory, but he uses it in action; the normal man, using his spiritual powers, can conquer the difficulties in observing the moral law; abnormal psychic dispositions are not compulsive in all instances and do not always take away from the subject the possibility of voluntary action; the dynamism of the unconscious and the subconscious are not invincible, but in great degree, man, especially a normal one, can overcome them; and the normal man is responsible for his decisions. 4. In order to understand personality, one must consider its eschatological aspect. . . . "From the moral and religious viewpoint, the decisive element in the structure of personality is his attitude before God, who is our last end given us by nature itself."

From the content of the discourse it is clear that Pius XII, basing himself on the metaphysical idea of man, speaks of the psychic, and particularly the ethical, personality and indicates its essential features. He spoke further on the obligations of the psychologist to the human person. The text is found in *Nouvelle Revue Théologique* 80 (1958) 630–639.

24. Leszek Kołakowski, "Katolicyzm i humanizm," *Po Prostu* 3 (1956) I, 15.

25. *Ibid.* "From the beginning of its history the meaning of the historical concept of humanism was always antireligious, laic, and earthly; in characterizing the concept of humanistic morality as opposed to a religious world view, I am trying to do nothing more than give a meaning to the term conferred upon it by its own authentic history."

26. Kołakowski refers to two texts from St. Augustine. "The maker of temporal laws, if he is a wise and just man, directs himself by that eternal law to judge which is not granted to any soul," *De Vera Religione* XXXI, 58; the Latin text of St. Augustine is "Conditor tamen legum temporalium, si vir bonus est et sapiens illam ipsam consulit aeterna de qua nulli animae iudicare datum est; ut secundum eius incommutabiles regulas, quid sit pro tempore iubendum vetandumque discernat," *De Vera Religione* XXXIV, 148. Kołakowski's Polish translation does not agree with the Latin text, in which it says that the just man "consults"—*consulit,* and not "directs himself." Moreover, the words "nulli animae iudicare datum est" were not understood by St. Augustine as though man made no judgment at all; indeed, the context says that man, according to the eternal law, distinguishes what is good and what is bad, except that man is not allowed to reject that law.

Kołakowski's second text to prove Augustine's antihumanist position is "When man lives according to man and not according to God, then he is like the devil," *Regnum Dei* XIV, 4. The text of St. Augustine does seem antihumanist, but we must see how he understood the expression "according to man." This is an allusion to the following text of Scripture: "For since there are jealousy and strife among you, are you not carnal, and walking as mere men?"— in the Latin, *secundum hominem* (1 Cor 3:3). St. Augustine explains the text in the following manner: "If he lives according to himself, that means according to man and not according to God, by the same token he lives according to falsehood; not that man himself is falsehood, for his maker and creator is God. But if he lives not according to the kind of life he was created to live, then that is falsehood. . . . That alone does man good which is from God; and a sinner, abandoning God, does not abandon that which is from himself, for then he lives according to himself," *Regnum Dei* XIV, 4. One cannot conclude from the above text that man is not free to live according to his nature and that man does not create moral values: as a responsible being and an image of God, he is the source of moral values, when he judges according to his conscience and the law, which, while it is also God's law, is also the natural law of man.

27. *S. Th.* I–II, q. 91, a. 2: "Lex naturalis nihil aliud est quam participatio legis aeternae in rationali creatura."

28. *Ibid.* I–II, q. 91, a. 2: "Rationalis creatura excellentiori quodam modo divinae providentiae subjacet, inquantum et ipsa fit providentiae particeps, sibi ipsi et aliis providens." In a somewhat different manner, man shares in the supernatural law of God through faith and charity, being conscious of his divine sonship.

29. The text is not cited very exactly. According to the author of the *Imitation of Christ* (III, c. 49, v. 3), Christ is instructing the man who would wish to die as soon as possible in order to enjoy the blessedness of eternity that he is bound to guide himself not by what is pleasant and useful to him now (that is, death and glory in heaven), but he must remember that for him there is still the time of warfare, the time of labor, the time of testing. The text speaks of man's true good upon the earth, on which he is to labor and accomplish his testing time; hence, it is a matter of man's twofold good, earthly and heavenly. Where is there the antihumanist meaning in the statement that man is not the object of moral progress? The will of God is that man is to arrive at his eternal good by doing good on earth.

30. Kołakowski supports this by citing John of the Cross that "all creatures are nothing, and attachment of the soul to them is worse than nothing, for it is a hindrance to transforming one's self in God—the soul cannot receive God, if it is attached to creatures," *The Ascent to Mount Carmel* I, 3, 4. A careful reading of the *Ascent to Mount Carmel,* and especially chapter 4 of the first book, certainly will not suggest the idea for which Kołakowski condemns the mystic. St. John of the Cross writes that attachment to creatures and being misled by their charms and attractions is a hindrance to union with God, and is thus a sin of treating creatures as an exclusive and highest goal.

31. The very expression about man as the object of moral progress is not clear in Kołakowski's article—if one took it in the sense that morality in general has no reference to man, the objection would be shockingly unfair.

32. Kołakowski, unfortunately enough, cites the text of a statement by the Council of Trent which teaches that man can by his good deeds achieve eternal life, but in a way that it is actually a grace and gift of God. The Church often condemned the opinion of pseudomysticism and quietism, which wished to demean human activity; hence, the Church rejected the characteristic statement of Molinos: Natural activity is hostile to grace, hinders divine action and true perfection, for God wishes to act in us, but without us.

33. Divine help does not come from without, but is an internal elevation of nature to a higher level. Theologians generally teach that grace is not cre-

Wincenty Granat

ated, but it is drawn from the potentiality of the soul—*educitur de potentia obedientiali animae.*

34. Kołakowski cites a text from St. Thomas' *Summa Contra Gentiles:* "How stupid would the man be, who suspected as false those things that have been revealed by God through the ministry of angels, because they cannot be investigated by reason," *S.C.G.* I, 3. Once again the text is mutilated and badly applied. The full text is as follows: "Just as an ignorant man would characterize himself with the greatest madness if he considered the things taught by a philosopher to be false because he could not grasp them, so much the more would man be servant to excessive stupidity if he suspected falsity in that which has been revealed by the ministry of angels, because they cannot be investigated by reason *(ratione investigari non possunt)."* One must note here that Kołakowski confuses two ideas: the irrationality of formulas and the impossibility of their demonstration.

35. The Church never recognized as its own the formula of Tertullian when he was defending the reality of Christ's body against the Manichaean Valentinian: "Mortuus est Dei filius; prorsus credibile est quia ineptum est; et sepultus resurrexit—certum est quia impossibile est," *De Carne Christi, PL* II, 760; *E.P.* 353. The Church does not teach us to believe in that which is absurd—*credo quia ineptum (absurdum),* but with St. Augustine says: "Intellige ut credas, crede ut intelligas," *Sermo* 43, 7.

36. "But the degradation of reason is even greater. Catholic doctrine presupposes that the content of revelation is such that we are obliged to believe it as true, although we are not capable of understanding its basic sense. It is further demanded that we support certain convictions whose meaning no mortal can know," Kołakowski, "Katolicyzm i humanizm," *Po Prostu* 3 (1956) I, 15.

Catholic morality is also attacked because of its leniency toward human nature. Pope Clement XI rejected as un-Catholic that view of the Jansenist Quesnel, who particularly condemned all actions as sins, if man was not guided by the motive of the purest and disinterested love of God. Kołakowski is scandalized that Clement XI condemns such propositions as "Where there is not charity, neither is there the God of religion," or "Whoever restrains himself from evil because of the fear of punishment, has already done evil in his heart and is guilty before God." If the Church had accepted these views, it would have had to abandon some good: in the first instance the good of faith in God and the good of an imperfect religion (they can exist with charity, even though they are imperfect); and in the second it would have been necessary to restrict very much the sphere of moral actions and to condemn a man who did not do evil, largely from a motive of fear (even though this does not exclude more perfect motives).

37. "A religious disposition and the state of a religious conscience favor not only a moral flight from the affairs of this world. In an even stronger effort religion hinders the intellectual endeavor of man," J. Kuczyński, "W kręgu chrześcijanskiej mądrości," *Po Prostu* 39 (November 27, 1955).

38. *Ibid.* The same ideas are in Kuczyński's book, *Chrześcijaństwo i sens życia* (Warsaw, 1958) 204–220.

39. *Ibid.* 204–220.

40. *Ibid.* 204–220. In this manner the author of the sketch repeats the opinion of Marx and Engels about the harm religion does to the development of man; then without any essential change he gives the theory of alienation—and

64

he forgets that in the last century a very rich literature has developed in the area of psychology and philosophy of religion.

41. Eugeniusz Kuszko, "Rozum przeciwnikiem rozumu," *Po Prostu* 8 (February 19, 1956).

42. *Ibid.*

43. Thomas did not teach that the articles of faith were demonstrated by reason, but that they are accepted rationally.

44. Kuszko, "Rozum przeciwnikiem rozumu."

45. *Ibid.* E. Kuszko thinks that if the Church would reject Thomism, the human mind would be independent of control and like a "free bird would fly rapidly to the sun of scientific knowledge, the more so since it proved impossible to lock it in prison or to burn it at the stake."

46. *Ibid.* "The biblical legend, one of the most profound and symbolic, declares that as long as man did not taste the fruit of the tree of knowledge, he was blessed in paradise. The tasting of that fruit became the greatest sin of man, original sin. Forgetful of the bitter testimony of Scripture, Thomas Aquinas planted another tree of knowledge in his theological garden."

47. *Ibid.*

48. *Ibid.*

49. *Ibid.*

50. Man "lives in his country, in his city, on his street, in his house; he lives not just with any people, but his own (those near to him), and then with his family, neighbors, and friends," Gerte M. Noetzel, *Persönlichkeit und Gemeinschaft* (Munich, 1957) 128–129.

51. *Ibid.* 128–129.

52. *Ibid.* 128–129.

53. "Man, growing in the civilization of his environment and taking part in the regulated relations and social groups, learns with the help of others rationally to organize his social personality, into its own particular system, and forms himself as a social personality," F. Znaniecki, *Ludzie teraźniejsi, a cywilizacja przyszłości* (Warsaw, 1935) 103. Znaniecki thinks it is impossible to speak of a technical, economic, religious, and aesthetic personality (p. 101).

54. *Ibid.* 117: "Every personal model includes four elements: the reflected self, the social status, the social function, and life meaning."

55. J. Chałasiński, *Społeczeństwo i wychowanie* (Warsaw, 1958) 34.

56. *Ibid.* 35. "An individual, knowing or surmising what features of mind and character a given social circle demands from his conduct and declarations, knows that for a given social role there is required a psychic self of definite characteristics, for instance, in certan roles one must be judicious and in others he must have a good memory. . . ." See also Znaniecki, *Ludzie teraźniejsi* 117–118: "The reflected self, when it becomes aware and fancies that it is the object of interest of a certain social circle (in the social and not the metaphysical sense, that is, in distinction from 'you,' 'he,' 'we,' and 'you,') there arises in the individual together with the impression a reflection of that picture which, in his opinion, others have of him."

57. Znaniecki, *Ludzie teraźniejsi* 120.

58. *Ibid.* 120: "The moral condition is the right (customary or statutory) of the social person to be treated as a more or less serious subject of obligatory moral actions, the right to demand that the participants of the circle in their behavior toward him manifest positive active social tendencies."

59. *Ibid.* 122: "The economic position depends basically on the recognition by the given social circle of the right to maintain a material existence on a certain level."

60. *Ibid.* 125.

61. *Ibid.* 110.

62. S. Baley, *Wprowadzenie do psychologji społecznej* (Warsaw, 1959) 174.

63. Znaniecki, *Ludzie teraźniejsi* 110: The conception of the "social person" differs profoundly from the concept of the "person" that psychology uses, wherein is implied a psychological unity of the conscious experiences of individuals.

64. S. Baley, *Wprowadzenie* 174.

65. C. H. Cooley, *Human Nature and the Social Order* (New York, 1902).

66. G. H. Mead, *Self and Society* (Chicago, 1933).

67. Baley, *Wprowadzenie* 174–175.

68. *Ibid.* 176.

69. E. Mounier, *Personalism* (London, 1952) 20.

70. Granted that the child begins to be aware that someone considers him well behaved and obedient. In this manner he comes to represent himself as one who in the perception of others is thus recognized, valued, and so forth. Only then the implied reflection of his own "I" in the consciousness of others is slowly transferred to himself as the particular distinct object that is at the same time a subject. Man begins to feel himself as a separate subject because he is treated so by others. See Baley, *Wprowadzenie* 176. One can ask here whence this necessity of treating others as subjects, and whence the ease with which one becomes aware of one's own "I"?

71. B. Suchodolski, *Wychowanie dla przyszłości* (Warsaw, 1959) 50. Here he evaluates critically sociological theories of personality; based on rich comparative material they tried to show that "the personality of man is formed not according to its internal foundations and powers, but entirely according to the demands and expectations of the group, according to the pressures of environment . . . the common feature of all these various sociological theories was precisely a disregard of historical factors."

THE THOMISTIC AND
EXISTENTIAL NOTIONS OF MAN

Józef Pastuszka

THE PRINCIPLE OF PROTAGORAS (IN THE FIFTH CENTURY BEFORE Christ) that "man is the measure of all things," considered the most ancient formulation of metaphysical and ethical relativism, is true from a certain viewpoint since it finds its confirmation in the hierarchical value structure of the cosmos. Man reflects the universe in himself; he combines in himself all the forms of being, which outside of man exist separately and independently; he is a microcosm, as the Greeks called him; he is—as St. Thomas Aquinas put it—"in some way all things" (*quodammodo omnia*): he is a small world, *minor mundus*.[1] Combining in himself the various degrees of being, man gives value to the world by the primacy of his own ego. The concept he himself formulates of man is a miniature of his own world view. In order to understand certain philosophers' ideas about the world or the ideas of a certain epoch, it is enough to know their idea of man. Their worth is not uniform. Some of them have a historical value conditioned by a specific time; others, significant for a given thinker or a certain epoch, are at the same time above time and valuable to all of humanity, because they express one of the basic forms of man in the world and in life.

The Thomistic and existentialist concepts of man can be considered such as being of general value for humanity.

Thomism is a creation of the thirteenth century, but it reaches retrospectively to Aristotle, and its perspectives extend into our own time and into the future, because it represents one of the permanent forms of man within the realm of reality.

Existentialism—and I am considering it in its typical formulation by Heidegger, Jaspers, and Sartre—is the creation of the twentieth century and hence cannot boast of a remote ancestry; but it also expresses a certain basic form of man in the world, even as it formerly found a partial expression in such tendencies as materialism, empiricism, and irrationalism.

In comparing the Thomistic and existentialist ideas of man we confront not so much two distant historical epochs as two basically different visions of the world and two forms of man in life—two forms that are not only historical, but are most relevant, contemporary, and vital in the past, and even today are the two leading ideals of contemporary man.

I. MAN AND THE WORLD

In the Middle Ages the view of the world was a hierarchical one: its center was God, around whom the world and man gravitated. Such an interpretation found its expression in the *Summa Theologica* of St. Thomas Aquinas, who speaks first of God, and then of man under the significant title—the tendency of the spiritual creature toward God.

In the period of the Renaissance this image of the world was destroyed. Man created new ideals for himself, and at the same time posed the problem of his own ego in all its acuteness. Difficulties began with the new interpretation of human knowledge.

Ancient Greek philosophy and Thomism, along with the tendencies that developed from it, were convinced of the cognitive powers of man and the possibility of reaching the essence of things. This was an essential form that accepted the primacy of knowledge before action, of thought before will. It declared that the human mind is not limited to knowing the phenomenal, the accidental side of reality, but that it reaches into the depth, penetrates the essence of things, and forms concepts about it. In the everyday scale of living we are subject to the influence of cognitive essentialism whenever we try to establish the structure of things, or ponder the "reasons," the ultimate principles, or when we penetrate into the meaning and goal of human action.

This essential form of philosophical thought—attacked even earlier by the Greek Sophists and medieval skeptics and questioned by Hume—was undermined by Kant, who prepared the way for phenomenalism and idealism. But Kant did not deny the existence of essences or "noumena," but actually arrived at them by the way of practical reason, morality. Finally only contemporary existentialism undertook a new, radical, and completely anti-essential solution of this problem, by saying that we do not know the essence (*esse*) of things, but only their existence (*existere*),[2] that we do not arrive at a knowledge of existence by way of metaphysical analysis of the world, but by reflection on our own existence, for it is something immediate, closer than the world which exists beyond us. Moreover, man understands his own existence not in a cognitive manner, not by way of thought and the necessary abstraction connected with it, but by feeling, disposition, and the experience connected with anxiety. The fundamental experience is the consciousness that man combines with the world, that he grows from it, that he takes from it the nourishing elements, that his existence develops in the world, that he is himself only because of the world. But in this case man is limited by the world, and the formulation of the view of man depends on the view of the world.

In Thomism the world is presented as an *ordo,* as a structure of material, vegetable, animal, and spiritual beings. Man is a creature lying in the midst (*positus in medio*) of irrational essences and pure spirits; he is a being that unites two worlds, and is thus a condition for the unity of the world. Being at once a part and the crown of the world, man does not lose himself in the world, but he has his own existence and his own goals with respect to his immortal soul, which is greater in value than the whole world ("What does it profit a man to gain the whole world if he suffer the loss of his own soul?"). The world of phenomena is for man the environment of perfection, the area of work and at times of trial, but always something other, alien, subject to his work and rule. Thus understood the world was created according to the exemplar of the Divine Idea, and therefore the things in the world possess a rational structure, since the thought of God brings harmony and order everywhere, and creates a cosmos. Moreover, the world is not only an actualization and bearer of ideas, but is an objectification of God's perfection. God's creative act is not the endowment of things with an abstract attribute to which we give the name existence, but it is an effusion of divine perfections into the things of this world. *Qui est infundens et creans bonitatem in rebus,*[3] says St. Thomas about God. Everything in this world is a reflection of some perfection, a visible sign of God's love and his image, even though it is imperfect. Each one has a share in a higher metaphysical goodness, and this fixes his role and title in the whole. On this basis rests the metaphysical principle, that all being is good (*omne ens est bonum*), and that being and good are convertible concepts in respect to content (*ens et bonum convertuntur*).

If we proceed from this supposition, it is impossible to consider the world evil; efforts at its improvement are good, and in a certain sense even obligatory. The world has a potential character; it is in continuous development, subject to change; it demands the cooperation of man, speaks of its own relativity and its own contingency; and over its own disasters and the evils of contingent beings rises the ideal vision of the contours of another reality, free from these defects. It is at once a veil and a glass, through which another ideal world is visible. Just as in any unspoken word there is a hidden, unexpressed but real content, so within the limits of this world there is hidden another reality, the infinite reality, symbolized by the contingent world: God.

By the same argument Thomism does not separate man from the world; nor does it introduce signs of equality between them. It underlines their distinctness, ontological and epistemological, and at the same time considers them correlatively, as two different but interrelated members of reality.

In existentialism the world plays another role. Man is only a part of the world, an inseparable element endowed with consciousness. According to Heidegger, man's relationship to the world is above all one of experience, not of cognition. The world provides the first impressions and first sensations, and by their means man becomes aware that he is involved in an environment, that his existence develops in the world. Without the physical environment, which surrounds man and which is imbibed through the senses, without dependence on the phenomenal world, and without the people with whom he communicates, man would be unable to live.[4] Moreover, in coming into contact with the world man finally becomes aware of his own existence, and thus his consciousness is, as it were, born. The first contacts with the world are a sense of resistance, opposition, limitation of the freedom of action; this forces man into attention and the tension of effort. In its struggles with the world, in the struggle with obstacles and difficulties the human ego arrives at consciousness. One cannot speak of a harmony between man and the world, or even of seeing the world as presented to man for conquest and transformation. Diverseness, incongruity, and hostility—these perhaps most completely characterize the situation of man in his relationship with the world. His existence in it involves unending difficulties and confronts him constantly with new problems. Man tries to solve these problems, to conquer the difficulties, but, in this very struggle with the world, human inadequacy and limitation appear. Existence in the world is a burden for man (Heidegger calls it *Lastcharakter des Daseins*)[5] because he feels threatened on every side, and it seems to him as if he had been "thrown" into the world, that is, on the edge of an abyss that threatens annihilation.

II. ACTIVISM AND THE FREEDOM OF MAN

In these circumstances, does not man ruin himself in this world? Is he a distinct being? Is he—to use a scholastic term—an *ens per se?* Existentialism gives an affirmative answer, but has another meaning for the term "distinctness." Man meets the world above all as an instrument and apprehends it from that viewpoint. The world is a collection of things, some of which resist man and must be overcome; others show themselves useful to human life; others are indispensable for human life. All appear in the form of an "instrument" which man constantly uses. This apprehension of the world has the character of an immediate experience, like an instinctive reaction in meeting the world. The rational understanding of the world and its interpretation come later, and are a derivative phenomenon, developing from the need of accounting for one's actions.

Important conclusions arise then for the evaluation of man's nature. Where Thomistic philosophy saw in man the *homo sapiens* and recognized his intellectual nature as his most important element, in existentialism man is above all an active essence, transforming the world, disposed to action: he is a craftsman. Conscious activity and the need for action, not thought, belong to his nature. The man is inseparable from the world, for only in man's union with the world, in its transformation and application to his needs, does the nature of man appear.

This activistic character of man appears not only in existentialism, but also in other philosophical tendencies, and its most characteristic expression is Bergson's definition of man as *homo faber.* Existentialism likewise underlines this activistic element in man. Not by knowledge but by action does man apprehend himself: eliciting an act of will, he becomes aware of obstacles and overcomes them. Moreover, man is involved in the conflicts of life,

71

but wishing to free himself from them and to avoid cognitive disquiet, he must work.

Using the world as an instrument, man does not cease being something different from the instrument and maintains toward it the relationship of a sovereign;[6] he is a conscious ego, he is a being distinct from the world, and he is not its accident or attribute. Activity enriches man and is the condition of his freedom. Heidegger even declares that human activity enables man to self-constitute himself, because it breaks the bonds of determinism that the world carries with itself, frees man from the world, and accentuates his individuality.[7] It is the creator of man's freedom, though this freedom is understood differently than in Thomistic philosophy.

According to Thomas, the will is subject to two limitations. One is a limitation on the part of the subject, since man cannot act blindly, but must weigh the possibilities of action, direct himself according to motives suggested by reason, and actually make a choice among them (hence, reason is the source of freedom, according to the principle *Liberum arbitrium est radicaliter in intellectu et formaliter in voluntate*). The limitation on the part of the object is the good to which the will tends as to its formal object, and which it seeks everywhere. Its turning to a concrete object is a search of a particular type for the absolute good, and it is the accidental and relative qualities detected in the particular that make the will free in choice. It can be said that all our acts of will are filled with desire and disappointment, for only after becoming aware of the relativity of the goods presented by the alternatives do we arrive at the choice of will which is directed to the absolute good.

In existentialism the freedom of the will has a metaphysical character, and not a psychological one. It is a specific type of necessity for action, and at the same time an escape from the boredom that man feels around himself, since nothing seems significant to him and things not only seem to lose their meaning but also fail to draw and entice to action. An act of will is then self-defense, a flight from oppressive monotony, and from vulgarity: it is an effort to introduce change in this condition and to break the determinism of the world. It is a free act, and at the same time an effort, for it is an unforced opposition to the course of events. The freedom of the will is also subject to limitations, but they have a different character from that in the Thomistic conception. One limitation of the will is melancholy, a fundamental feeling born of the understanding that to free one's self from boredom is impossible; for within things there lurks nothingness, and things are not of such a value that they can give man surcease in bearing the burden of existence. Sometimes melancholy ends in despair, which induces flight from life and a leap into another world.

It is possible to say that existential freedom of the will is a freedom in name, but basically it is a determinism of human life penetrated with an awareness of burdens and the necessity of constant resignation. This deterministic analysis of the freedom of the will, as taught by Heidegger and Sartre, is approved by Jaspers, who teaches that life is actually a constant resistance and effort, unforced but conditioned by a constant choice that can be loss or gain. Living in the world, man constantly meets opposition; he is always threatened; he is in constant conflict; he must constantly perform this or that act. But because of this he himself is constantly changing and actualizing himself: he himself decides about his life and exercises an influence on its formation.[8]

III. MAN – AN IRRATIONAL ESSENCE

Classical Greek philosophy and Thomistic philosophy, which grew from it, always saw the essence of man in his rationality. The ancient Greek *nous* and *zoon logosikon* were transformed in St. Augustine into the formula *Homo est animal rationale mortale,* a formula which was not free from ethical overtones.[9] From the spirit of Aristotelian philosophy there developed a definition of the human person in the sixth century, which was transmitted by Boethius: *Persona est individua substantia rationalis naturae.* This definition, accepted by St. Thomas and the Scholastics,[10] had quite a philosophical career, for even today it is usually accepted in Christian philosophy, and by other tendencies that consider it representative. It, too, sees the nature of man in his rationality and derives from this other properties emphasized by contemporary philosophy, namely, freedom, self-consciousness, creativity. Thus defining the human person, Thomas could say that the person as a rational essence is endowed with consciousness, that it possesses knowledge of its own existence, and that only the human person can give direction, since it is free in its choice of actions and is responsible for them.[11]

Existentialism placed itself in opposition to this philosophical tradition when it questioned reason as the source of knowledge, and saw the essence of man in his strivings and sensations, and thus in irrational elements. The very calling into doubt of the knowability of things and the limitation of the scope of the human mind for understanding existence imply a lack of confidence in reason. We arrive at a consciousness of our own ego through sensations, attitudes, and undefined personal knowledge, which only later receive an intellectual formulation.

Jaspers considers this cognitive helplessness a so-called ultimate situation, which cannot be avoided or changed, and which does not give man a choice. This sensation of helplessness originates in the conviction that human knowledge does not altogether exhaust things, that there always remains some secret frontier, something unknowable in all things, which neither intellectual acumen nor talent, nor knowledge nor technical skill can clarify. This same irrational character colors the fear of self-knowledge, which is actually a fear of the loss of existence. To know is the same as to conquer—and by the same token to deprive one of one's own existence, to tear away the mystery that protects the human ego, even from ourselves.[12]

This irrationalism is most evident in the supposition that the sensation of fear lies at the bottom of all conscious experiences. What is this existential fear? It is a metaphysical experience, arising from an awareness that man, in view of his contingent character, is in danger; that destruction and annihilation constantly threaten him; that he finds himself on the brink of the abyss, for the ghost of nothingness hovers over everything that man meets and threatens every situation in which he finds himself.[13] This fear contains something undefined and is different from that fright which is directed to a concrete object. One cannot explain or avoid this fear. Man feels himself constantly threatened, even though he himself does not know whence danger threatens, or where it lurks. Properly speaking, the "world as the world" is the source of fear; man experiences it by reason of his humanity and existence in the world.[14]

This metaphysical fear finds its concrete expression in anxiety, and that, says Heidegger, arises from "man's finiteness," which is anterior to man himself.[15] Man constantly senses new needs, seeks other means of quieting them, and by that very fact experiences new anxieties.[16] Even our cognitive acts are not free from them, for in performing them we experience anxiety as to whether the object is truly known and whether our knowledge is true. Anxiety, forming the dominant of our lives, turns to two directions: to our ego, which constantly feels itself threatened, and to the human environment, which shares a similar fate and is related to us. We are to give it our aid.

Individually, the anxiety experienced is twofold. The common man loses himself in the struggles of the present day, somehow grows into one with the world and loses the consciousness of his distinctness; this appeases the anxiety of life and clears it away, for then "all mystery loses its strength, and daily anxiety expresses itself in the efforts at reducing and contracting the possibilities of being."[17] The man who thinks more deeply is aware of his relationship to the world and feels the tragedy of existence, which reaches reflection in three forms: self-consciousness, evaluation, and speech.

Self-perception is marked by boredom and torment, along with moments of reflection—the experience of the burden of life, the sensation of being cast out on the brink of the abyss.[18] Moreover, understanding is not theoretical knowledge, but a practical form, because it is an effort with instruments, daily activity, experience of anxieties, the realization of certain tasks, the actualization of certain possibilities, and the projection of future forms of activity.[19]

In existentialism, speech—"dependent on the articulation of that which we understand"—is connected with understanding. Thus man can formulate intellectually the chaos of experiences and put it into harmony. Speech is the creator of social understanding and at the same time of the self-awareness of man.

Fear, which is the forecast of death that belongs equally to the essence of man, is not some episode in life but rather the highest actualization of potentiality, in which existence finds its ultimate expression.[20] Heidegger speaks of the "race of death" and of the tendency of all human existence toward it (*Sein zum Tode*). "Death is a form of existence, which existence accepts when it has been called into being."[21] It is at once the school of life, which unveils for man the sense of life, and then the metaphysical fear of existence is transformed into freedom in the presence of death. Thinking of it, man frees himself from trivialities and is not lost in details; but he must consider the problem of dying—to which he is forced by his very existence—since it develops between two poles: birth and death. Having been born, with inevitable necessity man approaches the opposite pole, death.

Human experiences, oscillating between existence and death, are irrational, filled with sensations and attitudes, and not apprehended in discursive thought. Human existence itself is given over to a particular irrational determinism. For it is a continuous process of self-annihilation and a "progress to death." Man loses himself in his daily activities, in a flood of new anxieties and undertakings, and loses even the awareness of his own distinctness; and if he rises above the ruins to self-consciousness, he experiences boredom, melancholy, and despair whenever inevitably approaching death becomes present. Sartre, the principal representative of French existentialism, goes even further, for according to him the chief sensation that penetrates all other human experiences is disgust (nausée), as only that can be man's reaction to the actual state of things—the contingency and relativity of the world.

From this pessimism in life—according to Sartre—action, activity, and the production of change in the world are supposed to rescue man; for they alone provide a forgetfulness of the environment and even a forgetfulness of one's self. Jaspers introduces another factor: love of other human beings, founded upon the depth of existence, because it is based upon the affirmation of another ego, which strives to unite with our ego and to strengthen our weakness and isolation. But love in this case is an experience quite different from what we usually consider it. It does not emerge from knowledge, or is it based on rational factors, for reason reveals only defects, uncovers the relativity of other values, awakens hesitations; these things cannot give birth to love. Love is born of faith, of trust; it comes from an irrational certitude— but this is not a free act.

Who knows whether Sartre's concept of our neighbor as enemy is the logical consequence from the suppositions of existentialism? Sartre declares that human contacts immediately reveal a clash of interests and efforts, and potentially contain conflict so that even an alien glance is a hostile act, for it seeks to intrude on our ego, draw out its mysteries, and use them for its own goals. Sartre proclaimed the paradoxical views that if hell exists, it must be so arranged that the damned live in groups in comfortable, luxuriously appointed rooms, but deprived of the possibility of leaving them and changing their companions.

This pessimistic notion of man is alien to Christian views. Christianity is a religion of hope, even though it speaks of the weakness and fall of human nature, and of death. Redemption, the love of God, and salvation give human life an optimistic tone. The highest moral and religious values are founded in God and give human life powerful support. The European intellectual currents, which evoked the Reformation, weakened not only the authority of the Church, but also undermined the religious and moral foundations of the old order. They gave a start to the ideas glorifying man and proclaiming his moral autonomy, at the same time producing a spiritual crisis for man: they led to his spiritual isolation; to the dulling of man's sensibility to spiritual ideal; to a conversion to the present—and evoked a fear of life, until then unknown.

IV. MAN AND THE ABSOLUTE

Every philosophical system takes some position with regard to the Absolute. Christian philosophy emphasizes the relativity and contingency of terrestrial things, which—according to St. Augustine—are a mixture of being and non-being. It points to the imperfection of man, considers human life a drama that not rarely passes into tragedy, speaks a great deal about the misery of man, the inquietude of his heart, and the insatiability of his will as well as instability of his thoughts. At the same time it declares that neither man nor the world exhausts reality, that there exists a superterrestrial Absolute that conditions the existence of the world. Earthly things are its imperfect images—a weak reflection of the Absolute—that form a barrier and a curtain, behind which there is God: they are at once his signs and his symbols. This relationship of the world with God appears most expressly in God, for (St. Thomas says it more than once) "each man is created according to the image of God," "is directed to the highest good," and "by nature is inclined to God as to his end."[22] The idea of God is at once the core and bond of all the sciences. The ultimate ground of harmony between being and human thought is God, as the *veritas prima et absoluta,* as the norm of morality and the goal of human life.

In existentialism reality is locked within the bounds of the temporal. Here, too, one can speak of the Absolute, yet it is not a superterrestrial Being, but it is Nothingness; only in Jaspers does it form a bridge to transcendence, but in Heidegger and Sartre it is a gate in the literal sense.

According to Jaspers, man and things are surrounded and encircled by an infinite void (*Das Umgreifende*), which is the reason of being for all things.[23] It is not filled with content, empty like the void, and without depth, and therefore it can be considered nothingness. Actually, it is reality fixed on transcendence, for it is fixed on "another actual reality," which is infinite and perfect. Earthly things are—according to the expression of Jaspers—slates, symbols, read by the human mind, which simply cannot penetrate the veil of the mystery of the world. Transcendence then means something which is hidden beyond the phenomenal nature of the world, which is a mysterious numen, or rather a symbol of numina, hidden in everything.[24] Things have their own eloquence, for they proclaim the existence of a being dwelling in inaccessible distance—a being that perhaps shall never become the object of our knowledge and will always remain hidden. This transcendence is not some knowable being, or even some accessible being, but rather it remains itself a mystery and the enigma of the world, a being that penetrates the world but itself is unintelligible and unknowable. Taken subjectively, transcendence means the marvelous adaptation of the human mind to infinity; it is the search for depth and the penetration to the very quick of reality, not some transearthly objective being. Truly, it does not exclude the existence of an infinite perfect reality that remains a problem, an unsolved mystery. Moreover, transcendence itself has an immanent character that truly rises above nothingness but expresses itself in the experience of the inadequacy of knowledge of the reason of being and in the foreboding of another reality. "Ecclesiastical religion," as Jaspers expresses it, does not change this situation; it only points the more popular, and hence more primitive way, to transcendence, but it does not guarantee the certainty of one's achieving it.[25]

Heidegger does not accept this transcendence as being subjective and immanent, but he sees the Absolute in nothingness. Making a travesty of the scholastic axiom *creatio Dei fit ex nihilo,* Heidegger formulates it as *ex nihilo omne ens quod fit.*[26] Man arises from nothingness, wanders through the nothingness of daily life, and proceeds to complete nothingness—death. "To exist," he writes, "is the same as being shoved to nothingness."[27] Nothingness is the ultimate vastness and the highest system that man finds himself in: he loses himself in it, loses his own individuality, and becomes man, an impersonal pawn. In reflection, in turning to the depths of the human ego the voice of conscience speaks, and man once again becomes himself. But even then nothingness persecutes him. The world seems to be a vastness—in which everything goes to ruin, in which he frees himself of the temporal, where he liberates himself from earthly bonds, and penetrates into the depths of his own ego, learning with wonderment that his greatness is lost in the common anxieties of life and that nothingness itself lurks there behind them. It is a curious thing that Heidegger ties nothingness with transcendence,[28] and thus perhaps there also appears in his work the effort to break through the iron chains of the temporal, some hope of finding beyond nothingness some ultimate, which is sensed, and he sketches as in a dream the transcendental reality.

Sartre proclaimed the ultimate consequences of existentialism by proclaiming extreme atheism and amoralism. At the basis of reality lies nothingness, and this denies the existence of God. If God existed, he would be consciousness, for that is considered the supreme form of being; but consciousness is actually steeped in nothingness. It is evidenced by the ability to ask questions, and a question implies the possibility of a denial and, hence, a lack of being. It is evidenced by the fact of awareness of one's own ego—hence a division, and even a kind of wilderness between the ego perceiving and the ego perceived; this suggests that consciousness is not perfection and enrichment of being, but is rather its degradation and the deepening of the alien in our ego. The surfeit of nothingness suggests the conclusion that nothingness forms the essence of all things, and that it also belongs to the nature of man and determines his course.

V. CONCLUSIONS

In conclusion we shall try to present a synthesis of these two notions and to take a position toward them.

The Thomistic man is a corporal and spiritual substance, rational, a miniature of the universe, whose sketch and synthesis he contains within himself. Man is "the horizon and frontier of the spiritual and bodily world." Placed between both spheres, and uniting their properties in himself, but without identifying himself with either, he is matter endowed with spirit and spirit endowed with matter.[29] He is a composite essence and yet a united one; internally divided, but harmonized; locked within the framework of the material phenomenal world; but by his consciousness be belongs to another world, the spiritual world. His life is based on matter, which enters deeply into all his psychic processes, but does not exhaust them. He is a rational, thinking essence ordained to know the essence of things. His knowledge is creative and spontaneous, and not merely receptive and passive, like that of the animals. Man possesses free will, since he executes actions which are not induced by physical processes or by psychic determinism. Developing within the terrestrial world and bound to it by many ancient links, man does not lose himself in it, but he preserves a certain distance and a sense of his distinctness. He is at the service of society, the family, and the state, but he cannot lose himself in them. He is a religious and moral essence. His life principles are ultimately founded in God, whose glory is also his ultimate goal. *Deus semper maior.* Indeed, inevitable death awaits him, yet it is not the end of existence but the exchange of time for eternity.

Quite different is the existentialist notion of man. Man is indissolubly bound up with the world, with nature, and is in union with it as with the only reality, and in activity he arrives at self-consciousness and growth. Neither thought nor action form his nature, but sensation, dispositions, and a particular activity called freedom. Ordained to action, he must oppose the hostility of the world, so that by breaking down obstacles he can continue to live. He must strive, work, worry about satisfying his needs, experience continuous anxiety, which forms the dominant of all his experiences. Melancholy, boredom, and even despair, are not alien to him. Lost in common vulgarity, man then experiences the pathos of life when he turns to his own ego, when in the daily course of his needs he begins to detect the dignity of life and comes to understand that the relativity and contingency of things are but nothingness, which surrounds him entirely. Then he experiences the fear of life, which is actually a reflection and anticipation of death that puts a term to all things.

It is the merit of existentialism that it called attention to certain aspects of human life, which in the last few centuries, when man was glorified and considered as the highest value, were either inadvertently or consciously neglected: the poverty and isolation of man, his continuous anxiety and boredom, his endless efforts to maintain his existence, and his "progress toward death." The existential man is not an abstraction, or a general concept, but it is man concretely, individually, struggling with his daily fate, whose contingency and relativity were expressed with complete realism and terror. From this viewpoint it is possible to speak of the agreement between the existential and the Christian, and more especially the Thomistic notion of man. Some of the arguments of Heidegger, Jaspers, and even Sartre, are stated in the tone of meditative studies and recall the chapters of the spiritual exercises of St. Ignatius of Loyola on the relativity of goods and the inevitability of death.

Moreover, the existentialist notion of man reflects certain aspects of contemporary man. Man has succumbed to his own depersonalization, for fundamental human matters were forced to the periphery of life, and matters connected with the daily biological and sensual existence were placed in the forefront; the essential meaning of life was lost in the thousands of endeavors of daily life, in the daily struggle for existence. Contemporary man is more temporal than the man of ancient times, because—as existentialism very properly emphasized—he involves himself in the circle of daily needs of life and experiences fear before general human ideals, especially those that transcend the earthly, for he has become suspicious of everything that transcends the limits of experience and is not bound directly with his living needs. Hence, he experiences fear in the face of religion. This is not so much a fear of religion itself as a fear of the problem it presents, its intellectual and even its conversational manifestation.

Another characteristic of contemporary man is his daily mediocrity: he is not only unwilling, but also finds it impossible to rise above the greyness of the day, above that which expresses the general opinion, and consequently the social leveling, while at the same time fearing that which is mysterious, unusual, vital in rank, and different from the customary pattern. Together with this goes the superficiality of the contemporary man, which finds expression, as Heidegger says, in unending empty conversations, in curiosity, in ambiguity. The world becomes a tarnished coin, which constantly preoccupies man and fills him with the boredom of life, but does not reach the depths, does not awaken significant thoughts, and does not shock him. Life becomes superficial: the sense of its depth is lost, its greatness, its dedication, and heroism; and thus vulgarity rises to the forefront. This form of life produces discord in man, for it creates a dualism between the deep core of his spirit and the superficiality of his interests and activities. Not without justice does C. Jung distinguish between the human ego and the person, which later he calls a mask that man puts on in social relations, a mask behind which man hides his true inclinations and goals.

All this is true. This picture of man, so dramatically presented by existentialism, is not a complete picture. It considers man only from one side of his relations with the world. The relativity of man and his finiteness possess other features—metaphysical features that speak of the infinity of God as the cause of the world, which also sustains man. Man has his own goals, he is distinct from the world, his life possesses a deeper meaning, and he is not filled only with anxiety and boredom. In spite of the various bonds that link man with the world, this relationship with the world does not exhaust the essence of man; the dynamics of his spirit have no analogy in the material and animal world, and his religious and moral life is entirely of its own kind. United with the world by thousands of bonds because he depends on it in his biological and sensory life, and even in his communicative and volitional activity, man is not locked within the world, but constantly transcends the limits of his biological existence, reaches into the sphere of the infinite, and creates ideals for himself which have their ultimate reason in God. This relationship with God justifies man's title as *mikrotheos,* a miniature reflection of God, empowered to govern earthly things. And it also demonstrates that man —according to St. Thomas Aquinas—is the most perfect being in the world, for he is a rational essence.

FOOTNOTES

1. *Summa Theologica* I, q. 91, a. 1.
2. The principal representatives of radical existentialism are: Martin Heidegger (born 1889), author of *Sein und Zeit* (Halle, 1927), *Vom Wesen des Grundes* (Halle, 1931), *Vom Wesen der Wahrheit* (1943); Karl Jaspers (born 1883), author of *Psychologie der Weltanschauungen* (Basel, 1925), *Philosophie,* 3 vols. (1932), *Von der Wahrheit* (Basel, 1948); Jean Paul Sartre (born 1905), author of *L'Être et le néant* (Paris, 1943), *L'Existentialisme est un humanisme* (Paris, 1946). See I. M. Bocheński, *Philosophie der Gegenwart* (Bern, 1947); Fr. Bollnow, *Existenzphilosophie* (Stuttgart, 1959).
3. *Summa Contra Gentiles* III, 19, 20.
4. Heidegger, *Sein und Zeit* 117, 374.
5. *Ibid.* 83, 137, 297, 368.
6. *Ibid.* 391, 384. A. Waelhaens, *La Philosophie de Heidegger* (Louvain, 1943) 58.
7. *Summa Theologica* I, qq. 82–83; I-II, qq. 6–17.
8. K. Jaspers, *Philosophie, passim.*
9. *De Civitate Dei* IX, 13, n. 3.
10. *Summa Theologica* I, q. 29, a. 4.
11. *Ibid.* I, q. 29, a. 3.
12. K. Jaspers, *Philosophie* II, 87.
13. M. Heidegger, *Sein und Zeit* 186, 343. J. Lotz, *Das christliche Menschenbild im Ringen der Zeit* (Heidelberg, 1947) 40.
14. Heidegger, *Sein und Zeit* 187.

15. M. Heidegger, *Kant and the Problem of Metaphysics* (Bloomington, 1962) 226.
16. Heidegger, *Sein und Zeit* 194.
17. *Ibid.* 127.
18. *Ibid.* 127.
19. *Ibid.* 134.
20. *Ibid.* 251.
21. *Ibid.* 254.
22. *Summa Theologica* I, q. 93, a. 2; I q. 93, a. 8.
23. K. Jaspers, *Existenzphilosophie* (Berlin, 1938) 4, 59, 66.
24. *Ibid.* 52, 53, 81, 22.
25. *Ibid.* 71, 81 n.
26. M. Heidegger, *Was ist Metaphysik* (Frankfurt am Main, 1949) 25.
27. *Ibid.* 19.
28. *Ibid.* 23.
29. *Summa Contra Gentiles* II, 68.
30. *Summa Theologica* I, q. 90, a. 3: "Persona significat id quod est perfectissimum in tota natura, scilicet subsistens in rationali natura."

PHILOSOPHY AND EVOLUTION

Mieczysław Krąpiec

THE THEORY OF THE EVOLUTION OF NATURE IS AS OLD AS SCIENTIFIC European thought. It appeared with the birth of philosophy and was its special expression or aspect.

Originally, when science was still only philosophy, the problems of evolution appeared in philosophical considerations on the nature of the world. This includes the period of ancient and medieval thought, and in some of its branches it reaches even modern times, that is, the middle of the nineteenth century. At that point the theory of evolution separates decisively from philosophical investigations about the cosmos and grows more closely connected with the exact natural sciences.

In this present exposition we shall examine evolutionary thought insofar as it is connected with the primitive philosophical concepts about the origin and nature of the world (from the beginning down to the times of Aristotle); then we shall examine the long period in which the theory of spontaneous generation was dominant, and we shall connect it with the philosophico-astronomical model of the world, as it was basically constructed by Aristotle and modified in some degree by other thinkers; and finally we shall examine the theory of evolution (biogenesis), as it appears in the field of natural sciences. This will form the foundation for independent philosophical solutions of the problem.

I.

1. Philosophical thought, whether in the form of pure philosophy or in the form of philosophical biology, actually always stood on the basis of one form or another of evolutionism. Thus

85

evolutionism had several forms: from a naïve—that is naïve in its answers and not in formulating questions—physical monism, through the dynamistic structure of Aristotle's world and all those who accepted Aristotle's philosophical assumptions, to the modern and contemporary monistic, or, at least philosophically monistic, biology.

Let us glance at some of the historical data of human thought.[1] At the turn of the sixth and seventh centuries before the birth of Christ, Thales of Miletus,[2] considering the original foundation of the world, developed the idea that water was the original element, the original cause, which is the ontological basis of all things. The philosophical physicists of Ionia—as confirmed by Aristotle—proclaimed that the original element "from which all things are made that exist, and from which everything originates and into which everything passes . . . hence, in general nothing really begins or ends, for nature is eternal."[3]

Anaximander, Thales' student, accepted as the cosmos' original element an indeterminate primitive matter, from which all things ultimately develop and of which all things are a manifestation: ". . . the indeterminate infinite (apeiron) is the universal cause or origin and end of all things. From it was born the heavens and in general all the infinite worlds. . . . He held, too, that the first man developed from animals of another kind; for other animals learn to live by their own means in a short time, but man alone needs a long period of time for his education. Hence, if from the beginning he had had such a nature as he has now, he would never have been able to stay alive."[4]

The third Ionian philosopher, Anaximenes,[5] "accepted air as the original element and said that everything originates in air and again turns into it."[6]

Diogenes Laertius stated the theory of Heraclitus: "The teaching of Heraclitus in general outlines it as follows: all things come from fire and return to fire. . . . Fire is the original element, and everything is a change in fire caused by condensation and expansion . . . all things originate through oppositions, and everything flows like a river[7] . . . ." Furthermore, Heraclitus held that everything is in motion, and by means of conflict, which is the parent of all, the world continuously organizes and reorganizes itself in nature as well as in society.[8]

With Empedocles, who lived in the fifth century before Christ, original matter appears as something (and we cannot analyze it more exactly, whether it be a property or another element) known as energy (which Aristotle called an efficient cause) in the form of attraction and repulsion, called love and hate. Was this a relic of the mythological theogonies, when Eros was ravished above Oceanus? In any case, the smallest parts of matter, appearing in the form of the four elements, actuated by love and hate, unite at first by chance until they produce an ordered and symmetrical organism: "Now hearken how fire, separating itself, produced the 'uprising' of the descendants of men and of miserable women dwelling in darkness . . . there arose many heads without necks; naked arms wandered about hither and thither without shoulders; eyes roamed about without faces. But when the two divinities (love and hate) blended in greater degree, the members united with one another, as chance provided. . . . Many beings arose with two countenances and two bosoms; there were beings with human faces, or human bodies with the faces of oxen, beings of confused male and female sex."[9]

In the fifth century before Christ, Anaxagoras, accepting the general evolutionalistic assumptions, deepened the theory by acknowledging the existence of a Creative Logos, which from the original chaos and confusion of all things with all things produced a rational cosmos; . . . he asserts that all things were confused with everything else, and the process of origination of things comes about through their separation. Besides this, he most probably accepted that view that other things originate from the very things that already exist, for instance, fire from stone, and air from boiling water. Perceiving that everything separates from some already separated thing (for instance, from bread there are meat, bones, and everything else) and that everything is at the same time in everything else, he concluded that all existing things originally were confused together, and then were separated from one another. For this reason he began his work: "All things were together." Anaxagoras, it seems, also taught that once all things were together and were at rest for an indeterminate time, Reason, which produced (the *Wypisy* mistakenly translated "create") the world and wished to separate their forms (called *homoiomeroi*), gave them motion."[10]

"According to Democritus, not only animals but also the vegetable world and all the worlds and every kind of perceivable body are continuously coming into being and continuously perishing. If the origination of things is produced by the unification of atoms and their demise by the separation of atoms, according to Democritus, this is but a change in the arrangement of atoms." Aristotle writes that "Democritus holds the view that the first organisms

87

were not born from one another, but they originated from a common matter. It differentiates itself in each of them by the size and form of its constituent parts."[11]

2. With Aristotle there begins a second great epoch in the understanding of the theory of evolution. If the earlier state of European philosophical thought was a rather naïve scientific effort at interpreting the world, with Plato and Aristotle there arise many-sided systems with wide-ranging interpretations of the structure, events, and processes, which earlier philosophical thought interpreted quite naïvely.

The question formulated by the Ionian philosophical physicists was the question properly stated: What ultimately explains the visible world? This question touched the discovery of the principle—*arche*—whose understanding would solve that which is puzzling in the world. For man the world presented, and still presents, a great problem. Philosophical thought, as the first dawn of scientific knowledge, sought within very being, in the very bosom of the world, some principle, some element, which would immediately and somehow automatically explain everything.

As in the life of the child, so in the life of humanity easy uniform answers explain all marvels. In terms of scientific learning—beginning with the seventh century of ancient Hellas—humanity was in its childhood. Naïve answers sufficed. It was imagined that for each question generally formulated, there would also be one general answer that would automatically explain everything at once. The world was understood naïvely—monistically. The world was supposed to be the result of only one material element. Everything was fundamentally the same, except that it was in different stages of evolution. Finally, it was an indifferent matter—how that primal element was apprehended; whether it is some particular form of matter or something indeterminate, some chaos or *apeiron*; whether that element was continuous or whether it is divided into atoms. Thus everything is the evolute of a primal matter.

The very mechanism of evolution, its laws, can be understood in various ways: the conflict of evolutionary elements, the natural process of condensation and expansion, or some other method. One thing is most important. The whole world, the entire cosmos perceived by us—which reveals itself to us in so many ways, composed so admirably and so enigmatically—is at bottom and in its ultimate essence something simple. It is reducible (chiefly in a genetic, historical aspect) to the one and same primal element, to one primal material. Germinally, everything is intelligible, and everything becomes clear. It suffices only to discover the mechanism of that evolution of chaos into the cosmos; it suffices to discover the laws of that progress whether upward or downward, so that ultimately and absolutely everything becomes intelligible. The very same wise men of ancient Greece, who so simply stated the categories of the world's fundamental elements, tried also to uncover the principal laws of evolution. For Heraclitus it was a dialectical conflict,[12] for Empedocles a prevision of Darwinian natural selection, for Democritus the mechanical laws of motion, for Anaxagoras cosmic thought, as yet unsolved—these were the first suggestions for the mechanism of the evolution of chaos into the cosmos.

Together with a naïvely monistic notion of the world hylozoism appeared among the first thinkers. For if the whole cosmos is an evolute of that primal element, then that primal element itself must in some way be living within itself; in some way it must contain life. For nothing comes from nothing. If the final evolutes of that primal element are endowed with life, then life itself cannot be separated from the original stages of the world, the stages of chaos, or of some earliest structure, of which everything else is but a multiplication or its evolute.

II.

The naïve monistic interpretation of the evolution of chaos into the cosmos did not entirely dominate the philosophical thought of Greece. By their investigations Plato and Aristotle transcended such a puerile vision of the world. The interpretations of Aristotle possess especial importance, for in his time he encompassed the whole body of knowledge; above all, he constructed a biological model, which is still usually used.[13] Certainly, evolutionary thought was not alien to the Stagirite. It appeared in the total philosophical system, which will have to be described generally and very sketchily.

The Stagirite in the first book of the *Metaphysics* criticized the views of his predecessors, who tried to explain the world in the light of only one principle (*arche, aitia*): some form of matter. The acceptance of matter only does not explain the nature of the world, for it does not permit the understanding of unchanging necessary structures. Moreover, the Stagirite introduced into being (the world, reality) a fixed element, a constant, which organizes matter and is the foundation of necessary knowability. The element which organizes changing and impermanent matter Aristotle called form, and he accepted it with matter as a co-element constituting every material thing.

Aristotle connected scientific investigation with the study of material being, in which, thanks to form, there exist permanent structures which enable one to formulate definitions and laws about the being under study. In this he differed from the idealistic views of Plato, who connected knowledge with the idea, which was a form separate from matter and exists in some transcendent worlds, in the *pleroma*. The material world is but a shadow of the perfect idea, and all knowledge is a reminiscence or intuition, which the soul possessed before it was plunged into a body for some sin. The concepts of the philosophizing physicists (the predecessors of Plato and Aristotle) did not provide a foundation for scientific knowledge, either because they originated in contradiction or led to it (as in cognitive relativism). The Stagirite took the position that the preceding chaotic state of the world was impossible; these were but myths of the theogony—for the world from its very beginning was an ordered world, was a cosmos, and is the collection of the greatness of independent beings bound together by motion and a common final goal, which is, as it were, the opposite of the first source of motion, the First Unmoved Mover.[14]

The Aristotelian world is a whole, a cosmos of various beings,[15] in which on the first plane motion appears as the absolutely first "stroke" of the cosmos on the human consciousness. All that is originally knowable is knowable by reason of motion. Motion is the factor which connects all things in the universe: from the most elementary local motion to the motion of the heavens, to the First Unmoved Mover. Motion (and through it also the end, for end is directive of motion) unites all beings with one another; thanks to motion the cosmos is ordered. Motion—understood as the means uniting the cosmos—must be taken as widely as possible to include all changes, substantial and accidental.

Among the various existing beings there is a hierarchy. Our material world is the lowest in all the sublunary world. Above the lunar world there exist other higher spheres—the heavens. The motion of the first heavens of the highest sphere is the most perfect, and it is the first drive wheel for all the other movements of the heavens as of all the movements in our sublunary world.

Particular beings, as we find them in the world, are composed of a material element, of matter,[16] indeterminate, without content, and unknowable, and of form, which forms, organizes, and gives content to matter. Neither matter as such nor form as such are beings. They form being by their mutual union, where the uniting, organizing, and perfecting element is matter. Matter is subject to organization and perfection by form, but no form completely comprehends matter, nor does it exhaust its potentiality. Hence, matter, thanks to motion and to change, continuously passes through and goes through the most various beings, in which together with form it creates new real contents. Matter, which yesterday was chicken, today by the process of eating and digestion becomes man. The procession and progression of matter in the sublunary world are unlimited. Matter passes from unorganized stages to other organized states—vital and human: it is quite indifferent to the kind of being it constitutes. Matter of itself is capable of becoming all things if there is but the corresponding cause, the source of motion, and the corresponding dispositions to be changed by matter. Matter can be everything. It is always capable of becoming something else. Only in the superlunary world, the heavenly bodies, being pure intelligences (like the angels) possess completely dominated matter. In the heavenly bodies the potentiality of matter is completely dominated, and the matter of the heavenly bodies cannot become something else. In the sublunary terrestrial world, matter by itself is without content: it can accept every content, and together with form constitute every being.[17]

Here we perceive the place for evolution. Actually, matter is the basis for the evolution of the world. True, in the eyes of the Stagirite the world from the beginning was a cosmos; true, there is no "progress upward" in the world; but this exists in distinction from the continuous change and evolution of the eternally existing world. All transformation takes place through matter. The world is subject to continuous changes, because its constituent co-element of being can transform into the most various forms of being. There is required only a corresponding factor, called "act" by Aristotle, to actuate the potentiality of matter for the corresponding stages of being.[18]

In the normal course of events, the evolution of the world, its internal change, is accomplished by the effect of univocal natural causes. In theory Aristotle accepted efficient causality, which is the source of evolution.[19] Only a sufficient cause can produce a man—that is, another man, specifically complete, man and woman; animal comes from animal. This is the general law.[20]

There was added to this, however, a naïve natural observation and a too ready acceptance that, namely, some of the smaller animals originate rapidly, for instance, lice, fleas. Hence, it was accepted (and Aristotle, the father of natural science, also accepted it) that the less perfect animals which do not possess blood can be generated from nonliving matter, either from the decomposition of living bodies or from dirt. It was thought that the animals without blood were so low in development that even the nonliving forces of matter could by chance construct such imperfect life.[21] This was the more readily believed, because the motion and power of a higher cause, namely, the heavenly spheres that were hierarchically higher in being could replace the act of the natural cause, the parent, and could supplement the power of the lower nonorganic, or nonliving cause.[22]

In this state of affairs the consistency of the theory is saved. There exists possibility and real change—evolution in the world by reason of matter—which in the Aristotelian concept has no content, under the condition that there be an efficient cause, corresponding in its perfection to the being which "becomes" in the process of change. This correspondence is either univocal, according to the law of synonym, or it is not, if a higher cause, a higher sphere, enters into it. Then we have a classical example of spontaneous generation, called from ancient times *generatio aequivoca*. There is no contradiction in such a theory, for all stages of being are established by other corresponding stages of being. Hence, even spontaneous generation, which seems so naïve to us today, was proportionately established and logical.

The Aristotelian picture of the world survived for many centuries, and in connection with it the theory of spontaneous generation; the theory of the origin of life from dead matter, immediate and abrupt, lasted even longer. The justification for such abrupt steps was always the higher spheres, according to the Ptolemaic picture of the world. It must also be remembered that the theory of Ptolemy was still held in the nineteenth century in some schools in Spain, as is evidenced by the nineteenth-century handbooks of philosophy, which still combat the theory of Copernicus.

On the basis of the above sketch it is possible to understand the statements of Aristotle on spontaneous evolution, as well as a series of texts from Lucretius, Pliny, Albert the Great, Thomas Aquinas, and finally Descartes and Newton.

It was Louis Pasteur who in his investigations destroyed the old theory of spontaneous generation, the theory of the spontaneous origin of life from dead matter. It is clear that there existed a whole series of thinkers and scientific researchers, such as Leeuwenhook, Redi, Linaeus, and Spallanzani, who at first timidly, and later more vigorously and with stronger arguments attacked the theory of spontaneous generation; but at the same time many still defended it in the nineteenth century, scientists such as the opponents of Pasteur in the French Academy, philosophers such as Schopenhauer, and philosophers of nature (philosophizing scientists) such as the Rev. Needham, an Englishman in the service of the Habsburgs. The latter believed that there was in nature a generative force, which is involved in every microscopic substance, animal or vegetable. (Needham connected the existence of the living force in a marvelous manner with the possibility of its destruction by the application of mechanical processes, such as heat; on this he based his criticism of the statements of Spallanzani.)[23]

It must be mentioned here that the theory of spontaneous generation which lasted until the nineteenth century was based not only on the Aristotelian model of the world, a philosophico-astronomical model, but also on the Augustinian theories of living seeds, scattered throughout matter and called *rationes seminales,* of the generative force later modified by Needham, which was believed to be implanted in every part of living matter (vegetable —in relationship to animal).

In drawing a general conclusion about the theory of spontaneous generation which originated with Aristotle and was accepted generally by antiquity, the Middle Ages, and modern times to the time of Louis Pasteur—we can say that this theory: (1) was generally accepted; (2) was based on the generalization of naïve investigations or observations; (3) contained many fantastic elements, unscientific, naïve, and at times embarrassingly stupid; (4) also fitted the general world view of the time and was an important element of the world view, philosophico-astronomical; ortheologico-astronomical, or astronomico-theologico-philosophical; (5) does not contain internal contradictions, for, in the light of the accepted systems, facts were eventually interpreted with the help of corresponding principles, either in the form of higher causes (heavenly bodies) or in the form of the theory of living seed disseminated by God in created matter, or in some form of panvitalism.

III.

After the investigations of Louis Pasteur, evolutionary thought so far as it concerned the possibility of nonliving matter being transferred into living matter, sustained a certain shock. On one side all thought of spontaneous generation was cast aside and the creation of life was accepted. Especially in the realm of philosophy there appeared the idea according to which Pasteur was supposed to have shown the impossibility of life originating in nonliving matter, and by the same argument he was supposed to have demonstrated "creationism" scientifically.

However, a great number of scientists, especially those who stood for a materialistic view of the world, transferred the problem of spontaneous generation and the evolution of nonliving matter into living substance several stages lower, namely, the origin of very simple albumen combinations.

Ernest Haeckl, a professor from Jena, was the particular propagator of spontaneous generation (called henceforth autogeny) of the original forms of life in the past periods of our globe. He opposed not only the generally accepted view about the impossibility of spontaneous generation, but he also opposed Darwin, who, himself the originator of the theory of the evolution of species, did accept original creation, as is clear from the conclusion of his work *The Origin of Species*: "It is certainly a sublime thought that the Creator breathed life, such as surrounds us, into several or even into one form, and while our planet, subject strictly to the law of gravitation, completed its circuit, from that simple beginning there developed and still continues to develop an unfinished series of the most beautiful and most wonderful forms."[24]

In his notes to his work on morphology in 1866, E. Haeckl wrote: "It seems to me (as has been considered by the opponents of Darwin) that the creation of the original organisms is a dualism completely in contradiction to the monistic spirit and work of the great English scientist; it is necessary simply to suppose that he deliberately avoided the question that would have involved him in many dangerous conflicts. For our part we must the more vigorously seek answers to the question, and there must be a causal statement of the theory of descendance; thus will the final completion be made in the cosmological system of monism."[25]

Under the inspiration of a monistic and mechanistic philosophy, Haeckl began to imagine a theory about the origin of life's first appearance on earth. The lack of evidence he disguised by using newly invented freak terms, although he did have interesting and, from a scientific viewpoint, very correct insights. Above all, he connects his theory of autogeny—what is undoubtedly interesting and in a large measure correct—with other cosmogonic theories and with Darwin's theory on the development of species. He thought that his theory was the missing link between the cosmogonic theories (in this case Kant and Laplace) and Darwin's theory.

For a model of autogeny he took the process of crystallization. For autogeny simple mechanical movements of organogenetic elements sufficed: "In the flow containing the scattered chemical elements that enter into the makeup of an organism as a result of the movement of the particles, there are formed centers of attraction, in which the atoms of the organogenetic elements (carbon, oxygen, hydrogen, nitrogen) come into such close contact that they unite to make constructed fragments. That first organic group of atoms, perhaps a fragment of a yolk, acts—as does a center of crystallization—to attract similar atoms in the surrounding environment, and these in turn come to create similar particles. The germ of the yolk develops and forms into uniform organic mass—a monera, or a lump of plasm (gymnocytoda) similar to some protoameba."[26] The development of such a *monera* can last a long time, and further it can go through more or less known stages of growth processes.

Haeckl's theory of autogeny underwent various modifications. The most important was that he thought mechanical laws of motion sufficed to explain the origin of life on earth. Although the differences between living substances and nonliving substances are great, they are not so great, according to Haeckl, that there could be no transition, based on the mechanical laws of motion, from nonliving matter to living matter. The foundation of these statements is a monistic world view. It was actually the only, and exclusively philosophical, argument for the possibility of the transition from a state of nonliving matter to living matter.

Haeckl's hypothesis, ultimately naïve, was subjected to severe criticism by philosophers as well as scientists who stood for the principle of an original autogeny of life, e.g., Naegel, Loeb, and others. However, the basic idea of Haeckl, as to the possibility of the origin and the historical origin of life from matter, was always a vital one among scientists, who, like Naegel, Pfluger, F. Allen, Verworn H. Osborn, Loeb, Lichtig, and finally Oparin, were working to discover the direction of the development of matter, and the investigation of the steps in the development of life.

Hypotheses and theories were extremely varied and they fill tomes. The most curious was Oparin's theory, which became well known and found many enthusiastic followers, as well as many critics. Clearly, I do not here intend to present the whole of that theory, but only consider its most important points.

A characteristic feature of Oparin's theory[27] was the connection of the formation of life with the complex of processes in the cooling of our planet, owing to which the preparatory stage for life lasted a very long time. Oparin emphasized the element of carbon and its evolution, its uniting with hydrogen, then with nitrogen, and oxygen. The next step was the condensation and stabilization of gases. Oparin investigated the weights of the carbons or chemical combinations of carbon with metals. They could have played an important role in the evolution of organic matter, since they are the natural and original form of carbon combinations in nature. In the course of time, the carbon metals could have been subject to the influence of heated matter, and thus to a hydrolytic process with the development of the corresponding hydrocarbons and hydroxides.

Besides the relationships of carbon, it is necessary to consider another element, nitrogen, as a basic constituent in albumen. Nitrogen, like carbon, would go through various chemical changes, and in the first periods of the earth's development appeared in the earth's atmosphere in the form of ammonia. In the period when the first hydrocarbons appeared, physical and chemical conditions on the surface of the earth were quite different from what they are now. In temperatures of several hundred degrees, owing to the hydrolitic reaction to which the metal carbons were subject, hydrocarbons appeared.

The next step included the formation of particles of water by means of the hydrocarbons; thence arose combinations of acids, alcohols, and finally in the presence of ammonia and water, the ammonium salts of acids, amides, and lastly amino acids. In the oceans the organic combinations would be subject to further chemical changes, as a result of which there developed more complicated organic particles. Oparin here calls attention to the chemical reactions known as condensation, polymerization, and oxide reduction. As a result of these reactions which shorten the construction of organic combinations, there developed slow evolutionary changes in matter that led to the appearance of chemical combinations that have immediate significance for the origin of living matter.

Furthermore, greater attention must be paid to the origin of the first albumens from the amino acids. Into the structure of albumen there enter various amino acids related in a long series. On the series of the appearance of amino acids, on the per-cent value, and on the series of polypeptides and other features of albumen depend its properties.

For combining the peptides among other particular particles of amino acids, there is required a rather great energy. If one thinks that the first albumens did not originate from combinations identical with today's amino acids, but from constituents endowed with great energy, the free combination of elements could have come spontaneously, as was suggested by the American scholar Lanham in 1952.

These albumen combinations are probably nonliving substances. Finally, only a change in matter can demonstrate their life. This is the subsequent necessary step in the evolution of matter, in which those bodies unite in a common construct.

The origin of albumen, according to Oparin, took place in accordance with the laws of the chemistry of colloids, since the albumen forms colloids in water. In the water solution there followed reactions dependent on mutual separation of various chemical bodies from one another. Oparin considered coagulation as the fundamental and most important reaction, or the coalescence of the particles of a given colloid, or the separation of colloids, depending on the separation of the colloidal substance. Bubenberg de Jong, the physiochemist, called this phenomenon coacervation. Particles of the colloids, which were subject to the processes of coacervation, formed droplets: coacervates. Only those coacervates in which the processes of synthesis predominated were able to survive. There occurred as it were a process of natural selection, as a result of which there arose—at first owing exclusively to physical-chemical forces—arrangements of coacervates which separated from the remaining fluid medium of organic matter.

Without going further into the detail of the processes which occurred in the separation of the droplets of coacervates, one can state generally that ultimately the origin of arrangements, made of larger particles of organic combinations, produced entirely new properties in the coacervates. Its most important effect was the acquisition of finality and harmony of chemical changes with the very coacervates, which gradually acquired the character of a biological change in matter. The coacervates, until then nonliving matter, transformed themselves into living matter, which could already play the role of precellular forms of life.

This phenomenon could have occurred only in a very long period in the evolution of matter, and this in entirely different conditions than we have today.

But how did the primitive organism continue its life? George Wald suggests a hypothesis to explain that problem.[28] At that time there was no oxygen. Hence, there existed only one means of acquiring the energy for growth and the maintenance of life. This was the process of fermentation. The second stage would have been the consumption of a rejected product, as was the dioxide of carbon, in the process of photosynthesis. Living organisms did not any longer need organic matter, accumulated in the course of the previous centuries. They could carry on the basic organic syntheses by getting energy from the sun. One of the side products of photosynthesis is oxygen. As soon as it appeared it was possible to pass to the process of oxydation or respiration. From that time life could emerge from the ocean, for with the appearance of oxygen high in the atmosphere there were also layers of ozone which absorbed the deadly ultraviolet rays.

Thus briefly stated, Oparin's theory—like other biochemical theories—was continuously improved, modified, and attacked. This is not the essence of the matter. What is significant here is the statement of a further stage of human thought after the investigations of Pasteur, who, as it appeared at first annihilated the theory of spontaneous generation. However, this concept did not disappear. It was transformed, and it transferred itself to more primeval areas, but it continues to exist.

Before we pass to its philosophical evaluation, let us consider the thoughts of the eminent Catholic evolutionist, Teilhard de Chardin. In his work *Le phénomène humain,* which aroused much discussion, he writes that the psyche is actually coextensive in relationship to matter and to time. Nothing appears in nature that has not been previously prepared: "We are logically forced to the admission that within each particle there is a rudimentary existence (in an infinitely small state, that is, infinitely diffused) of some kind of psyche."[29] If, then, there exists in man a consciousness, it must have always been there, prepared from the beginning in the form of a general consciousness diffused throughout matter, which evolves with finality into man; and man himself is to evolve further into the point of the most perfect "Omega."

According to Teilhard de Chardin, a universal consciousness appeared from the beginning in matter not in the form of energy, which he calls sensible and external, subject to the laws of entropy, but in the form of a radiant energy, an immanent[30] energy, which in man appears as a psycho-spiritual energy and which actually produces the organization of nature. In fact, all being, even material, possesses that immanent energy which is the motive force of evolution.

In such a condition there exists a continuity and development of evolution. Man and all species are only links in that evolution. Man is its last link. At the moment that man appears, evolution proceeds not in a biological direction, but in the "nousferous" direction, in the direction of the development of pure intellect, spirit.[31] Naturally there is a limit to that evolution, its final point. This is Christ, with whom humanity by a further process of evolution is to form one superorganism;[32] but it is unclear whether this is a natural or supernatural one.

The theory of Teilhard de Chardin received words of sharp criticism as well as of unusual praise.

Here at the end I purposely introduce the theory of a Catholic scholar (one not suspected of lacking orthodoxy, and one who died in a religious order) after the theory of Oparin and contemporary philosophical biochemists, in order to show that among their positions it is possible to find concepts from everywhere.

IV.

But let us now pass to a philosophical interpretation of the problems, presented in such narrow compass of autogeny and evolution, which is in some sense a general theory of the natural sciences.

Let us establish certain undoubted positions.

We cannot in any way underestimate scientific facts, discoveries, or findings of evolutionary forms in animal life.

We cannot in any way forbid biochemical scientists from forming theories dealing with the problem of the origin of life, especially the problem of autogeny.

We cannot forbid them from carrying out investigations, which would eventually discover in laboratories the hypothetical state of our earth many millennia ago when life originated.

On the other hand, philosophers can and must investigate the theories of biochemists and scientists and analyze them, explaining the philosophical data of such theories, which appear either in the foundations of such theories or in their generalizations. While we respect fully the rights of the scholars to form such theories, and even more their efforts—within the framework of the corresponding science—to give answers to the problem of the appearance of life as well as the problem of the transformation of living forms on earth, we are free and even obliged, for the good of science itself, to explain what in these theories is an immediate consequence of the generalizations of facts; what is merely a hypothesis explaining certain facts; and what is finally a generalization of a philosophical nature, or what is the philosophical foundation for such generalizations.

If it is permitted for a biochemist, or a theoretical scientist, to take in science a freely chosen research position, even on one philosophically incorrect (as long as his results will be very interesting and cognitively enriching), then philosophy must above all reveal such a foundation.

This paper has made clear that the positions of the supporters of autogeny (here we have in mind Haeckl and Oparin) were clearly monistic, and are a monistic materialism at that. Haeckl was, moreover, a mechanistic materialist, and therefore his theory is naïvely simple in interpreting the origin of life. Its life was also short. It was considered that between nonliving matter and living matter there is a fundamental difference, and therefore purely mechanistic laws of motion do not suffice to explain living phenomena, which possess their own specific laws.

Oparin accepts the position of monistic materialism but of a dialectical kind, and thus acknowledges the particular laws of living matter. He perceives the gravity of the problem and the enigma of autogeny, as we have seen, and he treats it under various conditions. Science has accepted this as extremely valuable. Although many points of Oparin's theory were criticized, still many scientists who have a different world view share the general direction of Oparin's interpretation. In his theory it is necessary to distinguish the philosophical foundation of his interpretation from the theory itself. The philosophical foundation is monistic in the sense of dialectical materialism. A philosopher is permitted to criticize such a position. It is possible to investigate the construction of the subject and the methods of a philosophy so accepted. This is done on a purely philosophical level and by a purely philosophical method.

Does not perhaps his philosophical position cancel out *eo ipso* the results of his work? But in the history of science we know instances where scientists, accepting some philosophical position and depending on such a system, established certain facts under investigation and announced a series of statements which have retained their value. Such was the case, for instance, with the theories of Newton, who formulated them on the basis of the mechanistic philosophy of Descartes. Besides, Newton's laws have a fundamental significance for classical mechanics. Thus, a scientist can formulate scientific laws on the basis of some philosophical theory, and, nevertheless, those laws can be shown to be valid. Does this demonstrate the validity of the basic assumptions? No. For there can be a purely accidental connection between the formulation of laws and the theory which enabled him to formulate the laws. The truth of the laws formulated and discovered does not confirm, nor does it refute, a philosophical theory which is autonomous, for it possesses its own distinct subject and its own distinct method of research. A philosophical theory can be discussed rationally and effectively only on the philosophical plane; or, on a prescientific level it can be discussed effectively, but less rationally.[33]

Hence, the theory of autogeny must be judged from the viewpoint of the natural sciences as well as from a philosophical viewpoint.

But an investigator not only can, but in his special science must, apply a method corresponding to his science and investigate the phenomena of nature independently of faith and philosophical system. Even if he accepts the position of idealism or monistic materialism, this is a quite accidental and indifferent relationship to this research in his own field of science. If a science is already formulated, then it is not dependent in its method on any philosophical systems. Hence, if the scientist uses the method of a given science, he will be a conscientious investigator without regard to his personal convictions, and the results of his work will pertain only to the given area of science in which he is working. Even if he himself considers or declares that his personal world view assisted him in achieving these results, this matter belongs to the psychology of discovery or creativity, and not to the field of the science cultivated by him.

Let us consider what kind of phenomena the biochemist investigates. The chemical processes of living phenomena engage his attention. He tries to answer the question as to what kinds of chemical processes occur in living cells. If he asks himself what life is, this question should always be understood within the framework of the chemical processes investigated by him; in other sciences, in terms of physiological processes, etc. No scientist will try to answer the question What is life generally? for he does not have the premises for an intelligent answer to the question. This question, touching the nature of being, pertains to philosophy. In a word, an investigator, applying a specific method of research, tries to determine how matter (studied under determined conditions) behaves in various—and in this case—living processes. If for the understanding of these material processes of life, a reconstruction of past nonexistent forms of life or its beginnings is necessary, the researcher, either for purposes of demonstration or for purposes of representation, is free to project such facts, whose description will permit him the better to understand the functions of living matter. The description of hypothetically existing facts is called the construction of a historical hypothesis. In such a hypothesis the scientist describes nonexisting processes as though they actually existed. He describes them in the same scientific language that he uses to describe his observation of actual living processes.

The scientist does not commit any scientific *faux pas* with regard to science, philosophy, or faith, if he describes vital processes of actually existing matter, or matter that existed a long time ago, for, strictly speaking, he describes and is trying to discover the operations of matter in its living or preliving stages. Then only would the scientist commit a blunder and talk nonsense from the scientific point of view if he asserted about the stages of being described by him that, for instance, the sufficient reason for life is the structure of the corresponding particles of matter. For he can only assert that in a certain structure of the particles of matter there appear some vital phenomena. The appearance of vital phenomena in a certain material structure does not determine the question of the adequate origin of life from matter. This question involves other aspects which must be considered in giving a general judgment, although there is the question of the consequent logical absurdities in such a general statement.

We shall illustrate this problem in terms of the origin of the individual human being. Theoretically we can investigate step by step the process of the formation of a human being in the mother's womb. We can begin with the description of the development of male and female cells, fertilization and the further development of the embryo, to the moment of birth. A scientist can describe in detail the phases of the human embryo's development, but he does not as yet give the answer to the question What is human life? What is its sufficient reason? He describes only the extremely various processes of living matter, but he cannot declare that human life consists only in the particular processes described. But philosophy, with weighty arguments, can show that the life of a human being is not explained by the processes of living matter in embryology, that there is required the intervention of a sufficient cause, providing a rational understanding of the life of man as man, and hence of a thinking and loving being.

The case is the same with the descriptions and hypotheses dealing with the functions of living matter or matter coming to life. All these descriptions and the establishment of laws undoubtedly belong to science, and they give us an enriched knowledge of the world, but they touch only the function of matter, either nonliving, or coming to life and living. But none of these descriptions or scientific hypotheses can give an answer to the question Does life ultimately settle itself into nonliving matter, and is it thus an exclusive function of a higher organization of matter? This question pertains only to philosophy, for it touches the origin of being and its causes. These can be established—as proportional— only at the price of a knowledge of the very structure of being, its structural and final constituent elements. Cognitive efforts aimed at establishing the constituent elements of reality are carried on in the field of philosophy, in dependence on precise philosophical analysis of a real subject in the light of established and exact principles: identity, contradiction, and the reason of being. Only this type of knowledge can determine whether the functions of living matter are proper and specific only to living things, or whether they differ essentially from the functions of nonliving matter. If the results of philosophical research are positive, this means that the phenomena of life are essentially different from all the other phenomena of nonliving matter, and that which we call a phenomenon is an emanation of a new substantial essence which possesses constituent elements proper to itself, and not found in nonliving matter. Hence, the origin of such an essence requires a sufficient reason—in accordance with the principle of sufficient reason—that would be ontologically able to produce the new constituent elements of living being different essentially from nonliving being. Everything that exists has the basis of its existence in being. For the being that is ontologically the basis of the existence of an originated thing cannot be the basis for and cannot grant that which it does not possess. Then nonbeing would create being. Hence, only being (or a group of beings), in the perfection of its being adequate to the act done by it, can be the cause of the appearance of new existential structures—in this instance, life. The material process of forming of coacervates does not adequately explain the appearance of a new essence: life. Otherwise, life itself would ultimately, in some one or other historical phase, be but the quantitative sum of the growth of matter. If this were really the case, life itself would originate in matter and with its laws of activity; this is contrary to fact.

Hence, the very description of the hypothetical origin of living matter is not an explanation of the origin of a new essence, a living being. The description of the change of nonliving matter into living matter deals with the means of life forming in matter, but it does not as yet indicate a sufficient reason and the ultimate ontological basis for a living being. Undoubtedly, the process by which nonliving matter is transformed into living matter, occurring in the course of history, can be considered as a partial co-principle, which engages the attention of the investigator, but it cannot be accepted as the sufficient cause for the origin of new being with features that did not exist previously in nature. Taking refuge in chance is but a confession of ignorance of the cause that produced life. We are free and even obliged to admit our ignorance in science if we really cannot find corresponding causes or if they lie beyond the reach of our research methods. But we cannot make chance, or more precisely our ignorance, the directing cause for the process of life's origin and its sufficient reason. Only philosophy indicates the cause by defining at least negatively the rational conditions for the existence of being essentially different from the previous forms of existence.

The natural sciences can and do give us descriptions and laws relating to the functions of matter. And this is extremely valuable, for by that means we know the material side of life. But we are not justified in making the leap: from understanding the functions of living matter to an assertion of the nature of life, the existence of a living essence. Such statements do not belong within the boundaries of the natural sciences. If a scientist does make such statements, he does this either as a philosopher or as a dilettante, even though he is a genius in his own special subject. The subject and method of the natural sciences do not permit him to make such a shift.

All natural descriptions of the origin of life from nonliving matter are very valuable, and they are subject to evaluation only within the framework of the science in which they are made. We philosophers accept them without any fears of contradiction. We are not qualified to judge whether things were actually so or not. We can accept and do accept the descriptions of the transformation of one species into another (here, naturally, it would be necessary to explain the meaning of 'species'): we accept the descriptions of the transformation of nonliving matter into living matter, but general conclusions pertaining to the problem of autogeny are already of a philosophical nature. These must be investigated from a philosophical viewpoint, in a complex of constructed theories, in the light of the first principles of human thought, and the eventually absurd consequences of the facts.

If then a biochemist or a scientist asserts that actually nonliving matter is an adequate cause for the origin of life, he clearly takes the position of materialistic monism. Indeed, some biochemists, like Haeckl and Oparin, do so. Even if we accept their scientific researches that describe hypothetical facts in the transformation of nonliving processes into living ones, we can, however, deny the scientific character of the general conclusion: this is the adequate origin of life from nonliving matter. Such a conclusion would be justified only on the basis of a monistic or pan-psychic concept of the world. For if the world in its present state is an evolute of some original, absolutely unorganized, and uniform primal matter, and if at the same time this primal matter was endowed with a psychic property—naturally, in an infinitely diffused state—the higher organization of matter would at the same time be the organization of higher organic stages and the phenomena of life. Then the very evolution of psychic matter (in which the degree of "psychicness" would be proportional to the organization of matter) would be identical with the spontaneous generation of life and the spontaneous development of living forms. The search by the philosopher (for the scientist neither asks these questions nor answers them, for he has no grounds to ask them and no reason to answer them if he insists rigorously on the subject and method of his particular science) for the only answer to biogenesis in the very fact of the evolution of matter is permissible only and exclusively on the grounds of a pan-psychic monism.

But pan-psychic monism itself is very difficult to accept, since on the one hand it takes the position that everything is an evolute of unorganized primal matter, and on the other it accepts the fact of evolution. These positions are contradictory, for how can something absolutely unorganized evolve? How can anything result from the development of something absolutely unorganized? Can multiplicity arise from absolute unity? To accept this one needs a faith which will not only move mountains, but which denies the very use of reason in its very first laws, in the very principle of contradiction. To make everything understandable at any price is to pay the highest price of all by entering the realm of the absurd.

There is, however, another possible explanation of the fact of life and the evolution of its forms; this explanation affirms completely all the statements of science and at the same time escapes the absurdities of pan-psychic monism. This is the philosophical explanation of a pluralistic world, which is a cosmos, an organic whole of distinct independent beings. This totality is not the identity of existence of apparently different beings, but results from the identity of the source of their being and the identity of the ultimate direction of their development, or the identity of the end.

The world is pluralistic. What does this mean? It means that many beings exist as independent, with their own individual features, unrepeated, endowed with a greater or lesser measure of autonomy in their dependence on their existential structure. How do I know that these beings are many, independent, unrepeated? Are they not the product of history, at this moment some sort of last link in evolution, an impermanent link, for at each moment it turns to the future, its whole history, its entire past? Indeed, it can be so. Perhaps it is so. However, these beings are not the evolutes of that same absolutely unorganized primal matter. Whence do I know this? In the beings presently existing I perceive structure, and that many-sided. The most visible form of that structure is the quantitative material difference. There is also something else. I perceive the most varied stages of being, such as multitude, mutability, difference of substance. These stages can be explained only by the beings' internal structure of various elements, discoverable only through the help of philosophical analysis, since these elements are not independent and self-existent and thus subject to investigation: for only that is subject to investigation that is in some sense self-existent. The most various existential elements that are not self-existing—called in the technical philosophical language "essence," "existence," "form," "matter," "substance," "accidents,"—are the constituent parts perceived only by purely intellectual analysis, which ultimately explains why they are manifold. Hence, if there is no unorganized being, and all beings are internally variously organized, then they are manifold, then they can evolve, continually create themselves in a great historical process of nature and tend to some limit and goal.

But this process of directed evolution is not inconsistent and blind, for the fact of pluralism, more exactly the structure of particular beings from many constituent elements, points to a First Being, God, as the actually sufficient and final existential cause of beings in general not organized, manifold, and accidental. But why does the problem of God appear at this point? We are concerned here not with the name, but with the ultimate real explanation of the world as it is. By its nature philosophy poses ultimate questions—and that is its property which results from its subject and method. Naturally, we first seek an immanent explanation of the world. Does there exist within the beings themselves something which will finally explain the world? Indeed, there would be such an explanation if the world were understood monistically; this means that it is either an evolute of primal matter (but the inconsistency of an evolution of primal absolute matter is obvious), or it is vivified by one "world-soul," as man is vivified by one soul. This last explanation is not inconsistent with itself, but it is inconsistent with the further consequences. For then the world, vivified by one soul-divinity, would be the subject of inconsistent properties, such as we actually see in the world of beings. Beyond this, there exists only the possibility of an ultimate explanation for the one world by a Transcendent Being, whom in religion we call God. His existence appears as actually necessary because of the internal structure of beings from heterogeneous parts, not reducible to one another either in a structural or genetic aspect. If we assert something, then we can distinguish in it as really existing that which constitutes it, as well as other elements which are not its constitutent factors. All that which constitutes a given thing, or the constituent elements, are intelligible by themselves. In order to understand them it is not necessary to have recourse to some other being, since they possess in themselves a sufficient reason of their given existential aspect, that is, of their identity. That reason is actually the form which constitutes being in a given essential sphere. All other elements, since they are not constituent elements, do not explain their presence in the being through the internal elements. And if they exist (the fact of their existence), they demand an external cause of being in relationship to themselves, or they demand the explanation of their existence by a causal element: either through the material cause in the case of natural properties, accidents, or through an efficient cause, if there exist other elements which are not a property emanating from the very nature of the thing. And this is exactly the case with the existence of being. Besides the content of beings which are intelligible in themselves, we perceive in beings existences causing a given concrete content to be truly a real content, and not only an intellectual one. The perception of the element of existence in beings (although it is an element proportionately one) places before our eyes the problem of the reason of being, the problem of a causative principle. The fact of existence (origin, continuance, a particular kind of existence, activity) is an unintelligible fact in philosophy as long as one does not accept pure being as an Absolute, which is the foundation of the relative, proportional state of existence in real, contingent, or constructed beings.

This deepest connection—because ontological and existential—of contingent beings with the Absolute is going on continuously in all the real processes, events, and stages of really existing things. Everything which exists, from the reason of existence and in the aspect of existence, is ultimately explained through the Absolute, which is pure Existence.

The existence of the Absolute and its distinction from the world (the distinction and its manner is undiscoverable for us by empirical methods) produces a pluralistic vision of the world; it is not some remote consequence, but a necessary element of the system, as a necessary reason, whose rejection reduces the very pluralism of being to absurdity. St. Paul's formulation, announced to the Greeks on the Areopagus, comes to mind: "He is not far from each of us. In Him we move, live, and have our being." In every action, in every existence of contingent being, He is immediately present as the First Cause. His presence and activity, undiscoverable by us through any empirical means, but demonstrated within the framework of a philosophical system, is the ultimate foundation and consistent interpretation of the fact of evolution. The operations of the First Cause supplement the imperfections of the secondary causes. In the case of biogenesis secondary causes, being material, were of themselves not proportionate to the production of effects higher than themselves. But if the First Being operates continuously from the side of existence on all of nature and is thus personally present in every natural process, then his power produces the origin of new, perfect forms of life, and produces the direction of evolution.

Is this creationism? Creation *ex nihilo?* In one case, yes, in the case of the human soul, which in whatever theory is an independent being (but incomplete specifically). But creation is the evocation of being from nothingness. If, then, the human soul is a spirit, an essentially substantial being, then it cannot originate owing to changes in preexisting matter. Hence, if it originates, it originates totally and at once without substratum. This is properly creation.

In all other instances the life of matter is not independent of matter. Therefore, all other cases of life originate through changes of a previously existing substratum. Hence, there is no creation, for it is a change. But there is a proportionate reason for the change. There is no change, or evolution unconditioned by a proportional cause. If change and evolution existed without a proportional cause, without a sufficient reason of being, then something less would establish something more; then nonbeing in some aspect would pass into being. But nothing comes from nothing. If evolution exists, if development exists, then also there exists a proportional factor which conditions and makes that development consistent. The First Cause and its presence in all world phenomena, in all processes, and in all stages of being is the sufficient reason of being that makes consistent the facts of evolution.

It must be further considered here that the presence and manner of action of the First Cause is not discoverable in the framework of the particular sciences; it is, finally, demonstrated in a pluralistic philosophy. God's manner of action is hidden from us. We do not know how it occurs. One thing is certain, there is no violence, for all nature proceeds from the First Being. In general, we can only say that the First Cause is present in every being and its operation is in accordance with the needs of that being. And the measure of its need is properly its own nature.

FOOTNOTES

1. A fuller picture is presented by the works of PAN (Państwowa Akademia Nauk), the Commission on Evolution, *Powstanie życia na ziemi* (Warsaw, 1957). I shall cite this work as *Wypisy.*
2. He lived probably c. 623–543, B.C. He is considered the first European philosopher.
3. Cited according to the translation in *Wypisy* 19.

4. *Ibid.* 20.

5. He lived c. 580–520, B.C.

6. *Wypisy* 21.

7. *Ibid.* 22.

8. See J. Legowicz, "Humanizm dialektyki metody myślenia u Heraklita," *Roczniki, U. W.* I, 9–39.

9. Cited from *Wypisy* 24.

10. *Ibid.* 26.

11. *Ibid.* 28.

12. Nussbaum called attention to this; see *Wypisy* 23.

13. The biological model of matter depends on conceiving matter as some substantial substratum, some being which exists by itself, and from which as from a branch of the tree there grow powers which produce fruit, acts.

14. In the sense that the final goal is that which is the first source of real motion.

15. Aristotle, *Metaphysics,* Ec. 4 1028 a. 5.

16. When we speak of matter in Aristotle, we must understand matter according to the Stagirite's whole system. This is not matter as we have it in the prescientific sense perception, but it is matter understood as an absolutely potential factor or reality. In general, with almost every philosopher the concept of matter appears as one of the elements of the system and can be understood only on the basis of the system. On the subject of Aristotelian matter see my work, "Teoria materii w aspekcie fizykalnym i filozoficznym," *Zeszyty Naukowe KUL* 2 (1959).

17. The Stagirite stated this theory in Book II of *De Coelo et Mundo,* and in Book I of *Metaphysics,* the introductory chapters and chap. 8.

18. See *Metaphysics,* Theta, c. vi.

19. See M. Jaworski, *Arystotelowska i tomistyczna teoria przyczyny sprawczej na tle pojęcia bytu* (Lublin, 1958) chap. 3.

20. This same philosophical picture of the world was accepted in principle by the Arab philosophers and by Thomas Aquinas, and a whole series of his later commentators from the sixteenth and seventeenth centuries. Thomas' innovation was the construction of a concept of being different from that of Aristotle. With Thomas the concept of Being as being possesses an existential character. Every being is real not because of form, as with Aristotle, but because of existence. Certainly form with Thomas fulfills all the functions of act, but in the essential order. However, the anterior condition for fulfilling those functions is existence.

21. In the first volume of *Wypisy-Powstanie życia na ziemi,* chaps. 2–4 present abundant and interesting material illustrating how general was the belief in spontaneous generation and how the ancient and medieval thinkers accepted the naïve theories.

22. St. Thomas, *S. Th.* I, q. 71, ad. 1.

23. See *Wypisy* I, z. I, chaps. 2, 3.

24. See *O Powstaniu życia hipotezy i teorie,* PAN (1957) 198.

25. *Ibid.* 199.

26. *Ibid.* 202–203.

27. I state Oparin's theory very briefly, according to the work of A. Jurand, *O Powstaniu życia hipotezy i teorie,* chap. 4.

28. See G. Wald, *Fizyka i chemia życia* (Biblioteka Problemów) (Warsaw, 1959) PAN, chap. 1, "Powstanie życia" 41–45.

29. Teilhard de Chardin, *Le Phénomène humain* (Seuil, 1955) 335.

30. *Ibid.* 363.

31. Teilhard de Chardin, "L'Avenir de l'Homme, vues d'un Paléontologiste," *Cité Nouvelle,* June 10, 1946.

32. de Chardin, *Le Phénomène humain* 321.

33. See my article, "Konfesyjność i wolność nauki," *Zeszyty Naukowe KUL* 1, z. 1, 8–10.

GUILT IN CRIMINAL LAW

Zdzisław Papierkowski

I.

1. AMONG THE FUNDAMENTALS OF CRIMINAL LAW, GUILT HAS A MOST proper place (for without guilt there is neither crime nor punishment). But criminal law is not the domain for norms governing social life, norms that give birth to the phenomenon and concept of guilt. In other words, guilt is not the invention of criminal law, that is, a system of norms established formally by governmental authority and transcribed through traditional forms in the public consciousness. The socio-psychological platform, creating the source and standing for every kind of obligation and responsibility, is morality understood as a complex of obligations in relationship to one's self (individual ethics) and in relationship to others (social ethics). In some way criminal law finds a ready concept of guilt and receives it for use in its juridical conceptions. Criminal law, like law in general, appears basically in the role of an editor who makes more precise the content of existing social norms, especially ethical norms. Indeed, it sometimes happens that criminal law sees guilt where morality does not see it. But in accordance with the definition of criminal law as the minimum of ethics, guilt in the understanding of that law exists where there is a deed forbidden by its nature, unlawful, and harmful, and showing other such characteristics which one can generally describe by the term "an immoral act" (unethical). That morality is a reservoir from which criminal law draws the material of guilt to make it a constituent element of crime is clear. There are situations in which, besides the existence of categorical legal prescriptions, the law is violated with full consciousness in the name of the prescriptions of moral law, which is the norm, as it were, of a higher rule. Life and literature provide situations that illustrate this (e.g.,

Sophocles' *Antigone*; in the name of moral law the sister buried her brother in spite of the legal prohibition by the king.)

2. *In maleficiis voluntas spectatur non exitus* (in criminal matters the will of the doer is to be considered, not the effect). Thus ran one of the rescripts of the Roman Emperor Hadrian on criminal responsibility. In the same spirit, Paulus, one of the distinguished lights of Roman law, explained his views on criminal law in the matter of murder: *qui hominem occiderit, aliquando absolvitur, et qui non occidit ut homicida damnatur; consilium enim uniuscuiusque non factum puniendum est* (he who kills a man is sometimes freed, and he who did not kill is sometimes condemned; for in each case, the intent, not the fact, is to be punished). In the considerations dealing with theft, the same jurist said *nam maleficia voluntas et propositum delinquentis distinguit*, that is, the criterion that distinguishes, or rather characterizes a crime, is intent and will.

From these and similar citations it is clear that in the matter of responsibility for a crime Roman criminal law agreed with subjectivism, that is, the principle depending on noticing—if not exclusively, then in very high degree—the psychic equipment of the doer. But we must recall that this characteristic of Roman criminal law appears only at the beginnings of the Empire. The first impulse toward rejection of the objective viewpoint that dominated from the time of the twelve tables to the end of the republic was the legislation of Cornelius Sulla, and in particular the *Lex Cornelia de sicariis et veneficiis*, that is, the law on murderers and poisoners. The question arises, what influenced ancient Rome to turn from objectivism to subjectivism in criminal responsibility? On the one hand, the scale was turned by circumstances and natural relations, which one can summarily describe as the rise of a strong government and the education of public interest. On the other hand, Greek philosophy played a role in this as the theoretical foundation for the essence of that public interest. In particular, the ethics of Aristotle was the vivifying breath, through whose influence by means of Cicero and Seneca there developed and was formed the concept of guilt in Roman criminal law during the period of the Empire. Aristotle states that the basis for the ethical evaluation of human actions is free will. He was the first thinker who took a decisive stand in favor of indeterminism. According to him, all considerations on the subject of virtue and guilt must lead to the distinction of *to ekousion*, that which a person desires, from *to akousion*, that which he does not want, that which did not lie within the limits of his intentions. This point of view, according to Aristotle, must govern the lawgiver as well as the giver of rewards and punishments.

As one can see from the citations in the introduction, the first form of guilt in Roman law was only deliberate guilt, that is, *dolus*. If it was impossible to impute to the doer of a socially harmful deed a *voluntas*, that is, *consilium*, or the will to commit a crime—it was then a *casus*, or an accident. Only in the measure of the development of social relations in the imperial period can one note that sometimes an individual, acting *sine dolo*, or unintentionally, caused serious social harm. From such crimino-political considerations there developed a second basic form of guilt, namely, unintentional guilt, or *culpa*. In this dual form the Roman concept of guilt became the basis on which medieval criminal law (with certain exceptions) was based, as was that of later times down to our own days.

3. In the Middle Ages the important opposition of the Roman notion of subjective guilt came from the objectivism of Germanic laws, expressed in the words "Man kann den falschen Mut nicht strafen, wenn die Tat nicht dabei ist," which means that it is not possible to punish an evil intention if it was not realized by some deed. The actual significance of the principle is in the attention given to the deed and its effects with an accompanying neglect of the psychic condition of the doer.

Medieval canonical criminal law revived and continued the Roman notion of guilt. There was the circumstance of the general relationship of church law to Roman law, expressed in the words *Ecclesia vivit lege romana* (the Church lives by Roman law), and of the particular character of a religious crime, emphasizing as strongly as possible the spiritual and ethical elements. Just as we observed in Roman law the influence of Greek ethics on the problem of guilt, so in medieval canon law we find a process of "ethicizing" criminal law, with the exception that in this case the source from which the influence came was not the natural ethics of Aristotle, but the religious morality of the Catholic Church as contained in the gospel. A tangible example of the influence of gospel morality on the subjective notion of guilt in canonical criminal law is the fragment of Jesus' statement dealing with adultery: "You have heard that it was said to those of old: 'Thou shalt not commit adultery'; but I say to you, that every one who looks upon a woman to lust after her has already committed adultery with her in his heart." It would be difficult to find a more forceful emphasis on the essence of guilt as a psychic disposition in terms of the moral evaluation of that disposition's content. We ought to remember, however, that here we are dealing with sin, and not with crime as an antisocial phenomenon defined by criminal law.

And yet, canon law, which was subjective par excellence in the matter of guilt, did not abandon certain elements of objective responsibility for unintentional deeds. There is the rule of the canonist Bernard of Pavia (from the end of the twelfth century) on murder, and expressed in the following words: *versanti in re illicita imputantur omnia quae sequuntur ex delicto* (one who does a criminal act is responsible for everything that results from the criminal act). And not only were *dolus* and *culpa* here considered guilt, but so was accident, if the accidental killing of a man was the result of an unlawful act. *Operam dare rei illicitae,* or engaging in some unlawful act, after centuries of evolution led to the conception of an indirect evil intent, *dolus indirectus,* still known today to some criminal codes.

4. The Roman, and then the Roman canonical, notion of guilt became the subject of elaboration by Italian glossators, postglossators, and commentators, who applied Justinian's *Corpus Iuris Civilis* to the needs of their time, and in this way they created the *usus modernus Pandectorum,* that is, a modernized Roman law. From the time that Roman Law was accepted in the sixteenth century by the *Constitutio Criminalis Carolina* (the criminal code of Charles V in 1532), through particular German legislation as well as that of other countries, the basic conception of guilt did not undergo further change. Doctrines of criminal law elaborated various species and subspecies, degrees and subdegrees of guilt, but the essence remained the same—intentional guilt and unintentional guilt. The evolution from objectivism to subjectivism sometimes gains strength, then again it weakens. This evolution and its product are the result of two forces: on the one hand the ethicization of criminal law, and on the other the slumbering objectivism of the human soul, which even during the most scrupulous examination of the psychology of the doer does not permit one to close one's eyes to the objective, effective social damage. Perhaps it will always remain the unfounded and arbitrary view that in the light of modern subjective criminal law it must be a matter of indifference, whether the object, for instance of theft, is a thing worth only a few cents or several thousand dol-

lars. For the *animus furti,* the psychic disposition directed to theft, is psychologically and morally the same in both cases. Essentially the *animus furti* of the thief is the same so far as title is concerned, but it is not the same if one considers its extent.

5. In the matter of guilt, criminal law underwent another development, namely, the evolution from collective guilt, or mass guilt, to individual or personal guilt. The original laws, which were colored by objectivism, did not make criminal responsibility dependent on the actual guilt and on the actual participation by a given individual in the commission of a crime, but they satisfied themselves by drawing into criminal responsibility the individual's belonging to the family group from which someone committed a crime, even from his residence in the place where the crime was committed. An especially expressive statement of that time of collective criminal responsibility was the old German principle *Mit gefangen, mit gehangen* (if one is captured with the criminal, one is hanged with him). In the course of time the very same process of ethicization of criminal law, which shifted the point of view from the responsibility for the act to responsibility for the subjective transgression, led to noting the circumstance, whether a given individual, involved to a certain degree in a crime, played some role in its performance, and if so, on what his role depended. Through such stages as accomplice, conspirator, a gang, and being an accessory to the guilt of the criminals, evolution led to individual guilt, or to a precise personal criminal responsibility for one's own actions. Summarizing the considerations on the subject of guilt, we can say that guilt in modern criminal law appears as the result of a twofold evolution, namely, from objective to subjective responsibility, and from collective responsibility to individual. The most proper idea of modern criminal law must include the following crimino-political consideration: it is proper to punish for crime, but it must be a true crime; it must be one's own crime, and not the crime of a fellow native or fellow member of a certain territorial unit, and finally, in the case of instigation and assistance, not for the crime of the principal.

II.

1. Having learned the origin of guilt as a problem of criminal law, let us look now at its essence and its species. In the contem-

porary science of criminal law we find three theories relating to the concept of guilt, namely, the normative theory, the psychological theory, and the theory of social danger.

The normative theory, or briefly, normativism, plays a great role chiefly in German science, and its chief point is that it understands guilt as a negative judgment of an illegal action. This theory emphasizes not the psychology of the criminal and its relationship to the criminal event, but stresses the impression and judgment of others evaluating the behavior of the criminal. It appears as though guilt grew not in the psychology of the criminal, but within the psyche of other persons. With regard to the genetic explanation of normativism in human guilt as a requisite of criminal law, it must be noted that this is a heritage from the philosophy of Kant. For Kant denied the possibility of knowing of the essence of a thing, of that which he called *das Ding an sich*; he admitted only the knowledge of phenomena, or appearances expressing the properties of a given thing (*das Ding an uns*). Applied to the problem of guilt, this epistemological criticism led to the view that the actual will or intent of the criminal is not the subject of judicial decisions, since that psychic experience is the unknowable essence of the thing. Only the external signs are subject to a decision, on the basis of which the judge surmises the existence of such psychic phenomena.

In the psychological theory guilt is actually something that exists substantially. It is a psychic fact depending on the relationship which exists between the spiritual disposition of the criminal and the criminal action or negligence. Dependent on whether the content of that relationship is the intent of committing a crime, or only the representation of the possibility of its existence, we have to do with the theory of will or with the theory of representation respectively. In both cases the consciousness of the criminal nature (and *eo ipso* its illegality) of the action of negligence is an integral part of guilt.

Finally, the theory of social danger represented by the positivism of the Italian school of criminal law understands guilt as *pericolosità*, that is, danger threatening social interests from an individual determined either anthropologically or sociologically toward committing a crime. In the light of that theory, guilt loses the character of moral responsibility and it becomes a purely juridical phenomenon (*ente giuridico*); in consequence, criminal law ceases to be the administration of penalty for an evil done (*malum passionis propter malum actionis*) and becomes a social hygiene *sui generis,* or administrative law with a preventive character, or a prophylactic one.

2. In evaluating critically these theories of guilt, it must be stated that none of them is acceptable in pure form. Normativism errs in identifying the guilt of the criminal with its condemnation by others. For social condemnation is a reaction to guilt, and it is not the criminal's guilt. If we can agree with the normatists that guilt—beyond the case of frank and certain admission by the criminal—cannot be simply proved, but only mediately on the basis of his external behavior, and thus that we work with certain presumptions and conclusions from external facts about the existence of a psychic experience, this in every instance is only the problem of the type of demonstrative process and not the problem of the essence of guilt. The circumstance that the intent or will of the criminal cannot be seen, touched, or observed in any manner by the senses, does not allow one to conclude that that intent or will, respectively, is not a real psychic experience of the criminal's. Moreover, it is unreasonable for the normatists not to know or establish guilt as a psychic reality in the criminal, but then to agree to a judgment for an evaluation of guilt, since that judgment itself is nothing else then a psychic reality experienced by those who condemn the criminal.

With regard to the theory of guilt as conceived by the positivist school of Italy, it must be rejected because basically this notion is dependent on determinism. For if we reject the idea of human will, then we cannot speak of any guilt. In that case society would not have any right to punish an individual who has committed a crime because he only yielded to some compulsive force.

It is precisely the psychological theory which resolves the problem of guilt; but one must stress strongly that not only is it a matter of the criminal's psychological attitude toward action or desistance, but in the same degree it is a matter of the awareness that such conduct is criminal. This consciousness of criminality obviously must not be equated with a knowledge of criminal law. Such an understanding of the consciousness of criminal action or desistance is in its proper light the principle of criminal law *Ignorantia iuris nocet* (ignorance of the law does not justify). The principle of demanding from the citizen a concrete knowledge of the articles or paragraphs of the criminal code would be a fiction always for the layman, and sometimes a fiction with regard to the lawyer who does not know legal prescriptions.

With these considerations we must declare that in speaking

about the consciousness of the criminality (illegality) of an action or desistance, we cannot separate this problem too much. Hence we cannot speak of an unawareness of the existence of the circumstance which makes the characteristic feature of the act forbidden by law, of an unawareness of the illegality of the act, or of an unawareness of the social harmfulness of the act. I think there is far too much of that. For, in the first case, what is significant here is not the circumstances taken by themselves, but rather their importance in becoming the signs of an act worthy of punishment in connection with the illegality (criminality) of a given form of behavior. Let us consider such a combination of circumstances, which together form the seizure of someone else's movable property in order to make it one's own. These circumstances become the signs of an act forbidden by criminal law only then when that seizure is illegal, that is, when it becomes theft. Beyond this instance, these circumstances are not the signs of a crime; they can even be the circumstances accompanying a legal means of acquiring property. One cannot, therefore, treat the formal signs of a criminal act independently of some general illegality or criminality of a given action or desistance which exists outside these signs. The second and third instance cannot be precisely separated, unless one is dealing with criminals who know the criminal law. In the case of the average criminal, his unawareness that he is committing a crime depends on his judgment that what he is doing, or what he fails to do, is not disrespectful, forbidden, evil, immoral, or socially harmful, and so on. Only in that sense can one speak of error, with respect to ignorance of the criminal law (*Ignorantia iuris criminalis*), about a deliberate crime that was, so to speak, a circumstance removing deliberate guilt.

3. When I consider that the psychological theory resolves the problem of guilt accurately, this is not to be understood as meaning exclusive accuracy. As frequently happens in other problems, it is not possible to solve the problem of guilt scientifically in a unilateral manner, that is, with the help of some theory which pretends to exclusive accuracy. It is one of the characteristics of the human mind that the investigator of particular phenomena also has, besides the tendency to generalizing conclusions, a tendency to understand given circumstances as the exclusive cause of a condition of things. A classical example illustrating this statement would be the legal and criminological studies in criminal etiology, or the science investigating the causes of crimes. The anthropologist insists that only the psycho-physical makeup of

the individual drives him to commit a crime; the sociologist sees the source of crime only in social circumstances, political or economic, in which the criminal lives. Neither the one nor the other of these views is exclusively true; and, in fact, both contribute to the discovery of truth. One must avoid extremes, and not be ashamed that the compromise solution of a particular problem, being unoriginal, is simply a mediocrity, unable to rise above the level of the average and to reach some special and hitherto unheard of result in the investigations. For an average mediocrity is one thing, and a judicious, synthetical view, based on objective judgment, is something else (*media sententia, media via*). Such cross-breeding provides useful results elsewhere than in genetics.

With regard to the essence of guilt as a condition of criminal responsibility, neither the psychological theory alone nor the normative theory alone explains it adequately. The psychological theory is inadequate insofar as it ignores certain normative elements essential to guilt which have their roots in morality; for instance, the individual's behavior is worthy of censure, reproach, negative evaluation. The psychological theory makes no difference between killing a man and eating a dinner in a restaurant. In the first instance and in the second there is the representation of a situation and the will to execute it. From a purely psychological viewpoint, the eating of a meal in a restaurant would be just as reprehensible as the killing of a man, theft, rape; each of these respective actions would be as guiltless as eating a meal in a restaurant or going to the theater. We see, then, that besides the psychic elements we need something else in order to speak of guilt. Equally inadequate for an understanding of guilt is the normative theory. In this problem it raises to prominence the element of censure (reproach, negative evaluation) with regard to human behavior; it fails to bring into prominence such psychological elements as consciousness (an idea of the crime, the desire to commit it, the consent to its commission) and unawareness (not foreseeing the crime, besides the possibility or obligation of foreseeing it). Only the combination of the psychological element with the normative element permits the fixing of the conceptional content of guilt as the psychic and censurable relationship of the individual to his observance (action or desistance) of a defined norm of criminal law (prohibition or command). Now, we can easily understand why the killing of a man, theft, or rape are criminal acts punishable by law (crimes), and why eating a meal in a restaurant or going to the theater is an indifferent matter for criminal law. It is easy to understand why in the killing of a man in necessary defense, or the executioner killing a man sentenced to death, or deprivation of freedom through arrest by a judge, or in any such situation, one cannot speak of guilt, and *eo ipso* of crime, without the existence of the psychological content of guilt (the spiritual relationship of these persons to their actions). In these cases guilt as the basis for criminal responsibility does not exist, for the normative elements of guilt are lacking.

III.

1. The Polish criminal code of 1932 (in force to the present with a few changes introduced by the postwar supplementary criminal legislation, and especially by the so-called Little Code) in the matter of guilt uses the psychological theory (while considering the necessary normative elements) with particular emphasis on the theory of will. The majority of theorists in Polish and foreign criminal law take the same position, as does the majority of criminal codes, among others, the codes of the Soviet republics. The prescription of the Polish criminal code that defines the content and kinds of guilt is article 14. It is found in the chapter entitled "The principles of responsibility," which describes guilt, criminal responsibility as the *conditio sine qua non*, as well as a series of circumstances that exclude guilt, and hence remove responsibility (e.g., mental retardation, mental illness, and other factors that hinder psychic activity; physical force, error, necessary defense, the condition of a higher necessity—some of these circumstances exclude illegality of action or desistance).

The prescription of article 14 of the criminal code deals with two different classical forms of guilt. They are, namely, two forms of deliberate guilt (*dolus directus*, or direct intent: the doer simply wishes to commit a given crime; and *dolus eventualis*, the consequent intent: the doer consents to the performance of the crime) and two forms of indirect intent (*luxuria*, or thoughtlessness: the doer foresees the criminal effect, but without grounds he hopes to avoid it; and *negligentia*, or negligence: the doer does not foresee the crime, even though he might be obliged to). From the methodological and editorial viewpoint it must be noted that the prescription of article 14 does not give a definition of these forms of guilt, but somehow skirts the definitions and treats the above mentioned types of guilt as known categories and defines two types of crime, dependent on the type of guilt with which they were committed. The prescription of article 14 of the criminal code does not express itself as "deliberate guilt occurs when," or "a nondeliberate guilt" depends on. But the prescription does state that a deliberate crime occurs when it depends on the will to commit it (direct intent) or on consent given for its occurrence (consequent intent); and that a nondeliberate crime occurs when it is accompanied by an unfounded hope of avoiding a criminal act (thoughtlessness), or when it occurs without having been foreseen, even though the doer could, or might have been obliged to, foresee it (negligence). Whether or not this manner of speaking in article 14 of the criminal code has a fundamental significance, I shall discuss later in connection with considerations of the project of a new criminal code.

2. In the earlier part of the present article I expressed the view that the problem of guilt is resolved fairly by combining the psychological theory with the normative theory. In the question of deliberate guilt and nondeliberate guilt in the form of thoughtlessness, the matter is entirely clear since in these cases the psychic relationship of the doer to his criminal action or negligence is clear. However, the matter is not so clear in the case of the second type of nondeliberate guilt, negligence, which, as we have said, depends on a failure to foresee the crime, except that the doer could, or was obliged to, foresee it. The opponents of the psycho'ogical theory see its Achilles' heel in negligence. They declare that once the essence of guilt is the psychic relationship of the doer to his conduct and his awareness of the criminality of his conduct, negligence cannot be a matter of guilt, because negligence depends precisely on a failure to foresee the crime and, hence, is a denial of a psychic relationship. This would have some semblance of truth, if we understood the psychic relationship as only an actual phenomenon. However, we know that various phenomena of the external world (the more so spiritual experiences) appear in a potential state and are actualized. Negligence, therefore, does not depend on the mere fact of not foreseeing the crime, but on the fact of not foreseeing in conjunction with the possibility or obligation of foreseeing it; hence, we must understand that possibility or obligation of foreseeing a certain situation as a psychological category in the form of a potential relationship to a certain event. In this way, without doing violence to the laws of psychology, we shall render great service to the social order, which is very interested in considering negligence as guilt and in

punishing persons, who, by their negligence, often do serious damage.

Nor is the possibility or obligation of foreseeing the criminal effect an Achilles' heel for the normative theory. As soon as anyone can or is obliged to foresee the criminal effect, and he does not foresee it, he deserves censure (reproach, negative evaluation) entirely as does the one who foresees the criminal effect and assumes without reason that he can avoid it. Censure must not necessarily be connected with the will to commit a crime, but it can apply and does apply to the possibility or obligation of avoiding its commission. The psychological theory makes it possible eventually to question the "psychic" nature of the possibility or obligation of foreseeing the criminal effect (with respect to the potential character of that psychic experience); in the light of the normative theory there can be no doubt about their "normative" character, because this possibility or obligation of foreseeing forms the basis for censure, reproach, negative evaluation, and condemnation, and by nature an element par excellence normative. According to the normative theory, the difference between deliberate guilt and nondeliberate guilt is not only a difference of species, but also a difference in the degree of censure. Since the thing censured is a deed contradicting the legal norm, it is censured without regard to whether it is dependent on a will directed to its execution, or on a prevision that from its execution there will result wicked effects, or on a thoughtless assumption that these evil effects will not result or, finally, on the failure to foresee the execution of that effect, quite apart from its possibility or obligation of being foreseen. And depending only on which of these eventualities occurs, the specific censurability is expressed in the greater or lesser criminal responsibility of the doer who behaves in a manner that violates the legal norm.

3. In connection with the change of the structure (social, political, economic, and so forth) of Poland, the necessity arose of adapting the legal status of the country to its socialist condition. Evidently this need touches—and that not in the smallest degree—the matter of criminal law. It must be noted that we are not concerned with a renewal of the old law and its application to the actual constitutional model, but rather a fundamental reform of the criminal law based on the most fundamental ideological, philosophical, and socio-political assumptions of a socialist state. For a number of years work has been progressing in the preparation of the project of a criminal code for the People's Republic

of Poland. At first the project was authored by the Ministry of Justice, which acted through a responsible commission (The Consultive-Scientific Commission of the Ministry of Justice). The project of the Ministry of Justice did not, however, pass the test; hence, the second phase of the work began in preparing the projected criminal code, namely, a special Codification Commission (also in the Ministry of Justice). This Commission's work is now in progress and undoubtedly in the near future the Commission will announce the project, which, like the former project of the Ministry of Justice, will be the subject of public discussion.

In the problem of guilt, all the versions of the Ministry of Justice's project (with certain editorial variations) accepted the position of the criminal code in effect, that is, depended so far as the content is concerned on the four types of guilt (direct intent, consequent intent, thoughtlessness, and negligence). The difference between the project and the code in force is that the project defined the kinds of guilt, while the code in force, as we know from previous considerations, defined the kinds of crime. The division of crimes into deliberate and nondeliberate is derived from the kinds of guilt. An act, socially harmful and forbidden by the criminal law, as an objective phenomenon, is not *per se* either deliberate or indeliberate. It acutally receives this subjective coloring from the kind of guilt, and only with respect to it does it become deliberate or nondeliberate. Criminal laws (like knowledge of criminal law) that avoid formulating the kinds of guilt as a metaphysical phenomenon which will not submit to positive determination, and then rush to distinguish crime into deliberate and indeliberate, act like the man who beats a thermometer with the idea that he will eliminate the frost indicated by the thermometer. The frost stays, in spite of his beating the thermometer. In spite of a refusal to formulate the kinds of guilt, these varieties have remained as a psychic and moral phenomenon deeply rooted in the nature of man.

I remarked earlier that the project of the Codification Commission has not as yet been officially made known to the public. However, from various pronouncements based on the project and published in the professional columns of the legal journals, we realize that the project of the criminal code of the Codification Commission operates with the four types of guilt known to us, and in essence and meaning it takes the position of its predecessors. From an editorial viewpoint the project of the Codification Commission is quite close to the last version of the project of the

Ministry of Justice. The relevant prescription reads: "A crime of deliberate guilt occurs. . . . A crime of unwillful guilt occurs. . . ." The question arises whether the project of the Codification Commission defines the concept of guilt or the concept of crime. I think it is a definition of the kinds of guilt. Finally, as to the practical goals of the codification and the practical tasks of the criminal code, I do not think that this matter is a fundamental problem. In fact, it does not matter whether the criminal code says "Deliberate guilt (indeliberate) occurs," or "A crime of deliberate guilt (or indeliberate) occurs . . ."; or finally, as in the code now in force, "A deliberate (indeliberate) crime occurs. . . ." One way or the other, the prime and decisive element is the kinds of guilt, and they determine whether an objective action or desistance (*per se* indifferent from the viewpoint of criminal law) is a deliberate crime or an indeliberate crime; whether the *verba legis* of the criminal code, dealing with the essence and kinds of guilt, will be taken in the form of the proposed definition, or will they play another role—this will be merely an editorial difference of legal expression. A just definition of guilt must be the dominant note in the considerations of the kinds of "act forbidden by criminal law."

THE INFLUENCE OF THOMISTIC

THOUGHT IN CRACOW

Marian Rechowicz

IN FORMULATING THE TITLE FOR THE PRESENT ESSAY I USED THE TERM "influence," and avoided the term "acceptance." The concept of "acceptance" of any doctrine, or any scientific system, is not as yet accurate enough. It could be taken to mean a formal acceptance, e.g., by means of an approval by the Academic Senate of some higher school, as well as an acceptance owing to merit, which actually can precede a formal acceptance. The word "acceptance" can suggest a certain exclusiveness, an absolute dominance of a scientific movement. Such an understanding of the term in relation to the thought of the Middle Ages, which is characterized by eclecticism, or rather syncretism, would lead to some confusion. Further explanations must deal with the phrase "Thomistic thought." By this term we understand the content of the works of St. Thomas, known and explained in numerous manuscripts, which during the Middle Ages were either brought into Poland or written in Poland. We shall not be concerned with the textual exactness of the copy, or with the degree of authenticity reached by the contending commentators in their interpretation of the Angelic Doctor's thought. The matter under study is something else— the actual reading, knowledge and exposition of the works of St. Thomas in university teaching.

In speaking of St. Thomas' influence on Polish theological thought, we do not intend to beg the question. To place the problem properly it would be necessary, first of all, to investigate the hundreds of manuscripts awaiting researchers in the Jagellonian Library and in other Polish collections. In the present article we intend to outline a working hypothesis and to describe the historical confusion in the circumstances and fluctuation of doctrinal thought. We would also like to call attention to danger of schematization, which can seriously impede an honest analytical investigation.

I.

In the research about the history of doctrine in the first half century of the existence of the Jagellonian University, interest has centered on the arts faculty and the philosophical tendencies in it. The fact that many archival records of the faculty are preserved has favored such research as have the relatively numerous researchers—from J. Sołtykowicz, M. Wiśniewski, and W. Wisłocki to Father K. Michalski, A. Birkenmaier, H. Barycz, J. Zathey, Z. Budkowa, W. Wasik, and S. Świeżawski.[1] With the exception of Father J. Fijałek and a few other authors, there was no interest in historical theological problems. The loss of contemporary books from the theological faculty made research on this subject more difficult, but even more significant was the lack of interest in the history of the discipline. Because of the lack of analytical works devoted to the writings of individual theologians, it seems that an outline of the historical environment, as well as an investigation of the analogies connected with the development of philosophical thought, would to some degree facilitate research into the history of theological thought.

Such a method involves many reservations, but its application is justified because we are entering an unknown area and are seeking the very primary factors.

Among such primary factors we include first of all the general statement that a certain syncretism characterized the theology of Cracow in the fifteenth century. No fundamental doctrinal tendencies (among which were Thomism, Albertism, Scotism, and Nominalism) dominated there exclusively. Syncretism was evident not only in the fact that Scotists and Thomists were lecturing on the same subject, but frequently the very same masters who commented on the writings of Ockam in philosophy would expound the ideas of St. Thomas in theology. This statement does not exclude the possibility of a greater or lesser preponderance of particular systems that set the tone in corresponding areas. In that sense it is possible to say that in the Cracow faculty of theology, from its foundation in 1400 to the fourth quarter of the fifteenth century, Scotism was very weakly represented. Evidence of this is the insignificant number of medieval Scotistic manuscripts, of which there are about eight in the Jagellonian Library.[2] Further evidence for this thesis is the lack of any information about an intensive intellectual movement among the Franciscans in the first half of the fifteenth century.[3] Perhaps the explanation of this phenomenon comes above all from the complicated doctrinal connections between Scotism and Hussitism. After its renewal, the University of Cracow owed its rapid development to the secession of professors from Prague. As a result of the conflicts among the nations and the intensification of the Wyclifite-Hussite quarrels, especially after 1409, the majority of the professors and students of the German nation (the Poles were also reckoned among them) left Bohemia.

Forty-six professors from Prague emigrated to the newly established university in Leipzig; and, as H. Barycz analyzed the data, of the forty professors at the Cracow Academy at the beginning of the fifteenth century, twenty-six were from Bohemia or had had their education in Prague.[4] Since Wyclif had been among the Scotists and had been an irreconcilable realist, Czech Wyclifism sympathized with Scotism. The Scotists began to be suspected of heresy. The theological faculty of Cracow prided itself on its irreconcilable opposition to Hussitism: therefore, it seems very probable that the emigres from Prague were especially followers of nominalism. But there were other doctrinal systems, not at all compromised by Hussitism. Which of them achieved primacy at the beginning of Cracow's activity?

If one were to take into consideration the state of research in philosophy at present, it would be necessary to say nominalism. It is in this sense that several of the students of the subject, with Father Michalski at their head, have expressed themselves. Michalski, the distinguished investigator of nominalism, reckoned that in the Jagellonian Library there were forty-one manuscripts of works by John Buridan, Albert of Saxony, Marsilius of Ingheim, and Nicholas of Oresme.[5] Considering the great number of nominalist manuscripts, he declared emphatically that "nominalist thought existed among us, and its beginnings go back to the first years of the fifteenth century."[6] To that stream of thought or circle of thinkers one must add Mieczysław of Cracow, Stanisław of Skarbimierz, Mikołaj of Gorzków, Jakób of Paradyż, and Benedict of Hesse.[7] In other words, a series of the most eminent masters in the first half of the fifteenth century were nominalists. It is true that there is a veritable legion of less well-known masters. It is impossible to classify them because their manuscripts have not as yet been investigated. Besides these arguments about the preponderance of nominalism, there are some historical arguments. Above all, nominalism was the very antipodes of Czech Scotism. Besides, there was the connection of the nominalists with conciliarism. Many distinguished conciliarists, such as John Gerson and Peter d'Ailly, were nominalists.[8] It is not necessary to add that conciliarism attracted wide circles in Poland. Benedict Hesse, Jakób of Paradyż, and Mikołaj Strzempiński were authors of valuable works at Basle, as Father Fijałek has shown.[9] The University of Cracow was the last to submit to Eugene IV. Since philosophical thought in the Middle Ages was generally connected with theological creativity, the suggestion arises spontaneously whether the influence of nominalism was equally strong in theological writing. But here we have reservations. For who else but Ockam by his critical writings separated philosophy from theology? Besides, we know that Ockam did not create any particular theological system, and that his theological influence, as compared, for instance, with that of Duns Scotus, was significantly less. It seems rather unlikely that in an area as sensitive to the orthodoxy of theological notions as Cracow in its fight against Hussitism, a doctrine could have been accepted that is in fact philosophically the very antipodes of Hussitism and from a theological viewpoint had awakened the gravest reservations in the Church.[10]

II.

What in fact was the image of Cracow's theology at the first part of the fifteenth century? Let us first try to analyze by analogy the prejudices that rise in this understanding.

Certainly one cannot refute the statement that the majority of professors who came to Cracow from Prague were hostile to Hussitism, and certainly were equally hostile to Scotism. Does the fact that they rejected Scotism imply that nominalism was dominant? For besides nominalism there was another current in Europe that also attracted wide circles. This was undoubtedly Thomism. All generalization without scrupulous research into the works of the individual authors would be a mistake. But another generalization is equally inadmissible. From the fact that a given writer was a nominalist in philosophy it does not follow that he pursued this system in theology. As we know, most of our masters cultivated syncretism. Michalski, for instance, declares that in the philosophical writings of Benedict Hesse nominalistic ideas are evident. It would seem correct to think that these ideas would also color his theology; but the latest research on Benedict's manuscripts permits the conclusion that the same author, who in philosophy cultivated nominalism, in theology based himself on St. Thomas Aquinas.

Just as weak is the argument that implicates the conciliarists in the nominalist position. Fijałek's investigations on Jakób of Paradyż and the latest research on Benedict Hesse show that both these eminent conciliarists from Cracow, whose work is no longer unknown to us, based their work principally on the writings of St. Thomas.

Nor is the statistical argument convincing. Against the 41 nominalist manuscripts in the Jagellonian Library, in the same period we can set 137 manuscripts of the works of St. Thomas, without speaking of the works by the later Thomists, for instance, the Dominican John Torquemada, Z. J. Versor,[12] and the learned disciples of St. Thomas, the Augustinians Aegidius Romanus and Augustinus Triumphus.[13]

The list representing the collections in the Jagellonian Library can be augmented by the collection in the Cathedral Library at Cracow, which is the richest collection outside Cracow.[14] The considerable number of codices found in the possession of many masters in the whole fifteenth century undoubtedly testifies to their spread and to the learned readers in the territory of Cracow. It does not follow from this that the majority were disciples of St. Thomas or that the masters who did not possess copies were opponents of this view. How deceptive statistics can be is illustrated by the fact that in our collection the names of the most eminent representatives of Thomism in Poland are missing, namely, Jan of Głogów and Jakób of Gostynin.[15] Also missing was the name of Jakób of Paradyż, whom Fijałek considered a Thomist.[16]

That in the theology in the first half of the fifteenth century not nominalism but Thomism, *toute proportion gardée*, was dominant, is suggested by certain positive data. We consider among them: (1) the influence of the Dominican school in Poland; (2) the foreign contacts of our masters; (3) the results of certain analytical investigations.

1. We have paid relatively little attention to the intellectual

movement among the Dominicans. This gap has been partially filled by the work of J. Kłoczowski.[17] This order, in constant contact with the West and especially with Paris, was the natural intermediary in obtaining Thomistic manuscripts. From the middle of the thirteenth century the Dominicans in Poland showed great vitality and scientific ambition. In fact, the Dominican *Studium Generale* arose in 1304, and a year later it was raised to the status of a *Studium Solemne,* that is, one that educated the brethren of one province only; that *Studium* lasted through the fourteenth century and showed particular signs of development during the years 1380–1419.

The order, being a general ecclesiastical institution, undoubtedly educated some of its more talented personnel beyond the frontiers, in particular in Paris, where the Dominicans studied at the University and at the College of St. Jacques. The fact that the reorganization of the University of Cracow after its renovation in 1400 was based on Parisian models speaks of vital contacts, cultural and scientific, between the Polish school and the first university of Europe.

It is very probable that the intermediaries between Paris and Cracow were actually the sons of St. Dominic. We know from other sources that the old quarrels between the Dominicans and the Sorbonne had somewhat calmed by 1403.[18] The influence of the Dominicans on the newly organized University could have been great. The fact that here and elsewhere there were conflicts, does not rule out other contacts. The united front against Hussitism could have formed the basis for friendship between the Dominicans and the University. For who else but the Dominicans controlled the administration of the Inquisition at that time?[19]

It is equally reasonable to assume that the professors of the newly established theological faculty, at least at the beginning, used the Cracow library of the Dominicans, which had already existed for half a century. Certainly, like Jan Szczekan[20] and other professors, they obtained at least part of their manuscripts through the priory of the Holy Trinity in Cracow.

2. In the first half of the fifteenth century, besides the contacts with the Dominicans, the journeys of our masters to the Councils of Constance and Basel caused the knowledge of Thomistic writings to spread. Actually, Paweł Włodkowic and Tomasz Strzempiński brought back codices of St. Thomas' writings.[21] From other sources we know that John Torquemada was active in the council of Basel; he was the general of the Dominicans, and the

author of the best scholastic work on the Church.[22]

3. The final argument on this matter is analytical investigation. Unfortunately, it is based on a few studies and therefore does not possess the convincing power of demonstration. Still the research done to date does not show that at the beginning of theological work at Cracow any system was more influential than Thomism. A typical example of this is found in the lectures of Master Benedict Hesse. This scholar occupied the chair of theology from 1430 and served as rector and vice-rector of the University; he became famous as the author of a *Tractatus Minor* on conciliarism, and his philosophical works were colored by nominalism.[23] In view of the doctrinal syncretism of the majority of the masters, this does not conflict fundamentally with the results of our researches, which show the great Thomistic influence on the theological writings of Hesse. A nominalist in philosophy, a conciliarist in the struggle for reform, Hesse for a quarter of a century disseminated Thomistic ideas from the chair of theology. The extensive commentary on the Gospel of St. Matthew in four tomes (BJ 1365, 1364, 1366, and 1368) was in fact a *reportata* of his lectures. The *Lectio* in the commentary is dependent on Nicholas Gorry, one of the eminent exegetes of the Dominican monastery of St. Jacques in Paris; there are also certain additions from the apparatus given by St. Thomas in the *Catena Aurea*. The problem of relations leads to the *Summa Theologica* and the *Summa Contra Gentiles,* as well as to the works of Aquinas' student, Augustinus Triumphus. As a whole, his work, the result of twenty-five years of teaching, shows a strong doctrinal flavor of the Dominican school and the specially strong influence of St. Thomas. In order to supplement these details, it must be added that Hesse used those texts of Scripture which came from the Parisian correctors, that his exegetical method is adapted to the Thomistic postulates, and that his preaching as well as illustrations lead to Dominican sources. In addition to the Dominican school, he turned most readily to the Scholasticism of the twelfth century, and principally to French Scholasticism, to Peter Comestor, the *Glossa Ordinaria,* the scholars of St. Victor, and the moralists of the type of Peter Blois. Closest to him were the reformers of the twelfth and thirteenth centuries—sober, concrete, and sometimes uncompromising. His view of theology and its function in life agreed with conciliarism. In conciliarism he saw the concrete way to reform, a matter which filled him with passion, as it did Jakób of Paradyż and many others in the period. Theological education and fondness for

Marian Rechowicz

legal matters opened the way to conciliarism. As has been shown by Brian Tierney, conciliarism developed by the penetration of corporate and canonical concepts into ecclesiology.[24] Above all, theologians and canon lawyers succumbed to the idea.

Hesse popularized his ideas from the university chair by means of sermons, writings, and administrative activity. It seems that Hesse was not alone in spreading Thomistic doctrine. Omitting the older Thomists like Jan Szczekan, we can include among them Stanisław Skałmierz, somewhat older than Benedict, known to us through the studies of L. Ehrlich[25] and Budkowa,[26] Hesse's contemporary Jakób of Paradyż, and St. Jan Kanty. Fijałek expressly calls the first of them a Thomist;[27] of the latter we know that he particularly delighted in copying the works of St. Thomas amid a multitude of copied manuscripts.

This circle was certainly extensive. At the end of the fifteenth century the ideas of St. Thomas were spread in Cracow by Jan of Głogów, *maximus sagax vir omni scientia,* partially by the influence of Albertinism, and later by the rector and vice-chancellor Jakób of Gostynin, of similar interest and doctrinal tendency.[28] There is no doubt that further investigations will broaden that circle.

In a general characterization of the epoch we can state that on the basis of the syncretism generally cultivated by the theological faculty in Cracow, it was not the works of Ockam or Duns Scotus, but rather the works of St. Thomas that were commented on widely and that exercised the principal influence on theological education until the triumph of Scotism in the year 1470.

III.

Even though the Thomistic school and its followers in Cracow, along with the writings of St. Thomas, were continually commented on, it seems that in the third quarter of the fifteenth century the influence of Thomism declined. The Polish Dominicans were unable to strengthen the doctrinal movement. Busy with missions to the East, the Inquisition, and frequently named suffragan or diocesan bishops, they took little interest in exact science. In the course of the fifteenth century it is possible to find only three sons of St. Dominic who were professors at the University of Cracow.[29] Their literary activity, too, reappears only in the seventeenth century.

At the turn of the fifteenth and sixteenth centuries the Franciscans obtained a somewhat stronger position in the intellectual movement. This condition was, however, a reflection of a general European phenomenon. In Paris during the last twenty-five years of the fifteenth century the nominalists were excluded from the University, and in 1473 the masters of the Sorbonne were obliged to lecture in the spirit of Scotism.

The fall of conciliarism in France buried nominalism in its ruins; but in Poland the defeat of conciliarism was the defeat of the series of Thomists, for instance, Benedict Hesse. The Scotists owed their success in some degree to the conflict over the Immaculate Conception, which was generally accepted in ecclesiastical practice. Moreover, former prejudices had ceased.

After 1436, that is after the agreement between the Calixtines with Sigismund of Luxemburg, the Hussite movement in Poland weakened systematically. The ghost of Hussitism, which had compromised Scotism, ceased to disturb theologians in the second half of the fifteenth century. At the same time the Franciscans, having gone through a process of renewal, produced several eminent scholars. In the second half of the fifteenth century Peter Tartaretto was active in Paris; and Francis Lychet, the later general of the order, was active in Lyons. Somewhat earlier Stephan Brulifero and Matthew Doering had achieved prominence. Particularly influential in changing the position of the Franciscans in Poland was John Capistran, who in 1453 spent several weeks in Poland and established there a flourishing branch of the Observants. Shortly thereafter younger Scotists, educated in Paris, arrived in Cracow: Michał Tworóg from Bystrzyków and Jan of Stobnica.[30] Albert Fantini, a Franciscan from Italy, supported their activity.[31]

With due respect to such fortunate circumstances, the Scotists gained great influence in the University. At the turn of the fifteenth and sixteenth centuries it is also possible to name eminent Thomists, Albertinists, and even nominalists. This was a period of renewed Scholastic flowering. At the same time, humanism conquered the minds of the younger professors and the majority of the students in the faculty of arts. Between the new tendency and the Scholastics a violent quarrel developed. The humanists caricatured the intricacies of the Scholastics, which seemed to them a game of words. The Scholastics, with the feeling of authority which they possessed, defended themselves against humanism as against a dangerous heresy.

The Erasmians especially belonged to the anti-Scholastic camp.

The Englishman, Leonard Cox, who had arrived in Cracow, became their rallying point. Eminent and influential people gathered around him, for instance, Jan Łaski, the brother of the primate of Poland, the future cardinal Stanisław Hosius, the future bishop of Cracow Andrzej Zebrzydowski, and some younger theologians. This group, not connected with the University, fought the Scholastics, and also undertook the struggle against Protestantism. Since the reforms in the University in the first half of the sixteenth century had produced no results,[32] the Scholastics were not prepared to struggle against the innovators, and there began a search for allies. This ally was found in the Society of Jesus. The Jesuits quickly adjusted. They realized that it was impossible to fight Protestantism, unless humanistic positions were adopted and unless theology were taught in the spirit of the time. Already St. Ignatius had found himself under the influence of Salamanca, where, owing to Francis Vittoria, the University accepted Thomism as its foundation and modernized the teaching of theology in the spirit of humanism. In his constitutions Ignatius ordered studies to be based on the writings of St. Thomas. This is the more significant, because the exposition of theology from Thomistic texts in the fifteenth century was gaining influence at the universities. Among them were Paris, Pavia, and German Freiburg.[33] The Dominican general chapter in 1551 named twenty-seven universities in which the brethren could obtain theological academic degrees.[34] After the end of the sixteenth century, the superior general of the society, Aquaviva, following the direction of Ignatius, ordered the composition of a new *ratio studiorum* for the order.[35]

In this work, as has been shown by Father S. Bednarski, the Polish province played a significant role; the majority of its recommendations was accepted. The *ratio studiorum,* approved in 1599, ordered the *Summa Theologica* to be the text of the lectures, but not without certain restrictions. These same Jesuit humanists and Thomists, in part, at the end of the sixteenth century waged a bitter struggle with the Cracow Academy about the monopoly of teaching in the country. In this way the Scholastic stronghold, besieged till then by the humanists, found itself in the presence of a new and more terrible enemy.

The University of Cracow, guarding its privileges, modernized itself and adjusted to the spirit of the time. In order to remain competitive, it began to reorganize itself on the Jesuit model and to reform its system of teaching.

The Influence of Thomistic Thought in Cracow

On March 23, 1603, the rector of the University, Dobrocielski, carried a motion that the University "proceed along the common way of St. Thomas as the basis of teaching," together with more or less restriction, such as that included in the Jesuit *ratio studiorum*.[36] In this way Thomism was received officially but not exclusively into the University of Cracow. This acceptance was the more characteristic, in that the Jesuits, above all, contributed to it.

FOOTNOTES

1. Since 1957 research on a larger scale in the medieval philosophical manuscripts was undertaken by the Institute of Philosophy and Sociology in the Polish Academy of Sciences. The results of these investigations are published in the Institute's *Mediaevalia Philosophica Polonorum* I, II (1958); III (1959).

2. See W. Wisłocki, *Katalog rękopisów Biblioteki Uniwersytetu* (Cracow, 1877–1881). This number could be increased by including the works of St. Bonaventure, of which the Library has about 30, but then one would have to speak of Bonaventurism rather than Scotism.

3. S. Kantak, *Franciszkanie Polscy, 1237–1517* (Cracow, 1937) I, 177–183.

4. H. Barycz, *Dziejów związku Polski z Uniwersytetem Karola w Pradze* (Poznań, 1948).

5. K. Michalski, "Zachodnie prądy filozoficzne w XV w. i stopniowy ich wpływ środkowej i wschodniej Europie," *Przegląd Filozoficzny* 31 (1928) 19; see also Michalski, "Jan Burdinus i jego wpływ na filozofie Scholastyczną w Polsce," *Sprawozdanie Akademii Umiejętności w Krakowie* (1916).

6. K. Michalski, "Tomizm w Polsce na przełomie XV i XVI w.," *Sprawozdanie z czynności i posiedzeń Akad. Um. w Krakowie za r. 1916;* Michalski, *Sprawozdanie z posiedzeń wydziału hist.-filoz.* (Cracow, 1917).

7. W. Tatarkiewicz, *Historia filozofii* (Warsaw, 1958) I, 422–423. W. Wasik classifies particular authors differently; for instance, he puts Mieczysław of Cracow among the Augustinians; see W. Wasik, *Historia filozofii Polski* (Warsaw, 1959) I, 32–34.

8. F. Cayré, *Patrologie et histoire de la théologie* (Rome, 1945) II, 662–663.

9. J. Fijałek, *"Mistrz Jakób z Paradyża i Uniwersytet Krakowski w okresie soboru Bazylejskiego,* 2 vols. (Cracow, 1900).

10. E. Amann, "Église et la doctrine d' Ockam," *Dictionnaire de la théologie Catholique* XI, c. 889–904; R. Quelluy, *Philosophie et théologie chez Guillaume d' Ockam* (Paris, 1947).

11. See M. Rechowicz, *Św. Jan Kanty i Benedykt Hesse w w. świetle krakowskiej kompilacji teologicznej z XV w.* (Lublin, 1958).

12. We omit the names of St. Albert the Great and Durandus de S. Porciona, for these authors do not represent the Thomistic tendency, even though they are Dominicans. See Cayré, *Patrologie* 666–668.

13. A detailed list of the medieval manuscripts of the Jagellonian Library includes the writings of St. Thomas Aquinas. See Rechowicz, *Św. Jan Kanty* 202–203.

Marian Rechowicz

14. J. Hornowska-Zdzitowiecka, *Zbiory Rękopiśmienne w Polsce średnio-wiecznej* (Warsaw) 206.

15. Michalski, "Zachodnie prądy" 19.

16. Fijałek, *Mistrz Jakób* II, 52.

17. J. Kłoczowski, *Dominikanie Polscy na Śląsku w XIII-SIV w.* (Lublin, 1956) 214–234; Kłoczowski, "Reforma polskiej prowincji dominikańskiej w. XV-XVI," *Roczniki humanistyczne* 4 (Lublin, 1953) 45–92.

18. J. B. L. Crevier, *Histoire de l'Université de Paris dépuis son origine jusqu'en année 1600* (Paris, 1761) 217–218; J. Fijałek, "Nasza Krakowska nauka o Niepokalanym Poczęciu NMP w wiekach średnich," *Przegląd polski* 34 (1900) 430.

19. H. Barycz, *Rys dziejów zakonu kaznodziejskiego w Polsce* (Lwów, 1961) I, 265.

20. J. Fijałek, "Studia do dziejów Uniwersytetu Krakowksiego i jego Wydziału Teologicznego w XV w.," *Rozprawy Akad. Um. w Krakowie, Wydział teologiczny* (Krakow, 1890) XIV, 71.

21. Fijałek, *Mistrz Jakób* II, 52.

22. M. Grabmann, *Geschichte der Katolischen Theologie* (Freiburg im Breisgau, 1933) 100.

23. K. Michalski, "Zachodnie prądy."

24. B. Tierney, *Foundations of Conciliar Theory* (Cambridge, 1955); see also the review by Dom Daphin, *Revue d'Histoire Ecclesiastique* 52, no. 1 (1957) 152–155.

25. L. Ehrlich, *Polski wykład prawa wojny z XV w.* (Warsaw, 1955); for the details on St. Thomas Aquinas see pp. 31–32.

26. Budkowa, "Najdawniejsze krakowskie mowy uniwersyteckie," *Sprawozdanie Pols. Akad. Um.* 52, no. 6 (1951) 57–575.

27. J. Fijałek, *Mistrz Jakób* II, 52. "He matured on Aristotelian ethics in the garb of St. Thomas."

28. Wasik, *Historia filozofii* I, 45–53.

29. J. Fijałek, *Studia do dziejów Uniwersytetu Krakowskiego* 116.

30. K. Michalski, "Michał z Byztrzykowa i Jan ze Stobnicy jako przedstawiciele skotyzmu w Polsce," *Arch. Kom. do badań hist. fil. w Polsce* I (1917) 21–92; St. Kot, "Michał Tworóg z Bystrzykowa i Jan Schilling, pośrednicy między ruchem filozoficznym paryskim i Krakowem na przełomie XV i XVI w.," *Arch. Kom. do badań* II, 150–155; J. Kędzior, "De Schola Scotistica in Polonia," *Collectanea Franciscana Slavica* (Sibenico, 1937) I, 81–116; Wasik, *Historia filozofii* 53–61.

31. H. Barycz, *Historia Uniwersytetu Jagiellońskiego w epoce humanizmu* (Cracow, 1935) 252–254.

32. *Ibid.* 147–159, 281–285.

33. On the renaissance of Thomism in the fourteenth and fifteenth centuries see the renowned article by P. Mandonnet, "Frères Prêcheurs," *Dictionnaire de Théologie* (Paris, 1924) II, cc. 905–910.

34. *Ibid.*, cc. 906.

35. S. Bednarski, *Jezuici polscy wobec projektu ordynacji studiów* (Cracow, 1935).

36. H. Barycz, *Historia Uniwersytetu Jagiellońskiego* 527–528.

THE POLISH DOMINICANS

IN SILESIA

Jerzy Kłoczowski

WE ARE CONCERNED NOT SO MUCH WITH MECHANICAL INFERENCES as with calling attention to the basic aspects of Dominican history in Poland and in Silesia in the thirteenth and fourteenth centuries. We have characterized the Dominicans as a religious organization that developed out of the Gregorian Reform and that was principally an instrument of that reform, an organization of a model and apostolic clergy. This aspect determined the character and structure of the institutions of the Preaching Brothers. From this followed the definite character of the economic bases of the Order; it defined the principles of the internal religious life and religious activity of the members of the Order. In spite of the initial opposition of the first Dominican generation, this aspect led the Apostolic See to place into the hands of the Preaching Order the Inquisition, which was to be such a fatal burden on the future history of the Church.[1] But not even the Inquisition, imposed on the Order and at variance with the spirit of the gospel, or the use of the Order as a papal militia in such or other activities of an ecclesiastical-political kind, can hide the fact that the Order in its most essential and basic assumption and essence was to be, and undoubtedly was, a group struggling for the realization of the principles of evangelical reform in society. In this lies its principal historical importance, in terms of Christendom in general as well as in terms of Poland and Silesia. In characterizing the Gregorian Reform, we called attention to its two aspects: one negative, that is, the effort to free the Church; and the other positive, most essential for the Church itself, which was fundamental reform of society in the spirit of the gospel. The

Dominican movement fits into the framework of the positive side of the Gregorian Reform thus understood. We shall grasp its full significance for Christian society and hence also for Polish-Silesian society, only when the recent studies on that aspect of the Gregorian Reform reach their completion. But even now it is possible to essay the task of defining the place of the Preaching Brethren in that complex process, so difficult for a historian to grasp.

1. From the beginning the Dominicans found support in clerical circles and the Christian episcopate that took a stand for the reform. Not only an ideological element enters here. Among the reform decrees of the Fourth Lateran Council in 1215 we find two canons that relate in a special way to the Dominicans.[2] Canon 10 commands the bishops to gather groups of persons capable of preaching, give them means of support, and use them as aids in their pastoral work—preaching, confessions, visitations, and so on. We recall that exactly in the year of the Council such a group had been organized in the diocese of Toulouse under the direction of St. Dominic, and undoubtedly it had been put forward at the Council as a model of a certain kind. Canon 11 dealt with the office of Master-Scholastic at the cathedral churches, and so far as possible at other churches. The master was to teach without charge the clergy of his church and the poor students. In the resolutions of Innocent III and his successors the Order of Preachers had as its actual goal the realization of both decrees of the Council. In establishing Dominicans the bishop fulfilled his obligation to canon law, and energetic support by the popes and their legates of the development of the Preaching Brethren was at the same time support for the realization of the Lateran decrees.

It is in this light that we shall understand best the numerous reports from all of Europe about the favorable attitude of the bishops toward the Dominicans. In observing the Dominican expansion in its first year a phenomenon of deeper significance must strike us. In France and Italy the greatest universities, Paris and Bologna, became the principal bases of operation for the Order. On the other hand, in the countries of northern and central Europe, the Brethren found support chiefly in the most important ecclesiastical centers, in the sees of the metropolitans and the more important bishoprics. Evidently, it was here that the best intellectual forces among the clergy were found; it was here that the advantages of the new institution were best understood. In England the first house was established in fact at Oxford, but from the very beginning Archbishop Stephen Langton was very favorable to the Brethren.[3] During the thirties of the thirteenth century a priory was founded at the metropolitan seat, Canterbury. In Germany, Cologne and Magdeburg belonged to the earliest and most important Dominican houses. Archbishop Engelbert established them in Cologne in spite of the opposition of all the clergy.[4] Archbishop Albert introduced them in 1224 to Magdeburg, the center of the Order in eastern Germany and the head of the Saxon province established at the beginning of the fourteenth century.[5] Denmark became the center of a province that included Scandinavia, Finland, and the island of Gotland.[6] Together with the political development of the country under the two Waldemars, the Danish Church, directed for a long period by Archbishops Absalon (d. 1201) and Andrew Sunesen, was passing through a period of intensive development. The first Dominican foundation arose in the metropolitan see, Lund, in 1223, and it was the work of Archbishop Andrew. Thanks to the support of the six other bishops in Denmark, the Dominicans continued to settle there during the twenties and thirties of the thirteenth century.[7] The first foundation in Norway was made in the metropolitan city of Nidaros about 1230. On the other hand, the Brethren met great opposition in Sweden, the most backward of the Scandinavian countries in ecclesiastical development. In the example of Sweden one can observe the fact that a lack of understanding for Gregorian ideas was connected with a lack of understanding and often with a hostile attitude toward the Dominicans. Only when Jarler, a reformer of Swedish ecclesiastical conditions, became the archbishop of Upsala in 1233–1234, did it become possible for the Order to establish a series of houses with the fullest support of the archbishop.

It is in the Polish province that the relations of the Dominicans with the bishops and the support of the ecclesiastical reform movement appeared most strongly. This is excellent testimony to the country's advance in ecclesiastical development. Iwo Odrowąż, who according to Polish Dominican tradition effected the introduction of the Order, belonged to the most enlightened and the most representative figures of Poland at that time. The pope appointed him as the successor to Henryk Kietlicz, who died in 1219.[8] The founding of the Dominicans in Cracow and Sandomierz, the two principal cities of the diocese, was the work of Iwo. In 1225 the lands of Władysław Laskonogi, the chief adversary of political and ecclesiastical reform, were omitted. The Dominicans were established in the principalities of Leszek Biały,

Henryk Brodaty, and Konrad Mazowiecki, as well as in the Pomeranian principalities of Światopełk of Gdańsk and Wracisław of Dymin, whose cooperation with the other rulers was expressed in the year 1223 in the common expedition of the five princes against the lands of Prussia.[9] With the exception of Płock, in all the priories founded as a result of the mission of 1225, the cooperation of the bishops in their origin appears very expressly in the sources.[10] We do not know the details of the foundation at Płock, but the information that Konrad introduced it comes from Długosz. In the Gdańsk the documents of establishment emphasize that Światopełk established the Brethren at the church of St. Michael at the request of Bishop Michał of Włocławek. A series of his documents for the newly founded house expressly confirms this. In western Pomerania the choice of the episcopal see of Kamień as the residence of the Dominicans testifies best of all to the attitude of the Bishop. Wracisław's document for the Brethren mentioned Bishop Konrad first among the witnesses. In Wrocław, as we know, the importing of the Dominicans was entirely the work of the Bishop; finally, in Prague Bishop Pelhrim was a special benefactor of the Brethren.[11]

In the course of the next years, two dioceses, neglected initially —the metropolitan see of Gniezno and the see Poznań—received the Dominicans. The house in Sieradz in the diocese of Gniezno arose in the thirties of the thirteenth century. We do not know anything from the sources about its beginnings, but it would be difficult not to relate them to the changes that were taking place in Great Poland and in the archiepiscopal see. In 1231 Laskonogi died, and in 1232 Pełka, an eminent reformer and leader of the Polish Church, took over the government of the metropolitan see after Archbishop Wincenty, who had been allied with Laskonogi.[12] Pełka's cooperation in the founding of the house at Sieradz cannot be doubted. In Poznań, according to a later and rather unreliable report, as early as the year 1230 Bishop Paweł had supposedly given them a residence at the church of St. Margaret at Środka. However, the priory was not built until the forties of the thirteenth century. With the consent and the active assistance of Bishop Boguchwała the princes of Great Poland granted the Dominicans the church of St. Gotthard on the left bank of the Warta.

Thus, in the course of twenty years, the Dominicans found themselves in all the dioceses of the metropolitan see of Gniezno, with the exception of the smallest, Lubusz; and everywhere they met a friendly and at times an extremely friendly attitude on the part of the episcopate.

The documents which the Polish bishops directed to the Dominicans indicated the very same role for the Order that it had in the whole of Christendom. Wawrzyniec of Wrocław charges them to lead his subjects to salvation, *verbo et exemplo*.[13] Most characteristic are the documents of Bishop Michał of Kujawy for the house in Gdańsk; they testify to the Bishop's full understanding of the importance of preaching and the institution of the Preaching Brethren.[14] Michał declares that he cannot personally fulfill the obligations of preaching and pastoral care incumbent upon him and therefore he grants "the beloved and pious brothers of the Order of Preachers in Gdańsk" the most extensive rights in this sphere. Hence, the Brethren received full rights to preach in the entire diocese, the right to hear confessions, impose penances, free from excommunication, and grant dispensations. From this it is clear that the Bishop transferred a significant part of his *officium* to the Dominicans, and in this way implemented Canon 10 of the Lateran Council. Concern for the effectiveness of Dominican preaching also appears in other episcopal ordinances. He authorizes the Dominicans to grant an indulgence of forty days on those days and in those places *"in quibus populo ministraverit verbum Dei."* The number of days of indulgence is to depend on the day and feast, but also on the number and piety of the congregation. It must be remembered that the Christians of those times attached great importance to penances and, consequently, to indulgences. The right granted the Dominicans intensified powerfully the attractiveness of their preaching. Other manifestations of Michał's concern are connected with the building of a community house and the erection or rather reconstruction of the church, in the course of which the Brethren met with obstacles that consequently made preaching more difficult. Declaring that "as long as a man is on this earth, he cannot live without a home," the Bishop granted ten days of indulgence to all who helped with the building, so that the Brethren would be able to establish their communities as soon as possible and devote themselves to sacred preaching, so useful for the salvation of men.

Sources are lacking to determine whether other Polish bishops granted their monasteries such far reaching rights. Without doubt, the most important aspect, preaching, found support. In Michał's documents we can see a concrete expression of the attitude taken by the reforming circles of bishops and clergy toward the Dominicans.

2. The Polish Dominicans, as elsewhere, entered at once upon the task of reforming the Church in Poland; and their history in Poland, especially in the thirteenth century, will be most closely associated with that work. The foundation of the Dominican priory in Wrocław by Bishop Wawrzyniec was a very typical phenomenon, and corresponded to the intentions of ecclesiastical law as well as to the practice of the entire European and Polish episcopate. The Dominicans' participation in the Silesian reform had permanent significance, and hence their rapid development in the thirteenth century must be considered in the framework of that reform. The reform of the Silesian Church and its great growth in strength and significance during the thirteenth century are represented by its three great bishops: Wawrzyniec (1207–1232), Tomasz I (1232–1268), and Tomasz II (1270–1292). The Dominicans' close bonds with these bishops are characteristic expression of their entrance into the Silesian Church.

The founding of a Dominican house at Wrocław by Bishop Wawrzyniec shows that the Bishop was concerned with having the Order at his side in the growing diocesan seat.[15] Purchasing the old parish of St. Adalbert from the abbey of the Immaculate Conception at Piasek—in exchange for a heavy annual rent of ten silver *grzywna* and eight measures of various kinds of grain—the Bishop won a freer hand in reorganizing the ecclesiastical life of Wrocław. He used this freedom to create two ecclesiastical institutions on the site of the old parish. He immediately gave the Dominicans the church of St. Adalbert but deprived it of parochial rights, and subsequently established a new parish of St. Mary Magdalen. Thus in Wrocław we see a repetition of what had been done some years earlier in Cracow by Iwo Odrowąż, and what was being done at the same time in Sandomierz, what was to be done some years later in Poznań, and what was to be done in Silesia during the second half of the thirteenth century in Głogów and Opole. The establishment of the Dominicans involved pastoral care for the people of the city: the house was to serve the needs of the entire population, and the new parish church was to serve a definite area. Increasing the network of city churches with pastoral tasks was one of the characteristic phenomena of the growth of the cities, just as was the ideological influence of the reform. We emphasized in the introductory remarks the baneful results of the Church's neglect of the urban centers in the eleventh and twelfth centuries. The Dominicans were chosen in great measure to unravel the effects of that neglect but, independently of their establishment, reform circles were striving to increase the number of parishes. For instance in 1213 the Bishop of Leodium divided the original parish in that city into eleven new parishes, and in the thirteenth century the total in Leodium grew to twenty-six parishes.[16] In Poland we deal with similar phenomena, but obviously on a much smaller scale.

The establishment of the Dominicans in Wrocław was not related simply to the local needs of that city. Bishop Wawrzyniec's activity in Wrocław was but a fragment of a general reorganization of the diocese, intended to systematize the pastoral work within its territory. Precisely in these very years the diocese was divided into three archdeaneries; we know that the principal task of the archdeacons was to oversee on behalf of the bishop the clergy's fulfillment of their pastoral duties.[17] We have every right to assume that Bishop Wawrzyniec, like Bishop Michał of Kujawy, counted on the Dominicans to be active over the whole extent of his diocese. Their preaching and their example were to assist the archdeacons in the fulfillment of their tasks. As Michał intended, they were to reach the whole diocese.

Attention must be called to one characteristic aspect of the new Dominican house at Wrocław, namely, the close cooperation of the bishop and chapter. In both documents regarding its foundation, Wawrzyniec emphasizes that he is acting with the advice and consent of the chapter. One of the documents mentions the members of the chapter as witnesses; the other is sealed with the capitular seal. It so happened that in the West the chapters violently opposed the arrival of the Dominicans, fearing their competition, influence, and loss of income.[18] In introducing the Dominicans, however, the bishops lost nothing; on the contrary, they obtained helpers and assured themselves, at no cost or at relatively little cost, of the fulfillment of the conciliar decrees. But, understandably, the material interests of the diocesan clergy were substantially curtailed. In the Polish sources we do not encounter this phenomenon until the end of the thirteenth century. The example of Wrocław and Cracow, where the first Dominicans actually came from the chapter, rather suggest the opposite, namely, the support of the Dominicans by the chapters. We must of course add that in both cases we are dealing with chapters powerfully penetrated by the Gregorian spirit.

During the time of Wawrzyniec's successor, Bishop Tomasz I (d. 1268), four Dominican priories arose in Raciborz, Przyłek, Głogów, and Bolesławiec. It seems that Bishop Tomasz played an

Jerzy Kłoczowski

important role in their foundation—not merely a formal and administrative one. The document of Prince Konrad for the Głogów Dominicans calls Tomasz their founder and patron. Obviously we are not to take the word "patron" literally, but in the sense of a protector of the monastery. However, the word "founder" cannot be subject to any doubt. With regard to Raciborz, there are evidences of the bishop's cooperation in that princely endeavor. Mieszko II names the bishop and the Dominicans of Raciborz the executors of his testament, and gives them at the same time, without division, the annual rent of the castellans of Raciborz and Cieszyń. This is sound proof of the close relationship Tomasz had with the Dominican house in Raciborz. The bishop confirmed the actual document of the foundation of that house in 1258 by attaching his seal.

In view of the lack of sources for the origins of the houses in Przyłek and Bolesławiec, we have suggested that they were the common work of the bishop and the princes, and we called attention to the role of the provincial, Szymon. Close bonds united Szymon with Tomasz; and several times he participated in important events of the diocese. While he was still prior at Wrocław, he, his superior Moses, and a canon of the cathedral mediated an agreement between the bishop and the adventurous prince of Legnica, Bolesław Rogatka. The prince in Legnica placed a document in their hands on Janurary 28, 1249, and granted a series of privileges to the church in return for being freed from ecclesiastical penalties.[19] The order of witnesses in the document is characteristic, and thus an evidence of the importance of the episcopal delegates; in it the Dominicans precede the canon. A year later, February 1, 1250, in Trzebnica the bishop and Szymon witnessed a document of Prince Henryk.[20]

Along with the archbishop of Gniezno and the abbot of Immaculate Conception in Piasek, Szymon became a papal legate for the definitive resolution of the conflicts between the bishop and Rogatka. Rogatka, dressed in penitential garb and asking for the lifting of censures, appeared before them on December 20, 1261.[21] Not much later Szymon functioned as papal commissioner to gather material for Princess Hedwig's canonization which occurred in 1267.[22]

Fragments from the sources testify expressly to the undoubtedly close relations of the Silesian Dominicans with Bishop Tomasz. In this light it is highly probable, according to an eighteenth-century chronicle by the Wrocław Dominicans, that Tomasz bequeathed a library to the monastery of St. Adalbert.[23] This seems to give extremely characteristic evidence of the intellectual contacts of that shepherd—highly educated according to the standards of his time and renowned for his learning—with the Wrocław outpost of that Order, which placed such great emphasis on study.

During the rule of Bishop Tomasz II (1270–1292) the Dominican organization in Silesia became basically definitive. Four or five new houses arose, and still another was begun. So far as we know, the Bishop was not the founder of any of them; but, nonetheless, the traditional cooperation of the diocese with the Order was entirely preserved, and in the course of the political and ecclesiastical conflicts among Bishop Tomasz, Konrad of Głogów, and Henryk II, it survived a test of fire with complete success. The attitude of the Dominicans in both conflicts and whole correspondence of Bishop Tomasz during the struggle with Henryk provide adequate proof for this.

In the course of the sixty years that separate the arrival of the Dominicans from the death of Tomasz II, the Silesian Church made vast progress. Corresponding to the growth of the creative forces in society and to the increasing population resulting from an intensive colonization of city and village, pastoral needs also grew and had to be satisfied. The Church was continually striving for a more complete inclusion of all society within the framework of its activity. The parochial network and the level of clerical activity were significant. In the course of the thirteenth century hundreds of parishes were established in Silesia, and together with that vast essential increment, the number of diocesan clergy increased; and so there came about the problem of training and educating the clergy. During the time of Tomasz I a fourth archdiaconate was established in Legnica.[24] At the same time in the course of the thirteenth century religious establishments of a different kind and with various activities spread throughout Silesia: Cistercians chiefly in the villages, the mendicant orders in the cities, as well as the Hospitallers. The personal role of the bishops of Wrocław in this movement was very important. In the episcopal principality of Nysko-Otmuchów the growth of parishes in the thirteenth century, a result of colonization but also of the episcopal concern, can be expressed numerically; there were three parishes at the beginning of the thirteenth century, and sixty-one parishes a hundred years later.[25]

The cooperation of the bishops in the creation of Dominican centers is very indicative—an evidence that they looked upon the

Jerzy Kłoczowski

Brethren as their own helpers. The legate Philip also regarded the Dominicans in Poland the same way, for in 1282 he granted them episcopal rights in the matter of confession.[26] No other Order was more closely bound to the bishops in the thirteenth century than were the Dominicans. Operating here were the same factors that guided the bishops who established the Dominican houses: the example of their lives, study, and preaching made them an instrument for influencing the population. The development of parishes and settlements caused the bishops to increase the Order's houses. These were situated near all the residences of the archdeacons, and in a planned and uniform manner the Brethren embraced the entire territory of the diocese with their activity and were enabled to reach all the parish churches. Panzram reckons that about the year 1300 there were 322 locations with churches in the territory of the diocese of Wrocław. For one Dominican house this would make approximately 30 locations, and a greater number of parishes—perhaps twice that number.[27] The Dominican preachers and confessors touched areas that the bishop could not reach and thus enriched the more or less routine work of the secular clergy.

3. From these facts it follows clearly that the Dominicans, at least in the beginning, received full support from the reform circles of the thirteenth-century episcopate, who saw in them an apt instrument in realizing the goals of the reform movement. We have tried to show that in Silesia the Dominicans were essentially such an instrument in the hands of the bishops during the whole thirteenth century. For a fuller understanding of the role played by the Dominicans in the Silesian Church, and in Poland generally, it is necessary to present it in terms of the whole process of Christianizing the country. We are concerned with what was done in the tenth-twelfth centuries, with what the thirteenth century added, and, moreover, with an examination of the role of the secular clergy and of the particular religious organizations in that area. We know how inadequately these problems are known and how little they are being investigated; hence, great caution is needed in forming general conclusions. Nevertheless, the results achieved by us show that in certain sectors of the reform the role of the Dominicans in Silesia, and probably also in Poland, was very far-reaching. Especially in pastoral care, broadly understood, the Dominicans were a focus of reform activity in some respects. The cathedral and collegiate chapters, made up of the elite of the secular clergy, primarily fulfilled other functions—administrative and

liturgical, rather than pastoral. Similarly, the Cistercian and Benedictine abbeys were in principal removed from activity in society.
In these conditions, besides the Dominicans, only the other mendicant orders devoted themselves exclusively to the realization of
the evangelical goals of the Gregorian Reform, which Orders, as
mentioned before, only gradually followed them to Poland. When
they arrived there, they were already to a great extent like the
Dominicans and had been pursuing goals and fields of activity
similar to those of the Dominicans. The Franciscans, settling in
Poland about twenty years after the Dominicans, were just then
completing their long evolution from an unorganized secular
movement into an order of priests, exempted from the jurisdiction
of bishops and devoted completely to pastoral work.[28] Their role
in the process of reforming the Church in Poland demands a
separate study. The current views, which are frequently repeated
and which raise the Friars Minor to the very front of activity in
Poland, require revision in every case. These views are based on
the great number of Poor Clares, who are associated with the
Friars Minor, and on the lives of these saintly women. Without
lessening the great significance of the Franciscans for thirteenth-
century Poland, it must, however, be emphasized that the Poor
Clares are above all a religious movement of women, and not of
the Friars Minor. The Friars' excessive preoccupation with the
pastoral care of the women's convents led to a distortion of the
Order's basic functions. The Franciscans of Wrocław will protest
against this,[29] but one can raise the question: To what degree
did the Friars Minor's relations with the princes reflect on the
Polish Friars Minor?

In comparing the development of Dominicans and Franciscans
in Poland, we called attention to a certain lack of expansion,
numerical and territorial, of the latter. In the territories of Little
Poland, Great Poland, and Mazovia, the Friars Minor filled the
gaps left by the Dominicans, and this very often in secondary areas.
Things were different in Silesia, but even here it was a far cry
from that threefold numerical preponderance of Franciscans over
Dominicans that is characteristic in the West. There is, besides,
the important problem of the relations of both Orders with the
thirteenth-century Polish bishops, among whom in Silesia and in
other dioceses we found so many reformers and persons of high
standing. We observed in the diocese of Wrocław the particularly
close relationship of the Preaching Brethren with the bishop-
reformers of that city, whereas the Franciscans not only took a

position hostile to the bishop, but also by their behavior provoked protests from the entire Polish episcopate with Archbishop Jakób Świnka at their head. The view, then, of the special position of the Franciscans among the mendicant orders in Poland does not have any foundation; on the contrary, the available data show that in Poland more than elsewhere such a special position belonged rather to the Dominicans. This is true especially in the matter of reform, undertaken by the Polish Church and its superiors; it was within this framework that the Dominicans established themselves upon their arrival in the country, and they continued to maintain this position for a long time. It must be added that besides the Dominicans and Franciscans, the other mendicant orders do not have any significance in Silesia and Poland in the thirteenth-fourteenth century.

How long the Preaching Brethren filled a special role in the Polish movement of the Gregorian Reform is another question. We must recall that the realization of the original Dominican conception of Innocent III and St. Dominic met from the very start with serious difficulties, especially among the parochial clergy. In the West, as early as the forties of the thirteenth century, the Order had to undertake new forms of activity, by no means compatible with the original conception. At the same time the Dominicans became but one of many mendicant orders which conducted a basically similar activity. It seems that in Polish conditions the problem developed differently from the West. Several times we have called attention to the breakdown of the Dominican position in Silesia in the fourteenth century.

In Polish historiography the problem of the significance of the mendicants—and in Poland, above all, of the Dominicans—evoked a definitely more profound but yet inadequate discussion. In his synthesis on Polish medieval culture, M. Friedberg ultimately understood the problem in this way:

> Frequently the opinion is repeated in literature that a new epoch on the Christianization of Poland was created thanks to the activity of the new orders, and the activity of the mendicant monks is contrasted with the inertia of the older orders. However, such a conception is not correct. The efforts of the old Orders, especially the Benedictines in the tenth-twelfth centuries, were equally effective, and in total perhaps more important in Christianizing and civilizing our country than the later efforts of the Dominicans and the Franciscans. The difference lies in this, that the monasteries of the older orders quickly lost their original apostolic zeal and ceased to

be an important cultural factor; the mendicant monks, in spite of neglect in certain spheres, were able to maintain a constant contact with society and to exercise an influence on it through the course of centuries.[30]

The above shows how imperfectly the literature was conversant with the problem of the orders. The basic differences between the particular religious organizations were not known; hence, everything was reduced to the zeal of the members of the orders. The entire dynamics of the Church's medieval evolution was not understood. Indeed, this was not a matter of activity or inertia, or even of the lesser merits of the monastic orders, but what is significant is that the Benedictine institutions and the mendicant institutions were dedicated to completely different kinds of activity, and that they were profoundly different in structure, assumptions, and mentality. In the light of the considerations in the present work, we can accept the view that the significance of the mendicants in the process of Poland's Christianization was undoubtedly important and decisive. We have tried to show on what the decisiveness depended. For only the mendicants began to promote Christianity among us on a large scale and to impose upon us their convictions of not being satisfied with an external veneer of Christianity. The religious ferment, which embraced wide circles of society in thirteenth-century Poland and which expressed itself in the fact that more or less one third of all Polish saints lived in that era,[31] centered expressly around the mendicants and provides sound evidence for the results of their activity.

Another matter, namely, the rapid development of the mendicants in Poland—primarily of the Polish Dominicans throughout the thirteenth century—is unintelligible without the 250-year development of the Church in Poland that went before it. The new institution progressed so splendidly and kept abreast with that in the West mainly because it corresponded to the religious and social needs of the times and found conditions that were conducive to its existence. These very needs, the recognition of influential factors, and the ability to mobilize its powers provide vital evidence of the precocious development of the Church in Poland. The first Christianization of our country, at the time of Mieszko or of Kazimierz the Restorer, was dependent on foreign strength and means, but now the Polish Church to a great degree succeeded in its own territory and by its own means to initiate the reform that had been worked out in the framework of the Universal Church. A mendicant order, of course, must rely on the generosity of society so as to maintain its character and can flourish only in a society capable of higher values and one possessing a developed commercial and money economy. The development of the Dominicans in Poland (and later of other mendicants) thus sheds light on that aspect of Poland's society and confirms once again the existence of urban areas in Poland, as well as of an advanced economy. The undeniable character of the Polish Dominicans throughout the entire thirteenth century and their close cooperation with the bishops testify further that the reform of the Church in Poland was not merely launched but systematically worked out, primarily by Poland's own strength.

One further aspect requires particular emphasis. What led us to these conclusions was the analysis of Silesian conditions, where these phenomena appeared more clearly than in other Polish lands. This is obvious from the source material that has been preserved as well as from historical reality. Hence, the significance of these conclusions for the Polish and German historiographical discussion of Silesia. T. Silnicki in his monograph on the Silesian diocese showed the fundamental significance of the thirteenth century in the history of that diocese.[32] Governed by Polish bishops, the diocese at that time built the framework of its powerful and independent position in the country. Relating this to the concept of the Gregorian Reform accepted by us, we can say that Silnicki considered the negative side of that movement. The present work has examined the most essential phases of the positive Silesian reform with a similar result. We have seen that the Poles were the initiators and executors of the principles of evangelization, that they effected the deepening of religious life in Silesia during the thirteenth century, and that the Polish environment was one of the centers of that movement. In summary, one can see clearly the vast and basic role of local Polish elements in the progress of the Silesian Church in the thirteenth century. The evidence reduces to absurdity the position propagated by German scientists in modern times, mainly that which ascribes to the Germans and to German colonists everything that is associated with the development of the Silesian Church at that time and in the following centuries. Like the problem of the cities, or the great properties in the period of colonization on the basis of the German law, so the problem of the Church at that time can be understood only in the light of earlier development. The Gregorian Reform of the Universal Church had been deeply rooted in the tenth century; hence, the reform of the Polish Church in the thirteenth century, conditioned by the development of Christianity in the country in the eleventh-twelfth centuries, grew on native soil made receptive to external impulses. At the beginning of the thirteenth century, the Silesian Church was no longer missionary in character but possessed its own Polish resources capable of accepting the reform and practicing it in spite of the influx of new German population. The Polish Dominicans of Silesia were an emanation of those resources. The fact that in Lower Silesia down to the fourteenth century, and in Upper Silesia down to the eighteenth century, they maintained their predominantly Polish character, is an eloquent illustration of the slow, never quite completed, process of Germanization.

FOOTNOTES

1. P. Mandonnet, *Saint Dominique: L'Idée et l'oeuvre* (Paris, 1938) I, 211. I. Guiraud, *Histoire de l'Inquisition au Môyen Âge* (Paris, 1935–1938) is fundamental for the history of the Inquisition. Around 1232 Gregory IX entrusted to the Dominicans the direction of the Inquisition's activity, *apostolica auctoritate,* in Italy, France, Aragon, and Germany. The centers of operation were the monasteries in Bologna for Italy, in Toulouse for France. From about the middle of the thirteenth century the Dominicans succeeded in transferring a part of the Inquisitorial jurisdiction to the Friars Minor. The history of the Inquisition in Poland and the history of heretical movements there still need study. See K. Dobrowolski, "Pierwsze sekty religijne w Polsce," *Reformacja w Polsce* (Warsaw, 1925) nos. 11–12, p. 78. The first Papal Inquisitors in Poland were named for the Cracow and Wrocław dioceses in 1318. In 1327 the pope entrusted to the Polish provincial the creation of an Inquisitorial administration (see Dobrowolski, p. 179); *Bullarium Ordinis Fratrum Praedicatorum* (Rome, 1729–1740) II, 174. From the fourteenth to the sixteenth centuries the Polish provincials named the Papal Inquisitors for the Polish province. See Dobrowolski (p. 185) for the characteristic text of the provincial chapter in 1505, about the naming of Inquisitors for the diocese of Poznań and the diocese of Cracow. In accordance with the resolutions of the general chapters, the provincials were to supervise the Brethren's conduct of the Inquisition. See, for instance, the general chapter of 1291, *Monumenta Ordinis Fratrum Praedicatorum Historica* (Rome, 1896–19. .) III, 261; for the general chapter of 1321 see *ibid.* IV, 134.

2. Mandonnet, *Saint Dominique* II, 237–238; A. Fliche, *La Chrétienté Romaine (1198–1274)* (Paris, 1950) 203–204.

3. W. Hinnebusch, "The Early English Friars Preachers," *Dominican History* (Rome, 1951) XIV, 60–61.

4. A. Hauck, *Kirchengeschichte Deutschlands* (Leipzig, 1931) IV, 411; H. Scheeben, *Der Hl. Dominikus* (Freiburg im-Breisgau, 1927) 361–363. It is worth calling attention to the fact that the Dominicans were arriving in Germany at the same time as in Poland, as well as in other central and northern

153

Jerzy Kłoczowski

European countries. In Cologne the Brethren were established in 1221, but the first mention of them occurs in 1224. There is no mention of German leadership in these countries.

5. P. Loe, "Statistisches über die Ordensprovinze Saxonia," *Quellen und Führungen* (Leipzig, 1910) IV, 11, 48.

6. J. Gallen, "La Province de Dacie de l'Ordre des Frères Précheurs," *Dominican History* (Helsingfors, 1946) XII. See also A. Taylor, "Absalon de Lund," *Dictionnaire d'Histoire et de Géographie ecclésiastique* (Paris, 1912) col. 199–201.

7. It was only in the diocese of Barglum, which had no city, that the Dominicans did not settle. The abbey of Premonstratensians in Barglum was the chapter of that diocese (see Gallen, "La Province" 28).

8. For a characterization of Iwo see S. Laguna, "Dwie elekcje," *Ateneum* (Warsaw, 1878) 164–167; Z. Kozłowska, "Założenie klasztoru 00. Dominikanów w Krakowie," *Roczniki Krakowskie* (Cracow, 1926) XX, 3.

9. J. Kłoczowski, "Dominikanie Polscy nad Bałtykiem," *Roczniki Humanistyczne* (Lublin, 1955).

10. J. Kłoczowski, *Dominikanie Polscy na Śląsku w XIII-XIV wieku* (Lublin, 1956) 291, for a list of monasteries.

11. M. D. Jakubiczka, "Przichod prvich Dominikanu do naszi vlasti," *Pamiętny spis (Prague,* 1916) 28.

12. For a characterization of Pełka, see K. Tymieniecki, "Kielce w wieku XIII jako ośrodek patriotyzmu polskiego," *Pamiętniki Kieleckiego* (1947) 52–53.

13. *Breslauer Urkundenbuch* (Breslau, 1870) 6. The Bishop granted them the church of St. Adalbert, "ut ibidem domino auxiliante in prepetuum moraturi verbo et exemplo populo nobis subjecto proficiant ad salutem."

14. Not counting the document of foundation, we have four documents, undated, published by P. Simson, *Geschichte der Stadt Danzig* (Danzig, 1918) IV, nos. 13, 14, 20, 21; previously published in *Preussisches Urkundenbuch, Politische Abteilung* (Königsberg, 1882–1939) I, nos. 921–924. Simson accepts their authenticity (Simson, see I, no. 20). The earlier editor, Esraphim, thinks that they originated around 1227, the year when the documents of foundation were issued for the priory in Danzig. According to Simson, only two, namely nos. 13 and 14, issued in Orłów on June 29, originated in 1227, and the two following documents, without date or place, originated only in 1239. He chooses this latter date because one of the documents (no. 20) mentions the altar in the church of St. Nicholas, consecrated by the legate, Bishop William of Modena, who was in Danzig in 1239.

These interesting documents of Bishop Michał, together with the documents of foundation issued by Światopełk and the Bishop (which are questioned in the literature) must be closely examined. There is the possibility of forgery in the fourteenth-fifteenth centuries, when the priory in Danzig felt itself threatened in its rights by the City Council and the Knights of the Cross (see W. Roth, *Die Dominikaner und Franziskaner im Deutsch-Ordensland Preussen bis zum Jahre 1466 (Königsberg,* 1918) 51. But even then this could have been a merely formal falsification, corresponding to existing relations in the thirteenth century. It is necessary to emphasize strongly that the content of the documents corresponds perfectly to those relations, and by no means can these documents be referred to later times, that is, to the four-

154

teenth century. For instance, document no. 13 is expressly related to the implementation of legislation by the Lateran Council IV, and the decisions of document no. 2 conform to conditions before the publication of the bull *Super Cathedram*, in 1299.

15. See the mention of the Silesian foundations in Kłoczowski, *Dominikanie Polscy na Śląsku* 50, as well as the list of monasteries, *ibid.* 291.

16. L. Lestocquoy, "Problèmes d'histoire réligieuses au Môyen Âge," *Annales, Économies, Sociétés, Civilizations* (Paris, 1947) no. 1, 117.

17. T. Silnicki, "Organizacja Archidiakonatu w Polsce," *Studia nad. hist. Prawa Polskiego* (Lwów, 1927) X, 152, stresses that the district of the archdeaconate is the district of visitation.

18. See for instance, G. Meersseman, "Les débuts de l'ordre des Frères Prêcheurs dans le comté de Flândre (1224–1280), *A.F.P.* 17 (1947) 19.

19. P. A. Stenzel, ed., *Urkunden zur Geschichte des Bisthums Breslau im Mittelalter* (Breslau, 1845) 18; *Codex Diplomaticus Silesiae* (Breslau, 1857) VII, no. 690.

20. *Codex Diplomaticus Silesiae* VII. no. 318.

21. T. Silnicki, "Dzieje i ustrój Kościoła na Śląsku do konca w. XIV," *Historia Śląska* (Cracow, 1939) II, 155.

22. *Codex Diplomaticus Silesiae* VII, no. 1139.

23. *Codex Diplomaticus Silesiae* VII, no. 1289.

24. B. Panzram, *Die Schlesischen Archdiakonate und Archipresbyrate bis zur Mitte des 14. Jahrhunderts* (Breslau, 1937) 50.

25. Silnicki, "Dzieje i ustrój," *Historia Śląska* II, 339.

26. See Kłoczowski, *Dominikanie Polscy na Śląsku* 254.

27. See B. Panzram, *Geschichtliche Grundlagen der älteren schlesischen Pfarrorganisation* (Breslau, 1940) 91, for a list of church locations.

28. P. Gratien, *Histoire de la fondation et de l'évolution de l'Ordre des frères Mineures au XIII siècle* (Paris, 1928) 111. For the arrival of the Franciscans in Poland, see K. Kantak, *Franciszkanie Polscy* (Cracow, 1937–1939) I, 13.

29. Kantak, *Franciszkanie* I, 23–24.

30. M. Friedberg, *Kultura polska i niemiecka* (Poznań, 1946) II, 101.

31. J. Woroniecki, *Hagiografia. Jej przedmiot, trudności, i zadania w Polsce* (Cracow, n. d.) 51.

32. Silnicki, "Dzieje i ustrój," *Historia Śląska* II, 128.

LUBLIN AND THE *DELUGE*

Aleksander Kossowski

I. INTRODUCTION

DURING THE "DELUGE" DISASTERS OF EVERY KIND OVERWHELMED THE unhappy people of the Polish Commonwealth. The massacres, the outrages, the extortions perpetrated by the aggressors, destruction of the seed grain, the burning of villages, the plunder, and the willfulness of the native detachments, frequent epidemics and conflagrations—all this still did not fill the measure of the people's agony.

Their distress was intensified by landowners' raids on neighboring properties, a type of greed lost to all human feeling. The gentry, drawing on real or imaginary rights, forced their village serfs to take part in armed expeditions. Their number ranged from about ten to over a hundred, and at times to some hundreds of persons. More than once did soldiers from enemy detachments, called up by the landlords or the leaseholders, take part in such raids. Frequently conflicts stemmed from disputes about a sum of money owed because of a lease or the pledging of lands as security.

Actually, the fundamental source of the raids was the weakness of the executive government organs in face of the turbulent and willful landed gentry. The length of the judicial process and the stubbornness of the litigating parties caused an affair to be dragged out, claims and complaints to be raised by children and granchildren after the death of those who had begun the process. At times they went from generation to generation. The sentence of the court did not actually end the process, for often it was not executed for various reasons (determined opposition by the losing side, bribery, and abuses of every kind). Besides the legal process, illegal means were used, left or right;[1] recourse was had to judges and to raids, violent and armed expeditions.

The residences of the gentry were usually well fortified, protected against side-arms and fire-arms. Hence, it was the serfs who suffered most from the raids. They had to take part in the attack or the defense and to bear heavy material losses. The conflicts often required sacrifices among the people.

Much of what has been recorded about the raids in the territory of Lublin is preserved in the Provincial Government Archives in Lublin, under the title of *Manifestationum, Relationum, et Oblatorum.*

II. KOSSECKI

Stanisław Pruszyński, of noble birth (the son of Paweł the judge of the land of Sandomierz, and owner of the village of Bliskowice, located in the county of Janów) on May 14, 1658, charged before the city government of Lublin the nobleman Dobrogost Kossecki, the hereditary possessor of the above property, with the nonpayment of two installments amounting to 2,500 złotys. From the proceedings of May 16, 1658, found in the Lublin city records, we learn that Dobrogost Kossecki, confessing the same faith as the Swedes, lived in friendship with them. In 1656 he conducted the enemy to the hereditary lands of the plaintiff at Bliskowice, which had been granted to the defendant. The Lithuanian army, learning of the Swedish officers hidden by Kossecki and enraged at the enemies of the fatherland as well as at the defendant who supported them, slew a number of Swedes in the lands of the plaintiff and devastated the lands and the whole village.[2]

As early as January 7, 1654, Kossecki had announced his readiness to pay the sum owed for that year, but Pruszyński had not presented himself.[3] At the orders of Kossecki, the bailiff, Jan Gajowski, along with two nobles, Andrzej Pawłowski and Stanisław Łubkowski, entered the village of Bliskowice, and on September 4, 1656, lodged a report on the devastation and burning of the village by enemies of the crown in that year.[4] A decree issued by Jan Kazimierz in Danzig on November 28, 1656, granted to Jan Toszkowski—aide to the ensign, who had a certain sum of money with Stanisław Pruszyński—the village of Bliskowice, in the light of Kossecki's treason.[5]

III. SPINEK

Hostile relations existed between the Kotarbskis, the hereditary owners of the village—Łańcuchów, Łańcuchowska Wola, and

Ciechanek—[6] and Henryk Spinek, the owner of the village Ostrówka in the county of Lubartów. After the death of her first husband, Paweł Spinek, brother of Henryk, Katarzyna Kotarbska married Mikołaj Latalski. After the death of both husbands, she accepted Catholicism, in order to bring up her son of the first marriage in that faith. Henryk Spinek, on the other hand, was a determined Calvinist. He joined the Swedes as his correligionists. Learning of the Swedish king's arrival and short stay in Lublin, he hastened to the city. From him Henryk obtained the privilege of a grant of the lands of Łańcuchów, Wola Łańcuchowska, and Ciechanek.[7] Taking his armed household with him and summoning his serfs to take part in the expedition, he attacked these lands. He seized the grain and money he found there. A part of the loot he brought to the Swedish commander *in Stationem* at Lublin. The soldiers of the Lithuanian army expelled Spinek from the properties he had seized.

On April 27, 1656, at three o'clock in the morning, with his armed retainers Spinek attacked the village of Ciechanek in the absence of its Kotarbski owner, who had been summoned by a royal "universal" for military service; and he carried off eight heads of peasant cattle to his own estate.[8] When the plaintiff sent his friends to lodge a complaint in the village of Ostrówka at the estate of the defendant, the latter gathered from among his retainers and serfs a group of sixty persons. They showered the messengers with insults, shot at them as they were leaving the estate, and performed various acts of violence.[9]

IV. THE KOTARBSKIS

Nor were the Kotarbskis innocent lambs. In 1656 Wojciech Kotarbski conducted soldiers to Łańcuchów, where they confiscated the hay. In that same year during an enemy raid the Kotarbskis sent their household and their serfs to the upper village. Jan Szewicz, who lived there by the church, was beaten with clubs and wounded.

Father Jan Sikorski, parish priest of Leźny and Łańcuchów, as well as custodian of Lublin, sent his vicars Jan Bobrowski and Kasper Lawecki, along with household servants and wagons, to gather his barley. The Kotarbskis summoned their own servants and serfs: a Gustałowski, Dąbski, Kowalczyk, Pierożek, Sadzik, and many other peasants from the village of Łańcuchów. This mob, armed with firelocks, pistols, battle axes, and javelins moved on the parish house of Łańcuchów to seize the barley. The vicars with their retainers had to flee across the river Wieprz. The crowd called after them: "Go while you are still healthy. Don't stay here. You don't have anything here. Now everything here is ours, because His Majesty the Swedish King has given us all."

In 1657 the servants and serfs of the Kotarbskis, with their consent, broke into the Łańcuchów church and carried away the grain that had been stored there. From the parish house they took beer and whisky.[10]

Henryk Spinek, on May 11, 1658, lodged a complaint with the Lublin city authorities against his sister-in-law, Katarzyna Kotarbska, Mikołaj Kotarbski, and Walenty Kłopotowski for an armed raid on the property of the plaintiff, the village of Ostrówek, the killing of a horse on which he used to ride, and the killing of serfs. The defendant Katarzyna railed that Henryk Spinek must be exterminated. The Kotarbskis invited Tartars and Wallachians to take part in this raid. They confiscated grain that belonged to the estate, as well as grain that belonged to the peasants; they carried off fifteen oxen, killed a horse, plundered the movable property to the value of 20,000 złotys. They raped women and beat the serfs, two of whom died.[11]

In the Lublin city records of May 29 and June 4, 1658, a royal letter was copied, dated May 13, summoning Kotarbska, Wojciech Kotarbski, and Szamuel Spinek on a complaint by Henryk Spinek. The defendants had attacked his lands, village, and estate of Ostrowek with armed force. The servants and serfs of the villages of Łańcuchów, Ciechanek, and Wola Łańcuchowska had been forced to take part in the raid. On August 3, 1658, Mikołaj Kotarbski was granted intromission for the properties of the village of Ciechanek and the estate of Ostrówek.[12]

V. THE LUBIENICKI FAMILY

The litigation about the village of Jabłonna, located in the county of Lublin (at present in the county of Bychów) and the city and village of Wysokie (presently in the county of Krasnystaw) along with the raids on these properties during the period of the "Deluge" were closely associated with the fortunes of the family of Lubienicki H. Rola, settled in Lublin, in Wołyń and Ruś, and so well deserving for services rendered to the Polish Brethren.

On May 27, 1658, a nobleman, Szymon Węgliński, appeared before the Lublin city authorities against Katarzyna Lubienicka, widow (since 1648) of Krzysztof, an Arian minister,[13] and against her son Krzysztof, who, having joined the Swedes, had devastated the village of Jabłonna in the county of Lublin, held in security *modo obligatorio* for the sum of 16,000 złotys by the plaintiff from the defendant and her sons. The counterclaim contains many interesting details about that "Arian" family during the time of the *Deluge*. Aleksander Lubienicki perished as a traitor during the conquest of Tykocin.[14] Stanisław, later the author of *Historia Reformationis Polonicae,* held the office of preacher in the synod of Cracow and remained at the side of the Swedish commandant until Cracow surrendered in August 1657 to the legal authority.[15] Krzysztof Lubienicki joined the Swedish king when he took Lublin in 1656.[16] He joined the garrison in Wysokie (presently in the county of Krasnystaw), the property of his paternal uncle Mikołaj, who also perished *perduellis* in Tykocin. From Wysokie Krzysztof Lubienicki almost daily rode in the village of Jabłonna and "disposed of those properties as though they were his own, boasting that the Swedish king, his lord, had conferred them on him."

He appropriated household utensils, cattle, grain, calves, "and other things relating *ad victum.*" He chose "stations from the peasants." However, a royal forces' rally surprised him. By the favor of the king and the guarantee of relatives, Krzysztof was returned to liberty—but this pardoned transgressor again joined the Swedish king.

In 1657 the accused traitor ordered the burning of a threshing floor in Jabłonna containing 1,100 stacks of wheat, winter and spring, as well as the barns. In that year, too, he came with Swedish and Hungarian detachments to the neighborhood of Lublin and did great damage to the inhabitants of the village of Jabłonna. He took all newly purchased movables "with cattle, horses, and pigs." He ordered all the serfs, for the sake of greater safety, to go to Wysokie for a "Cossack garrison." He soon realized that in view of the Swedish withdrawal from Polish lands he would have to abandon his own home; he went to Jabłonna with a Cossack garrison, fired the whole village along with the estate, and ordered the digging of a dike so that any one holding his property would not be able to draw income from it.[17]

On February 21, 1657, Katarzyna Lubienicka, nee Rudnicka, widow of Hieronim, along with her son Paweł charged the nobleman Orzechowski, the holder of the property of Leczny in the county of Lublin, with armed attack. According to the complaint, the defendant seized 188 head of cattle and 68 sheep, taken by the Tartars in the village of Starościce.[18]

VI. PAWEŁ BOGUSŁAW ORZECHOWSKI

Paweł Bogusław Orzechowski, a fervent Calvinist and son of Paweł, member of the Polish Brethren, also joined the enemies of his country. On May 10, 1658, Szamuel Obodziński and Krzysztof Dzierzek appeared before the city authorities of Lublin against Paweł Bogusław Orzechowski, the landlord of Bełżyce, Jan Bychawski, and Henryk Wonschelen (in some documents Wanschelen). Orzechowski had joined enemy detachments. Depending on protection by the enemy, he attacked the property of the plaintiff, plundered it, and destroyed it.[19]

More information on Henryk Wonschelen appears in a royal summons of July 1, 1658, sent because of a complaint by Piotr Bliszkowski to Michał Słupecki from Konar. Wonschelen as *rebellis* and an enemy of the fatherland had in 1656 borne arms with the Swedes against the Commonwealth. The plaintiff threw him into prison. In order to free the traitor from imprisonment, Michał Słupecki gathered a crowd of people and attacked the estate of the plaintiff—the village of Kierz (at present in the county of Bełżyce). Unable to resist, the plaintiff released the prisoner. The defendant obliged himself to pay Wonschelen 20,000 Polish złotys for liberation; then he inflicted damage of 3,000 złotys.[20]

From the complaint of Father Wawrzyniec Piecznatkowicz, parish priest of Matczyn, we learn that the latter part of April[21] 1657, Paweł Bogusław Orzechowski dispatched a motley group of landless persons and vagabonds against the property of the village of Matczyn and of the plaintiff. They seized two bells from the church, the larger and the smaller one, carried them to Bełżyce, and placed them in the synod there.[22]

The nobleman Jan Gołębiowski, the steward of the properties of Adam Pszonka, Babin, and others, including the steward of these properties, Wawrzyniec Wach, on July 1, 1657, lodged a complaint against Paweł Bogusław Orzechowski on the score of armed attack in May 1657 against the property of the villages and estates of Babin, Matczyn, Jarochowicz, Członów, Radawyczka, from which grain was carried off to Bełżyce and to Lublin. Counting on impunity and the protection of the enemy, Orzechowski used vagabonds for this action (. . . *spe impunitatis atque protec-*

tionis hostilis).[23] On April 22, 1657 (or thereabout) he attacked the village and estate of Radawiec, which belonged to Jacek Michałowski, the *starosta* of Krzepice.[24] On October 31, 1658, a complaint by Katarzyna Szornelowa from Piotrowice, cup-bearer of Sanock, was entered into the Lublin city records against the same Paweł Bogusław Orzechowski. The defendant had dared in May 1657 to send an enemy detachment of about one hundred Swedes and Hungarians together with his serfs against the village and estate of Kreźnica. The attackers stole some 50 head of horned cattle, 90 sheep, and 30 hogs, and drove them to Bełżyce. As a result of the raid and the draining of the pond the plaintiff sustained damages which she reckoned at 2,000 złotys.[25]

This series of crimes and, above all, the crime of treason are charged against Paweł Bogusław Orzechowski according to a document entered in the city records of Lublin March 15, 1659. By a document of February 6, 1659, Jan Kazimierz summoned him to appear before the royal court in the Diet. Jan Pieniążek, the treasurer of Przemyśl, appears as the plaintiff. Moreover, the defendant had conspired with George Rakoczi, the prince of Transylvania. The heresiarch and enemy of the country had aimed at the overthrow of the Constitution of the Commonwealth. He had dared to reveal to the enemy all the secrets of state, and to inform him of the roads and byways. He joined the enemy in attacks, burning cities, villages, castles, fortresses, and churches. On May 2, 1657, he had attached his own troops to and provided guides for two thousand armed Hungarian and Swedish troops who were approaching the hill country. The armed detachments took the city of Gorlice (presently located in the province of Rzeszów), half of which belonged to the plaintiff, burned it, and murdered the inhabitants without sparing anyone. The property of the inhabitants was seized. Many inhabitants were placed in Calvinist prisons (*in carceres calvinisticos*). The city was leveled to the ground and the ashes scattered. The shrines also were given over to flames. The Eucharist was cast out of the tabernacle, trampled underfoot, and many other sacrileges were perpetrated. The ecclesiastical vestments were torn. Remains were dug out of the graves. The plaintiff reckoned his losses at 100,000 Polish złotys.

VII. SMALLER RAIDS

Jan Śliński, the master of Wołyń, on May 7, 1659, had charged Aleksander Mokasiej Bakowiecki before the city authorities in

Lublin with bringing Cossacks and Hungarians against properties belonging to the plaintiff, the villages of Siedliszcze and Wola Korybutowa in the county of Chełm.[27] Father Wojciech Malinowski, vicar of the bishop's church, and the nobleman Stefan Tuszowski, on July 3, 1659, complained against the famous religious dissidents Paweł and Mikołaj Mościejowski, Sabestyan Śląski, Stanisław Rozwalski, and Jan Krzymowski for ridiculing the Catholic Faith, and cultivating religious practices forbidden by law. At night these opponents of the church attacked the village of Siedlisk, the property of the landowner Mikołaj Suchodolski, master of the Table from Chełm. They perpetrated an armed attack in an understanding with Hungarian detachments, their co-believers, who were plundering the province of Lublin at that time. Stefan Tuszowski, administrator of the above properties, frightened by the attackers and in fear before the enemy, saved himself by fleeing with his wife and children, having spent the night in the hedges. The attackers seized things preserved in chests.[28]

VIII. RAIDS ON TERRITORIES BEYOND LUBLIN

Armed attacks with the participation of enemy soldiers, instigated by greedy and brawling individuals, obviously troubled not only the population of the province of Lublin, but also other places in the Commonwealth. This plague also affected the population of Great Poland. Particularly notorious among the traitors and plunderers of that region was the squire of Skoki, Mikołaj Rej from Nagłowice, the great-grandson of the author of *Żywot człowieka poczciwego*. Leon Białkowski gives a colorful sketch of him in his study *Szkice z życia Wielkopolski w siedemnastym wieku* (Poznań, 1925): "A whole series of complaints presents him as an informer in regard to his fellow citizens, cruel to other people, a persecutor of Catholics and a destroyer of churches (for he was a Calvinist). Faithfully attached to the Swedish army, he remained under the spell of its invincible might."[29] Rej "in the year 1656 was persuading Adam Padniewski to disobey the king, and when the latter did not give him any answer, he sent a hundred horses of the Swedish cavalry, and Padniewski was taken into custody (and held in fortresses for eighteen weeks (RP 182 [c] f.299); with his retainers he killed a number of Łukasz Anhiemojewski's serfs, and with the Swedes he plundered his property and his rich estate in Poluchów. The parish priest of Świętków and Władysław Padniewski complained against him for persecuting Catholics and churches; finally the government charged him with treason (RP 182 [A] f. 114, 144, v. 204, 206)."

Rej entertained the Swedish king splendidly in Skoki.[30] We can name others as satellites of the Swedish murderers and robbers: Krystyan Dziembowski with his sons Jan and Baltazar, Krzysztof and Aleksander Unrug. Krzysztof Unrug had requested benefices from the Swedish king, had called Jan Kazimierz "last year's king," and had restrained the nobility from revolts against the Swedish king (RP 182 [c] f. 220).[31] Treason and open service in the Swedish army were charged against Henryk Loss, Jan and Baltazar Zajlic, and Wacław Sadowski.[32]

Nor did the disaster of the raids miss the northern Ruthenian lands. For instance, in 1643, Ludwik Lazar Wolczkiewicz, using a detachment of four thousand—made up of Cossacks, dragoons, and his serfs—expelled his neighbor Tumowski from his Korystyszów properties in the village of Minijek. Colonel Stanisław Krzyczewski (Krzeczewski) with numerous helpers and citizens from Krzemieńczuk, Potok, Maksymówka, and Omelnik perpetrated an attack in force "with banners, drums, cannon, hooks, and other instruments of war, on August 23, 1647, and a crowd of under two thousand against Horodek, Przewłoczna, the property of W. P. Jerzy Niemierzyc, the chamberlain of Kiev."[33]

This Niemierzyc was an extraordinary figure. At Raków he accepted the teaching of Socinius, which he then propagated in later discussions. At his own cost he organized a squadron of cavalry and infantry, and fought under Hetman Koniecpolski against Moscow, Turkey, and Sweden. In order to save his property he sided with Chmielnicki in 1648. After Charles Gustav attacked Poland, he sided with the Swedes and plundered the country together with them; subsequently he supported Rakoczi. After the Unitarians were expelled, he went to the Cossacks where he accepted Orthodoxy. As a "heretic" and as "accursed" he perished at the hands of the peasants near Byków in 1659.[34]

In speaking of the brawls of those times we must mention Stadnicki, the grandson of "The Devil of Łańcut," who captured Biecz and the surrounding area, and proclaimed Charles Gustav the king of Poland. Jan Wielopolski, the castellan of Cracow and the *starosta* of Biecz, seized the traitor and turned him over to the executioner.[35]

The nobility in Muscovite Ruthenia, in Germany, in France,

and in other countries was also accustomed to attacking the properties of their neighbors.

IX. CONCLUSION

From the rich archival material that gives a colorful picture of the raids *armata manu,* sometimes of battles, I have chosen those particularly characteristic for the "Deluge of Blood." As a singular feature of those turbulent years I consider the summoning of enemy soldiers to cooperation, or at least to execution of force, in an understanding with enemy detachments. Nor can an express charge against the defendant of such a shameful deed be accepted as evident proof. One must reckon with the plaintiff's desire to overwhelm the opposing side. A generalization about these crimes and all exaggeration would be equally wrong.

On the contrary, the failure to mention the summoning of the enemy for an understanding with him does not of itself exclude some contact with him. In the Lublin city records of May 14, 1658, there is a royal document dated April 29, 1658. It was issued by the king at the request of Andrzej Gołuchowski against Stanisław Dunin-Borkowski, the lord of the villages of Celejów, Stok, Karmanowice, Rabłów, Wierzchniów, and Bochotnice, as well as against Mikołaj and Jadwiga Włoszek, wife of the holder of the village of Bochotnice, charging them with an armed attack on the village of Celejów in the county of Puławy. The defendants perpetrated the attack on or about October 15 (*circa festum s. Hedvigis electae*), 1655. On that very day Muscovite and Cossack detachments besieged Lublin. The supposition of a connection between those two events seems very probable. In this raid there were peasants from the following villages: Celejów, 6 persons; Stok, 24; Karmanowice, 21; Rabłów, 21; Wierzchniów, 20; Dębin, 4; Bochotnice, 43. The attackers seized twelve barrels of excellent Hungarian wine, a vat of distilled brandy, ten vats of plain brandy, two beer kettles, eight brandy bottles, six Cordovan chairs, seven small chairs, other matters and privileges from a chest in the storeroom, along with many other things.[36]

In 1657 Jan Franciszek Skolimowski, captain of a cavalry squadron from Halicz, having gathered a great number of persons, attacked the properties of Andrzej Jelowiecki, half the city of Wysokie, and the surrounding villages. Besides other loot, he took arms of all kinds: muskets, hooks, and over a hundred pieces of artillery.[37] Remigian Andrzejewski, captain of the hunt in Lublin, in 1656 and 1657 organized attacks on the city and village Wysokie; he marched out with two large cannon, twelve hooks, and iron weapons.[38] At the time of the Intromission of Jelowiecki to the property of Wysokie (March 20, 1657), the bailiff Andrzej Sadło stated that after the devastation perpetrated by Skolimowski, "neither guns nor cannon of any kind remained on those properties."[39]

The materials contained in the city records give a colorful, interesting picture of the internal condition of Poland, but one that is also one-sided. Since only the darker hues are presented here, one cannot accept all the recorded complaints and charges as a basis for evaluating the society of that time, any more than one can assume the cited contemporary judicial processes to be the principal source. Besides, at the very time of this great humiliation and abasement there was a growing consciousness of the need for raising the fatherland from the deep decline, and it found expression in the decisions of the dietines.

FOOTNOTES

1. Wł. Łoziński, *Prawem i lewem* (Cracow, 1957) I, 3–76, and especially 38–45, 54–63.

2. Wojewódzkie Archiwum Państwowe, Lublin, Castr. Relat. 83/21241, k. 372v.–373: "Tu nihilominus Kossecki hosti suecco uti religione similis ita intime quotidiana conversatione familiaris eundem sueticum hostem oblitus amore patriae et proximi dellatoris hostem ad bona dellatoris hereditaria villam Bliszkowice tuae vero possessionis obligatoriae consulto et industrio animo invitasti. . . ." *Ibid.* 409–410v. 526–527, 527–527v., 532v., 533v.–534. A. Kossowski, *Protestantyzm w Lublinie i w Lubelskiem w XVI–XVIII w.* (Lublin, 1933) 190.

3. W.A.P.L., Lublin, Castr. Relat. 80/21238, k. 93–94.

4. *Ibid.* k. 192v.: "Curiam magnam in loco dicto *nad jeziorem* sitam cum omnibus aedificiis circum circa existentibus cumque tota suppelectili domestica tum horreum granarium et id genus alia aedificia tam villam integram Bliszkowice (exceptis tribus gazis) per hostes Regni tempore non pridem praeterito anno presenti combustam et in cineres redactam viderunt."

5. *Ibid.* k. 189–189v.: "Ob eiusdem perduellionem et de aliis causis."

6. In the county of Lublin.

7. W.A.P.L., Lublin, Castr. Relat., 83/21241, k. 219v.–220.

8. "Tu existens eiusdem fidei et religionis sectarius habensque cum eodem hoste coniunctionem suam utpote cui iam paulo ante perduelli audacia adhaeseras, accepta notitia quod rex Sueciae civiatem Lublinensem cum suo exercitu intraverat ibidemque dies aliquot moraretur, illico huc accurens

Aleksander Kossowski

facta cum aliquibus ex hostili exercitu cointelligentia eosdem in bona villarum Lacuchow, Wola Lacuchowska *(sic!)* et Ciechanki superinequitare consuluisti." From the royal letter of April 15, 1658. *Ibid.* k. 219v.–220, 220–220v. See Kossowski, *Protestantyzm* 189–190.

9. *Ibid.* k. 220–220v.

10. *Ibid.* k. 247–250v., 319v.–320, 320–321, 321v.–322, 1147–1149v., 1152–1153v. See Kossowski, *Protestantyzm* 189–190.

11. W.A.P.L., Lublin Castr. Relat. 83/21241, k. 319–321: "Foeminis subditis maritatis quam et virginibus vim intulisti et flore virginitatis virgines privastis deflorastis *(sic!)*."

12. *Ibid.* kk. 574–575v., 624v.–626, 1121v.–1122.

13. The terms "Arians" and "Arian" as applied to the Polish Brethren do not apply, for these Polish opponents of the doctrine of the Trinity protested, and quite properly, against being called Arians, since they did not profess the doctrine of Arius. However, I use this name here and elsewhere as being current and convenient, for it is difficult to form an adjective from "Polish Brethren."

14. W.A.P.L., Lublin, Castr. Relat. 83/21241, k. 558v.: among the first, Alexander, *cum praesidio regis Suecorum,* at the taking of Tykocin as *perduellis occubuit.*

15. *Ibid.,* k. 558v.

16. *Ibid.,* k. 558v. Krzysztof Lubienicki, his son, who *adhaerendo* to the Swedish King, when that said Swedish king for the first time in *anno millesimo sexcentesimo quinquagesimo sexto proxime praeterito* took Lublin, *tempore Turbulenti status Reipublicae et expeditionis generalis bellicae.*

17. *Ibid.* k. 559v.–560, 560–561, kk. 652–654; Kossowski, *Protestantyzm* 190–191.

18. W.A.P.L., Lublin, Castr. Relat. 80/21238, k. 242–243.

19. W.A.P.L., Lublin, Castr. Relat. 83/21241, k. 733v.: "Quia tu existens beneficii Regni immemor ausus esse *(sic!)* te copiis hostilibus adiungere atque protectioni hostili innixus bona delatorum . . . invasisti expilasti, et omnem substantiam ipsorum distraxisti."

Paweł Bogusław Orzechowski, in spite of the crime of treason, received forgiveness of his guilt and a return to royal favor: "Gratiam et clementiam nostram largiremur eaque omnia quae commiserit contra Nos Regnumque Nostrum cum hostibus nostris egerit et commiserit condonaremus."

20. W.A.P.L., Lublin, Castr. Relat. 83/21241, k. 1170–1170v.

21. *Ibid.* k. 833: "Circa dominicam Jubilate ante vel post."

22. *Ibid.* k. 833v.

23. *Ibid.* k. 848–849v.

24. *Ibid.,* k. 880v.–881.

25. *Ibid.* k. 1574–1574v.

26. W.A.P.L., Lublin Castr. Relat. 85/21243, k. 329v.–330v.: "Quia tu facto in anno millesimo sexcentesimo cum principe Transilvaniae Georgio Rakoci contra Nos totamque Patriam et Regnum contra omne fas et aequum conspirans, cui cum aliis tuis asseclis et conspiratoribus contra iura Regni sine omni causa in regem Poloniae et solo religioni Catholicae orthodoxae ipse existens heresiarcha odio statum Reipublicae convertere et permutare intendens, promovere ausus es illi omni secreta regni revelasti, armamenta comuni-

casti, defectus docuisti itinera et transitus ac ingressum in Regnum prodidisti. . . ."

27. *Ibid.*, k. 556: "Enimvero facta rebellione conspiratione et coniunctione cum hostibus Patriae praefatis cosacis et Hungaris ipsos ad villas Siedliszcze et Wola Korybutowa superinduxerunt."

28. W.A.P.L., Lublin, Castr. Relat. 84–21242, k. 24v.–25.: "Supervenientes in bona villae Siedliska generosi Nicolai Suchodolski, dapiferi Chelmensis haereditaria, quo tempore actor eorundem administrationem habuit, nocte intempestata nocturno tempore varios insultus in vitam eiusdem actoris et consortis eius facientes et conspirationem aliquam cum hoste Ungaro protunc in Palatinatu Lublinensi et visceribus Regni grassante intuitu coniunctionis ex aedem sua professione habentes, cum vario armorum genere supervenientes." See A. Kossowski, "Dokumenty z życia różnowierców polskich w latach 1658–1663," in *Odrodzenie i Reformacja w Polsce (1957)* II, 195–196, 203–204.

29. L. Białkowski, *Szkice z życia Wielkopolski w siedemnastym wieku* (Poznań, 1925) 98.

30. *Ibid.* 99.

31. *Ibid.* 101.

32. *Ibid.* 101.

33. W. Lipiński (ed.) *Z Dziejów Ukrainy* (n. p., 1912) 339, 347, 493–497.

34. J. Jerlicz, *Latopisiec* (1853) II, 6; L. Kubala, *Wojna Brandenburgska (1917)* 156; Lipiński, *Z Dziejów* 612.

35. W. Łoziński, *Prawem* II, 394.

36. W.A.P.L., Lublin, Castr. Relat. 83/21241, k. 382v. 386.

37. *Ibid.* k. 49.

38. *Ibid.*, k. 479v.

39. W.A.P.L., Lublin, Castr. Relat., 80/21238, k. 272.

MAN AND SOCIETY

Jan Turowski

I. THE HISTORY OF THE PROBLEM
AND ITS RELEVANCE [1]

MANY AUTHORS TREAT THE PROBLEM OF THE INDIVIDUAL'S RELATIONship to society as an imaginary problem and as the result of a misunderstanding.[2] In their view, the "individual" and the "social" are included in social reality: and in every phenomenon, if it be individual, social elements appear; and if it be social, individual elements appear—the more so since in their view society forms man's personality, and society is the work of human individuals. This view is valid as being opposed to an absolute ontological confrontation of man and society, and vice versa. However, one cannot agree with this view if it proclaims the impossibility of studying and defining man's relationship to society. The existence of dependence between the person and society does not deprive them of their distinction, nor does it identify them, but, on the contrary, it implies their subjective distinction. The existence of links between man and society even demands the fixing of the mutual sphere of dependence and subordination. In theory, as well as in practice, the relevant questions arise whether and in what sphere the clan, family, race, village, state, class, profession, or party can subordinate the individual to itself, how far the individual's obligations extend toward the group and what rights the individual has with regard to society. For various conflicts that have come up in practice do stem from the basis of these limitations.

Nor is it strange that from the dawn of scientific reflection on man's social life, the problem of the principles governing relations between man and society has been a subject of continual discussion. From the time when in ancient Greece the Sophists, the creators of humanistic philosophy, focused their studies on man, the problem of the individual's relationship to society and the city— and subsequently to society in general—appeared in the history of human thought. All ancient philosophical thought in Greece studied among numerous other philosophical and social questions the essential relationship between the human individual and society. We meet this in the science of Protagoras, in the views of Socrates, in the great creativity of Plato, and in Aristotle's vast synthesis of political philosophy. The later schools of ancient thought—the Cynic, the Epicurean, the Skeptic, and the Stoic— showed a diversity of views in social philosophy, and thus differences in considering man's relationship to society. At the same time the meaning and the content of the problem were being expressly formulated. In what, from the nature of things, the viewpoint of ontology, or the theory of knowledge, does the relationship of man and society consist?[3]

In the Middle Ages mutual rights and obligations between society and the human individual were formulated in the writings of Augustine and Thomas Aquinas. Beginning with the work of Hugo Grotius in the seventeenth century, the problem of the individual and society appears in all philosophico-social theories, as well as sociologies.

The definition of relations between society and the human individual was not only a matter of theory, but involved practice as well. Thus practical needs evoked the necessary discussion. All movements, social, political and intellectual, as well as all efforts in the economic, cultural, and governmental sphere, raised the matter of limitations on the rights of the state, and the obligations and rights of the citizen. The basic problem in the programs and ideologies of the social movements was in social structure: the question of defining the relationship of the individual to society. Hence, many thinkers recognized man's relationship to society in practical social life as so basic that the process of the individual's assimilation by society or society's subordination to the individual and his interests was considered the principal historical process in human history. Historiographical views on this subject developed in several directions. The "linear" theories recognized a steady direction in the development of human history, either in the realization of constantly greater freedom of the individual, or the deepening and expansion of the individual's subordination to society in the course of historical development. The "cyclical" theories teach that human history depends on a changing and repeated transition of society from stages of individualism to stages of collectivism, community, and even socialization.[4]

This is the character of Hegel's historiographical theory on the direction of historical development, which proceeds from an absence of freedom for the individual to these stages: freedom for the individual, freedom for the few, and freedom for all. The conceptions of De Greef and Maine have a similar character insofar as they teach that historical development proceeds from the complete dependence of individuals in primitive societies, dependent on patriarchal authority, to the state of full freedom and cooperation among people based on voluntary agreements.[5] Keller-Krauz, the Polish sociologist, formulated the sociological law of social retrospection: social development proceeds according to two antagonistic principles, which "turn the wheel of dialectical consequence, individualism and socialism,"[6] that is, the predominance of the individual's interest over the interests of society in one period, and then the predominance of society's interests over those of the individual in the following historical period. According to Krauz, after an epoch of subordination to the individual, societies react by passing to the following form in which the human person is absorbed by society. And so we have *corsi i ricorsi*, as Vico formulated his law on the cycle of human history.[7] Societies pass a certain stage in social structure, based on a defined relationship of the individual to society; then they enter a period of its denial, and finally they repeat that course, but in different form, and constantly perfect themselves.

The contemporary sociologist Popper does not permit himself such great historiographical simplifications; but, nevertheless, on the basis of an analysis of the chief philosophical and social doctrines and political history, he says that efforts at creating an open society that serves the individual and his freedom instead of a closed society, a total society, form the principal stream of the history of human social life.[8]

All these theories show how certain historically stabilized systems of relations between the individual and society exercise influence and give character to the whole of social life and the culture of a given epoch. They also prove how dominant in the history of nations and states are the efforts to find the best and most exact system of relations between the individual and society. For this reason they appear to students of society as the basic social processes.

Truly, one can say with Welty that the problem of the relationship of the individual to society is "the problem of humanity,"[9] that is, universal, and somehow eternal and permanent, continually solved anew in practice, as the forms of social life change. On the other hand, defining the place of man in society and establishing the relationship between the group and its members basically prejudges the whole social system. Hence, Maritain describes precisely the problem of man and society as a fundamental problem of political philosophy; and Linhardt defines it as a basic problem in social ethics.[10]

For these reasons the human individual's relationship to society has never lost its relevance. In particular, the problem is an open one in our epoch. During the lifetime of the present generation, great reconstructions of social life are occurring. Obviously, we must not fall into the error of seeing our own age as a turning point or one of an epochal character; but we must declare that the social changes of history occurred mostly in a spontaneous manner, whereas at present they depend on the execution of a great sociological experiment, since the construction of new systems is carried on in a conscious manner and according to definite ideologies based on sociological theories. Not without reason does Mannheim—the eminent scholar of contemporary life and culture—call the twentieth century one of social reconstruction.[11]

Hence the question arises: What is man's future and place in the new society that is being created? On what principles of defining man's relationship to the collective are today's social reconstructions based, and on what principles ought they to be based? Our age demands to call itself the period of the new humanism. It is, therefore, time to probe the efforts of human minds through the centuries, as well as to recall and visualize the declarations of social movements, principles, and framework which define not only the rights and obligations of society toward man but also the natural rights of the human person.

Today, as well as in times past, theoretical thought is confronted with the question: Are human society and the human individual naturally coordinate, as Welty writes,[12] or is the natural relationship of man and society something other than this? The answer is important, since it decides the direction of the practical solution. Practical activity is faced with executing a task, which depends on the obligation of creating a social system wherein the relationship of man to society is based on principles rooted in the essence and nature of the human person and of society. How to achieve this follows from the nature of the thing, from the law of nature.

II. THREE THEORIES ON THE INDIVIDUAL'S RELATIONSHIP TO SOCIETY

Welty and Piwowarczyk properly point out that the solution of the human person's relationship to society is conditioned by the idea of society's essence and the definition of the human person's place in it.[13] For the exposition of the relationship between two magnitudes undoubtedly depends on the exposition of the nature and variety of those two magnitudes. In the history of social thought there are three conflicting notions about the nature of society—even in our own days—just as there are three different notions in understanding and defining the relationship between man and society.[14]

In antiquity Plato, and in modern times Spencer, recognized society as primary, as original and superior in its relationship to man; they saw society as an organism and hypostatized the state. In his way they created the foundations for the organic theory of society and the totalitarian theory of the individual's relationship to the state. The views of Herbert Spencer were continued by A. Schaffle, R. Worms, J. Vovicov, A. Fouillée, and P. Lilienfeld; O. Spann and Hegel, even though they proceeded from other suppositions, ultimately recognized society as a substantial being, as the primary totality, as an organism, and the human individual as a part of that whole.

In the light of these views, society as a prior whole, as an organism, determines the nature and the essence of its part, which is man. Related to these views are the views of Durkheim and all the views of other sociological systems which recognized society as the original reality, and the human individual as a part and creation of society. In this concept of society the human person has no goals of his own. Only society as a whole and as an organism has its goals, and it exists by itself. The human individual acquires a sense of his own existence only to the degree that he fulfills functions in the whole and to the degree that he fulfills functions within the framework of society. Man, therefore, does not have his own personal rights, but only those granted him by the organism, by the whole. The organic notions of the nature of society always led to totalitarian theories in resolving the individual's relationship to society, in which the human person was absolutely subject to the rights of the nation, the state, the party, since these rights were granted by the groups that directed these societies.

Parallel to the first attempts regarding an organic notion of society, there developed in the history of human thought indications or outlines of a mechanistic, atomistic, or even nominalistic theory, still called the theory of social contract.[15] The foreshadowings of this theory came from Anaxagoras and Democritus, who declared that only individual things exist, that wholes and systems are the creation of human thought. The Sophists transferred this theory to the social arena; then the Cynics saw the happiness of man in independence from the world and especially from society; and the Epicureans declared that only human individuals really exist, and that society is but the sum of individuals who have united by agreement for the abandonment or achievement of some activities. But these agreements do not create some distinct subject, or whole, or a being in relationship to the individuals who have agreed. Society is the creation of human thought; it is a name to which no subject in the real world corresponds. The conflict about the essence of society continued. Hobbes, Rousseau, and Locke propagated the nominalistic or atomistic theory; and although the problem of society's origin or the problem of man's relationship to society lay within the sphere of these considerations, at the basis of these views was the position that society means only the fact of executing certain similar or supplementary activities by people in accordance with the agreement concluded. According to this theory, when students of society observed the fact of human beings agreeing not to injure one another, or to undertake some similar or supplementary activities, the people erroneously interpreted this fact as an evocation of a distinct subject in their social life that could not be reduced to or identified with the individual's party to the agreement and with their individual interest. According to the nominalistic theory, the common good is the sum of the goods of the greatest number of individuals; hence, there is no such thing as a common good that is distinct from the goods of the particular individuals. The relationship between the individual and society is constructed naturally in this way, that society (if it exists, and it is not necessary to personify society as a distinct subject) is entirely subordinated to the individual. This natural system, resulting from the essence of things, must also be the ideal in social relations. The task of society, and actually the goal of all the collective tasks undertaken by the individuals, is the removal of those difficulties and obstacles which make impossible the achievement of the private good of the greatest number of individuals.

The organic theory as well as the nominalistic theory have shown themselves to be antihumanistic. They both ultimately led to the suppression of the rights of man and his dignity, and they made it impossible for human individuals to develop their personalities. By hypostatizing society and especially the state, the organic theory led to a complete subjection of man by the collective and made of man an instrument for the collective, and, practically, for the group of persons who direct the life of the collective. The individualistic theory, by misunderstanding the common good and society through its rejection of social bonds, made the majority of people an instrument and tool in the hands of a few individuals.

Extrema se tangunt. The organic and nominalistic theories waged polemics against each other. Both these theories produced a reaction, a realistic position, called by Sorokin "the functional theory." The realistic theory developed from empirical studies conducted on social groups, but nevertheless its full conception already existed in the works of two representatives of realism. We have in mind St. Augustine and St. Thomas Aquinas. Considering the many definitions of society and social groups by the sociologists of the nineteenth and twentieth centuries, we can say without fear of any prejudice that the exposition of the nature and essence of society formulated by St. Augustine and St. Thomas describes social life with exactness, simplicity and conformity with reality,[16] for their definitions point out the essential elements of human society, confirmed by research based on an empirical analysis of the life of real social groups. In the words of Augustine, "Populus est coetus multitudinis rationalis rerum quas diligit concordi communione sociatus. . . ."[17] And Thomas Aquinas says: "Cum societas nihil aliud esse videatur quam adunatio hominum ad unum aliquid communiter agendum."[18] These words express the idea that society is not a substantial being, but it is the individual human beings who make up society or societies that are society.[19] These definitions indicate the weakness of the organic theory. Nor is society the creation of human thought, to which there corresponds no real subject in the world of reality. Human societies really exist, and are wholes distinct from the persons who form them. Society is an accidental real being and originates in the union and dependence of a group through relationships of subordination and cooperation by the persons who are creating a given society. This union takes place in order to achieve some definite good. It also demands the creation of a corresponding group government and requires activities to be performed by individuals on behalf of and for the good of the whole. Hence there is no doubt that, besides the particular individuals who have united to achieve a common goal, there now arises from this union a distinct subject, a social group different from the particular individuals who form it. The kind of bond that unites human persons in society is not a physical unity, as the biological theory claimed, but it is a spiritual bond. The factor uniting human persons in society is always some type of good, goal, or common need which the individual seeks to achieve by way of common, more or less organized, effort. Since human persons do not form societies in order to achieve full humanity, man therefore does not exist for society, but society is to assist and serve the goal of the human person. Human individuals create societies as a necessity resulting from their rational nature. Man must live in society and develop by means of society. Every society, organizing human individuals for their good in the family, village, state, and nation, has as its principal task the achievement of the common good of all. The common good, the goal of a given group, is different not only quantitatively but also qualitatively from the individual good of the particular persons. In the sphere of a common good of the same order, the individual good is subordinate to it. In their efforts the individuals then have the right with regard to the group to realize their individual good by means of the common good. Thus in a definite area the human person is autonomous and rises above the collective, but on the other hand he is in a definite area subordinate also to society. Hence, the realistic theory, and within its framework the Thomistic theory, reject the Platonist organic theory in which the human person is subordinate absolutely to society; and it also opposes the individualistic position, which once again tore the human person from its bonds with society.

Is it possible to arrive at a closer definition of the mutual relations between the person and society? Is it possible to define more completely the limits of mutual obligations and rights between the human person and society?

III. THE CONFLICT OVER THE THOMISTIC CONCEPT OF THE INDIVIDUAL'S RELATIONSHIP TO SOCIETY

Recently, in Thomistic social philosophy a conflict arose over two positions in an effort toward closer definition of the mutual rights and obligations between the individual and society. Basically, until now the dominant position was that which analyzed the problem of the individual's relationship to society in terms of the rights of the human person and defined the relationship that exists between the good of the individual and the common good. Against this was presented the view that based its analysis of the individual's relationship to society on distinguishing two aspects within the framework of the given problem, namely, the relationship of the *individuum* to society and the relationship of the person to society. Many eminent representatives of Thomistic philosophy have accepted the new method. Such thinkers as P. Gillet, R. Garrigou-Lagrange, and P. Schwalm introduce the distinction of individual and person and assert the correctness of understanding man as an individual and as a person in explaining the relationship between the human individual and society.[20] J. Maritain, however, introduced the distinction in a more logical way, but he also recognized it as indispensable and as the only means for an actual solution of the human person's relationship to society.[21] In his discussions Maritain emphasizes that not only does this distinction follow from the views of Thomas Aquinas, but it is irreplaceable in philosophical efforts at defining the relationship between the individual and society. He quotes the celebrated definition of Boethius, accepted by St. Thomas, which says that man is an "individuum rationalis naturae." Analyzing the concept of individual and person, he establishes the significant content and limits of these concepts, and then defines the relationship of man as an individual and as a person to society. Furthermore, Maritain says: "The concept of the *individuum* is common to man, animal, vegetable, microbes, and atoms. And since personality depends on the existence of the human soul (an existence independent of the body and communicated to the body, which is maintained in existence through the very existence of the soul), individuality as such is dependent—as Thomistic philosophy teaches—on the proper requisites of matter, which is the principle of individuation. . . ."[22] Here we must emphasize Maritain's view that matter is the principle of individuation. Hence, in

Maritain's thought, man as an individual is only a piece of matter. It would follow from these views that, according to Maritain, *individuum* would define only the material, the corporal side of man. Further on we read: "The person is a complete individual substance, of an intellectual nature, governing itself by its own laws, autonomous, *sui generis* in the actual meaning of the word." The concept of person is applied to a substance which has something of God within itself—and that is spirit.[23] Having established such a distinction, Maritain then argues that "St. Thomas' whole theory of individuation shows that the individual as such is a part. . . ."[24] He says further that "the individual as a part of the human race is subordinated to society and by that reason is subordinated also to the good of society," and that society is subordinate to man as a person, which is the highest value.[25] In Polish literature the ideas of J. Piwowarczyk[26] and Karol Górski[27] tend in a similar direction.

Many theorists dealing with society and ethics took a stand against this position. They based their opposition on the principles of social philosophy as formulated by Thomas Aquinas.

Jacques Croteau in his *Les Fondements thomistes du personalisme de Maritain* carried out a fundamental analysis of the distinction between individual and person and their contrast by Maritain. Using previous criticism, the author showed that the contrast made by Maritain between the individual and the person had no foundation in the writings of St. Thomas Aquinas. Croteau rejected the formulation and explanation of the social problems in terms of the contrast between the concepts of *individuum* and person, even though he himself accepts the position of Thomas Aquinas' along with Maritain's personalism. He shows that the rejection of the distinction and contrast in understanding the concepts of *individuum* and person, which are only formal aspects of man, not only fails to reconcile anything, but, what is more, makes it possible to extract and to show the meaning and the degree of transcendence granted the human person by Thomas Aquinas and Maritain.

We must still mention the names of Polish theorists Fathers I. Bocheński[28] and W. Granat.[29] Their opposition is entirely proper and complete. Quite correctly Bocheński calls attention to the fact that the distinction of two aspects in man, individual and social, the individual and the person, creates misunderstandings and leads to an artificial and theoretical division of man, who is an indivisible unit. Independently of these consequences, it must

be noticed that Thomas Aquinas, to whose authority both Garrigou-Lagrange and Maritain appeal, in many places considers the
relationship of the citizen to the state, or the individual to other
societies, or societies in general, but there is not a single passage
in Thomas where the distinction of individual and the person
would serve as the basis for explaining other philosophical social
problems, for instance, the natural character of social life. While
considering it as very fruitful for the solution of a series of knotty
problems in social philosophy, the supporters of this distinction
failed to notice that the concepts of individual and person are
indissolubly connected in Thomas' writings and both enter into
the definition of the human essence, the definition of man as
being. Thomas actually accepts the definition of man and declares
that he is an *individua substantia rationalis naturae*.[30] The
term *individuum* defines the generic features of man. He says:
"Individuum autem est quod est in se indistinctum, ab aliis vero
distinctum."[31] Let us mention another definition: "Particularia
vero dicunter individua, inquantum nec materialiter nec formaliter ulterius dividuntur."[32] Hence, distinction from other
members of a given genus and indivisibility are the essential elements of the notion of *individuum*. An individual is that which
is not subject to division either materially or formally. The principle of individuation is matter, but not exclusively. Stefan
Świeżawski expresses this idea and emphasizes the fact that the
term *individuum* affirms and includes individuality, the concreteness of a given being, that "the principle of individuation,
according to St. Thomas, is not prime matter . . . but matter as
remaining in potentiality for numerical definition and *quantitate
signata*. It is matter which, having been united with substantial
form, appears in a given individual being constituted by the union
of substantial form with prime matter."[33] Thomas expressly states
that *materia sub quantitate signata* is the principle of individuation, and not prime matter.[34] Since substantial form actualizes
prime matter, the notion of *individuum*, although dependent on
materia signata, is related also to substantial form, by virtue of
which prime matter can be actualized in a concrete being.[35] In
an exhaustive study, Welty devotes much space to the problem of
the individual and the person according to Thomas Aquinas, and
shows that the definition of individual as the sense side of man is a
great error. The notion of *individuum*, as that of person, includes
the whole man, and they form one "verschiedene Sens . . . betra-
chtete im Menschen."[36] Basically, the notion of individual is not

a matter of doubt. Linhardt states that the material side of man, as well as the spiritual, are aspects of man which the notion of *individuum* includes.[37] Hence, *individuum* does not signify the material side of man exclusively. The individual or the *individuum* is a concept that indicates concrete being in contrast to the universal. Thus, within this erroneous interpretation of *individuum* as the material side of man and in this definition of the principle of individuation lies hidden the error that under the concept of *individuum* a conceptual content is accepted different from that given it by Thomas Aquinas.[38] Consequently, this definition of the content and the extent of *individuum* is the basis for an erroneous analysis of the individual's relationship to society.

If we abstract from this conflict over the criterion of individuation, there is no doubt that only the fixing of the specific difference—the rational nature belonging to a human individual —brings us to a description and definition of man. Therefore, it is possible to ask those who support the distinction between person and individual as a solution of the individual's relationship to society: Precisely what does this distinction provide and how does it help in the exposition of the problem "the individual and society"? Garrigou-Lagrange, Maritain, and Piwowarczyk assert that with this distinction we can arrive at the great discovery that man as an individual is subordinated to society, and that man as a person subordinates society to himself.[39] But does it mean to say that man as an individual is subordinated to society? In what sense is this so? And, ultimately, what are the limits of this subordination? And on what is it based? If *individuum* signifies the material side of man, this would mean that man as a biological organism is subordinated to the family, the state, and the party. Does the family have the right to subordinate a child entirely as a member of the family and because of its bodily aspect? And what does this mean? In some experiences, obligations, efforts, and hence in the spiritual sphere (which is supposed to raise the child above the group), is not the child subordinated to the family in a certain measure? Certainly. On the other hand, the child as a biological organism is not absolutely subordinated to the family as a whole. In opposing this view, Hoban quite correctly says this concept leaves much to be explained: Whence and why is society a phenomenon of spiritual unification among people? Whence does it draw spiritual forces and means in its existence and activity, if we accept the principle that society is based on the fact that man as an individual in his bodily aspects is subordinated to society, whereas, as a person, man is entirely above nature?[40]

If the *individuum* means distinctness, separation, and internal indivisibility even in the spiritual sphere, and if we accept the view of the supporters of the distinction, then we arrive at an *absurdum*. Since the *individuum*, as a part, is absolutely subordinated to the whole, then society subordinates man to itself absolutely and entirely as an *individuum*, and hence in the spiritual as well as bodily sphere. Those in defense of the distinction do not arrive at this conclusion. The matter becomes obviously complicated. The distinction of the *individuum* from the person is quite purposeless and adds nothing to the clarification of man's relationship to society by considering first the individual's relationship to society, and then subsequently the person's relationship to society. For this reason neither Maritain nor Piwowarczyk define the meaning or the extent of man's subordination as an individual to society, but actually and finally establish the limits of the rights and the subordination of man to society only by considering the relationship "person and society" and not "individual and society." The statement that man as an individual is subordinated to society explains nothing at all. It is apparently a matter of logic and inference. Since the concept of "man" includes the concept of individual and the concept of person—stating also that man is *genus individuum*, which possesses rational nature and so is properly man—he is an individual with a rational nature. Hence, establishing the relationship between the person and society, or between an *individuum rationalis naturae* and society, at the same time clarifies the relationship between the individual and society. Therefore, in reply to the question concerning the limits of man's subordination to society, both Maritain and Piwowarczyk consider the relationship between the human person and society, and only then do they establish the rights of the human person, or the relationship of the individual good to the common good.[41] They do not apply their earlier position at all or can they do so, namely, that man as an individual is subordinate to society. For this position is useless. The relationship between man and society is ultimately resolved by an analysis of the relationship between the human person and society and the relationship between the individual good and the common good.

Hence, the notion of a distinction between the individual and the person and its use in the analysis of man's relationship to society must be rejected as purposeless, useless, and as contributing nothing to a clarification of the problem. On the contrary, it adds to the problem by leading to mistaken interpretations of the notion of individual and to an artificial bifurcation of man's essence.

THE RIGHTS OF THE HUMAN PERSON AND THE COMMON GOOD

A more precise definition of man's relationship to society is possible only by fixing the limits of society's rights in relationship to the individual and by fixing the converse. In social theory and in social practice it is only a statement of the human person's rights that permits one to define the sphere of man's subordination to society.

The approach to defining the human person's rights can be twofold. It includes a deductive analysis and empirical definition. By means of the first, we arrive at a statement of the person's rights through analysis and reasoning, with the point of departure being the definition of the essence and nature of society and the human person.[42] This deductive analysis should not be identified with the rationalistic method of establishing natural rights used by Locke, Hobbes, and Rousseau, who treated them as the result of a social contract.[43] In the second case, we arrive at a knowledge of the human person's rights by observation of social practice, the description and systematizing of rights which various social and political movements demanded for man and which have become the subject of declarations and resolutions by international institutions.

The rights of the human person deduced from a definition of the essence and nature of man and society are systematized in various ways, depending on the foundation that is accepted. Bocheński groups and defines them as the right to existence, and the right to achieve man's goal.[44] Maritain arranges them in three groups as the rights of the human person in general, the rights of man as a citizen of a state, and the rights of man as a working individual.[45] E. Chenon accepts as the basis for the division of the person's rights the goods or the person to which the rights refer, and he speaks of the rights of the person with regard to himself, to things, to other persons, and to the state.[46] Many authors generally do not list systematically the rights of the human person, but simply list them in various orders.[47] Pope Pius XII also presents the natural rights of the human person by way of enumeration.[48]

Basically, these rights can be reduced to two groups of rights of man, which include the particular rights. They are the right to existence and the right to one's final goal, which is also called the right to development.[49]

As we have already said, only the human person is a substantial being, which exists *per se* and *in se*. Man is a rational essence, has his goal to achieve, and directs himself by his free will.[50] Independence in being and independence in activity characterize the human person.[51] The human person is an "independent subject with a rational nature,"[52] and it signifies the most perfect being in all of nature.[53] The spiritual and corporal nature of the human essence, expressing itself in its free and rational operation, is properly the constituent characteristic of man.[54] From these viewpoints, the human person is higher than society, since he is the creator of his own activities. The human person does not lose his ontological superiority by uniting with other persons in order to achieve a common good.

Society as an accidental being receives its existence from man. Since society does not grant substantial being to the human person, but owes its own existence to the human person, the right to existence is the basic right of the individual, which society cannot trample, and only so far do the limits of the individual's subordination reach. The right to existence is violated by taking life, applying the death penalty (except as punishment for murder), orders to kill children of a certain kind, pressure to limit the birth of children. But not only interference of this kind violates man's right to existence; man's right to existence is violated also by any kind of contempt for man, by trampling on his dignity, by physical torture, by conducting experiments, by depriving man of any part of his organism, and by acting on his psychic powers, the will, or the mind. The right to life means every person's right to life from the moment of conception, the right of personal immunity, and the right to preserve one's existence.

But existence is not man's only right. Man as a rational being has also the right to realize his goal, the right to development, the right to act as a human person, the right to develop his personality. Maritain calls it the right to strive for the eternal good, the right to perfect one's moral and rational personality.[55]

Society cannot deprive the human individual of his right to development, or his right to achieve his goal. It is society's task to make possible man's development of his personality. The goals of society are defined by the goals of man, and not the reverse.[56] Society draws its functions and goals from the definition of man's ultimate goal. Society exists naturally and necessarily to satisfy man's material needs, as well as his spiritual needs, on a constantly higher level of civilization.[57]

The right to development includes a series of special natural rights; above all, the human person has the right to respect for his human dignity and his freedom, and hence to his autonomous conduct according to his own will. The right to freedom includes also the freedom of conscience, as well as the freedom of speech, work, association, establishing a family, entering matrimony, the freedom of scientific research, and the search for truth.

The right to development also includes the person's right to natural equality independently of social origin, nationality, faith, or sex. This means equality before the law and the government, as well as social and economic equality. This view does not deny the existence of natural inequalities and individual differences among people. However, all legal privileges and the factual structure of relationships, in virtue of which a certain group of people remains unfree, injure equality in law insofar as one group of the population remains privileged in one way or another with respect to another group, whether it be in political or economic aspects. In the light of contemporary views, equality before the law means the uniform attitude of the constitution and the state administration toward the individual, the removal of all legal and actual distinctions in the treatment of citizens, and the nullification of differences among them with respect to their being party members or nonmembers, believers or nonbelievers. A state that deprives the human person of the right to equality thereby limits or deprives the human person of the right to development—and hence does not realize the principles of a humanistic society.[58]

The right to development also includes the right to the choice of profession and type of work, and includes the right to a share in the social income and in the ownership of the means of production and consumption, which make possible an ever growing civilized satisfaction of needs. This participation must also guarantee the satisfaction of human needs at those times when the person is incapable of work.

The rights of the human person have been formulated and are actually practiced.[59] From the beginning of social life in the form of agreements, declarations, and ideologies of social and political movements, people have defined the rights of the human person, codified them, and indicated the goals and goods which cannot be subordinated to society. The Great Charter of Liberties (Magna

Carta) of 1215 is often mentioned as the first and most famous declaration and guarantee of political liberty. In modern times the rights of the human person achieved their full definition in several historical acts. The Petition of Rights in 1628 and the demands of the English Revolution, the Bill of Rights, in 1689 belong to those partial codifications of the person's rights that defined the citizen's relationship to the state. Similarly, in Germany or in Poland one can mention a series of historical acts, whether it be the law *Neminem captivabimus nisi iure victum* (1430–1433), or some of the resolutions of the *Constitution of May 3, 1791,* as partial definitions or guarantees of the rights of the human person to existence, immunity, and equality in terms of the political society. Perhaps the most famous codification of the rights of the human person is the *Declaration of the Rights of Man and Citizen* in France in 1789, even though it does have certain class limitations;[60] there are also the American *Declaration of Independence* and the *Bill of Rights.*[61]

Independently of these general acts, the constitutional laws of particular countries also proclaimed the special rights of man. As various political or social movements developed, special rights were put forward and solemnly proclaimed; for instance, the right to work was proclaimed in the February revolution in France in 1848. In formulating the rights of the human person a very great role was played by the *International Declaration of the Rights of Man* approved by the International Institute of Law on October 12, 1929, in elaborating precisely and defining those rights,[62] and by the *International Declaration of the Rights of Man* proclaimed by the General Assembly of the United Nations on December 10, 1948.[63] In the first of these declarations the rights of man are presented by way of synthesis. They declare that human societies and especially the state are obliged to recognize the equal right of each individual to life, freedom, and property and to treat all as equal before the law, independently of nationality, sex, race, language, or religion. The state recognizes the right of every human person to freedom of confession and religion and to the practice of religion. The state guarantees to every individual the right to use his native language, the right to work, the right to choice of vocation, and the development of economic activity. The United Nations *Declaration,* in a most detailed, exhaustive, and practical manner, defines and specifies the rights of the individual and society and fixes the person's rights and social obligations.

All these codifications formulate those very same laws that

follow from an analysis of the essence or nature of the human person and of society.

The rights of the human person indicate the type and the extent of rights which the human person possesses with regard to society; but at the same time they indicate the obligations imposed on social beings. Human societies are not something absolutely separate from human persons; they exist and operate through human beings in association. In order that societies might guarantee to the individual the realization of his right to existence and his right to development, they must unite men in common action and have the right to oblige the individual to perform definite activities for the common good of all. Only by means of and with the help of the common good, achieved by the activity of individuals, can society guarantee the realization of the individuals' rights. We see, therefore, that the rights of the individual are accompanied by an equal obligation toward the group. The common good of society is a very important concept in the analysis and definition of man's relationship to society. For the rights of the human person, as an individual and personal good, cannot be understood as irrespective and absolute and free of all limitations with regard to the good and the very same rights of other persons.

The human person's natural rights form the basis for defining the human person's relationship to society. However, the realization of those rights in the concrete actuality of human social life is changeable. If we would call the realization of the right to existence and the development of the human person its personal good, we would even then state that it is subject to limitation by the common good. Actually, the common good is the only factual guarantee for the realization of the personal good of the individual, that is, of his right to existence and development in a concrete time and place; and it is the criterion which defines the limits and the sphere of the individual's obligation toward society, as well as the sphere of intervention and the possibility of the limitation of the individual's rights by society. The common good also indicates in what degree and in what sphere the rights of man to existence and to development in a given time and place can be realized within the particular rights of the individual. It is possible to say that the individual's relationship to society is controlled, on the one hand, by the rights of the individual, and on the other by the common good.

What is this common good? Without entering into the age-long discussion on the essence of the common good, we can state that from the objective point of view the common good signifies the total of means, values, and things, by which society can satisfy (within the limits defined by the goal of society) the definite needs of its members. From the subjective point of view, the *bonum commune* indicates the goal of particular societies.

The individual's defined goal which he hopes to realize through the family, the nation, the state, the class, and the party is contained within the goals of these particular social groups. The realization of the needs, the efforts, and the individual goal is achieved through and by creating just those means, values, and objects common to all in which the associated individual shares. There is obviously no ontological conflict between the individual's good and the good of society.[64] However, this goal—in the objective sense or the good—is in the subjective sense generically identical; however, not only in the quantitative but also in the qualitative sense it is different from the individual good.[65]

Obviously, the common good of a given society is higher than the good of a given individual contained in that society. For the individual good and the defined goal of a given individual can be achieved only through the common good, and this common good is achieved not only by one person but by the generality of the associated individuals.[66] Hence, in the case of the common good being threatened and in the case of a necessary choice between the common good and the good of the individual, the good of the individual is subordinated and is sacrificed for the benefit of the common good. In the case of a threat to the existence of the state or the fatherland, the individual's right to being and existence is sacrificed in order to maintain and to defend the existence of the state. Therefore, the individual sacrifices his life to preserve the existence and independence of the country. But such a subordination of the individual to the common good applies only within the framework of goods or goals of the same genus: "Bonum commune potius est bono privato si sit eiusdem generis."[67]

Man enters into each society only within a defined area and, namely, within such as is the defined goal of each society. Every social group has a defined goal or good, "the group nucleus," which it realizes. Only within this sphere and only with the application of goods of the same genus is the individual good subordinated to the good of a given society. Hence the entire man with his personality cannot be subordinated to a given society if he belongs to it only within the area of his goals or needs. Hence, man as a member of a family is dependent only in those

189

matters which are included by the society of the family. Hence, he is dependent on the party in his political ideology, on the professional union only in his professional activities, and so on. St. Thomas Aquinas writes: "Homo non ordinatur ad communitatem politicam secundum se totum et secundum omnia sua."[68]

Therefore, the individual good can be sacrificed to the common good only in the case of collision and the threat to the common good within the same genus of the individual good and the common good. This is the first limit of the ultimate interference of society with the human person's natural rights. A higher good, and especially a good of a spiritual nature, cannot be subordinated to a material good. Independently of this limitation, there exists the natural right of the human person, that is, the good, the goal of the human person, in which the human person cannot ever be subordinated to the common good. "Bonum animae non ordinatur ad aliud melius bonum."[69] The good of the human soul, the right to eternal life, the right to freedom of conscience and to the development of moral values, the freedom of thought—is a good of such a nature that it cannot be subordinated to anything else, since it is the highest good. This is the second ultimate limit of all interventions by society in the rights of the human person and the admissible limitation in sacrificing the individual good to the common good.

This limitation of society's intervention in the natural rights of the human person is justified only within the limits stated above and only in case of a threat to the common good. This is a transient and exceptional case in the relations between the individual and society.

The normal state, arising from the nature of the thing, is the defense and maintenance of the person's natural rights by particular social groups, such as by societies, understood as complexes of social groups, subordinate to one basic group (e.g., the society of government, of the Catholic Church, etc.). Thus, the ideal or the model for the individual's relationship to society must be one that follows from the nature of the human person and society, that is, a condition wherein the natural rights of the human person are realized and protected in their full extent. Only such societies can be said to be societies which fully implement humanism. For humanism in the life of societies depends on such an organization of social life, culture, and civilization in the needs of man, and their fullest and most perfect satisfaction, that human value and human dignity are the goals of all activity and its foundation. The degree of "humanization" of a given society, or the degree of humanism achieved by a given society, can be measured only within the extent of the realization of the rights of the human person.

Therefore, quite properly did the United Nations proclaim a universal declaration of the rights of man as a common ideal for all peoples and all nations. Quite accurately did the United Nations' *Universal Declaration of the Rights of Man* recognize man's dignity as the basis of freedom, justice, and peace in the world, and at the same time recognize that ignorance and contempt for and the disregard of man's rights lead to acts of barbarism, and that the realization of the human person's rights through economic and moral progress is the basic goal of all human societies.

In every political society the rights of the human person must be guaranteed and realized through an obligatory order defined by law, and by an administrative state system in accord with that law, as well as by the fulfillment of obligations in accordance with the prescriptions of the law and by a use of rights by the citizen.

Hence, all social reconstructions and reforms, as well as revolutionary changes in the social order in accord with the relationship that follows from the nature and essence of the human person and society, must aim to create conditions for the development of the human personality by establishing the common good while preserving the natural rights of the human person.

FOOTNOTES

1. The terms human person, person, man, human individual are used interchangeably. The terms society, social group, collective, group, and society are used in the same meaning to indicate any spiritual association of people for a common goal. The term society is also used here to indicate a complex of social groups subordinated to a fundamental group. In this case the meaning is clear from the context. We must also keep in mind that the term person is not used here in an analogical sense. Stefan Świeżawski has called attention to this (see *Znak* 5 [1950] 374).

2. F. Mirek writes: "In various sociological books this one problem wanders about like the Eternal Jew: the problem of 'individual-social,' 'the individual-the nation,' the 'individual and society,' the 'individual and the superindividual' (Durkeim). I think that this is all a misunderstanding. The antithesis of 'individual and society,' 'individual and social,' is a pseudo antithesis, such as the pseudo antithesis of 'mine and thine,' 'one and five,' 'cold-and colder.'" See Mirek, *Zarys Socjologii* (Lublin, 1949) 266–267, where he establishes the fictitious nature of the problem of "individual and society" by show-

Jan Turowski

ing that in every interhuman activity the original contribution of the individual appears, but it uses the communal contribution as well. This is quite true, but nevertheless the problem of the individual's relationship to society does not involve the structure of social action, but the mutual limits of rights and obligations.

3. See W. Kornatowski, *Rozwój pojęć o państwie w staro-Grecji* (Warsaw, 1950); K. Diehl, *Der Einzelne und die Gemeinschaft* (Jena, 1940) 22–34; J. A. Leighton, *Social Philosophies in Conflict* (New York, 1937) 507.

4. P. Sorokin, *Dynamique socio-culturelle et Évolutionisme, Sociologie au XX Siècle* (Paris, 1947) I, 96; P. Sorokin, *Social and Cultural Dynamics* (New York, 1941) IV.

5. C. C. Zimmermann, *Patterns of Social Change* (Washington, 1956) 57; P. Barth, *Die Philosophie der Geschichte als Soziologie* (Leipzig, 1915) 229.

6. Kazimierz Krauz, "Socjologiczne prawo retrospekcji," *Ateneum* (Warsaw, 1898) 14. See also Edward Abramowski, "Kazimierz Krauz: Socjologiczne prawo retospekcji," *Dzieła* (Warsaw, 1924) II, 386–400.

7. J. B. Vico, *Nowa Nauka* (Warsaw, 1916).

8. K. R. Popper, *The Open Society and its Enemies* (Princeton, 1950).

9. E. Welty, *Gemeinschaft und Einzelmensch* (Salzburg-Leipzig) 11. "Die Frage nach dem Verhältniss von Gemeinschaft und Einzelmensch ist eine Menschheitsfrage. Sie betrifft und bewegt jeden Menschen. Denn das Leben von und in Gemeinschaft gehört zur Menschengrösse und zum Menschenschicksal."

10. J. Maritain, *The Rights of Man and Natural Law* (London, 1945) 5; R. Linhardt, *Die Sozial-Principien des hl. Thomas von Aquin* (Freiburg, 1932) 132.

11. K. Mannheim, *Man and Society* (London, 1940) 12; H. W. Odum, *Understanding Society* (New York, 1947) 419, says that the central problem is the achievement of a balance between freedom and society.

12. Welty, *Gemeinschaft und Einzelmensch* 16.

13. J. Piwowarczyk, "Podstawy personalizmu," *Towarzystwo* 35 (1951) 337; Welty, *Gemeinschaft und Einzelmensch* 16, 48.

14. Sorokin distinguishes four principal theories: the mechanistic, the nomalist or atomistic, the organic, and functional. However, the mechanistic and the atomistic theories differ only in the method of establishing their views. See P. Sorokin, *The Contemporary Sociological Theories* (New Jersey, 1928) 195. T. Szczurkiewicz, *Rasa, środowisko, rodzina* (Poznań, 1938), also distinguishes four theories. Mirek, *Zarys Socjologii* 491, distinguishes seven theories, but they can all be reduced to the three principal views of the essence of society.

15. The different names for the nominalistic theories on the essence of society are connected with the various means of establishing their view, or with the particular changes of the theory about the origin of society.

16. M. E. Healy, *Society and Social Change in the Writings of St. Thomas, Ward, Sumner and Cooley* (Washington, 1948) is an interesting comparison of the definition of society in the writings of St. Thomas with the views of contemporary sociology.

17. *De Civitate Dei* XIX, 24. Father Mirek discovered this definition.

18. *Contra impugnantes Dei cultum et religionem*, chap. 3.

19. Welty, *Gemeinschaft und Einzelmensch* 178: "Die Gemeinschaft ist

keine Substanz, auch keine Quasi-Substanz, sondern—so sonderbar das klingen mag—ein Akzidens. Das soziale Sein gehört nicht in die substanziale, wohl aber in die akzidentelle Seinsordnung. Die Einheit der Gemeinschaft darf nimmermehr als Wesenseinheit, sondern nur als Einheit der akzidentellen Ordnung begriffen werden." Linhardt, *Die Sozial-Prinzipien* 136, emphasizes that St. Thomas distinguishes various kinds of unity that appears in being. The association of people in society is an *unitas ordinis*.

20. W. Granat, "Integralna definicja osoby ludzkiej," *Roczniki Filozoficzne* 2, 3 (1941, 1950) 102–103.

21. J. Maritain, "La personne et le bien commun," *Revue Thomiste* 46 (1946) 238; J. Maritain, *Three Reformers* (New York, 1929) 19.

22. Maritain, *Three Reformers* 21.

23. *Ibid.* 20.

24. *Ibid.* 19.

25. *Ibid.* 24.

26. Piwowarczyk, "Podstawy personalizmu" 337; Karol Górski, *Wychowanie personalystyczne* (Poznań, 1936); Karol Górski, "Jednostka i osoba," *T.P.* (1952) 355.

27. Jacques Croteau, *Les Fondements du personalisme de Maritain* (Ottawa, 1955).

28. I. Bocheński, "ABC Tomizmu," *Znak* 23 (1950) 23.

29. W. Granat, "Indywiduum a osoba," *T.P.* 41 (1951); W. Granat, "Integralna defincja" 102–103.

30. S. Th. I, 29, 3, ad 2: "Omne individuum rationalis naturae dicitur persona."

31. S. Th. I, 29, 4. The same idea is expressed in *S.Th.* I, 13, 9: "Sed singulare ex hoc ipso quod est singulare, est divisum ab omnibus aliis."

32. See J. H. Hoban, "The Thomistic Concept of Person and Some of Its Social Implications" 6–7.

33. St. Thomas Aquinas, *Traktat o człowieku,* Stefan Świeżawski, ed. (Poznań, 1956) 726–727.

34. Hoban, "The Thomistic Concept of Person" 16, 20: "The principle of individuation is in the union of matter and form. . . . The *individuum* is established as one individual substance by the union of prime matter." This is also the view of Thomas Gilby, *A Philosophy and Theology of the State* (London, 1953) 201.

35. *De Ente et Essentia,* chap. 2: "Materia non quomodo libet accepta est principium individuationis, sed solum materia signata."

36. Welty, *Gemeinschaft und Einzelmensch* 126–129. "Individualität und Personalität, dürfen keineswegs aufgefasst werden als zwei getrennte Sphären. Individualität und Personalität teilen den Menschen nicht in zwei Hälften. . . . Das wäre eine grobsinnenhafte Vorstellung. . . . Trotz der Individuierung aus der Materie wäre es grundfalsch, die Individualität zu beschränken auf den sinnenhaften Teil im Menschen. Die Einzigheit umfasst das ganze Sein des Menschen, auch den Geist."

37. Linhardt, *Die Sozial-Prinzipien* 134.

38. Piwowarczyk seems to say that the *individuum* means only the generic features of man, as a being distinct from other human individuals and a being undivided in itself, that it touches all the spheres (corporal and spir-

Jan Turowski

itual) of man, the full endowment of man; but *rationalis naturae* means the unique characteristic of man—man's own eternal goal.

39. Although Welty expressly says that the *individuum* means individuality, distinction, and indivisibility of man with regard to other human individuals and not man's material side, still he takes an erroneous position and uses the notion of individual and person in defining the relationship of man to society. In this view he formulates the same idea, that man as an individual is subordinated to society, and that as a person he rises above society. However, this statement does not contribute anything to the solution of the problem of the individual's relationship to society.

40. See Hoban, "The Thomistic Concept of Person" 65.

41. It might be worthwhile to note at least marginally that the whole thesis of man as an individual being is subordinated to society in some degree based on a play of words. It is based on the view that man as an individual is part of the human species; since a part is subordinate to the whole, and exists through and by the whole, man as an individual is subordinated to society, exists through and for society. See J. Piwowarczyk, *Katolicka etyka społeczna* (Cracow, 1948) Part I, 85; Piwowarczyk, "Podstawy personalizmu"; J. Maritain, *Those Reformers* 193. Maritain cautions that he does not say that the person, the individual responsible for its actions and capable of virtue, is not a part of society. This man, as an individual by reason of his character as a part of society, is entirely subordinate to society; and man as a person—according to Maritain—remaining a part of society because of his character as a part of society, is not entirely subordinate to the whole. He declares that man as an individual is a part of the human species. However, he is not part of a species, since the human species is not a whole, neither a moral whole (since it is not united as a state, nation, or any other social group, and an international society is but now developing), nor a physical unity, nor a unity of external association, but is rather an exemplar. If he is a part of the human species (if we assume this for the moment), he would be subordinate only to the species as a whole. On what basis can we conclude that he is subordinate to the family, the party, and class? For we have not established that he is a part of these groups, but only a part of the human species. The supporters of this distinction fail to see this lack of precision between person and individual and its use in the solution of the individual's relationship to society.

42. "The rights of man flow from his very nature," is quoted from *Kodeks społeczny*, translated by I. Górski and A. Szymański (Lublin, 1934) 33. J. Maritain, *The Rights of Man* 45: "The awareness of the person's rights really has its origin in the conception of man and of natural law established by centuries of Christian philosophy." Linhardt, *Die Sozial-Principien* 134, says that the rights of the human person are "angeborene Rechte der menschlichen Natur."

43. Joad properly says that the views on natural rights can be divided into two groups. The first is based on the theory of social contract; the other is derived from the goal of society. See C. E. M. Joad, *Guide to the Philosophy of Morals and Politics* (London, 1948) 539.

44. Bocheński, "ABC Tomizmu" 354.

45. J. Maritain, *The Rights of Man* 41.

46. E. Chenon, *Le Rôle social de l'Église* (Paris, 1921) 178.

47. See Linhardt, *Die Sozial-Prinzipien* 134; E. Jarra, *Socjologia katolicka*

194

Man and Society

(London, 1953) 111, lists the right to existence, to freedom, to equality, to property, to work, and to education.

48. Pius XII, in a 1942 discourse, defined the rights of the human person. See Pius XII, "Rundfunkausprache an die ganze Welt an Weinachten 1942," *Acta Apostolicae Sedis* 35 (1943) 637. Pius XII mentioned the following rights: the right to maintain and to develop a corporal, spiritual, and moral life; the right to private and public confession and honor of God; the right to marry and to have a family; the right to work; the right to a free choice of vocation and type of work, in particular the priestly vocation; and the right to use material goods.

49. Manser distinguishes the two rights, the right to existence and the right to development. See his *Angewandtes Naturrecht* (1947).

50. *Kodeks społeczny* 33: "In reality man has his personal destiny, and society is for him a necessary means, which facilitates the achievement of his own goal."

51. Welty, *Gemeinschaft und Einzelmensch* 134.

52. S. Świeżawski, *Byt* (Lublin, 1948) 282.

53. I am citing the famous definition of Thomas Aquinas: "Persona significat id quod est perfectissimum in tota natura." See S. Th. I, 29, 3.

54. W. Granat, "Integralna definicja osoby ludzkiej" 108.

55. Maritain, *The Rights of Man* 44.

56. *De Regimine Principum* I, c. 14: "Idem autem oportet esse iudicium de fine totius multitudinis et unius . . . oportet eundem finem esse multitudinis humanae quod est hominis unius."

57. C. H. Miron, *The Problem of Altruism in the Philosophy of Saint Thomas* (Washington, 1939) 77.

58. Jarra writes that equality before the law means "the possibility for all to share in the material and spiritual goods of the nation, supplying all with the possibility of providing for one's self and one's family honorable work in living conditions worthy of man; the exclusion of all persons or groups politically privileged as well as of immunity for crimes; the assurance of legal protection for all." See Jarra, *Socjologia katolicka* 120.

59. The relative data for the history of human rights are contained in F. Karrenberg, ed., *Evangelisches Soziallexikon* (Stuttgart, 1956) 717.

60. M. Beer, *Historia socjalizmu i walk społecznych* (Warsaw, 1924) Part IV, 27.

61. *Basic American Documents* (Aines, 1956) 71–91.

62. J. Maritain, *The Rights of Man* 62–63.

63. *Déclaration Universelle des Droits de l'Homme* (Publications des Nations Unies, 1949) I, 3.

64. There is no contradiction between the good of the individual and the good of society. Hence, the position of Thomistic social philosophy is called "solidarism." Thomas Aquinas thus establishes this harmony: "Ille qui quaerit bonum commune multitudinis ex consequenti etiam quaerit bonum suum, propter duo: primo quidem quia bonum proprium non potest esse sine bono communi vel familiae vel civitatis vel regni . . . secundo, quia cum homo sit pars domus vel civitatis, oportet quod consideret quid sit sibi bonum ex hoc quod est prudens circa bonum multitudinis. Bona enim dispositio partium accipitur secundum habitudinem ad totum." II–II, 47, 10, ad 2.

65. S. Th. II–II, 58, 7, ad 2.

195

Jan Turowski

66. E. Kurz informs us that Thomas Aquinas emphasized this principle in his writings, and he found about sixty passages in which Thomas repeats the formula "Bonum commune multitudinis est maius et divinius quam bonum unius." See E. Kurz, *Individuum und Gemeinschaft beim hl. Thomas von Aquin* (Munich, 1932) 47.

67. S. Th. II–II, 152, 4, ad 3.

68. S. Th. I–II, 21, 4, ad 3.

69. S. Th. I–II, 87, 8; but there is another formulation in S. Th. I–II, 113, 9, ad 2: "Bonum universi est maius quam bonum particulare unius, si accipiatur utrumque in eodem genere. Sed bonum gratiae unius maius est quam bonum naturae totius universi.

POSTWAR INDUSTRIALIZATION

IN POLAND

Jerzy Ozdowski

THE PHENOMENON OF INDUSTRIALIZATION HAS BECOME THE DOMI-
nant feature of civilization in the twentieth century. The great
development of industry in the contemporary world, with mass
production based on the use of the machine and the division of
labor, has led to the growth of the participation of industrial
production in social income and to the growth of the number of
workers engaged in industry in comparison with other areas of the
economy. The basic role of industry in the contemporary economy
depends not only on the consumption of mass-produced items at
a relatively low price, but also on the manufacture of every kind
of means of production not only for itself but for the other areas
of the economy. The process of industrialization began in western
Europe at the end of the eighteenth century and the beginning
of the nineteenth century, owing to the introduction of machines,
which made possible the transition from hand manufacture to
large-scale industry. Some scholars, such as N. Wiener, J. D.
Bernal, and J. Schumpeter, attempt to divide the evolution of
industrialization into two or even three "industrial revolutions."
However, quite properly, O. Lange has declared that there was
actually one industrial revolution which called into being large-
scale industry; the later development, that including automation,
is basically only a process of completion.[1]

The significance of industrialization for each country is evidenced by the fact that in general the states with a developed
industry play a great economic and political role in the contemporary world. This fact is related not only to the higher standard
of living of industrialized societies, but also to the developed

197

Jerzy Ozdowski

economic infrastructure, social stratification, and cultural level. There is nothing strange, therefore, in the fact that an industrial civilization has become the goal of the undeveloped states, which by industrialization hope to overcome their condition of age-long backwardness.

The concept of industrialization is generally understood univocally. Although the sociologists consider industrialization a "complex of technical, economic, and social processes," still the economic content of that complex plays a fundamental role and is the actual *definiens* in the characterization of the concept.[2] Moreover, we agree that "industrialization is a process enclosed within time limits, evoked by a continuing increase in the degree of productive investment in industry."[3]

O. Lange expresses the view that only by the accumulation of capital and its transfer to industrial investment can the economy be brought out of an undeveloped state.[4] The English Marxist economist Paul Sweezy is of the opinion that industrialization is a process characterized by directing the greater part of the economic potential of a country into the construction of new means of production.[5]

The American economist W. A. Lewis considers that the beginning of the process of industrialization indicates a growth in the degree of investment from 5 to 10–12 per cent.[6]

As the prime condition for a "beginning of independent growth" W. W. Rostow places the growth of the degree of investment at over 10 per cent of the national income.[7] Consequently, the value of technical equipment per worker increases as does the per capita production, and the industrial structure is changed by a rapid transfer of laborers from agriculture to industry. Some investigators, interested in the problem of economic growth, place such great weight on this change in the employment structure that they apply the expression "industrialized" only to countries having a relatively low employment in agriculture as compared to industry. In our opinion, it would be improper to identify the concept of the "process of industrialization" with the concept of "the process of accumulation of capital," for in this way one can also characterize as industry a more intensive method of agricultural production.[8] Hence, strictly speaking, industrialization will be characterized by the growth of the share of industry in the value of national property and income and in the employment structure, owing to which there is a subsequent growth in the productiveness of labor and income in the general social scale.

However, is industrialization the only method that makes possible economic growth and social progress? H. W. Singer, United Nations expert for aid to underdeveloped countries, answers this question. He makes the choice of method of development primarily dependent on the relationship between the number of people and the natural resources.[9] If a country is overpopulated, then the development of agriculture is more expensive than industrialization; the opposite is true where the density of population is small, so that the development of agricultural production is cheaper. Nine years earlier H. W. Singer and Czesław Strzeszewski expressed the same view, that "for an agricultural country with a significant density of population there is only one way of development—industrialization."[10] According to the author, in the interwar period Poland was a relatively overpopulated country, with ninety inhabitants per square kilometer, leading the other agricultural states of Europe. As a result, hidden unemployment of several millions in the villages and of several hundreds of thousands in the urban centers was a permanent phenomenon in the Polish economy before the war. In the world-market our country, suffering from an undeveloped industry and a backward and unproductive agriculture, served as a source of cheap labor and an exporter of raw materials.[11]

After World War II Poland faced the urgent need of transforming her economic structure by industrialization.

The party and government authorities in Poland developed a program of industrialization for the country based principally on the rapid construction of a new heavy industry. According to Marxist assumptions, the program of rapid industrialization involves a reconstruction of agriculture and the creation of the economic bases of a socialist state.[12] The basic source of strength for socialist industrialization was the development of the socialist sector of the national economy, expressed by the dominant role of public investment in the process of industrialization.[13] In order to evaluate meaningfully the industrialization of Poland, it is necessary to describe in a few words the economic situation of the country after World War II.

Economic conditions in Poland in 1945 had changed basically in contrast to the interwar period. On the one hand, the war and the occupation had caused catastrophic losses in population and in the national economy. It has been estimated that during the war six million persons perished and about 38 per cent of the national wealth was destroyed.[14] On the other hand, the change of

Jerzy Ozdowski

frontiers after the war and the acquisition of the western territories with their potential wealth created better conditions for the process of reconstruction and of transforming the national economy. A measure of the industrialization in the recovered territories before the war in comparison with the lost territories can be seen in the statistics of the number of persons employed in industry for every one thousand inhabitants. In the recovered territories 80 persons were employed in industry in 1939, whereas in the lost territories 35 persons were so employed in 1937.[15] Indeed, the advantages resulting from the shift of frontiers could not be exploited rapidly because of the particularly heavy destruction and devastation in the western and northern territories. Certain economists, who underestimate the acquisition of areas with greater industrialization in the dynamic development of our industry after the war, compare the present state of the country's industrialization with the state of industrialization before 1939. After October 1956 such reports met with proper criticism as a habitual falsification of the real picture of development.[16]

A characteristic feature of industrial development in Poland during the postwar period was the rapid tempo of the growth of production. In the first years after the war's end that growth was conditioned by the rapid restoration of establishments that were inoperative or partially damaged; the use of the economic potential of the recovered territories played a fundamental role. Owing to the direction of limited sources of investment to areas that in a relatively short time would produce results—and owing to the rapid growth of employment outside of agriculture—industrial production by 1949 approached the 1938 level of production in the present territories of Poland.[17]

The process of industrialization gained additional momentum in the years 1950–1955. The average annual rate of growth in industrial production for the Six-Year Plan was over 16.2 per cent, and surpassed the rapidity of growth in socialist as well as capitalist countries.[18] Taking into consideration the very inexact statistics for total production reckoned in unchanged prices, we obtain for that period a growth of industrial production of about 112 per cent.[19] If the calculation is conducted by another method, and if namely the quantitative growth of the production of the principal industrial products is considered, the actual growth of industrial production in that period is approximately 120–130 per cent of the production for the year 1949.[20] In any case, the statistics all indicate the great acceleration of industrialization for the years 1950–1955.

The principal source for realizing this forced industrialization was large government investments, which demanded a high share from the accumulation of the national income. In the Six-Year Plan it was proposed that the growth of the encumbrance on the national products' accumulation would by 1955 reach the peak level of 28 per cent of the national income. But as a result of the deterioration of the world situation in 1950–1951, the creation of an armaments industry was undertaken, which together with the efforts toward achieving the original goals led to a less than planned growth of the share of accumulation in the national income. In the prices of 1950 the encumbrance on the accumulation grew in the year 1952 to 32 per cent of the national income, and in 1953 to 38.[21] Consequently, the rapid tempo of industrialization, which in the early years of the Six-Year Plan had received a further acceleration, necessarily led to a breakdown of the non-industrial production of goods and services and was reflected negatively in the level of current consumption by the public. Omitting here the structural, placement, and organizational problems we see that what contributed to the acuteness of the situation was the immoderate expansion of investment and the notorious delay in periods of new construction.[22] Under the pressure of public opinion, with the year 1954 there began a transitional stabilization of investment funds at the level of 1953, the number of realized objectives was lessened, and efforts were made to shorten the construction periods.

Consequently, the annual average rate of industrial growth dropped significantly in the years 1955–1959 to the level of 9.5 per cent; the plan for 1960–1965 envisaged the rate to be 8.7;[23] in the long range, however, the share of accumulation in the national income continues at a level of over 20. There is also a tendency of growth in the degree of accumulation.[24] From the report on investment funds per one inhabitant, if we take the funds for the year 1950 as 100, we reach a growth of 154 in 1955, and 219 in 1960.[25] Whereas in the Six-Year Plan industry received 44.9 per cent of the investment funds, in the last five years its share dropped to 41.7.[26] The lessened dynamism of growth in income was the price which had to be paid for neglect of the division of investment in agriculture and the economic infrastructure. In the last Five-Year Plan as compared with the Six-Year Plan, a serious effort was made to increase funds in agriculture (its share

Jerzy Ozdowski

of the funds rose from 9 to 11.3 per cent) and nonproductive investment (from 21.8 to 29.6), but it is difficult to consider that effort adequate.[27]

The second characteristic feature of the process of industrialization in Poland was the state's assumption of definite tasks in the direction of industrial development. The basic postulate of economic policy was proclaimed to be the absolute necessity of the rapid growth of investment goods rather than of consumption goods. In accordance with this postulate, 85 per cent of the investment funds in the Six-Year Plan was set aside for the development of heavy industry, namely, steel production, electrical energy, industrial machinery, chemistry, and construction materials. Accepting the total production of the year 1949 as 100, for the year 1960 in the production of capital goods we obtain the figure of 486.5, and in the production of consumption goods the figure of 376.7.[28] Such a great concentration of funds in heavy industry, and especially in steel production and industrial machinery, was justified by the impossibility of basing Poland's industrialization on ties with the world market. The tempo of Poland's industrial growth having been accepted, and there not being a chance of getting the machinery by import, it was necessary to choose the extraordinarily difficult way of a rapid construction of our own industry for investment goods. The model for the realization of this industrialization, borrowed from the Soviet Union, in the first phase of industrialization placed the chief emphasis on the development of a heavy industry, and only in the second phase was there to be a development of consumer goods production. Thus, the high degree of investment in conditions of limited autarchy led under the influence of ideological assumptions to deferring the growth of the production of consumer goods, and, consequently, also of consumption to the moment of completing the many-yeared cycle of the entire economy's development. In this manner, to the immoderate tempo of industrial construction was added the one-sidedness of its structure, expressed in a lack of investment in light industry and consumer industry, as well as in many branches of heavy industry. In heavy industry during the Six-Year Plan, besides the overinvestment in steel and machine production, there appeared the inadequate growth of funds for the construction of chemical and electrical industries, as well as mining, especially coal. The need of development in these branches of industry was dictated in Poland by the possession of the corresponding raw materials, the demands of economic

202

planning, and the postulates of technical progress. In the Six-Year Plan the situation of the light and consumer industries was even worse, for they did not receive adequate resources, even to reconstruct their productive ability.

The serious lack of investment for the production of consumer goods led to the fall of real wages and to the impossibility of satisfying the fundamental needs of society; and in production it led to failure in exploiting the country's raw material resources and to a decline of the average effectiveness of funds generally.[29] The partial warping of Polish industry during the Six-Year Plan originated in the immoderate share of investment funds or resources set aside for the construction of new office buildings, while the possibility of construction and renovation of existing establishments was not exploited.

The first Five-Year Plan for the years 1956–1960 was in great measure a program to correct the lack of harmony in the structure of industry that developed during the Six-Year Plan; the basic principle accepted was the equal growth of accumulation and consumption. As a result of the undeveloped consumer goods industry, in the early years of that Five-Year Plan acute economic tensions developed because of the rapid growth of nominal wages. The disproportions in Polish industry continued to affect the following period by making impossible the full utilization of the technical base and making difficult the satisfaction of needs in many areas of the production of goods and services. In reality, the investment plan for the years 1956–1960 was characterized, above all, by the continuation and extension of objectives initiated in the Six-Year Plan. Actually, for this reason, in the five-year period there continued, although in a lesser degree than in the earlier six-year period, the growth of heavy industry in comparison with the industry that produces articles for consumption. It must be admitted, however, that the years 1956–1960 brought two new phenomena to industrial production, namely, the appearance of mass production of new goods made at home for long-term use and efforts at a better utilization of the economic potential of industry.[30]

Wiktor Buch, the chief editor of *Gospodarka Planowa*, vividly described the evolution of the auxiliary structure of Polish industry: "In our industry the former dominant role of coal and textiles has declined; instead the production of every kind of machine, means of transport, and electrical products developed."[31] Unfortunately, this change, quite proper in its basic essence, was carried through at the cost of great renunciations by the living generation and led to a weakening of important areas of the national economy, such as small industry, various services, communal and domestic economy, and, above all, of agriculture. It seems that these areas of the economy are still inadequately considered in the investment plan for the years 1961–1965, as well as in the assumptions of future development.

The third feature of Poland's industrialization involved changes that occurred in the distribution of industry. In accordance with the doctrine that proclaimed the equal distribution of productive forces in socialism, it was expected that somehow automatically the development of industry in the country would cause the activization of regions poorly developed and would equalize the disproportions on the economic and cultural level in the different areas of the country. This unrealistic assumption led to a neglect of industry's distribution in the Six-Year Plan, particularly of new establishments in equalizing the differences of economic development on an area scale. Moreover, the slowing of industrialization at the end of the Six-Year Plan and in the early years of the Five-Year Plan was reflected negatively in the originally intended investments in economically backward regions. Indeed, the Cracow province, owing to the placing of Nowa Huta in its territory, increased its share in the country's general industrial production, but at the same time on the scale of that one province there grew up new disproportions, caused by the further concentration of production in already industrialized areas.[32] An analysis of the distribution of 156 new industrial establishments during the Six-Year Plan leads to two conclusions: the new goals were located to an excessive degree in provinces already strongly industrialized; in the choice of locations preference was regularly given to the provincial centers over the small cities and towns.[33] The best illustration for the first conclusion is the situation of the province of Katowice, whose share in the total investment funds of the country was 18.2 per cent in the Six-Year Plan, while the undeveloped province of Białystok received only 1.9 of the funds. This policy led not only to the loss of opportunities for a rapid development of backward regions, but in addition created difficulties in the infrastructure in the regions of excessive concentration of industry (e.g., lack of water in Śląsk, Częstochowa, and Łódź.)[34] The second conclusion especially concerns Warsaw and other provincial cities, where about one third of all new enterprises constructed during the Six-Year Plan were located. The consequences of favoring the large cities in the policy of industrialization were the great movements of population, the acuteness of the housing problem, and the need for additional communal investments. A symptom, harmful to a certain degree, was the obvious economic decline of the small cities and towns, which ceased to fulfill the functions of local centers of industry and commerce.[35] If we turn from the data about provinces to the data collected by the Planning Commission of the Council of Ministers in 1958 about the development of the counties, we find evidence indicating the economic backwardness of certain smaller regions; for instance, in 1957 the yearly income of one inhabitant in the county of Leżajsk was 2,026 złotys, but in Katowice it was 23,700 złotys.[36] It seems that here we are dealing with some defect in the process of industrialization in Poland, which, forcing the development of large objectives in key industries, neglected a whole series of other possibilities for activating underdeveloped regions, principally in agriculture, small industry, and the development of the apparatus of services. The responsibility for this state of affairs lies not only with the excessive centralism in the direction of the Polish economy, but also with the lack of competence and initiative in the regional apparatus of the national councils. For, as August Losch says strikingly, "A good mayor is proud of the manner of administering his city, not of its growth."[37]

An obvious sign of the improper policy in distribution of industry was reflected locally in the increased number of job seekers during the first years of the five-year period. Actually, a result of the failure to adjust the building of new enterprises to the needs of the labor market was manifested in some provinces by a greater number of unemployed than jobs available for them (1956), and an excessive acceleration of migration, particularly from the village to the city. It seems that in the future the size of the labor supply in a region will dictate the location of new industrial objectives if location is not dependent to great degree on other factors.[38] Investigations of the 1961–1965 tendencies in employment indicate a relatively higher rate of growth in the labor supply in the western and northern provinces, and hence they suggest the need of developing industry in that area. In every case the needs of development in some regions of the country ought to be considered in a just policy of industrialization and ought to influence the choice of location, and to a certain degree the tempo and structure of industrialization.

Industrialization is characterized not only by space and time changes in property and social income, but also by changes in the structure of employment, productivity of work, and the level of wages. The accepted tempo of industrialization required above all the rapid growth of the population employed outside agriculture. Whereas in 1931 only 29.6 per cent of the population generally was employed outside of agriculture, after the war this sector grew rapidly, so that in 1950 the percentage was up to 42.3, and in 1955 to 46.4.[39] The chief element in the rapid growth of employment outside of agriculture was the growth of mean employment in industry, which was 859,000 in 1937, but by 1950 had reached 2,050,000; by 1955 2,702,000; and by 1960 3,012,000.[40] A characteristic feature of the dynamics of employment was the significantly more rapid growth in the Six-Year Plan than in the Five-Year Plan; from 1958 the slowing of the growth is especially clear.

The sources from which industry drew new labor power were, above all, the village, and then the reserves in the city. According to a provisional count, in the years 1950–1955 alone "over a million persons of working age left agriculture, and of this number an important part (50–70 per cent) found employment in industry."[41]

Taking into consideration the direction of industrial development characteristic of the first phase of industrialization, we obtain an uneven growth of employment in the individual sectors of production. In the years marked by the most rapid tempo of the growth of accumulation, in the period 1948–1953, employment in the sector of the means of production grew about 110 per cent, but employment in the sector of consumer goods only about 14.[42] According to other figures, during the period of the Six-Year Plan in the principal areas of industry serving consumer production, employment remained at an unchanged level.[43]

An interesting interpretation of the growth of employment in Poland was presented by J. Pajestka at the Polish Academy of Sciences in 1959, during a special session devoted to the problem of Poland's development in the last fifteen years.[44] According to him, the economic policy followed in Poland after the war, in particular during the Six-Year Plan, can be called the policy of maximum employment. On the one hand, it was based on certain economic conditions, for instance, the existence of labor reserves, the possession of unexploited productive powers (the potential of the recovered territories), and on the other hand, on institutional conditions connected with the socialist system of economy.

In this situation it was possible to transfer the reserve labor forces from the village to the city, to employ them in greater measure in the production of investment goods, and to acquire an unusually high degree of accumulation. Briefly, the maximalization of employment became the source for the maximalization of investment and the chief factor in the great acceleration of economic growth. Except for a certain one-sidedness, this interpretation is adequate chiefly because of the emphasis placed on the role of the human factor in the process of industrializing the country. In production, maximal employment brings about derationalization in the utilization of the labor force. The measure of that derationalization is the decline of efficiency in numerous establishments, and even in entire branches of production. In the general economic scale this meant the shift from full employment to a state of overemployment in certain phases of industry, while the lack of a labor force in agriculture was increasing. Estimates indicate that about 0.5 million people were employed in industry beyond the actual need.[45] Although the established work day was eight hours, people actually worked from five to seven hours.[46] On a small economic scale the irrationality of employment was expressed by the establishments' efforts at achieving maximum employment and a full utilization of permitted limits. Consequently, the growth of industrial production in the most intense period of growth was based on increasing the number of workers with almost complete neglect of the possibility of the better use of the human factor.

The conditions that made difficult the increase of efficiency were the one-sided system of planning and direction in the whole economy, the low level of qualification in the work crews as well as in the supervision, and the neglect of the necessary changes and the modernization of machinery. However, the fundamental reason for the low efficiency of work in the peak years of industrialization in the Six-Year Plan was the lowering of living standards owing to a decline in the real income of the population. The inescapable consequence of the rise in the degree of accumulation, as well as the one-sided direction of investments and the labor reserve force chiefly into heavy industry, was the decline of the mean real wage. Neglected and rapidly collectivized agriculture, from which the best element of the population was going into industry, in the years 1950–1954 went into a period of decline in production. At the same time the industry producing consumer goods was deprived of an increase in human labor as well

Jerzy Ozdowski

as of investment resources. In comparison with the growing purchasing power of the increasing population employed outside of
agriculture, the consumer market in the years 1951–1953 was
always poorly supplied in articles of prime necessity as well as in
luxury items. Consequently, industrialization led to a decline in
the real wages along with a lowering of consumption per capita
of population. Truly, the second phenomenon has a transitional
character if one considers the given averages, but one must stress
most emphatically that here the statistical analysis hides the real
picture.

Beyond the statements of average consumption of the basic
articles per capita of population, particular consumption problems
of the population in various regions of the country and various
areas of employment—but, above all, the basic problem of the
consumption per capita by the member of the family—remained
hidden. And here we see actually the impropriety of burdening
certain groups of the population with the principal cost of industrializing the country. In the year 1956 the percentage of physical
workers earning up to 600 złotys in the particular sectors of the
national economy was as follows: social and cultural arrangements,
56.3; administration, 53.0; financial institutions, 34; forestry, 28.6;
agriculture, 18.5; and state industry, 3.6.[47] If on the other hand we
consider the dynamics of nominal wages, this shows that in the
course of industrialization wages in industry and in construction,
compared with other sectors of the economy, were characterized
by a more rapid growth. Hence, the evident conclusion follows
that workers in the nonindustrial sectors of the economy and in
the areas deprived of industry bore to a great extent the consequences of transforming the economic structure of the country.
Mutatis mutandis—this reasoning can be applied to the particular
branches of industry, among which in terms of level of nominal
wages are the specially privileged branches of heavy industry.

An important area of the unfair decline of income was the situation of the families with many children, especially those whose
only source of sustenance depended on the wages of one person.
These families, especially if the parents worked outside industry,
were faced with the tragic problem of how to sustain and educate
their offspring. Most painfully concerned with this state of affairs
were particularly the mothers who, as interviews have shown,
needed gainful employment in order to supplement the excessively low wages of their husbands. Consequently, since 1936,
the percentage of unmarried workers outside agriculture rose to

70, that of married persons to 320, while that of married women—who in 1931 formed 15 per cent of the workers in general—to 30.[48] According to the investigations made by the Department of Sociology of the Institute of Social Economy, the higher the income of husband in a marriage with children, the less wives seek employment. Hence, in families with incomes from 800–1200 złotys 60 per cent of the women work; in families with incomes from 2,000–3,000 złotys 30 work; and in cases of incomes over 3,000 złotys, 20.[49] This was also an important source of the labor force for the hungry labor market in industry. But ultimately, did not society, in the competitive employment of wives and mothers, lose more than it gained?

What made the lowering of the level of consumption and the unfavorable situation of families even worse was the steadily more acute housing problem: the lack of housing rose from 290,000 dwellings in cities and settlements to 440,000 in the year 1960.[50] Society had to endure a lowering of its standard of living, the limitation of funds needed for communal and socio-cultural establishments, and particularly great neglect in the small cities, settlements and in the villages.

In view of the growing dissatisfaction resulting from the program of industrialization, there followed at the end of the Six-Year Plan, especially from 1956, a rapid growth of nominal wages and an improvement in supplying the market. The wage reforms led to a halt in the decline of the low income and the growth of high wages. At the same time there appeared on the market the long awaited fruits of the process of industrialization in the form of long-term consumer goods from the country's production. Such basic instruments of domestic economy, for instance, electric washing machines, ceased being a luxury. The number of families possessing such machines grew in the years 1955–1960 from 0.5 to 18 per cent.[51]

In the sector of employment from the year 1958, the tempo of growth in industry fell to the level that corresponds to the natural growth of the population, and with this there followed a halt to the process of migration from the village to the city. At the same time productivity increased more slowly at the beginning of the Five-Year Plan than did nominal wages, but more rapidly from 1958. Generally, after the somewhat chaotic period of growth during the Six-Year Plan, the last five years have been a period of returning to balance, which was proved possible to achieve in more than one sector (e.g., the general balance of the market).

Jerzy Ozdowski

However, a whole series of matters related to the changes in the structure and social culture of the nation—and produced by the process of industrialization—still awaits regulation. On the rapid recognition of these social problems and on their proper solution depends the successful development of our nation, economic as well as cultural. Concerned as we are with the full technical progress in our country, we must not forget that the basic goal of all technical arrangements and social institutions is the service of man, who is the subject "of inviolable and universal rights."[52] The achievement of this goal through the process of industrialization in Poland is the fundamental criterion of its humanistic value.

FOOTNOTES

1. O. Lange, "Społeczny proces produkcji i reprodukcji," Ekonomista I (1962) 21.
2. J. Szczepański, "Industrializacja i socjologia," Przegląd Kulturalny 37 (1961).
3. J. Rutkowski, "Z zagadnień industrializacji socjalistycznej," Zagadnienia ekonomiki politycznej socjalizmu (Warsaw, 1959) 69.
4. O. Lange, Pisma ekonomiczne i społeczne 1930–1960 (Warsaw, 1961) 208.
5. P. M. Sweezy, Teoria rozwoju kapitalizmu (Warsaw, 1957) 345.
6. W. A. Lewis, The Theory of Economic Growth (London, 1956) Chap. 5.
7. W. W. Rostow, "Start do samoczynnego wzrostu," Problemy wzrostu ekonomicznego krajów słabo rozwiniętych (Warsaw, 1958) 78.
8. P. Rosenstein-Roden, "O uprzemysłowienie krajów ubogich," Ekonomista 1 (1947) 35.
9. H. W. Singer, "Problemy uprzemysłowienia w krajach słabo rozwiniętych," Problemy wzrostu ekonomicznego krajów słabo rozwiniętych (Warsaw, 1958) 318.
10. Cz. Strzeszewski, "Zagadnienia uprzemysłowienia Polski," Ekonomista 2 (1947) 73.
11. E. Kwiatkowski, Dysproporcje (Cracow, 1932) 224.
12. P. A. Baran, Ekonomia polityczna wzrostu (Warsaw, 1958) 251.
13. O. Lange, "Społeczny proces" 186.
14. J. Pajestka, "Rozwój ekonomiczny i przemiany strukturalne w gospodarce Polski Ludowej," Zeszyty Problemowe Nauki Polski (Wrocław-Warsaw, 1961) XXIC, 207.
15. A. Kukliński, "Uprzemysłowienie Polski w perspektywie historycznej," Przegląd Polski i Obcy 4–5 (1957) 7.
16. See A. Kukliński and M. Najgrowski, "Naciągane wskaźniki," Życie Gospodarcze (November 11, 1956).
17. See J. Pajestka, "Rozwój ekonomiczny" 201.
18. W. Buch, "Przemysł polski na tle przemysłu świata," Gospodarka Planowa 3 (1961) 13.

210

19. *Rocznik Statystyczny 1961* (Warsaw, 1961) 81.

20. A. Karpiński, *Zagadnienia socjaliztycznej industrializacji Polski* (Warsaw, 1958) 49. See also the author's penetrating criticism of the report on total production (pp. 46–48).

21. *Ibid.* 11.

22. *Ibid.* 92: The value of unfinished investments at the end of 1955 was placed at about 14–18 milliards of złotys, that is about 25 percent of the investment in the years 1950–1955.

23. W. Buch, "Przemysł polski" 13.

24. *Rocznik Statystyczny 1961* 56.

25. *Ibid.* 68.

26. *Mały Rocznik Statystyczny 1961* (Warsaw, 1961) 38.

27. J. Pajestka, "Niektóre problemy minionego 5-lecia," *Życie Gospodarcze* 40 (1960).

28. *Mały Rocznik Statystyczny 1961*, 46.

29. A. Karpiński, *Zagadnienia* 76–77.

30. A. Karpiński, *O Gospodarce Polski* (Warsaw, 1961) 57–59.

31. W. Buch, "Przemysł polski" 18.

32. J. Kruczała, "Zmiany w rozmieszczeniu przemysłu kluczowego w wojew. krakowskim oraz uwagi o obowiązujących zasadach rozmieszczenia przemysłu," *Myśl Gospodarcza* 4 (1958).

33. A. Karpiński, *Zagadnienia* 221.

34. T. Mrzygłód, *Planowanie regionalne* (Warsaw, 1958) 219.

35. M. Kielczewska-Zalewska and J. Kostrowicki, "Problem aktywizacji małych miast w Polsce," *Nowe Drogi* 7–8 (1956).

36. B. Winiarski, *Aktywizacja regionów gospodarczo nie rozwiniętych* (Warsaw, 1961) 8.

37. A Losch, *Gospodarka przestrzenna* (Warsaw, 1961) 349.

38. J. Obodowski, "Tendencje w dziedzinie zatrudnienia w latach 1961–1965," *Jak pracuje człowiek* (Warsaw, 1961) 407.

39. M. Kabaj, "Warunki ekonomiczne racjonalnego zatrudnienia," *Jak pracuje człowiek* 382.

40. *Rocznik Statystyczny 1961* xxvi–xxvii.

41. A. Karpiński, *Zagadnienia* 118.

42. J. Pajestka, "Rozwój ekonomiczny" 226.

43. A. Karpiński, *Zagadnienia* 108.

44. J. Pajestka, "Rozwój ekonomiczny" 218.

45. A. Karpiński, *Zagadnienia* 123.

46. M. Kabaj, "Warunki ekonomiczne" 378.

47. E. Vielrose, *Rozkład dochodów według wielkości* (Warsaw, 1960) 48.

48. J. Piotrowski, "Praca i rodzina," *Jak pracuje człowiek* 296–297.

49. *Ibid.* 299.

50. W. Mieciuński, "Sytuacja mieszkaniowa ludności," *Życie Gospodarcze* 41 (1961).

51. A. Karpiński, *O Gospodarce Polski* 87.

52. John XXIII, *Mater et Magistra*.

ALIENATION AND HUMANIZATION

IN INDUSTRY

Jerzy Ozdowski

THE TERM "ALIENATION" APPEARED IN VARIOUS MEANINGS IN ENGLISH economics, in some theories of the law of nature, and in German philosophy in the nineteenth century. It was from Feuerbach and Hegel that Karl Marx took the concept of alienation, and in his early writings he gave it a general meaning as an inseparable feature of every human creative process.[1] The further development of Marxist thought restricted the notion of alienation to the estrangement of work and its product in the conditions of the capitalistic system. Finally, some Polish socialist writers show the tendency to treat alienation as a concept affecting not only labor and its product, but the very relationship of man to man and the meaning of human existence, which is threatened by contemporary industrialism.[2]

Catholic thought also searches for the meaning of alienation when it reviews the weaknesses of contemporary culture, sensed painfully by the "grey" man. Bishop Fulton Sheen gives a profound moral meaning to alienation, for he sees the cause of human misery in the breakdown of the relationship between man and his neighbors and his own nature.[3] The Cardinal Primate Wyszyński, in writing about the spirit of human labor, tends to relate labor with the totality of human living, so that "labor will not be something divided from life, but will create a harmonious whole."[4]

It is considerably easier to agree on a definition of the humanization of labor, inasmuch as essential differences appear only secondarily in the concept of man's nature and the purpose of his labor. We approve W. Missiuro's definition, which in his opinion embraces "all the means of adapting circumstances, and hence of

213

the mechanical factor of labor and its immediate environment, to the physical and psychic properties of man, guaranteeing him the protection of his health and the unfettered possibility of developing his spiritual and physical powers as well as the satisfaction of his material and cultural needs."[5] Clearly, an acceptance of his definition does not free us from the obligation of a stricter definition of these characteristics, powers, and needs of man, which must be accepted in their total fullness—individual, social, bodily, spiritual, natural, and supernatural. Hence, not only alienation as the point of departure for our considerations, but the humanization of labor as the goal of social policy, create the need of distinguishing world views.

Why is this problem considered only in the framework of industry? For the structure of contemporary society is undergoing an evolution, in which the majority of those employed in productive work is transferring to service employment; hence, it would be necessary to consider above all the problematic of this type of work.

However, the association of this subject with industry is justified not only from a general viewpoint, but also from the Polish viewpoint. Daniel Bell properly states that the contemporary factory is in some sense an exemplar, for its rhythm is being transferred to other areas of social life.[6] Again, Poland's situation as a land undergoing rapid industrialization demands that special attention be directed to the human factor in industry.

Our considerations will begin with a genetic consideration of the phenomena of alienation in contemporary industry; then we shall analyze the principal means of labor's humanization, so that, after a short review of the social perspectives of automation, we can suggest some conclusions of a general nature.

The structure of the new industrial enterprise is conditioned basically by the development of two factors, namely, machine technology and the organization of labor—briefly stated, mechanization and the rationalization of production. This does not mean that we consider these factors the total of forces influencing contemporary industrial life, since they do not appear in isolation for general cultural, social, and economic conditions. Nevertheless, a dominant role in the development of industry belongs to technology and organization.

Mechanization is a form of technical progress of the capital-absorbing kind, which expresses itself in the lessening of the quantity of human, physical labor or its productive processes through mechanical arrangements.[7] By rationalization we understand the general application of organizational, in-production efforts that maximalize the economic results.[8] Technological progress in the first decade of the twentieth century made possible the application in industrial production of special machines, made for specific operations and powered by electrical energy, and the discovery of methods that permitted great precision in measurements. As a result of these discoveries, the demands made on the talents and abilities of the worker were significantly reduced, and the process of labor could be analyzed into a series of partial activities. This process was accompanied by rapid growth into great combinations working with a large accumulation of capital and employing masses of workers.[9]

At the same time, in the field of organization of labor, there appears the concept of scientific management, called in Poland (not quite exactly) the scientific organization of labor, which was an attempt to transfer to human labor the methods modeled on the mechanical technical sciences.[10] The actual creator of this tendency in investigation and application was the American engineer Fredrick Taylor, who first completed the analysis and fragmentation of labor into components, so as to recombine them in the most effective manner.[11] Taylor's method consists chiefly in measuring the time of particular operations and elaborating on that basis a rule for the worker. In Taylorism the worker left to himself is in no condition to work properly and needs complete direction from the organizing staff of the enterprise.[12]

Another American engineer, Frank Gilbreth, pushed Taylor's analysis a step further. He conducted so-called motion studies and revealed in the whole variety of human activities eighteen micro-movements, which he called "therbligs," a derivative from his name. In this way human labor is subjected to complete depersonalization, and the participation of the worker in the productive process is reduced to a collection of movements that are purely mechanical. The contemporary critics of scientific management emphasize its creators' complete misunderstanding of the basic physiology and psychology of man, which they say necessarily leads to a painful violation of the dignity of the human person.[13]

The third state in the rationalization of production was Bedeaux's system of payments, wherein he based wages on measuring human power with the aid of the "unit B." Here we have an attempt to introduce into social life the laws of physics, and to treat the workers as a neurophysiological mechanism.

The unification of machine production development with the

suggestions of scientific management leads to the generalizing of continuous production on the principle of the assembly line. Omitting the technical aspect of this form of production, we can, following G. Friedmann, indicate the four characteristics which human labor in this way acquires: the work is repetitious, fragmented, subject to a forced rhythm, and dependent upon the rhythm of a group.[14] After the first enchantment with this form of production, many-sided studies in various countries showed absolutely that work on the assembly line is injurious to the majority of workers from the physical as well as psychical viewpoint. On the basis of broad investigations the Swiss psychologist Walther showed that the forced rhythm of labor generally collides with the rhythm natural to man and produces exhaustion, neuroses, and contributes to frequent accidents.[15] American scholars from the Industrial Health Research Board state that "only some types of individuals are able to conduct themselves as mechanically as the machine at which they are working, but many of them consider such conditions of work intolerable."[16] The best proof of the contradiction between continuous production and human nature is the reaction of workers in the first phase of the introduction of assembly-line technique; this was expressed in the great growth of change-over in the work crews, which reached 80 per cent of the workers annually. Indeed, after a time the crew stabilized, but this stabilization is a result of the fatal influence of the work done in assembly line as the workers accustomed themselves to the new type of work and lost the spirit of initiative.

These effects of assembly production are a particular example of the consequences to which every exaggerated division of labor leads if it does not take into account the demands of human nature. The fragmentation of labor leads to a lessening of man's participation in production. The "pulverized" movements, as G. Friedmann expresses it, become entrusted to machines, and the direction of production in the Taylor Thinking Department is conducted outside the actual center of production. The worker remains sentenced to the monotony of his occupation, to a lack of interest in his work, to a degradation of his professional skills, even to psychic disorders—and to the oblivion sought in recreations and hobbies with which he fills the time free from work. Some investigators of contemporary culture consider quite utopian all efforts to introduce joy or meaning into contemporary industry. David Riesmann even says that the worker gains more from going along with the nucleus of depersonalization than by opposing it.[17]

Consequently, in the structure of contemporary industry there appears a characteristic phenomenon that affects the worker. Until recently he was classified as either skilled or unskilled. Now there is a break in the continuity of learning a trade and as a result difficulty in advancing one's self in the hierarchy of workers. One can perhaps find comfort in the thought that the efficiency taken away from the workers has only been transferred to another sphere, namely, from the production of goods to the field of invention and organizational ability; however, these are not currents of equal importance, and the preponderant phenomenon is the degradation of the hitherto skilled workers.

A further consequence of contemporary mechanization and scientific management is the growth of disintegration in the staff of the enterprise, the growth of antagonism between the formal organization and the informal organization, and the expansion of a conflict-situation.[18] Conflicts and struggles develop among various groups in the enterprise: between the work force and supervision, between the administration and the so-called operator, among groups of workers, among specialists and the rest of the staff, and among various departments.[19] The worker—dissatisfied with his work, disturbed with the directors and his fellow workers, weary and bitter—carries his frustrated attitude from his place of work and reflects it on his family and social life. An American sociologist presents the example of an assembly-line worker who made it his habit to attack Negroes on his way home and then to abuse his wife. There is some exaggeration in that example, but it does show that contemporary industry in its whole development and in its technical and organizational perfection depraves man, awakens in him his lowest instincts, and alienates him from the whole of social life. With good reason does A. Huxley write that "today every well-ordered factory is a panoptical prison and the workers suffer, since they are aware that they are in the midst of a machine."[20]

Let us use the example of the Ford establishments. Their founder—a typical example of an American captain of industry—based the organization of his establishments on a system of complete centralization and an especially privileged corps of engineers. The worker, though well paid, was treated as a blind performer who was not to show any independence of thought or action. This system of organization, after initial successes that lasted until the middle 1920's, proved in the long run to be fallacious. Just before World War II Ford faced such difficulties that eventual government intervention or absorption by another firm was being considered. A new period in the greatness of Ford came in 1944, when the grandson of the founder took over and introduced a complete change of organization. In place of the centralization, the enterprise was broken down into several autonomous establishments. Dominant positions in the enterprise went to people trained in economics, and the attention of the directors was transferred from the technical tasks to social problems, in particular the problematic of human work.[21] The Ford enterprises in this transformation of their organization used fully the achievements of the new tendencies in investigations of industrial labor and of the experiments undertaken in that field during the interwar period.

In citing the history of the Ford enterprise, we wish to emphasize what in capitalist industry basically determined the growth of interests in its human problems, namely, the need of considering a problem which had begun to have a negative influence on the economic results of the enterprise. The phenomena of a growing anarchism in its social structure, the disruption of the tempo of labor, the outbreak of wild strikes, and the growth of unemployment—all this forced the Ford people to break with orthodox Taylorism and to support research into the human factor.

In the first place, the physiology of labor brings relief to the worker. Biological rationalization, whose object is to provide the best working conditions for the human organism, removes technical rationalization. In the actual working conditions there is the application of proper lighting for the places of work, ventilation, attractively painted interiors, rest periods, the adaptation of machinery and factories to the human organism, consideration of the workers' environment, isolation from the noise, and so on. Studies on weariness had a particularly important significance; distinctions were established in the areas of exhaustion, fatigue, and lassitude; at the same time there was a broad application of means to reduce weariness, and these means led to increased productivity and to a drop in accidents.[22]

The second stage of the humanization of labor was the criticism of fragmented labor, which led to investigations of the possibility of integrating labor and toward efforts in the field of combining the operations fragmented under the system of Taylorism. The first experiment in this field was undertaken by the American concern IBM, one of the largest producers of office machines in the world. It was shown that this tendency of returning to labor its healthy unity required certain conditions: the approval and understanding of the workers, professional training, and a definite increase in wages. It was also discovered that there are precise limits to integration that cannot be crossed with respect to the number of parts and instruments. But in every case the experiments showed that the worker, in consequence of job integration, did his work with satisfaction, had a sense of the subjective shortening of the time of work, and felt a greater need of schooling.[23] As a result of this movement, there developed the system of changes of workers at their place of employment and the system of using so-called utility men at the assembly line.

The third stage in the progressive humanization was the discovery and study of the social structure in the labor ranks; this led to the development of the practice of human relations, or the regulation of interpersonal contacts, in industry. Preliminary studies came from the famous experiment in the Hawthorne factory of the Chicago Western Electric Company, under the direction of Elton Mayo, over a period of twelve years.[24] This experiment showed for the first time the great significance of the worker's attitude toward the group of which he is a member and which to a great degree determines his conduct and productivity in labor. This movement placed before the Company's directors a new task, dealing not only with people and labor, but above all with groups of workers and the staff made up of them.[25] In this way a new science arose—the psycho-sociology of industry—and these industrialists gained valuable insights into manipulating the social relations aspect. In practice, the new system of personnel management permitted psychological persuasion in worker relations so as to achieve greater utilization of the staff in achieving the formal goals, especially by means of organized team work.[26]

In its concern over the worker's satisfaction with his job and his so-called morale, whose chief criterion is the degree of cooperation reached in the group, the human relations movement suggests four means: employing the services of a consultant and the application of his suggestions; placing a specialist, a so-called efficiency expert, in the trouble areas threatened with disturbances; the establishment of an industrial adviser, whose capacity is to resolve problems that a worker might have either in the factory or outside it; stimulating the interest of employees in company problems by summoning staff meetings for the discussion of concrete issues.[27]

The great merit of the theory and practice of human relations is the placing of the social factor as the center of interest in the study and direction of the industrial field; however, its weak side is that it makes the group a fetish, particularly a small group, considered by specialists of industrial relations as a hermetically sealed little box (to put it sarcastically), as an absolute that defines the attitude of its members and is subject to socio-technical manipulation by a competent administration. For the worker who has been liberated from the role of a part in a machine, a new danger of dehumanization threatens in the form of being reduced to the rank and file of a productive group, in which the ruling principle is the subordination of the human person to the formal instrumental goal of industrial organization. This type of formulation of the task of the new science and practice provoked the complaint of Daniel Bell, who said it was a sociology of cattle rather than a sociology of human beings.[28]

Another negative aspect of human relations is the fact that many of its representatives ignored the role of economic factors as though the worker did not expect the reformers to improve his material situation. On the other hand, gearing the wage system to economic achievements (for example, the proportional wages of the Scanlon plan) introduced relaxation, and even cooperation in the social relations of industry.

The last of the four means for regulating human relations in industry, namely, interesting the workers in company problems by taking part in conferences, brings us to the fourth stage of humanization of labor in industry, to the various types of participation of the workers in the organization and ownership of the company. Unfortunately, the concept of sharing and participation is not fixed. The attempt to agree on the content of the notion and the classification of various forms of participation, undertaken at the Paris conference of the International Sociological Society in June 1957, did not produce the hoped-for results.[29] According to one group, participation means that the directors reckoned with the workers. Another group felt that participation is simply a share in the organization; a third that participation implies, besides a share in the administration, a share also in the development of the firm; and finally, the view was also represented that participation can occur only in collective structures. Nor did the members of the conference, Dharendorf and Tourain, succeed in having their attempt to classify employee participation accepted by the majority of the conference. This fact is a consequence of the fertile development of this type of humanization in industrial relations in various countries, so that at the present time it is not possible to elaborate a general scheme.

In the West the movement for workers' participation in the organization and exploitation of industry was particularly active after the last war and took on the various forms of industrial democracy. Except for Yugoslavia (which was the first to introduce workers' councils), the socialist countries, as a consequence of the social and economic experiences in the period of centralism in nationalized industry, tried to realize the form of a direct workers' democracy. In each case, in the West as in the East, the principal goal of the development of various forms of participation was the need of a certain compensation for the social results of modern mechanization and organization of production, as well as the need of drawing the workers into a realization of production tasks.

Particular countries, depending on the actual structure of social forces in them and the general situation in industry, worked out organizational forms of participation. England produced an indirect form of participation (joint consultation), in which the workers elected representatives for mutual communication, and not for direct participation in administration. The representation fulfills an advisory role in the daily life of the factory, in particular in the matter of working and living conditions. This representation does not lessen the rights of the trade unions, who are the representatives of the workers in negotiations with the employers. Moreover, the English trade unionists take a negative stand to other forms of workers' participation in profit or ownership, because they cause a blurring of the opposite relationship of capital and labor and lead to conflicts.[30]

West Germany developed a form of direct participation (*Mitbestimmung*), which depends on various forms of participation by the workers' representatives in management. In this way trusted men are chosen as the workers' representatives with the employers; the workers carry out the election of their representative, a so-called director of labor, who is interested chiefly in the factory personnel policy; finally an economic committee is created, half of which is chosen from the workers and half from the representatives of management. Independently of this, Western Germany originated the movement of "People's Actions of Labor," a new effort to realize the form we know as "actionary of labor."

A distinct type of participation, sometimes formalized and other times not, was created in the United States, in which the dominant

221

feature of the social life of industry is the role of the trade union, which appears as a partner in the direction of all affairs dealing with labor and wages. Indeed, the American trade unions did not succeed in revolutionizing the industrial social structure, but they did succeed in gaining for the workers an improvement in working conditions, shortening of working hours, and the introduction of broad social benefits. On the other hand, as R. Dubin says, the American trade union movement limited itself actually to the problem of wages and labor, and it does not give the workers any chance for activizing their role.[31] In America often it is not the trade union but management that initiates plans to increase staff participation. It seems that the critics of the American trade union movement are justified in describing the bureaucratization and corruption of the unions, which sometimes are transformed into interest groups that harm the social good.[32]

Unfortunately we cannot in the narrow confines of this paper describe other special forms of participation, particularly those that involve a share in profit and ownership. We shall limit ourselves to mentioning only the four basic forms, namely, share in profits without responsibility for losses and without influence in direction; a share in the profits with responsibility for losses; a share in the profits with title of ownership and with responsibility for losses, as well as a share in the direction; and, finally, workers' cooperatives. However, we must emphasize that participation in profit and ownership meets numerous difficulties in the condition of the capitalist economy, so that in the United States only 2 per cent of the workers achieved ownership of shares.[33]

New possibilities for the humanization of work in industry were opened with technical progress, or rather with the revolution in technology known as automation. This term in the strict sense describes the processes in which self-correcting instruments control the operation of other machines. Automation was used to construct electronic brains, which in seconds collect and select masses of information, so as to move production in a continuous flow and perform automatically a series of combined operations; and, finally, it was applied to the automated assembly line. Automation has an enormous significance for the human factor in labor. After the limitation of man's physical effort by the machine, and the reduction of mental effort by the division of labor, we are arriving in automation at the elimination in great part of the effort of the will. The students undertaking the issue pose the problem: Is automation the ultimate enslavement, or the ultimate liberation of man? Quite properly G. Friedmann warns against haste in giving an answer to this question, and he attacks N. Wiener sharply for his naïveté in describing self-operating factories, whose production no one can buy.[34] The latest investigations seem to confirm the thesis that automation will not be able to take over all branches of industry, for in technology's present state it seems to apply to mass production, a process that is continuous or repeated. Besides this, the introduction of automation in some factories does not mean that the factory is thus changed into one that can be run by pushing a button. There will always remain factory departments that are not adapted to automation. Finally, even in an automated department of production, there will be operations which, in terms of profitability, will be better left unautomated.

In spite of the above mentioned limits of automation, basic changes in employment will necessarily be involved. By freeing a part of the workers from production, automation will need them in other service-type occupations that cooperate with production.[35] In an enterprise that is being automated, it is possible, according to P. Drucker, for 95 per cent of the workers to find employment, obviously after the passage of some time and after training the former staff.[36] Workers engaged directly in automated production will have to show special characteristics: alertness, adaptability, aptitude, and a sense of responsibility. Generally, the occupations of the future will be many-sided, that is, they will be able to find application to various branches of production. The operations, which not a technician but a specialist will have to perform, will be based on the characteristics and talents of the man, and not on the characteristics of the materials and machine. This indicates in industry a healthy return to human nature, whose potential talents it will be necessary to develop according to the needs of production itself. However, employment in automated industry has an ambivalent character: along with the possibilities of humanization there exists also the danger of an excessive psychological burden on the workers employed in the supervision of automated machines under circumstances of complete isolation, which tend to produce nervous tensions.

Further social consequences of this second industrial revolution may be the following: the lessening of the optimum of factories; decentralizing their location in relationship to the great urban agglomerations; and, finally, the elimination of the differences between city and village. Daniel Bell grows fanciful when he says that factory society may even return to the example of dependence on the village manor.[37] However, one of the most important consequences of automation is the real possibility of a significant reduction in working hours. Here again, with more free time for the population, arises the question of an ethical and educational preparation for the use of such leisure time, above all, by way of personality development and the awakening of cultural needs.[38]

Generally, by evoking in man new possibilities of progress through prosperity that can give him leisure time, automation is a great new opportunity for true human progress. But what is to be done so that the opportunity will be fully used, that the possibilities offered by technology will develop the individual culture and society? G. Friedmann answers this question by postulating the return of its threefold value to labor: intellectual, moral, and social.[39] But Daniel Bell ends his very fine essay with a skeptical question mark.

What will be the Catholic answer? Permit me, in view of offering an answer to this question, the use of a beautiful picture from the letters of St. Augustine. In it he compares man with the industrious bee, which thanks to its wings does not become burdened by the honey which it manufactures.[40] It is not only the articles of consumption that are this honey for man, but above all the whole apparatus of production, which is destined to serve man. And man, thanks to his spiritual powers and supernatural calling, must always and in all places be the goal of the productive processes. The perversion of the natural hierarchy in contemporary industry necessarily led to the evil phenomenon of alienation, which then reacted negatively on the morality and prosperity of society.[41] The return of humanization to industrial labor through the stages of biological rationalization, the integration of labor, interest in human relations, and the development of participation —all must be recognized as a healthy return to a natural order, which is obligatory on all the levels of growing industrial civilization. For instance, the integration of labor is, as it were, a realization of the Thomistic philosophy of labor, of which one is its characteristic of unity, totality, and its union with all the powers of man.[42]

Automation will produce the hoped-for results only when it serves man in his twofold economic role as a producer and consumer; and the contemporary growth of mechanical and organizational technology must be brought to serve as auxiliary forces in realizing man's temporal and supernatural ends.

We can cite in conclusion the words of Cardinal Wyszyński: "There are no such goods that can be alien to man," but these goods are for man, and man is for God.[43]

FOOTNOTES

1. K. Marx, *Ökonomisch-Philosophische Manuskripte* (1884); Marx-Engels, *Kleine ökonomische Schriften* (Berlin, 1955). See H. Popits, *Der Entfremdete Mensch, Zeitkritik und Geschichtsphilosophie des jungen Marxs* (Basel, 1953).
2. B. Suchodolski, *U podstaw materialistycznej teorii wychowania* (Warsaw, 1957) 105–113.
3. Fulton Sheen, *Sursum Corda* (London, 1956).
4. Stefan Cardinal Wyszyński, *Duch pracy ludzkiej* (Poznań, 1957) 8.
5. W. Missiuro, "Industrializacja a czynnik ludzki," *Przegląd Techniczny* November, 1959.
6. D. Bell, *Praca a jej gorycze* (Paris, 1957) 47.
7. See K. Wandelt, *Istota i rodzaje postępu technicznego* (Poznań, 1960) 66.
8. See Ch. Adamiecki, *L'Organization scientifique et son rôle dans là vie économique* (Warsaw, 1932) 13.
9. M. Reynaud, "Ewolucja pracy przemysłowej," *Antologia wiedzy o pracy ludzkiej* (Warsaw, 1959) 94–95.
10. G. Friedmann, *Maszyna i człowiek* (Warsaw, 1960) 12.
11. See F. Taylor, *Scientific Management* (New York, 1947).
12. F. Taylor, *Shop Management* (New York, 1911) 59.
13. See J. March and H. Simon, *Organizations* (New York, 1958).
14. G. Friedmann, *Où va le travail humain* (Paris, 1950).
15. L. Walther, *La Psychologie du travail* (Geneva, 1947).
16. G. Friedmann, *Maszyna i człowiek* 153.
17. D. Bell, *Praca a jej gorycze* 50.
18. M. J. Vincent and J. Moyers, *New Foundations of Industrial Sociology* (Princeton, 1959).
19. See A. Matejko, "Socjologia a przemysł współczesny," *Kultura i społeczeństwo* 1 (1958) no. 1, 96.
20. D. Bell, *Praca a jej gorycze* 19.
21. See J. Kwejt, *Elementy teorii przedsiębiorstwa* (Warsaw, 1959) and P. Drucker, *The Practice of Management* (New York, 1954).
22. See J. C. Larson, *Czynnik ludzki w zapobieganiu wypadkom przy pracy* (Wrocław, 1961) 63–64.
23. See G. Friedmann and M. Carre, "Czy zmierzch podziału pracy?" *Antologia wiedzy* (Warsaw, 1959).
24. E. Mayo, *The Human Problems of an Industrial Civilization* (New York, 1933).
25. F. J. Roethlisberger and W. J. Dickson, *Management and the Worker* (Cambridge, 1949).
26. D. C. Lynch, *Leading and Managing Men* (New York, 1950).
27. See M. L. Blum, *Industrial Psychology and its Social Foundations* (New York, 1949) and J. Tiffin, *Industrial Psychology* (New York, 1952).
28. D. Bell, *Praca a jej gorycze* 39.

Jerzy Ozdowski

29. For a report on this conference see *Kultura i społeczeństwo* 1 (1958) no. 1, 221–234.

30. See H. A. Clegg, *General Union* (Oxford, 1954).

31. See R. Dubin, *Working Union Management Relations* (Englewood Cliffs, 1958).

32. See A. Matejko, "Od służby społecznej do businessu," *Kultura i społeczeństwo* 3 (1958) 4.

33. C. W. Mills, *The Power Elite* (New York, 1956) 120–121.

34. G. Friedmann, *Maszyna i człowiek* 178.

35. R. Caussin, "Przeniesienia czynności wykonywanych przez człowieka na maszynie," *Diogène* (1958) no. 28.

36. P. Drucker, *The Practice of Management*.

37. D. Bell, *Praca a jej gorycze* 64.

38. B. Suchodolski, "Wychowanie a perspektywy rozwoju cywilizacji technicznej," *Zeszyty problemowe nauki polski* 17 (1960).

39. G. Friedmann, *Maszyna i człowiek* 384.

40. W. Zdaniewicz, "Augustyńska filozofia pracy," *Roczniki naukowe KUL* 7 (1960) no. 2, 139.

41. See Cz. Strzeszewski, "Obowiązek pracy ludzkiej," *Zeszyty Naukowe KUL* 7 (1960) no. 1, 3.

42. See Cz. Strzeszewski, "Praca źródłem szczęścia," *Roczniki filozoficzne KUL* 6 (1958) no. 2, 10.

43. Stefan Cardinal Wyszyński, *Duch pracy ludzkiej* 40.

THE SOCIOLOGY OF

RELIGION IN POLAND

Józef Majka

IN THE LAST SEVERAL YEARS A DEVELOPMENT IN THE SOCIOLOGY OF religion occurred in the West. This manifested itself in an increased sociographic and statistical investigation as well as in a revitalized discussion of method and ways of arriving at theoretical formulations. This succeeded in throwing positions into relief and in developing at least three tendencies,[1] which will undoubtedly come closer together as the discussion and investigations expand.

This growth of interest in the sociology of religion found a very lively echo in Poland; and especially from the year 1957 our investigations and publications on this subject have gained momentum. This does not mean that previously we were completely unaware of sociological investigations on the subject of religion. On the contrary, Polish sociologists' interest in religion is traced to the very beginning of the twentieth century. In view of the present efforts in research and discussion it would be worthwhile to review the work done thus far and to strike a general balance (since space does not permit a detailed description and analysis) of their results. A comparison and evaluation of the work to date will suggest the probable thrust of future investigations.

All our authors who in some way worked in the sociology of religion can be divided into three groups.

The first group includes those who were interested in religion as an element of social culture, especially popular culture. As researchers, they were interested in ethnology but did not retreat from efforts at broader syntheses and the formulation of theories on religious development and the mutual influences between religion and social life. In this some of them overlap into the philosophy of religion and declare themselves representatives of sociologism, either of the Durkheim or the Marxist school;[2] others are interested principally in the cultural and not the religious-cognitive aspect of the problem, and they usually refrain from formulating theses in the philosophy of religion.

The second group is made up of sociologists from the school of Florian Znaniecki, who are chiefly interested in the sociological aspects of religion, more precisely, religious institutions, activities, and social groups. Among them, too, one can perceive two tendencies. The one undertakes to study the influence of religious institutions and groups on social life, in particular the forming of social, national bonds; the other tries to analyze religious groups, institutions, and social activities, in this way trying to arrive at some generalizations along with the formulation of theoretical statements. These authors are especially interested in the internal structure of the religions and social phenomena under investigation.

The third group of investigators is interested in the religious condition of the Poles. With the aid of sociographic and statistical investigations they try to discover what role religion plays in the daily life and in shaping the life attitudes of particular groups in the Polish population. Here one perceives two clearly different methods of investigating the subject. One group, mostly laymen, concentrates on testing, the subject of which is religious attitudes among the various statistical groups. This deals with a general orientation, namely, to what degree the members of the group under investigation feel themselves bound to religion and the Church. The second group, represented by Catholic centers, tries to detect whether and to what degree Christ is present in the lives of the faithful, and also to what degree religious social groups (above all the parish) unite their members with the Church, as the Mystical Body of Christ. Thus, these investigations have an analytical character.

The sequence preserved in listing the groups not only has a logical but also a historical significance. In the same sequence we shall examine their accomplishments somewhat more thoroughly.

I. INVESTIGATIONS OF THE RELIGIOUS CULTURE OF THE POLISH PEOPLE

Popular culture has been and is a subject of interest for ethnographers, who describe and gather its various manifestations.[3] At the moment we are not concerned with ethnographic works that form a veritable mine for sociologists. What concerns us are the sociologists' efforts, often based on this very material, at syntheses and general characterizations of the religious culture of the Polish people.

We must mention here before all else the name of Stefan Czarnowski,[4] whose sociological eduction occurred under the influence of the school of Durkheim, since he was a student of M. Mauss and H. Hubert.[5] This is evident especially in his early works in sociology and religion, for instance, in his work about St. Patrick, the national hero of Ireland.[6] The author tries to show that saints and religious heroes are the representatives of a social event or group, the personification of some social value.[7] Furthermore, he does not oppose the historical existence of St. Patrick, but rather distinguishes the historical Patrick from the mythological Patrick —thus he considers that the legends which grew up around that person have a social significance and seem to answer definite social needs. This characterizes his entire analysis of the life and cult of St. Patrick, as well as the comparison of his history with analogous situations in other religious cults. This tendency toward "mythologizing" appears also in Czarnowski's other works dealing with the history of religion. In Czarnowski myth always corresponds to some social need, for even religion itself, in his conception, has a social character and a social beginning. According to his opinion, this is so with everything that is in man.[8]

The sociologism of Durkheim appears most expressly in his definition of a religious fact. Czarnowski does not doubt that "religious phenomena are a distinct category of fact,"[9] but at the same time he emphasizes that "in religious facts there appears not only the influence, but also the effective cooperation of the whole social group"; and he concludes that religious facts are "social facts, and the representations on which they depend are collective representations."[10] It follows from this that for him religion is an element of social culture, created by a given collective, more exactly by a series of collectives, since "culture is essentially an intergroup phenomenon."[11] For Czarnowski religious culture and the religion of a given group are interchangeable terms.[12]

Here we are interested above all in what Czarnowski wrote about the religious culture of the Polish people.[13] In a small work devoted to this subject[14] he states the characteristics of the Polish peasants' religion at the beginning of the present century. The Polish village is obviously Catholic, but the author proceeds from the supposition that there exists a mutual adaptation between religion and the group which professes it, and hence the Catholicism is of a particular type.[15] According to Czarnowski this adaptation occurs automatically; it is not planned but arises from the mutual influence of religion on the collective and of the collective on religion. The result of this mutual influence actually engages Czarnowski's interest. He tries to describe the typical manifestations of the content and form of the Polish peasant's Catholicism:

1. It is a "confessional nationalism" of a special kind,[16] depending on a combination of Polonism and Catholicism, that it not only leads to the conviction that every Pole is a Catholic, but it also expresses itself in such statements that any Catholic who is not Polish is a poor one (dajczkatolik).

2. The second feature of this religious attitude is its social, communal character. It is connected with the local group through cooperative, communal participation in devotions, with the regional group and with the national group through a bond of religious consciousness of regional and national centers of cult to which they conduct communal pilgrimages and from which they bring souvenirs carefully preserved, and so forth.

3. The religious attitude of the village is closely bound up with daily life and penetrates it. "In this way," writes Czarnowski, "all moments of the peasant's life from his birth to his death, all domestic and field work, all the cares and joys of the villager, his home and family life, the village and the community—all this is protected by Blessed Mother of Częstochowa, before whose picture at Jasna Góra occur the solemnities expressing the devotion of the whole people."[17] Thus the cult's very character and its content impose themselves upon the family life and the agricultural tasks of the faithful.

4. The Catholicism of the village conditioned by the senses is of a practical kind. Mystical flights are rare, and even rarer are theoretical conflicts and philosophical considerations. All religious representations have a realistic form and are relevant to the senses (lifelike statues of the saints). Moral and cult aspects play a most important role. An expression of this sense orientation, according to Czarnowski, is the vivid cult of images, the connection of cult with certain localities, and the tendency to dramatization.

5. Finally, the religious attitude of the village is traditional and ritualistic. The attachment to traditional ceremonies is so great that any change provokes violent opposition. This is closely related to the forms of communal social life. "The peasant would

cease to be himself, would cease feeling as a particular member of a particular community and as fulfilling certain functions in it, if he did not scrupulously perform those religious actions which were traditional in that collective."[18]

These observations are undoubtedly interesting and even valuable as a presentation of the problematic. The stated characteristics, however, are not adequately documented. The author limits himself to producing a series of examples. The characterization does not represent the actual state of affairs at the time it was made (1937), for the author gives an account of the changes that were occurring in the Polish village in the interwar period. He writes: "The Polish village in the last thirty years, and especially in the postwar period, is in a fermentation of spirit; and this fermentation grows more violent, is penetrating more deeply, and is intimately associated with the changes that are occurring in the whole national organism. It is possible to predict a transformation of religious life that will be far-reaching in the direction of dividing the totality of collective life as well as a deepening of an ethical and doctrinal kind."[19]

Moreover, these characteristics have a purely plastic character. The author does not detect here any distinct geographical variations or social levels. He does not detect any difference in the religious attitude of a mountaineer, a person from the Poznań province, or Podlasie; he does not consider that it is possible to speak of a more or less intense religious life, or of different degrees of Catholic orthodoxy, as was indicated by Thomas and Znaniecki.

Czarnowski's observations recall in some points the comments of L. Krzywicki, made earlier in his sketch *Do Jasnej Góry*.[20] Krzywicki's views on religion resulted from the influences of Durkheim, enhanced by historical materialism and his interest in ethnology. Krzywicki investigated the manifestations of the religious life of the ancient inhabitants of Żmudź,[21] and his interpretation of the data (the same as observed in the sketch *Do Jasnej Góry*) is Marxist. Krzywicki thinks that the forms of religious attitudes result from the social and economic structure, and that a close link exists between the religious life of man and the general conditions of his existence, namely, that "the manner of work, environment, and the conditions of subsistence"[22] are decisive in forming a religious attitude. Thus Krzywicki sees the evolution of village religious attitudes quite differently from Czarnowski. At the time when the latter was seeing the beginnings of religious deepening and foretelling its progress, Krzywicki, in accordance with the theses of Marxism, predicted the demise of religion in proportion to the growth of culture, and especially to the development of technology.[23]

The author of the book *Culture and the Religious Village* tries to combine the two views, as well as to develop them and expand them with the results of his own observations.[24]

W. I. Thomas and F. Znaniecki, authors of a well-known work on the Polish emigrants, present an interesting characterization of the religious life of Polish peasants.[25] The sociographical material on which they base their conclusions is the letters of peasant families living in Europe and America, but in their characterization of the religious attitude they appeal to the ethnographic materials gathered by O. Kolberg and the Polish Academy of Arts in Cracow. They distinguish four types of religious attitude among the Polish peasants, but they are not certain whether these distinct types correspond to distinct groups of people, or whether they are but four stages in the development of religious life. Nor do they exclude the possibility that particular people, or groups respectively, can to some degree combine the four types.[26]

1. The first type is a particular kind of religious-magical adaptation, depending on a tendency to animate all natural subjects which people in a village meet in their everyday life. This expresses a solidarity with nature and a kind of devoted coexistence with her. It appears in the individualization of the simplest objects; in ascribing to an animal the ability to understand man, and even a moral evaluation of its conduct; and the attaching of special importance to certain places, things, and animals—respect for some, dislike and even fear of others. With this is connected the authority of certain people (auguries, wise men). Religious elements blend here and are not distinguished from magical elements or from elements of esthetical experience (which the authors do not seem to appreciate).

One receives the impression that the authors of this description lack a good definition of religion. Without such a definition, the sociologist is not in a position to distinguish certain religious phenomena from others, no matter how similar they are.[27]

2. According to these authors, the second type is characterized by a belief in spirits associated in some way with various material objects. These are either good spirits who help man, or wicked spirits prepared to injure man. The authors mention a series of such spirits and relate this to a belief in the appearances of deceased souls, angels, and devils, something that had its beginning

in Christianity. They believe that faith in spirits includes religious elements but the practices accompanying it are simply magic,[28] and the authors declare that people with this type of religion sometimes understand Christian practices in a magical manner. Consequently they reduce Christianity to a primitive state.

3. The third type is completely Christian, purified of all pagan elements. It is characterized by a strong bond with the parochial group, understood as an enlarged family; a vital participation in parochial and communal religious practices; participation in solemnities, pilgrimages, and devotions; a typical religious attitude toward God, the Blessed Mother, and the saints. The attitude toward the devil shows some elements of magic. The final feature is a recognition of and emphasis on the high authority of the priest as a representative of God.[29] This also affects strongly and positively the moral attitude of the person and his altruistic relationship to his neighbors.

4. The rarest is the final type, an individual mysticism, marked by a deep experience of a personal relationship with God and a tendency to personal perfection. This does not conform with the practical attitude of the Polish peasant. These phenomena appear in large numbers only in exceptional periods, in times of particular misfortune, and in particular experiences of fate. However, it is frequent with country women who have gone from the village to the city.[30]

This presentation gives a somewhat richer and stratified picture of the religion of the Polish peasant. However, the confusion of certain religious elements with others and the failure to place them in time and space darken the picture. Not even the object of the religious types is adequately determined, so that basically it is a characterization rather than a typology in the strict meaning of the word.

J. St. Bystroń should also be included in the group of sociologists interested in religion as an element of culture. Principally this concerns his works of synthesis, which present the features of Polish religion in the past[31] as well as provide a glance at the Church's influence and its role in the shaping of popular culture.[32] In fact, these are considerations from the history of culture and ethnology rather than from the sociology of religion, but they include considerable material, problems, and theses that necessarily interest the sociologist of religion.

Today all these generalizations must awaken serious methodological reservations. They include statements that are too general, frequently not precise enough, and lacking adequate documentation. The challenging problem presented in them is not stated systematically enough. They do not transcend the range of a generalized description. However, they possess great value insofar as they suggest directions of research and establish a point of departure. The methodological value of Thomas and Znaniecki's studies is so much the greater because they are the result of working definite sociographic material; but even the statement of Czarnowski has sound value at least as a synthetical sociographical description.

II. INVESTIGATIONS OF THE INFLUENCE OF RELIGION ON SOCIAL LIFE AND ANALYSES OF SOME RELIGIO-SOCIAL CATEGORIES

The investigations of Thomas and Znaniecki concerning the Polish emigration in the United States gained several continuators, who in their works take into account the influence of religious factors—especially the parochial bond—on the social life and national consciousness of the emigrants. According to Znaniecki, the parochial bond is one of the chief features of the Polish peasants' religion. It is no wonder that in their investigations his disciples stay close to the role of the parish, be it their native one or the national one in the life of the emigrants. J. Chałasiński[34] conducted such investigations; T. Makarewicz analyzed the role of the native parish;[35] and S. Nowakowski[36] considered the problem in his researches. The subject of their interest deals with the emigration's particular conditions of life. In these circumstances the bond with the native as well as with the national local parish is most powerful, and the parish itself necessarily assumes a series of nonreligious functions. This area of nonreligious influence by the parish and its functions chiefly interests the above mentioned authors.

In accordance with the methodological suggestions of F. Znaniecki,[37] these authors try to discover how the particular function of the parish appears in the eyes of the emigrants themselves, and how they represent that role in their testimonies.[38] Hence, the principal source of these investigations is interviews with the emigrants, the emigrants' letters written to their parish priests, the reports of the emigrant press, its commentary, and so forth. The results of these investigations confirm not only Znaniecki's thesis about the "parochial" character of popular Catholicism but also Czarnowski's thesis about its "national" coloring. The most drastic expression of this was the establishment of the Polish National Church among the emigrants.

A second group of authors, under the influence of the Znaniecki school, concentrated their efforts on the analysis of some categories, the activity of respective social groups. The works of Fathers F. Mirek,[39] E. Wojtusiak,[40] and W. Zdaniewicz[41] deserve attention. Mirek tries to formulate a sociological theory of the parish as a social group. First of all, he makes an analysis by comparing several parishes, their origin, and their development in different regions and at different times, and by trying to detect the essential elements of each—the result of which brought about his definition of a parish.[42] To support his research he used the analysis of the Church-State conflict in France, with the emphasis on the role of the parish in that conflict. The detailed elements of his findings lead to an emphasis on the role of the priest in the parish and to a definition of the significance of social relations and activities in the life of the parish. Social relations include also the instruments of these relations, among them naturalization, ideology, accommodation, assimilation; finally he interests himself quite broadly in the problem of the institutionalization of social relations in the parish.

Although the author tries to arrive at a definition of the parish through induction, the work basically retains an analytic character, and its chief significance lies in the fact that it sketches a great part of the sociological problem connected with the parish. If one considers the momentous pioneering character of the work, one refrains from complaining that the author does not present the problem completely.[43]

The work of E. Wojtusiak on the sociology of the priesthood is purely analytic. The author represents the type of writer who, having fixed a problem for himself, tries to gather absolutely everything that has been said on the subject from different points of view, in every kind of literature, and in every area; then, making a selection of this rich material, he tries to form a total picture of the problem relating to vocation, the social personality, and the state of the priesthood.[44] In this manner he gives a broad view of the problem, not only in sociological terms but also in psychological, theological, and canonical terms, related in some way to the general notion of the priesthood. Undoubtedly, a more critical evaluation of the materials the author relied upon would certainly have helped his work. True enough, the author makes the reservation that his work is only the presentation of a problem. But the posing of a problem is nothing other than the total of

235

Józef Majka

working hypotheses, which the author basically advances and which he somehow establishes, unless perhaps he maintains only the position of a historian by simply recording their development.

It is worthwhile to note that in Wojtusiak's work, as in Mirek's, one of the principal and important sources for the investigator is personal testimony. This is understandable if we consider that we have here the representatives of the school of Znaniecki, who in his methodological suggestions leaves no small place to this source in sociological investigations and researches.[45]

The works of Zdaniewicz have a different character, although they remain within the circle of the Znaniecki school. He borrows from Znaniecki not only mere methodological principles, but also the very theory of social action. On the basis of abundant material gathered from all of Poland in the interwar period, and documentary material dealing with the origin, development, and operation of Catholic Action, the author carries out a sociological analysis of it as social action. He investigates the assembled material in relationship to the normative system which in this case he finds in the directives of the Apostolic See in the matter of Catholic Action. The general theory of social actions[46] serves as a point of departure and a schema of considerations. Their principal task is the analysis, in the light of the normative system, of that collection of religious social actions occurring in time and place—which made the total of Catholic Action—from the viewpoint of their religious correctness, sociological correctness, their social usefulness and, finally, from the point of view of their function in the Church as well.

The author's conclusions dealt with the effectiveness of this activity and included an effort at defining that combination of factors which was decisive in that in the given circumstances (historical, socio-cultural and socio-political) Catholic Action assumed precisely this form in Poland and developed a definite style of social action. The work is at once a development of Znaniecki's theory of social action and an attempt at its verification. One can find in the work a series of statistical and cartographic data which illustrate the dimensions and scope of the phenomenon.

The common feature of all the works described is the search for some way to investigate socio-religious phenomena in dependence on and in connection with the assortment of methodological means proposed by Znaniecki. In spite of their differences, all of them belong within the limits of the sociology of religion, although not all the authors mentioned expressly and consciously placed themselves within that discipline. They believe that their works fit simply into the framework of general sociology. Hence, some specific methodological problems of the sociology of religion are unsolved, or they are solved "by feeling." But these works testify that at that time the problem of religion was already very vital in the consciousness of Polish sociologists, and some of these works (e.g., Mirek) have a pioneer character even in a world at large.

III. STATISTICAL-QUESTIONNAIRE AND SOCIOGRAPHIC INVESTIGATIONS ON RELIGIOUS ATTITUDES

In Poland today sociological research in the sociology of religion is under a dual influence. There is the influence of the statistical, cartographic, and sociographic investigations of Catholicism, begun in France by G. Le Bras. In addition, the present-day interviews, based chiefly on religious attitudes, have become quite popular.[47] This latter method of research seems to be particularly close to sociologists trained under Znaniecki's influences, since it answers to a certain degree his notion of the "humanistic co-factor," and at the same time is the result of the theory of Znaniecki and Thomas, who saw in the investigation of social attitudes the most important area of sociological investigation.

The first to suggest the need of undertaking such investigations in Poland was L. Halban.[48] Only ten years later, under the immediate influence of literature and contacts from the West, absorption in that problem grew and informative and methodological articles in this field began to appear.[49] Following this, certain circles undertook regional investigations of Polish Catholicism.

These investigations can be divided into three groups: investigation of religious attitudes (mostly questionnaire); statistics on the practice of religion; and religious sociography. These three tendencies overlap in certain cases.

In the first group, special attention is merited by the investigations of the religious attitudes of students in Warsaw, conducted by the Department of Sociology of the University of Warsaw under the direction of Professor S. Ossowski.[50] They were conducted twice (1958 and 1961) with a representative group, chosen by lot; in each case there was also another group. The organizers of the investigations believe that the results obtained in the two investigations provide a basis for comparisons and conclusions dealing with the dynamics of attitudes. The questions dealing with the students' attitudes toward the Catholic religion and morality were placed in the questionnaire in the midst of many other questions. The content and character of the questions together with the percentage of the results are illustrated in the table below.[51]

Content of Question	Category of Answer	1958 %	1961 %	Difference %
To what category do your religious beliefs most nearly belong?	a. Belief deep and systematic practice.	7.4	4.9	−2.5
	b. Belief and systematic practice.	25.3	15.7	−11.6
	c. Belief but irregular practice.	34.6	34.2	−0.4
	d. Belief but no practice.	6.3	12.3	+6.0
	e. Agnostic.	7.4	8.1	+0.7
	f. No belief but practice.	4.1	4.9	+0.8
	g. No belief, no practice.	10.4	14.9	+4.5
	h. Decided opponent of religion.	1.9	3.2	+1.3
	i. Without interest or views.	2.2	2.7	+0.5
	x. Lack of data.	0.1	0.8	+0.7
What is your relationship to the moral principles of the Catholic Faith?	a. The moral principles of Catholicism are the best and most sufficient.	20.1	8.9	−11.2
	b. All the moral principles of Catholicism are just, but must be supplemented by other principles.	33.1	30.9	−2.2
	c. Most of the principles are just, but I do not agree with all of them, hence they do not suffice for man.	36.4	42.7	+6.3
	d. Religious morality is alien to me, but I consider some principles just.	8.2	15.6	+7.4
	e. The moral principles of Catholicism are completely alien to me.	2.2	4.5	+2.5
	x. Lack of data.		0.8	

First of all, the questions themselves require a critical analysis. It is true that they were so formulated that the answers do not give a factual picture of the religious attitudes of the respondents, but rather a picture of their current personal convictions. It is usually difficult to define and evaluate one's own religious status. A conviction about one's own religious condition within brief periods is subject to greater hesitations than are the attitudes themselves, for so much depends on momentary dispositions or misfortunes in one's religious life. We add, too, that the questions lacked flexibility, and the suggested answers were so formulated that, dependent on the disposition of the respondent, they could be applied as statements of fact or as acceptable evaluation. Besides, the classes of answers (especially the first three classes and even the first five classes) contained distinctions so subtle and only slightly measurable, that it must have been very difficult for the respondent not to select answers accidentally. We may admire the determination of nearly 10 per cent of the students in 1958 who admitted that they believed deeply and were practicing faithfully, but we might not easily agree that their religious attitude was actually four classes higher than that of the student who described himself as "agnostic," for at the given moment he was suffering difficulties in the faith.

Similar caution can be suggested for the second question, in which it was not made clear to the respondent whether the question dealt with his theoretical evaluation of Catholic morality or his practical relationship to it—for these two matters do not always go together.

Nor are we entirely certain whether the comparison of the results of the two investigations (separated by only three years) of different groups will allow the formulation of conclusions on the subject of the dynamics of religious attitudes. Perhaps, too, it is merely a test of the growth or decline of one's readiness to declare personal convictions. It would seem, then, that investigations of such delicate matters would prove more effective if the test questions were carefully planned.

It is unfortunate that the defects in the questionnaire brought about such inaccurate results of these very interesting investigations, the more so since the analysis by A. Pawełczyńska, conducted to discover a series of correlations, merits attention from every viewpoint.[52]

Fewer reservations are aroused by the investigations conducted by the OBOP of Polish Radio on the views of youth in correlation with their membership in social and political organizations.[53] In this study, which included 2,746 persons, there was no demand for precise declarations, but, nonetheless, the effort was made to discover whether the respondents were consistent in their Catholic convictions. In our judgment, there were two well-chosen supplementary questions, one theoretical and one practical, the tabulation of which is given below.

Results %
I consider myself a Catholic 78.2
I consider myself an atheist 4.3
These matters do not concern me 5.0
I do not have a definite stand in this matter 11.3
Lack of particulars 0.2

The question designed to test the coherence of theoretical views dealt with faith in the creation of the world by God. The answer "yes" was given by 70.6 per cent; "no," 9.3; "I do not know," 20.1 of the respondents.

The test of the practical coherence of convictions was in the matter of marriage. Of the respondents 70 per cent were in favor of ecclesiastical marriage; only 7.4 in favor of civil marriage; 16.0 would allow the mate to decide; and 6.3 did not know how they would act in the matter.

The inquiry method was also used in the investigations of religious attitudes of persons engaged in scientific work.[54] Questionnaires were directed to such workers in Poland (about 5,000), 33.2 per cent of whom sent replies (1,366).[55]

Results %
Believing and practicing 25.19
Believing but not practicing 15.16
Attached to tradition 12.00
Indifferent 10.90
No belief 22.03
Opponents of religion 7.69
Individual system of beliefs 1.25
Believing and anticlerical 1.62
Others 1.16
Lack of responses 3.01

The investigations, although allowing greater freedom in the answers than that given the students, were much more lacking in their particular classification of attitudes than were those carried out previously. Yet professors, in terms of age and classification, were in a better position than the students to specify more precisely their relationship to religion. Even if we take into consideration all the difficulties of classifying voluntary responses, on the basis of the investigation we can declare that 54 per cent of the scientific workers maintain a relationship to the church, and 55 per cent acknowledge some religious bond. Over 33 per cent maintain an indifferent relationship toward religion, while 7.7 oppose religion. The correlation of these attitudes with the particular scientific specialties is also interesting; however, at present we do not know the exact status of the problem in presenting the results.

The investigations of religious attitudes conducted among the guests of the workers' hotels in Silesia also deserve attention.[56] The method of interviews was used here, and in this way about 700 persons, between 16 to 30 years of age, were questioned; about 90 per cent of these came from villages or towns of no more than 20,000 inhabitants. In these investigations there was a correlation with age, origin, education, area of residence in the city, and attitude toward persons thinking otherwise. The small number interviewed in the correlated group means that the results cannot be considered as fully certain.[57] But the general picture is interesting, even though its ultimate value depends on the manner of conducting the interviews and on the respondents' confidence in the interviewer.

Results	%
Practicing zealously	2.5
Believing and practicing	48.5
Believing but practicing irregularly	28.5
Not practicing because of indifference	7.0
Not practicing because of anticlericalism	3.0
Unbelieving	9.5

One can see that the schemata of research in religious attitudes in all the above mentioned investigations are quite close. The investigation conducted by OBOP of Polish Radio is an exception. Investigations of this type can only give a general orientation in the adjustment of particular groups to religion. Efforts at a more detailed analysis of these attitudes and the discovery of correlations give problematic results. This leads to a demand for a revision of method in these investigations and in every case a renewed analysis of the questionnaire. But this does not mean that these efforts failed to produce useful and even interesting results. At

Józef Majka

least, they confirmed the opinion that between 80 to 90 per cent of Polish youth feel themselves bound to religion in some way, at least through this that they believe. The cases of the scientific workers present a special problem, and it would be an interesting investigation to compare the religious attitudes of scientific workers with those of the Polish intelligentsia in general.

Certain possibilities of comparison are provided by investigations of the religious practices of teachers in one of the largest cities in Poland (Łódź).[58] From them it appears that 60.3 per cent of those studied participate in religious life—the percentage of women being some higher (63.2). The percentage is higher among teachers having intermediate education (62.0) than among those having a complete or incomplete higher education (58.1). There is an interesting correlation between the age and the religious practice of those who were studied:[59]

Age Group	% Practicing	% Not Practicing	% No Answers	% Total
18–24	75.2	24.0	0.8	24.0
25–29	54.8	44.4	0.7	26.8
30–39	63.8	35.1	1.0	18.6
40–49	57.1	40.0	2.8	6.9
50–	49.6	40.3	10.0	23.6

In the same manner, that is, by investigating those interested, a survey of religious practices was made among the Lyceum youth.[60] These investigations were conducted in 1958 and 1959 in two cities. In the first case the questionnaire was sent to all the students of the tenth class of the lycees in a city of about 200,000; the second dealt with youth in professional schools of the Technicum type in a city of about 100,000. From an analysis of the results it is clear that in the first case only 76.8 per cent of the boys fulfill their fundamental religious obligations, while among girls the percentage is 97.8.[61] In the second instance both figures are some percentage points higher. The frequency of particular practices in the first instance is as follows:

Type of practice	% Boys	% Girls	% Together
Sunday Mass	68	90	82
Easter Communion	94	98	97
Daily prayers	55	85	75

After comparing all the results of the investigations mentioned so far, a twofold hypothesis suggests itself: the younger generation is more closely bound to religion than the older generation, and practices it more faithfully; persons of higher education are less bound to religion and practice it less fervently than persons on a lower level of education. The confirmation or correction of these hypotheses would demand further investigations, broader and more complete statistical material, a more penetrating analysis of the character of the religious attitudes among particular groups and, especially, its general circumstances and structure. This demands a further and better conducted investigation of attitudes and broader statistics for practice as well as particular sociographic investigations of carefully chosen groups.

These investigations are being conducted in various centers. For instance, efforts to determine the statistical frequency of attendance at Sunday services by the faithful are being made. Data from the region of Warsaw indicate that 53 per cent of those obliged to do so attend Sunday mass, whereas in the archdiocese of Warsaw the frequency is 73. Calculations made in two other rural dioceses show that the frequency there fluctuates between 75 and 100 per cent in certain parishes.

Another tendency in the research deals with priestly and religious vocations,[62] their dynamics, as well as the social conditions of their development. These investigations are continuing. Besides this, the social function of the priest in Polish society is an object of interest,[63] as is the social role of particular clerical positions and the relationship of particular social groups with the clergy.

The third tendency includes monographical research, whose subject is religious social groups (parish, deanery, diocese, religious order, and the like). This research leads to an understanding of the structure of these groups and to a definition of the function of particular activities and institutions in these groups and in the church. The findings also permit the fixing of the influence of various social factors on religious attitudes and, finally, offer a more perfect characterization of the religious attitude itself and the direction of its various tendencies.

The sociologism of Durkheim and the economic determinism of Marx burdened Polish sociology of religion at its very beginning, but they exist today only in lay circles. Znaniecki's influence on Polish sociology determined the fact that Polish sociologists, interested in religious phenomena, kept their conclusions strictly in the realm of sociology without forming any theses in the philosophy of religion. This was undoubtedly progress. In addition, the achievements of the other camp have been rather slight.

Józef Majka

Investigations, as they developed after 1957, presage an interesting future, in spite of some methodological failures.[64] Although, perhaps, not yet as advanced, these investigations remain in close contact with the development of similar research in the West. The results arrived at so far give only the general orientation in religious conditions of some statistical groups. The generalized hypotheses, suggested by the presentation and comparison of these results, demand further confirmation, which will be possible only with the further development of many-sided investigations.

FOOTNOTES

1. See J. Majka, "Socjologia religii w ujęciu niemieckiej szkoły strukturalnej," *Zeszyty Naukowe KUL* 2 (1959) no. 3, 53–69; "Socjologia religii w ujęciu Prof. G. Le Bras a socjologia duszpasterska," *ibid.* 3 (1960) no. 1, 91–108.

2. In the field of religious knowledge Marxism is undoubtedly sociologism, but with this feature that it raises the influence of economic factors to the level of first importance. See Ch. Hainchelin, *Pochodzenie religii* (Warsaw, 1954).

3. The results of their work are not only the ethnographic museums, but also their numerous publications among which one is especially worthy of attention: O. Kolberg's *Lud,* published by PAU, *Materiały antropologiczno-archeologiczne i etnograficzne.*

4. He lived 1879–1937. In the academic years 1935–1936 and 1936–1937 he lectured at the University of Warsaw on the sociology of religion. A collection of his writings appeared only twenty years after his death: Stefan Czarnowski, *Dzieła* (Warsaw, 1956) 5 vols.

5. N. Assorodobraj, "Życie i dzieło Czarnowskiego," in Stefan Czarnowski, *Dzieła* V, 122.

6. See S. Czarnowski, "Kult Bohaterów i jego społeczne podłoże, Święty Patryk bohater narodowy Irlandii," *Dzieła* IV.

7. *Ibid.* 30.

8. Czarnowski, *Dzieła* I, 15: "Everything which is in man has a social character."

9. *Ibid.* II, 235.

10. *Ibid.* II, 238.

11. *Ibid.* I, 19.

12. *Ibid.* p. 88.

13. Besides the work on St. Patrick, Czarnowski wrote a series of similar works on the history of mythical cults (see *Dzieła* III, 139–160, 161–217). Worthy of consideration are also his studies on the subject of religion and magic (*Dzieła* III, 221–241).

14. Czarnowski, "Kultura religijna wiejskiego ludu polskiego," *Dzieła* I, 88–107.

15. *Ibid.* 88.

16. *Ibid.* 91.

17. *Ibid.* 94.

18. *Ibid.* 106.
19. *Ibid.* 107.
20. L. Krzywicki, "Do Jasnej Góry," *Studia sociologiczne* (Warsaw, 1923) 147–164.
21. L. Krzywicki, *Żmudź Starożytna* (Warsaw, 1906).
22. Krzywicki, "Do Jasnej Góry" 163.
23. *Ibid.* 159.
24. E. Ciupak, *Kultura religijna wsi* (Warsaw, 1961). The author published a series of articles in the periodical *Euhemer,* but they are mostly another version of the book. I review it in "Książka o religijności wsi," *Tygodnik Powszechny* (1961) no. 25.
25. W. I. Thomas and F. Znaniecki, *The Polish Peasant in Europe and America,* 2nd ed. (New York, 1958) 2 vols.
26. *Ibid.* I, 206.
27. Znaniecki sees the need for separating these phenomena. See F. Znaniecki, "Przedmowa," in F. Mirek, *Elementy społeczne parafii rzymsko-katolickiej* (Poznań, 1928) xi.
28. Thomas and Znaniecki, *The Polish Peasant* I, 235.
29. *Ibid.* 275.
30. *Ibid.* 286.
31. J. St. Bystroń, *Dzieje obyczajów w dawnej Polsce wiek XVI–XVIII* (Warsaw, 1960) I, 295–350.
32. J. Bystroń, *Kultura ludowa* (Warsaw, 1936) 128–199.
33. It would be proper to mention here the investigations by B. Malinowski on the religion of primitive societies; but since he did not investigate the subject within Poland, we are not interested in them in the present article.
34. J. Chałasiński, "Parafia i szkoła parafialna wśród emigracji polskiej w Ameryce," *Przegląd Socjologiczny* 3 (1935) 633–711; "Związek parafialny a świadomość narodowa emigranta," *ibid.* 4 (1936) 547–549.
35. T. Makarewicz, "Emigracja amerykańska a macierzysta grupa parafialna," *Przegląd Socjologiczny* 4 (1936) 521.
36. S. Nowakowski, "Polonia Chicagowska," *Kultura i Społeczeństwo* 1 (1959) 63–97.
37. See F. Znaniecki, *The Method of Sociology* (New York, 1937); J. Szczepański, "Koncepcje metodologiczne socjologii F. Znanieckiego," *Przegląd Socjologiczny* 14/1 (1960) 57.
38. F. Znaniecki, *Wstęp do Socjologii* (Poznań, 1922) 244.
39. F. Mirek, *Elementy społeczne parafii rzymsko-katolickiej* (Poznań, 1928).
40. E. Wojtusiak, *Socjologia kapłaństwa* (Lublin, 1959), mimeographed.
41. W. Zdaniewicz, *Wskazania Piusa XI w liście "Quae Nobis" a ich realizacja w Polsce* (Lublin, 1958), mimeographed.
42. The author mentions the following essential elements of the parish: "1) A priest sent by higher authority that is in union with the bishop of Rome. 2) The association through a social relationship of the priest with a defined (territorial) group of people, with the help of various instruments of social contacts. 3) Acceptance by particular individuals and the assimilation (naturalization) of the ideology announced by the priest. 4) The institutionalization of the functions of the priest and the faithful." See F. Mirek, *Elementy społeczne* 90.
43. Father Mirek gives the essentials of his work in his article "Parish

Józef Majka

Research in Poland," in C. J. Neusse and Th. J. Harte, *The Sociology of the Parish* (Milwaukee, 1951) 341–346. He deals with the investigations undertaken in the dioceses of Cracow and Wilno at the request of the bishops during the interwar period. But they had to be quickly abandoned. A series of monographs on the parish, treating its religious and moral condition, was prepared by the theological faculty of the Jagellonian University after the war. Unfortunately, these monographs are not available.

44. Independently of this, Father Wojtusiak investigated the subject of the social origin of the clergy of the Tarnów diocese.

45. See Szczepański, "Koncepcje metodologiczne" 62.

46. See F. Znaniecki, *Social Actions* (Poznań, 1936).

47. A. W. Green, *Sociology* (New York, 1960) 460.

48. See L. Hałban, *O Potrzebie badań etno-socjologicznych na religijnością* (Lublin, 1946).

49. Some works are: S. Nowakowski, "Religia jako przedmiot badań socjologicznych," *Kultura i Społeczeństwo* 1 (1957) no. 1, 229–233; T. Mrówczyński, "Socjologia i socjografia katolicyzmu w Francji," *Euhemer* 3 (1959) 333–342; J. Majka, "Socjologiczne badanie parafii, *Homo Dei* 28 (1959) 704–715; see also Majka's, "Religia jako przedmiot badań socjologicznych," in *Ateneum Kapłańskie* 60 (1960) 71–81, and his "Socjologia religii w ujęciu Prof. G. Le Bras" in *Zeszyty Naukowe KUL;* W. Zdaniewicz, "Ku socjologicznym badaniom powołań kapłańskich i zakonnych w Polsce," *Homo Dei* 29 (1960) 51–55; E. Ciupak, "Parafia wiejska jako przedmiot badań socjologicznych," *Studia Socjologiczne* 2 (1961) 262–283.

50. A. Pawełczyńska, "Dynamika i funkcje postaw wobec religii," *Studia Socjologiczno-polityczne, no.* 10; see also her article "Studenci a wiara," in *Argumenty* 4 (1960) no. 49; A. Pawełczyńska and S. Nowak, "Światopogląd studentów w okresie stabilizacji," *Przegląd Kulturalny* 10 (1961) no. 46; A. Pawełczyńska, "Les Attitudes des étudiants Varsoviens envers la religion," *Archives de Sociologie des Religions* 12 (1961) 107–132.

51. We produce it according to A. Pawełczyńska, "Les Attitudes" 109. The number investigated was different in each case. The comparison refers to students of the Warsaw Polytechnicum, from whom 269 answers were obtained in 1958 and 335 in 1961.

52. *Ibid.* 111.

53. See *Światopogląd młodzieży a przynależność do organizacjii młodzieżowych,* completed by M. Szaniawska on the basis of materials from Z. Skorzyńska, Public Opinion Research Center of Polish Radio, Warsaw, 1960; J. Maître, "Un Sondage polonais sur les attitudes religieuses de la jeunesse," *Archives de Sociologie des Religions* 12 (1961) 133–144. The data is taken from the latter publication.

54. See I. Nowakowska, "Światopogląd pracowników nauki," *Argumenty* 5 (1961) no. 32. In all the cases mentioned the questions dealing with religious attitudes were included with those relating to political attitudes, among other things.

55. *Ibid.*

56. See R. Kijak and N. Chmielnicki, "Postawy religijne mieszkańców hoteli robotniczych w Gliwicach," *Euhemer* 3 (1959) 668–686.

57. *Ibid.* 677.

58. See A. Wędrychowski, "Przyczynek do badań udziału nauczycieli ludzkich w praktykach religijnych," *Euhemer* 5 (1961) 49–53.
59. *Ibid.* 50.
60. See K. Pychlik, "Religijność męskiej młodzieży licealnej," *Sprawozdanie,* no. 1, Zakład Socjologii Religii KUL (Lublin, 1960), mimeographed.
61. The numerical proportion of boys to girls in the lycees is 1:2.
62. We must mention the investigations of W. Zdaniewicz, "Zagadnienie kryzysu powołań kleryckich w zakonach męskich w Polsce," *Homo Dei* 29 (1960) 525–534; O. R. Wawro, O.F.M., "Powołania kapłańskie a środowisko społeczne," *Sprawozdanie,* no. 2, Zakład Socjologii Religii KUL (Lublin, 1961), mimeographed.
63. E. Ciupak, "Proboszcz wiejski a grupa parafialna," *Euhemer* 5 (1961) no. 2, 67–76. St. Lisowski, "Zagadnienie dystansu społecznego między księżmi a inteligencją w Polsce," *Sprawozdanie,* no. 3; Zakład Socjologii Religii KUL (Lublin, 1962) carried out investigations on the same subject, mimeographed.
64. The investigations described do not entirely exhaust everything that is being published on this subject in Poland. We omitted less important works, either because they are not based on new material but reflect efforts at reworking from a religious viewpoint sociographic materials gathered for other purposes, or because the materials gathered are quite accessible. For instance, some newspapers and periodicals published interviews and then published detailed replies and analyses of the results. Often enough this was not done with sufficient competence and sense of responsibility.

Worthy of particular notice is the work on the historical geography of the Church in Poland, whose object is the preparation of a Historical Atlas of the Church in Poland. This work is being completed by the Institute of Historical Geography of the Church in Poland at the Catholic University of Lublin, under the direction of Prof. Dr. Jerzy Kłoczowski. The studies do have a historical character, but their significance for the sociology of religion, in particular for the sociology of Catholicism, needs no emphasis. A detailed description is not possible, but the work has to be mentioned in order to provide a total picture.

THE EDUCATIONAL TASKS

OF A UNIVERSITY

Stefan Kunowski

THE VIEW THAT THE CONTEMPORARY UNIVERSITY IS ALSO AN EDUCA-
tional institution is daily gaining ground. The most ardent
researchers seek refuge in scientific institutes,[1] but even there,
while they may avoid the problems of training students, they
nevertheless must deal with forming a cadre of younger scientists.
Wherever one has to do with the training of children, youth or
even adults, human relations and the educational needs of man
complicate the task of teaching. These aspects must be considered
even in every business undertaking.[2]

Human endeavor and effort at development necessarily lead to
cooperation with others: the professor with his student, the director of an enterprise with the worker. This cooperation occurs not
only on the level of social relations, but also rises to the higher
plane of direction to a goal and the corresponding influence on the
development and formation of personal internal attitudes, which
bring about a harmonious coordination of work, strengthen the
common good, and confer benefits on the weaker side that is
subject to direction. Such human reactions affect relations in
education and demand a theoretical formulation for the mutual
dependence of people, be it in the school or in a productive
enterprise.

In times past various sanctions provided the norms for the
greater part of social relations. Today the democratization of
social life aims above all at arousing the individual activity of
cooperative units to inculcate such education that they voluntarily
and consciously cooperate with their educators or the directors of
their collective life. For this reason the educational tasks of the

249

university are increasing at an unheard of pace; and together with this there has been a great increase in the practical and theoretical educational study of the higher schools of learning, an academic pedagogy. On this subject a number of periodicals has appeared.[3]

In the present sketch, it will be necessary to consider these five points in order to analyze systematically the educational tasks of the university: know in outline the origin of university pedagogy; examine the growing crisis of university pedagogy and the proposed solutions of the impasse; survey the educational needs of the student in connection with his general development; establish the social-educational tasks of the university; survey the basic methods that the higher school uses in its pedagogical tasks.

I. A sketch of the origin and development of university pedagogy is related immediately to the history of the universities from their beginnings to the present day.[4] In the course of history four basic types of higher institutions of learning developed, namely, the *studium generale,* the medieval university, an autonomous and privileged corporation of teachers and students, directed by the Church, striving for a synthesis of philosophy and theology as the crown of knowledge;[5] the French type of state university, established in Paris by Napoleon in 1808, with a monopolistic task of specialization, to prepare the basic specialists (lawyers, doctors, chemists, etc.);[6] the German type of a scientific-research university, established in Berlin in 1810, in Wrocław in 1811, and in Bonn, for a national development of industry, economy, and culture;[7] and, finally, the English type whose objectives are social enlightenment, after the model of the university of London, which from the year 1836 made possible the obtaining of academic degrees without actual attendance at the university.[8] Indian universities, functioning as examination centers, followed this example in Calcutta, Bombay, and Madras.[9]

Obviously the most common type is the university which in the course of the centuries adjusted itself to the times by drastic reforms. In Poland the Jagellonian University is an example of this. Its six-hundredth jubilee recalls the Diploma of Reform issued by Władysław Jagiełło, the reforms of Rector Dobrocielski in 1603 adopting the system of study to the humanistic *Ratio Studiorum* of the Jesuits, the reforms of Kołłątaj, the reforms of Dietel, and finally the changes of the university in People's Poland.[10]

All types of the universities mentioned above formed and educated the students in a definite direction—be it the ideal of the

Christian, a member of the liberal professions, the scholar and researcher, an educator of society, or at least a member of the *intelligentsia* as a child of his time. For this reason, in the correlation of the university with its chief aims, there were special elements that formed an academic pedagogy in answer to the needs of the school. Thus the Christian Middle Ages began to prepare scholastic handbooks of studies, e.g., Hugh of St. Victor's *Didascolicon,* Dennis the Carthusian's *De vita, moribus ac eruditione scholasticorum,* and Nicholas of Cusa's *Dialogus de recto studiorum fine et ordine,*[11] and finally to formulate the basic principles of study and rules for students, as St. Thomas Aquinas did in his letter on the method of study.[12]

During the Enlightenment the universities, preparing professionals for the royal service, created *encyclopedic compendia,* e.g., Morhof's *Polyhistor* (1688), or Gesner's *Isagoge* (1756), and were concerned with examinations and even with examination questions and answers that sometimes took the form of a catechism, such as that composed by Czartoryski in 1774, *Katechizm moralny dla uczniów korpusu kadetów.*

The scientific universities in Germany developed a new concept of higher schools in the spirit of nationalism, e.g., Fichte, Schleiermacher, or Henry Stefens in *Über die Idee der Universitäten* (1809),[13] but at the same time emphasized the introduction of the student to the methodology of science and the method of study, which Schelling began in 1802.[14] However, it was only at the end of the nineteenth century that E. Bernheim demanded the transformation of the passive methods of study into an activization of the student's work in a seminar.[15] Finally, for the first time, H. Schmidkunz in 1907 distinguished among the tasks of the university the supervision of the students in the form of boarding schools; education in terms of character, truth, criticism, and preparation for life and a profession; and the art of teaching, including method, consultation, lectures, exercises, and independent study.[16]

Then the liberal universities, by a process of democratization, turned their attention to the socialization of knowledge[17] and the tasks of enlightenment in the educational needs of adults, thus underlining the social functions of the higher institutions of learning.[18]

As a result of the cultural influences of the present century, a new university has developed in which the four fundamental tasks are combined in one center: scientific investigations; the training of researchers; professional specialization; and propagating the results of scientific research in society by popularization and the education of youth.[19] The renowned Spanish philosopher Ortega y Gasset described the "Mission de l'Université" as the transmission of culture, the professional training of students, and scientific research. With this synthesis an emerging contemporary academic pedagogy created an amalgam of the several problems, among which the following are prominent: the ideology and theory of the university, emphasizing the dignity, freedom, and social significance of knowledge;[20] advisers and guides for students, including counsel and suggestions with the obligations of university youth;[21] the methodology and technique of intellectual work as well as scientific work;[22] the didactics of higher education in terms of lectures, exercises, practice, and examination;[23] and, finally, subject training, to prepare for study by one's self and to initiate study in some particular field, chiefly by means of bibliography.[24] It would seem that such a general and rich pedagogical theory would already include or embrace the essential needs of the student; that it would provide him with so many motives, stimuli, suggestions and instruments; and that the task of training university youth would not involve any special difficulty. However, after the Second World War signs of dissatisfaction began to appear and much was written about "the crisis."

II. The crisis of the university in Western countries began to appear in its structure. Quite apart from the temporary financial crisis, namely, the one experienced by higher institutions in France,[25] attention was given to the internal problems: the loss of the humanistic viewpoint in the humanities, the destruction of the unity of knowledge, and the increase of specialization caused by the training of specialists for military needs.[26] With the rise of technology and nuclear studies to the first level of interest, universities lost their scientific significance: the *universitas scientiarum* which in the past century had replaced the *universitas magistorum et scholarum*, was dissipated. This destroyed the social bonds, which until then united knowledge and teachers with the students and with the whole of society. Thus, too, the methodological bond of the sciences dissolved. Hence began the search for a way out of the impasse in the university: integration and creation of a "whole," whose goal is to be the development of internal culture.[27]

The basis of this integration and "wholeness" of sciences was to be found in educational work itself. The student was not only to devote himself to his specialized studies, but—as Livingstone formulates it—he is to meet with the problems involved in human life, and by meditation regain the lost sense of wholeness. Therefore, the university is to create a contact with life by developing a conception of life and defining the goals of human existence through the study of philosophy and religion.[28] This view emphasizes the development of humanistic values in education by reading the classics of literature, history, and philosophy from Homer to Whitehead, in order to counterbalance technological training with moral and spiritual attitudes.[29]

Others see the tasks of education in formulating an ideological integration. For instance, the Soviet revolutionary universities develop their struggle for scientific materialism in the spirit of Lomonossov, Sechenev, Timiriazev, Pavlov, and other Russian scholars.[30] At least they try to permeate all sciences with one dialectical methodology.[31]

In this critical situation there has come in the West a return to the "idea of a university," formulated by Cardinal Newman, who, going beyond the classical education of the gentleman, indicated the need for a broad education of the mind on the basis of a real philosophy of life and theology, as the scientific foundation of the unity of human knowledge.[32] Catholic universities, following the ideas of Pius XII,[33] had no need to seek any other basis of integration beyond the denominational character of the institution of learning and its effort to combine with contemporary learning.[34]

Thus we see how the need of integrating the students revivified the philosophical-ideological assumptions of knowledge that are evident in the cultural systems of liberalism, socialism,[35] and Christianity. Yet this way of integrating the atomized scientific specialties is only a means to the immediate object of education, which creates the internal personal integration possible for each student through an all-sided development wherein the psychic phases would be harmonized: the scientifically and practically trained professional; "socialized" citizen; a vitally developed moral character; and a humanistically educated and cultured person.

III. The university, in the student's full development, tries to solve the crisis provoked by the early professional specialization or by an education that is too one-sided from an intellectual standpoint. Ideological excesses in education—for instance, in Hitlerism—which were elevated above independent thought and the need of mastering the objective bases of the sciences, were also a warping of the universities. All these deviations cannot be cured solely by a deepening of the didactics of the higher school,[36] or by the development of the technique of intellectual work and the investigative skill of the scientific disciplines. These ingredients do not exhaust the content of integration in academic pedagogy, for they do not consider all the needs of developing students and do not include the totality of human relations that exist in the academy between the professors and students. The educational tasks of the contemporary university have evolved in so many directions that their realization would result in a universal personal development of youth. At present pedagogical theory considers that the full development of the human being demands his perfection under bodily, intellectual, professional, and moral and esthetic aspect (a total spiritual synthesis).[37] For this goal the university must realize a program for the student's complete development, which in accordance with the historical development of the university's hierarchy of values must include: (1) development of awareness, comprehension, and ability (intellectual education); (2) development of experience, ability in practice and resourcefulness, (practical education); (3) the development of a fine sensitivity, vitality, health, and pleasure (hygienic and physical education); (4) the development of character and principles of human behavior (moral and social education); and (5) the development of creative sensibilities and talents in cultural recreation and the use of leisure time (cultural and esthetic education). Let us examine, in order, what the realization of these educational aims demands from the university.

1. The intellectual training of students is the center around which the other supplementary goals of the university develop. The scientific and investigative activity of the professors and the assistants creates this hearth of light and warmth. This permeates and irradiates their entire didactic activity in lectures, exercises, consultations, examinations, and publications. Only the creative activity of the teaching body can vivify relations with the student and actually eliminate routine; for it produces new results, directions, and methods of research. With all due respect to this creativity, the student's interest in scientific research is formed, a methodological foundation is established, the direction of intellectual development is fixed, zeal for engaging in their own efforts is established, and their creative powers and abilities are developed. The crown of intellectual training in the university is a philosophical synthesis in which respect for truth, objectivity,

tolerance of others' convictions, healthy criticism, and methodical doubt express the real development of the student's thought. Only in such an atmosphere can students grow into candidates for scientific research.

However, the intellectual development of youth cannot be confined to any one method of research, or any one sphere of knowledge. On the contrary, in all studies it is necessary to maintain a sensitivity to related areas or to the bond of a special discipline with the totality of humanistic studies, philosophy, or universal knowledge. Integration of the sciences can best be served by an exchange of professors and students among the universities, series of lectures by foreign scientists, seminars or sessions of an inter-university nature, discussions of the diverse directions of the sciences. Without these means for the exchange of ideas, results, and methods there cannot be created within the walls of the university a live intellectual movement, nor can the intellectual stagnation of students be arrested. The satisfaction of intellectual education usually is reflected in the intensification of the other areas of academic education.[38]

2. The practical training of students ought to increase in intensity with the passage of years. Students must see more clearly the distant perspectives and practical usefulness of their efforts. Professional specialization, growing from one's chosen field of knowledge, demands its preparation and introduction to practice. However, the practical preparation is not to be limited by future professional obligations, but also must embrace social and civic obligations generally imposed upon every man's life. Generally speaking, the need of preparing the student for his future life includes (a) the training of the student through his completion of pedagogical study, which prepares him theoretically and practically for the teaching profession by lectures and exercises and school practice;[39] (b) preparation for marriage and the future establishment of a family by mastering the arts of home economics or the science of household management, that is, cooking, hygiene, esthetics of domestic life, and so on; (c) technical preparation in motorization, communications, and production through a variety of courses which prepare a person for superior performance in life. Thus the contemporary university has grave responsibilities, so that by fulfilling its pedagogical tasks—military, technical or domestic— it will make possible the full development of the student's practical life.[40]

3. Hygienic and physical education is one of the oldest tasks in

the concern of the universities for academic youth. In the past it took the form of guardianship, discussed by Schmidkunz, which from medieval times took an interest in creating burses and residences, and even separate hospitals for the students.[41] Today the task goes beyond medical, dental, and sanitary care of the students. Sanitoria and semi-sanitoria for consumptives need psychic and pedagogical assistance in the struggle against the frustrations of illness in order to ease the process of recovery.[42] The protective tasks of the university include the living conditions of the students, e.g., dining conditions and a system of scholarships, most profitable in the form of a living stipend. These tasks now embrace the totality of physical education, which today includes general physical culture (morning gymnastics, bathing, hiking, living in the fresh air, swimming and sun-bathing), training in sports and camping. All these areas of physical education make possible the satisfaction of individual needs in sport, recreational or medicinal, correcting the deficiencies of a sedentary life, but providing always joy, health, and rest. Contemporary universities have grave obligations in the fulfillment of these tasks.[43]

4. The moral and social education of the student is another aspect of the intellectual formation of the student and goes far beyond scientific and intellectual work. Personalism, or a humanism based on contemporary science,[44] must have permanent support in a personal and social natural morality of the individual student. Just at this time academic youth is most in danger of corruption. Alcoholism, gambling, idleness, and sexual activity are generally recognized as the dangers that most threaten the students. Therefore, work on one's self—on forming the ethical features of character—is an absolutely necessary element in education. The disciplinary commission of a university intervenes in student violations without regard to the dignity of the student. But it will not help much if it is not respected by the permanent commissions that distinguish students for their academic work or for their social action.

The contemporary university must care for the moral and social education[44a] of the students by creating self-governing organizations for student life, beginning with scientific circles and the academic press, and culminating in organizations of more general utility. The university must provide direction, and moral as well as financial assistance. Besides forms of general or self-help, the moral education of youth requires some kind of direction in the form of character or psychological counseling. Pastoral care plays a comparable role in Catholic universities, which have created this form of activity long ago.[45]

5. Finally, cultural and esthetic education supplements moral training. It can devise positive methods for preventing the corruption of individuals; it creates the possibility of sublimating feelings and at the same time uses youth's creative impulses. The traditional forms of the academic theater,[46] or choral singing, do not suffice today. In order to form the esthetic taste, concerts are necessary, especially on records, as are films, television, as well as demonstrations and expositions of the plastic arts.

Competitions, recitative and oratorical, poetic and musical; painting and photographic exhibits; chess tournaments; student publications—all these can open a field for writing and for the development of varied talents.

Esthetics within the universities[47] and the culture of everyday life ought to create an atmosphere of harmony and beauty, thus ennobling thought and activity. Finally, academic solemnities—commencement, matriculation, and doctoral promotions; also the closing of the school year, diversified by recreational performances with cultural entertainments by the students—give charm to academic life by basing it on the esthetic framework of social culture.

Developing the many forms of intellectual, practical, physical, moral, and esthetic education, the present-day university must remember that these numerous tasks must not violate the basic pedagogical principles, which are the principle of autonomy of student activities organized always within the framework of cooperation with the university; the principle of correlating all the supplementary directions of academic training around its core, shaped by the formative and cultural tasks of the university; and the basic harmony between the principal and supplementary areas of education, so that enthusiasm for sports or for the theater will not absorb all the student's energy with resulting damage for his learning, character and even his health. In this way prudence and moderation in achieving life goals have their fundamental validity even in academic life.

IV. The university's task of social education. Beyond these tasks of general education the universities are burdened with deeper and wider responsibilities that involve the radiation of knowledge and culture to society beyond the walls of the university. The maintenance of ties with the life of the country secures advantages for both the university and society.

Above all, there is the need for popularizing scientific achievements and scientific progress among wide social circles, e.g., parents, teachers, special professions—and this by means of university lectures; scholarly societies, scholarly publications; and adult education for the general public and for the working class. Another field for the universities' activities is research into and popularization of historical knowledge about the region where a university exists. Then there is the need of scientific and technical assistance in industry and production. Here not only the polytechnical schools but also the universities can accomplish much, for instance, in psychology and pedagogy and in economic and sociological education. The universities must also cooperate in combatting the social calamities and diseases of its time, for instance, alcoholism, demoralization, corruption, and juvenile delinquency.

It is necessary to organize in the universities the corresponding research, popularize the achievements of science, adapt the suggestions of science in psychological, pedagogical, economic, and sociological counseling to the needs of marriage, parents, children, and family life in general. The initiative and the conceptual work must originate with the professors, but it is always the particular domain of auxiliary forces; for its realization it will be necessary to engage the students who are active in social matters as well as senior students as members of the various societies, for example, the Society of Universal Knowledge, which needs lecturers; the Temperance Society; the Society of Ethical Culture, which needs young organizers; the Polish Red Cross; or the Society for the Protection of Youth. The best student youth must also provide social guardians, court trustees, scout masters, and educators in the struggle against illiteracy or demoralization; readers for the blind; tutors to do their social work for some wages or for their stipends. Such participation in the social work by the university creates the best circumstances for educational work among students. In this manner the educational tasks in a broad education of youth combine with the social and educational tasks of the university, conducted by the professorial body as well as by academic youth under their direction.

V. The university's most important educational methods and means. After establishing the pedagogical tasks of the university, it is necessary to sketch the means for their realization. Since the object of university education is the whole man and his general development, the methods of educational activity must embrace the conscience of the student as well as his convictions, his intellect as well as his activity. Today it is understood that not only the head goes to the university to be "furnished" with knowledge, as Rector M. Kasprzak expressed it, but the whole man comes to the university with all his growing needs, which demand satisfaction. Therefore, we shall consider principally two methods of education applied in academic pedagogy, namely, active and passive methods, which must be reciprocally balanced.

Among the passive methods, based on the reception of impressions, it is necessary to include, above all, the lectures of a general and specialized nature. The direction of the lecture and the reading of the student become the task of literary pedagogy, which struggles against the restriction to anthologies or articles—even more against the use of summaries—and recommends the experience with and contemplation of only the best works of *belles lettres,* history, philosophy, and ethics, etc.[48] Library training cooperates in this by leading the student to independent study,[49] in which the library has a special role in documentation, information, counseling, and propagation of reading.[50] These passive methods include audio-visual aids,[51] in which the films, slides, television, and recordings create a rich collection of modern technical means used in automated museums that combine sound and light on a revolving screen. Because of this, the application of the principles of objectivity has a greater significance, not only in the teaching activity of the university[52] but also in educational work.

By themselves the reading and audio-visual methods do not suffice for the general development of the student. Therefore, they must be supplemented by action and activity, in which certitude rests on contact with living persons rather than merely on books and pictures.[53] Among the active methods, the university disposes of various theatrical productions, with students assuming their future roles, for instance, that of teacher by giving exercises or lectures to their colleagues, the role of defending or prosecuting attorney in court, and so on. Above all, there is the active participation in discussions and in the activity of various groups, in scholarly and social organization in the university.

Taking the matter generally, we say that the organization and activity of university youth, along with directing that activity to noble goals, belong to the educational tasks of the university as a common method and means of realizing its high postulates, which are based on the total role of the university in relation to its students, to national culture, and to the whole of society.

Stefan Kunowski

FOOTNOTES

1. French research institutes associated with universities are mentioned by J. B. Pobietta, *Les Institutions Universitaires en France* (Paris, 1951) 117–126; Polish institutes of the Polish Academy of Sciences are listed in *Informator nauki polskiej 1959–1960* (Warsaw, 1960) 14–43.

2. K. Davis, *Human Relations in Business* (London, 1957); J. Lutosławski *Człowiek w przedsiębiorstwie przemysłowym* (Warsaw, 1960); G. Friedmann, *Maszyna i człowiek* (Warsaw, 1960).

3. *Szkoły wyższe,* a quarterly publication of the Section of Higher Schools of ZNP (from 1938, and restored in 1946); *Życie nauki,* a scientific monthly, Cracow (from 1946 to 1949); *Życie nauki,* a monthly, Warsaw (from 1950 to 1952); *Życie szkoły wyższej,* a monthly, Warsaw (from 1953 to 1957, and in changed form from 1958). German university periodicals are numerous: *Colloquium* (from 1947), *Deutsche Universitäts-zeitung* (from 1946), *Forum* (from 1947), *Hochschuldienst* (from 1948), *Leuchtturm* (a Catholic periodical, restored in 1948), *Studium Generale* (from 1947), *Universitas* (from 1946), *Hochschulwesen* (from 1953).

4. R. Aigrain, *Histoire des Universités* (Paris, 1949).

5. H. Denifle, *Die Enstehung der Universitäten des Mittelalters* (Berlin, 1885); H. Rashdall, *The Universities of Europe in the Middle Ages* (Oxford, 1895); N. Suvorov, *Srednovekovye Universitety* (Moscow, 1898); S. D'Irsay, *Histoire des Universités françaises et étrangères* (Paris, 1933–1935); R. Aigran, *Les Universités catholiques* (Paris, 1935).

6. R. Aulard, *Napoléon et le monopole universitaire, origine et fonctionement de l'Université imperial* (Paris, 1935).

7. G. Kaufmann, *Die Geschichte der deutschen Universitäten* (Stuttgart, 1888–1896); F. Paulsen, *Die deutschen Universitäten und Universitätsstudium* (Berlin, 1902); M. Lenz, *Geschichte der Königlichen Friedrich-Wilhelm Universität zu Berlin* (Halle, 1910).

8. R. Dyboski, "Stulecie Uniwersytetu Londyńskiego," *Przegląd Współczesny* (1927), no. 67; J. Chałasiński, *Społeczeństwo i wychowanie* (Warsaw, 1958) 171–176; D. Logan, *The University of London: An Introduction* (London, 1956) 7–20; its social character was underlined by the fact that from 1856 the convocation of graduates shared in the government of the senate. See P. Dunsheath and M. Miller, *Convocation in the University of London* (London, 1958).

9. S. R. Dongerkery, *History of the University of Bombay (1857–1957)* (Bombay, 1957)

10. H. Barycz, *Historia Uniwersytetu Jagiellońskiego w epoce humanizmu* (Cracow, 1935) and *Alma mater Jagiellonica* (Cracow, 1958); M. Chamcowna, *Uniwersytet Jagielloński w dobie Komisji Edukacji Narodowej. Szkoła główna w okresie wizyty i rektoratu Hugona Kołłątaja, 1777–1786* (Wrocław, 1957).

11. J. Dolch, "Hochschulspedagogik," *Lexikon der Pedagogik* (Freiburg, 1953) III, 726–729.

12. S. Thomas, *Opuscula omnia . . . cura et studio P. Mandonnet* (Paris, 1927), IV; V. White, *How to Study—Being the Letter of St. Thomas Aquinas to Brother John—De Modo studendi. Latin Text with Translation and Exposition* (London, 1956).

13. E. Spranger, *Über das Wesen der Universität* (Berlin, 1910).

The Educational Tasks of a University

14. F. W. Schelling, *Vorlesungen über die Methode des akademischen Studiums* (Stuttgart, 1802).

15. E. Bernheim, *Der Universitätsunterricht und die Erfordernisse der Gegenwart* (Berlin, 1898).

16. H. Schmidkunz, *Einleitung in die akademische Pedagogik.* (Halle a S., 1907) 82–90, 112–125.

17. W. Jerusalem, *Die Aufgaben des Lehrers an höheren Schulen* (Vienna-Leipzig, 1912).

18. R. Livingstone, *Oświata przyszłości* (Warsaw, 1947) 89–95; H. Hetherington, *The Social Function of the University* (London, 1953).

19. T. Czeczowski, *O uniwersytecie i studiach uniwersyteckich* (Toruń, 1946) 5–6.

20. T. Ziegler, *Über Universitäten und Universitäts-Studium* (Leipzig, n. d.); K. Jaspers, *Die Idee der Universität* (Berlin, 1923) and *The Idea of the University* (Boston, 1959); L. Petrazynckij, *Universitet i nauka: Opyt teorii i techniki universitetskago dela i nauchnogo obrazovaniia* (St. Petersburg, 1907); J. Donat, *Die Freiheit der Wissenschaft* (Innsbruck, 1912) and *Wolność nauki - obraz nowoczesnego życia umysłowego* (Cracow, 1930); K. Twardowski, *O dostojeństwie uniwersytetu* (Poznań, 1933); S. Hessen, *Podstawy pedagogiki* (Warsaw, 1935) 361–393; A. Wójcicki, *Co to jest współczesny uniwersytet?* (Wilno, 1938); J. D. Bernal, *The Social Function of Science* (London, 1944) and *Nauka w dziejach* (Warsaw, 1957).

21. J. K. Szaniawski, *Rady przyjacielskie młodemu czcicielowi nauk i filozofii pragnącemu znaleźć pewniejszą drogę do prawdziwego i wyższego oświecenia* (Warsaw, 1805); K. Brodziński, *O powołaniu i obowiązkach młodzieży akademickiej* (Warsaw, 1826); J. Kremer, *O zadaniu młodzieży polskiej kształcającej się na Uniwersytecie Jagiellońskim* (Cracow, 1871); H. Struve, *Wstęp krytyczny do filozofii* (Warsaw, 1903).

22. L. Fonck, *Praca naukowa. Przyczynek do metodyki studiów uniwersyteckich* (Warsaw, 1910); A. Nippoldt, *Anleitung zum wissenschhaftlichen Denken* (1928); J. E. Heyde, *Technik des wissenschaftlichen Arbeitens* (Berlin, 1935); E. Dimnet, *Sztuka myślenia* (Warsaw, 1936); S. Rudniański, *Technologia pracy umysłowej* (Warsaw, 1950); K. Wojciechowski, *Praca umysłowa* (Warsaw, 1947) and *Technologia pracy umysłowej w Polsce* (Warsaw, 1947); S. Żurawski, *Technika pracy umysłowej* (Warsaw, 1947); J. Pieter, *Praca naukowa* (Katowice, 1957).

23. J. Rutkowski, "Z zagadnień dydaktycznych wyższego szkolnictwa," *Księga pamiątkowa ku czci S. Michalskiego* (Warsaw, 1937) and *Z zagadnień dydaktycznych wyższego szkolnictwa* (Poznań, 1948); *Dydaktyka szkoły wyższej. Księga pamiątkowa Sesji Naukowej w Katowicach 1958 r.* (Gliwice, 1961).

24. J. Starnawski, *Warsztat bibliograficzny historyka literatury polskiej* (Warsaw, 1957); L. Małunowiczowna, *Wstęp od filologii klasycznej wraz z metodologią pracy umysłowej i naukowej* (Lublin, 1960).

25. J. Lacrois, "Kryzys uniwersytetu" *Esprit* (1946) no. 7; W. Kuteynikoff, "Anemia szkolnictwa wyższego," *Myśl współczesna* (1947) no. 2, 247–256.

26. H. E. Sigerist, *The University at the Crossroads* (New York, 1945); A. S. Nash, *The University and the Modern World* (London, 1945), reviewed by B. Suchodolski, "Podstawy i zadania nauki," *Życie naukowe* (1946) no. 3, 172–179; W. Moberly, *The Crisis in the University* (London, 1949).

27. W. Naf, *Wesen und Aufgaben der Universität* (Bern, 1950) 35–42.

Stefan Kunowski

28. R. Livingstone, *Some Thoughts on University Education* (London, 1948) 25–28.

29. S. R. Dongerkery, *Thoughts on University Education* (London, 1955) 106–109.

30. *Iz istorii Moskovskogo Universiteta (1917–1941)* M. W. Garibowa ed. (Moscow, 1955) 6–8.

31. J. B. S. Haldane, *La Philosophie marxiste et les Sciences* (Paris, 1947); M. Cornforth, *Nauka przeciw idealizmowi* (Warsaw, 1957) 278–291; S. Kulczyński, "Organizacja nauki procesem dialektycznym," *Życie nauki* (1948) nos. 35–36, pp. 366–370.

32. J. H. Newman, *The Idea of a University Defined and Illustrated* (London, 1925); F. De Hovre, *Le Catholicisme, ses pédagogues, sa pédagogie* (Brussels, 1930) 193–238.

33. Pie XII, *L'Éducation, la science, et la culture* (Paris, 1956) 20–30; *Relations Humaines et Société Contemporaine. Synthèse Chrétienne directives de SS. Pie XII* (Fribourg-Paris, 1956).

34. M. Pollakówna, "Myśli o uniwersytecie," *Katolicki Uniwersytet Lubelski w oczach wychowańców* (Lublin, 1958) 9–18; M. A. Krąpiec, "Konfesyjność uczelni i wolność nauki," *Zeszyty Naukowe KUL* 1 (1958) 5–19.

35. J. Szczepański, "Problemy współczesnych uniwersytetów," *Życie szkoły wyższej* (1955) no. 12, 127–128.

36. M. Siemieński, "Problemy dydaktyki szkoły wyższej," *Życie szkoły wyższej* (1957) no. 6, 30–37.

37. R. Hubert, *Traité de Pédagogie Générale* (Paris, 1952) 307–456.

38. On the other hand, teaching has a stimulating influence on the creativity of scholars; see L. Hirszfeld, "Rola dydaktyki w życiu i twórczości ucznego," *Kultura i społeczeństwo* (1957) no. 1, 44–5.

39. S. Truchim, "Zagadnienia pedagogizacji na uniwersytetach," *Życie szkoły wyższej* (1957) no. 4, 53–56.

40. E. Palyga, "O humanizacje szkolenia na studium wojskowym," *Życie szkoły wyższej* (1957) no. 7/8, 124–125; S. Wanat, "Rola studium wojskowego w pracy wychowawczej wyższej uczelni," *Życie szkoły wyższej* (1958) no. 4, 92–98.

41. Z. Turska, *O kąt dla żaka* (Warsaw, 1960); see C. Bąk, S. Sitko, and J. Waszkiewicz, *Dawny szpital scholarów w Krakowie* (Cracow, 1959).

42. S. Zdębska, "Problemy psychologiczne w polsanatorium," *Zdrowie publiczne* (1959) no. 4, 333–337; T. Zakowa-Dąbrowska, "Z zagadnień opieki psychiatrycznej nad młodzieżą akademicką," *Życie szkoły wyższej* (1959) no. 2, 107–115.

43. J. Wróblewska, "O zagrożeniu tężyzny fizycznej młodzieży studiującej," *Życie szkoły wyższej* (1957) no. 3, 50–52.

44. M. Kasprzak, "O humanizmie dawnym i obecnym," *Życie szkoły wyższej* (1960) no. 5, 76–84.

44a. *Problemy wychowania w szkole wyższej. Ogólno-polska konferencja rektorów w Poznaniu* (Warsaw, 1958).

45. B. Bozowski, "Duszpasterstwo akademickie we Francji," *Tygodnik Powszechny* (1959) no. 48, 5; *Apostoł młodzieży ks. E. Szwejnic* (Poznań, 1936).

46. S. Sawicki, "Uwagi o teatrze studenskim," *Zeszyty Naukowe KUL* (1958) no. 2, p. 125–135; P. Mroczkowski, "Teatr Akademicki na sekcjach neofilogicznych," *Roczniki humanistyczne KUL* 6 (1959) z. 6.

The Educational Tasks of a University

47. J. Woźniakowski, "O Wychowaniu estetycznym na uniwersytecie," *Zeszyty Naukowe KUL* 1 (1958) no. 2, 136–143.

48. E. Planchard, *Études de pédagogie universitaire* (Coimbra, 1956) I, 221–257.

49. J. Stemler, *Praktyczna pedagogika biblioteczna* (Warsaw, 1938); L. Bykowski, *Zakres i zadania pedagogiki bibliotecznej* (Warsaw, 1938); M. Walentynowicz, *Działalność pedagogiczna bibliotekarza* (Toruń 1956) 67–72.

50. *Bibliotekarstwo naukowe*, A. Łysakowski, ed. (Cracow, 1956) 347–363, 401–421; A. Kochańska, "Stan i aktualne potrzeby bibliotek szkół wyższych," *Życie szkoły wyższej* (1959) 13–21.

51. H. C. MacKnown and A. B. Roberts, *Audio-visual Aids to Instruction* (New York, 1949), see "Using audio-visual aids in the High School" 470–531; W. A. Wittich and Ch. F. Schuller, *Audio-Visual Materials, Their Nature and Use* (New York, 1957).

52. M. Lipowska, "Zastosowanie zasady poglądowości w pracy dydaktycznej na uniwersytecie," *Życie szkoły wyższej* (1958) no. 8, 38–57.

53. R. M. Cooper, ed., *The Two Ends of the Log-Learning and Teaching in Today's College* (Minneapolis, 1958).

THE FRIAR'S TALE

Przemysław Mroczkowski

I.

IT IS A STRIKING FACT THAT "THE FRIAR'S TALE" HAS, COMPARATIVELY speaking, escaped comment. This has usually happened to the less conspicuous among *The Canterbury Tales;* yet it can hardly be denied that the story of Frere Hubert ranks high among the contributions of the individual pilgrims.

One of the explanations may be that consideration has chiefly been given to the plot parallels which Archer Taylor[1] has collected with such assiduity and from such a wide range of space and time: they are somewhat discouragingly numerous, and yet they provide no obvious immediate source or analogue that agrees in all essentials. Taylor concluded that ". . . one cannot hope at present to determine whether the curious shape it takes is wholly Chaucer's own reshaping of an exemplum, or whether it is in large measure the result of oral transmission."[2]

It now seems possible to indicate where the probable inspiration for the form of *The Friar's Tale* came from—and in that connection, precisely, with "oral transmission," perhaps in an unexpected sense of the term. It would still come from the field of the exempla literature (quoted also by Taylor in several instances). The important aspect to be considered, however, is not so much the actual stories analogous in varying measure to *The Friar's Tale,* but rather the sermon tradition of the High Middle Ages and its *loci communes.*

By the latter I mean the recurring ideas, comparisons, accumulations of moral and moralizing observations, the great stock of which supplied the stage and the visual arts. I do not mean pulpit rhetoric in its formal aspect such as was studied by C. E. Shain,[3] though this, too, may prove to be very useful in its way—especially after some further research.

The paradoxical claim advanced here is that some new light thrown in a less explored direction on Chaucer's indebtedness to his epoch may enhance our appreciation of his creative genius. For it seems that his contribution to, or modification of, the skeleton plot in the story of Frere Hubert consists in drawing masterfully on the traditional commonplaces of the friars' preaching, noted with amazing perspicacity: in this way he made "brilliantly plausible" the outline of the narrator's personality and the bias of his thought. The tale will remain a high achievement because of various features which will here be touched upon. Now this achievement seems, to a considerable extent, the development of the nucleus seen with penetration in the potentialities of the pulpit practice of the late medieval mendicants.

II.

All readers of Chaucer know that *The Friar's Tale* is an exemplum. Few seem to have given closer attention to the attendant questions: What is the significance of such a statement? And, especially, for what is it an exemplum?

Later medieval preaching appears to have been sufficiently spontaneous to admit a variety of applications of a story and combinations of *motifs* (not merely narrative). Besides, one subject may be "fed" by echoes of a different nature; one "example" may contain several moral "points." On the other hand, it does appear possible to group the characteristic elements of a story around one idea, to consider one inspiration as central.

At one time F. Tupper advanced the thesis that in *The Friar's Tale* Chaucer gave an exemplum for "the cursing stage of wrath."[4] To others it appeared to be a story illustrating the distinction between unpremeditated and conscious sin. Dissenting from these views, I want here to submit that it is basically a study of greed, although easily deviating to a few other topics, specifically topics of sins, recurrent in the pulpit literature of Chaucer's (and earlier) time.

III.

The method adopted here will be relatively simple. I intend to follow the story as it is unfolded to the reader, pointing to the connection of specific themes (often very brief) with the preaching tradition insofar as we can reconstruct it from its compendia. On more than one occasion I shall permit myself a comment on the literary effects obtained by such echoes.

I want to provide evidence of the *Tale* being rooted in homiletic soil of a particular kind. My authorities will be the *Summae* on moral subjects, those especially of the two Dominicans, Peraldus[5] and the still insufficiently explored Bromyard;[6] collections of exempla, such as that of Caesarius of Heisterbach[7] as well as other anonymous ones;[8] partial literary parallels to certain situations as in Deguileville's *Pelerinage*;[9] lastly, fragments of ecclesiastical writers not always directly connected with preaching, though certainly illustrating trends of ideas popularized by it.[10]

IV.

It is part of my argument that Chaucer's Friar must be of the type that used the popular and partly radical kind of preaching, which became widely known in Europe with the spread of the mendicants: a reader of Chaucer would be aware of the Friar as representative of the great upheaval, at one time so fresh and uncompromising, directed against the acquisitive spirit. A *limitour*, whether Franciscan or otherwise, would be expected to inveigh chiefly and primarily against riches and the disasters they caused in human souls as well as against those, clerical or lay, who suffered from the vice and yielded to its attraction.

V.

With this in mind let us look at the first lines of the *Tale* to see if we can immediately find something characteristic. It begins with the description of an archdeacon. The words "a man of heigh degree" (1. 1302) in the mouth of a mendicant might already put a knowing listener on his guard. Prelates were not exactly minions of the begging friars,[11] and archdeacons are mentioned at least twice in a derogatory manner in collections of exempla.[12] There is, accordingly, a good possibility that the praise of the boldness with which this dignitary pestered sinners (1. 1303) is another instance of Chaucer's pervasive irony. But it is obvious that

For smale tithes and for smal offrynge
He made the peple pitously to synge (11. 1315–16)

take us in the direction of the accustomed targets of the friars'
attacks. Here is one more case of an inconsiderate or oppressive
magistrate.

This magistrate has at hand a man ready to be sent on errands[13]
(1. 1321). Here is what Peraldus can tell of such a situation in
the course of one of his attacks against *avaritia*.

> Thirdly it is reprehensible in those receiving gifts if they have
> godless servants who exert themselves in every way possible to extort
> something from the subjects: which is a very great sin.

This is followed by a brief story showing where this kind of vice
can be found most easily, the story of a man who in a blasphemous
fury was looking for a way in which to offend God most grievously.
Somebody present advises him: "If you wish to offend God more
than any sinner, become the collector of a bishop's palace."[14] In
a similar way the anonymous *Vices and Vertues* defines, as the
third branch of the sin of covetousness, robbing the poor, *raueyne,*
of which a subdivision "is in thes grete prelates that pilen and
taken so harde upon here sugetes," as wolves devouring sheep;
immediately after that we have the next subdivision which is

> in thes baillies, reues, constables, schereues, bedeles, seriauntes, and
> others suche, officers and purueyors, what so they be, that pilen and
> raunsomen men and wommen . . . ,

especially "pore men and pore widues and children. . . ."[15] Thus
the initial situation in which a ruthless (ecclesiastical) dignitary
has at hand a corrupt and greedy agent was familiar to the preaching treatises. It struck a note of condemnation of the omnipresent
sin of greed, *avaritia*.

As to the summoner himself, it is not difficult to see that corruption coming from the same sin constitutes the dominant note
of his unregenerate personality: ". . . on it he sette al his entente"
(1. 1374). That a summoner passed for a notorious figure in this
respect, we learn from the so-called *Ludus Coventriae* where we
even have a minor self-revelation in the style of some lines in
Chaucer (1. 1578). The summoner sent by a "spiritual court" to
Mary and Joseph is ready to withdraw the false accusation for a
bribe. He wants "gold or sylvyr," "as all somnorys."[16] From the
homiletic field we find a relevant passage in Bromyard describing how certain officials, both lay and ecclesiastic, allow prosti-

tutes and rascals to sin in return for gifts.[17] Our summoner has an established policy about the sinners of his district, calculated to raise his income; within this policy "wenches" guilty of fornication escape most easily.

All this, together with the final statement that our summoner is going to accuse an old widow on a trumped-up charge, to get some money, makes his inward state completely clear. He is spiritually ill in a most dangerous way. Peraldus makes such a case plain: "The fourth point which makes avarice detestable is that among spiritual diseases it is the worst or one of the worst. . . .;"[18] its victim, we read further, is marked with a poisonous kiss of the world which invites the devils to "take him."

Therefore, when the figure of an armed rider in green is introduced, an experienced listener probably already knows whom to recognize, and the narrator certainly knows what he is about, for we are now facing the fairly well-known figure of *diabolus venator,* the hunting devil. He can be found in manuscript illuminations[19] and in spiritual treatises.[20] Guillaume de Deguileville shows him attending to his various nets and ropes waiting eagerly for the imprudent passers-by (or rather swimmers).[21] As to his attire, Dr. Robertson seems to have been the first to offer a plausible explanation: on the authority of a fourteenth-century encyclopaedia he thinks that the green dress is the symbol of hypocrisy on the part of the hunter-tempter.[22] It seems simpler to point out that a green costume was in general a frequent garb of the devil in later medieval iconography,[23] here additionally suitable for a pseudo yeoman, while the black fringes of the hat may have contained a premonition of his real character.[24]

It is a pregnant moment. The green rider suggests the character of his companion by his question: Could he be a bailiff? To this the wretch assents readily (and probably overambitiously for his actual status). Thus another key word has been spoken. A bad bailiff appears almost proverbial, a stock figure in the jungle-picture of a wicked world. The etymology of his name may be interpreted, we are told, as "one carrying in himself disturbances for the common people" (*Ballivus dicitur quasi bajulans lites vulgi*). These he pesters by calumnies and accusations, robberies and extortions. Thus, literally, the *Speculum Laicorum.*[25] Elsewhere bailiffs are compared to sturgeons which lead smaller fish right into the whale's mouth. The whale (the lord of the bailiff, as the text explains) swallows the smaller fish and lets the sturgeon go. *Sic ipsi adducunt pauperes ad devorandum dominis suis.* All this under *ballivus,* in an alphabetical *Tabula Exemplorum.*[26]

It is not surprising that the tempter can hint at the identical occupation which he shares with his new acquaintance.[27] The devil can all the more easily make friends with him,[28] a no less standard trick.[29]

We soon note how eagerly the man responds to hints: this will be his attitude throughout. Here in particular he wants to show himself the "social equal" of his new friend. Yes, he is a bailiff, like his companion. He is no whit behind this smart "yeoman" who has chosen, accordingly, the most suitable disguise, likely to appeal to his fellow's way of thinking.[30] (Our summoner sins, among other sins, by *ambitio.*) In analogous cases the devil appears to a monk as an abbot,[31] and the like.[32]

But, of course, the main appeal will be made to the summoner's main concern. Gulielmus de Pagula, in his treatise *Oculus Sacerdotis,* explains that "the devil tempts a man to the sin to which he knows him to be inclined," and compares him to a besieger storming a castle from the weaker side, and to a hunter hiding in ambush in the place which he knows to be frequented by game.[33] St. Bruno the Carthusian will be more specific for us. Commenting on the lines of Psalm 90 with their reference to hunters' nets, he says that ". . . evil spirits are called hunters by similitude" and ". . . their net is gold and silver."[34] A *Meditatio de Humana Conditione,* too, assures its readers that Satan "has set his nets in gold and silver."[35] What, therefore, could be more in accordance with a well-established tradition than the pseudo yeoman's assurance, "I have gold and silver in my chests" (1. 1400)? Again, a listener with some experience might feel a shudder (not wholly unpleasurable) running down his back on hearing the following promise that those riches will belong to the summoner when he comes to "oure shire." He may have heard the story of the miser so fond of gold that on his coming to hell he was made to drink it liquid.[36]

Here we note how quickly the acquaintance turns into friendship. It is sworn between two rascals and is not likely to last. Oddly enough, there exists a story about *falsa amicitia,* told by Bromyard. It is struck up there between a "devil" and a "scoundrel" and is meant to illustrate his thesis that such fellowship is bound to end sadly. The two meet, exchange information about their respective errands, decide on mutual help and friendship: they are to kill and rob a hermit, the demon being after his soul and the *latro* after his cattle; but they quarrel at the hermit's door about priority, and each spoils the other's business. This comes of associating with God's enemies:[37] thus Bromyard ends his high-spirited anecdote, remarkable for the comedy of its situations. Similarities here do not, of course, go very far, but the point is that without some such echoes in the listeners' minds it is difficult to imagine their enjoying the constant innuendoes, ominous allusions, and double entendre with which the conversation of the "yeoman" and the summoner is really strewn and which presage a bad end to the relationship.

One of the chief reasons for the listener's amazement is the blindness of the summoner. He can know, with Peraldus, what, for the sinner, looms beyond the line: "In daliance they ryden forth and pleye" (1. 1406): "the stupidity is that, whilst he plays, in the court of the heavenly judge his death warrant is patent."[38] Yet he enjoys himself and enjoys his dubious company, falling into another obvious danger, that of inadvertent talking and curiosity ("ful of jangles," "evere enqueryng upon every thyng" [11. 1407–09]). The man, says the treatise of *Vices and Vertues,* who does not control his tongue, "he falleth lichtliche into thee hondes of his enemys, that ben the deueles of helle"; the tongue is the gate of his castle and "the deuel, that werreth the castle of the herte, whan he fyndeth the grete gate up, that is the mouth, he taketh lichtliche the castel";[39] and Peraldus states that "unless the tongue is diligently watched, it rages in the first place against its master."[40]

The summoner does everything but keep watch on himself. Thus, although the conversation is shot through with the allusions already mentioned, he misses their meanings. This is true of the ominous promise in 11. 1415–16:

> Er we departe, I shall thee so well wisse
> That of myn hous ne shaltow nevere misse.

Nay, the summoner at once displays eagerness to be in fact thoroughly instructed. This is true of the mysterious hint about the yeoman's dwelling being "fer in the north contree" (1. 1414). On this point it is worth adding to Robertson's commentary that more could be involved than just the association of *aquilo,* the northern wind, with hell. Adam Premonstratensis, in his treatise *De Tripartito Tabernaculo,* connects the terrible wind, *aquilo,* with an obscuring cloud, spread from the head of the monster figure of Satan. The head is very black (*caput nigerrimum*—we here recall the yeoman's hat with black fringes), and it hides truth. "For the ancient enemy first obscures the minds of the reprobates, taking away from them the light of truth and afterwards inflames," says Adam.[41] Still less, of course, will such an obscured mind take a hint about the conditions reigning in the "north contree": "My lord is hard to me and daungerous" (1. 1427). There is more than one story about the sternness of Lucifer with his subordinates: one of them, in the exempla of Odo de Cheriton, shows that even such "achievements" reported to the archdevil as bloodshed or shipwreck could be judged insufficient and deserving of punishment.[42] Elsewhere Turtivillus is hanged for not turning up at once when summoned by his master.[43]

Instead of recognizing the danger, the summoner only recognizes such features in his interlocutor as make him feel the kinship. This centers round the vice I have suggested as crucial in the story. The pseudo yeoman frankly declares that he lives by extortion and takes anything by any means. This coincides quite remarkably with a piece of instruction in dialogue in Guillaume de Deguileville—the pilgrim instructed in various spiritual dangers hears the allegorical figure explain the nature of his hands. The first has claws:

> La premiere qu'est armee
> D'ongles de grifon, nommee
> Rapine est qui gentil se fait,
> Et dist que sa proie li lait
> Penre ou elle la puet trouver.

The last two lines are revealing. For *rapina,* indiscriminate robbing, it does not matter where the prey is found (the pseudo yeoman says: "I take al that men wol me yive" 1. 1430). Now the speaker, in Deguileville, is *Avarice,* of which *rapina* is the most directly dangerous variety. The summoner, so far from being frightened, is at home. He immediately finds his way of living identical: "so fare I" (1. 1434).

This must be so because, even apart from the newly struck up brotherhood, *mali acquisitores sunt socii demonum,* the unjust acquirers are devils' associates, as Bromyard is ready to assure us.[44] Elsewhere in Bromyard people of that kind are denounced with greater vehemence as worse than devils, and Peraldus declares: *quia raptores peiores sunt diabolo,*[45] Which the coming stages of the association, with the devil's caution and restraint, will prove.

The complete lack of restraint in the summoner, emphasized

in the next lines of his speech, will now be more obviously boasting. In itself boasting, *iactantia,* one of the vices of the tongue, is already a great sin which makes of man God's thief (arrogating the glory due to Him): such is the case made by the author of *Vices and Vertues.*[46] Things get very much worse if it is sin that is the object of boasting; and such is our summoner's case. He probably represents

> obduracioun, that is hardenesse of herte, whan a man is so harded and beten in his euele that ther may no man make hym bowe ne come to amendment.[47]

The next branch of the same sin is "despit of penaunce," and we know that the summoner is already infected with it. It is this kind of heart that is "reckless of dangers" (*impavidum ad pericula*), as St. Bernard finds.[48] How this obduration can be caused precisely by greed, certain fourteenth-century exempla can easily show.[49]

With this preparation it ceases to be surprising that, on learning the real identity of the pseudo yeoman, the summoner displays no shock or fright. The only effect is increased curiosity (which has already been shown to be excessive in him). Even the less informed reader by now understands all the previous strange sayings. But the summoner is unmoved. He "sleeps at the door of hell," as a title in Bromyard puts it.[50] He is one of those sinners who have deliberately blinded themselves (as the same compiler explains elsewhere[51]) by their desire of gain. So now he belongs to those who do not "see hell fire nor the devil always waiting near them."[52]

Those flames from below again and again intermingle in the reader's perception with genuine amusement: this is the special and unique flavor of *The Friar's Tale.* The devil reaches virtuosity in describing his procedure to his prospective victim. In one of the most thrilling lines of the tale he refers to himself as a superior juggler. It is difficult to imagine that the arrangement of the passage and the use of the theme could belong to anybody but Chaucer; the theme itself, however, is an exemplum:

> Item, the world and the devil play with those who love them like a conjurer that seems to be putting a lot under the hat, but when the hat has been raised, nothing is found under.[53]

So, unabashed, the summoner continues in his inquisitive mood. For,

> in fact the madness of an avaricious rich man may be shown in many

ways. First in that he is looking for hidden nets in order to strangle himself. Thence Prov. XXVI: The heart of the wicked seeketh out evil things. The wicked can be understood as the avaricious. . . .[54]

This may contribute to our understanding of the enquiry now opened by the summoner as to the shapes that devils may choose. The devil's reply that the shapes assumed are adapted to the character of the person tempted, while it remains another masterpiece of psychological irony, now confirms from the tempter's mouth the previous suppositions about his *exterieur,* as calculated to rouse social ambitions (supported by economic *arrivisme*) of the would-be rich yeoman-summoner.

At the same time this reply opens the theological excursus on demonology, in the form of a monologue, with a couple of additional questions from the summoner. This portion of the tale has been less neglected than the other. There have been two articles quoting parallels in certain Latin writings to particular points in the "lecture," by Pauline Aiken[55] and Sister Mary Immaculate.[56] Owing to the interesting material collected there, we know that the devil in *The Friar's Tale* reflects the relevant lore quite faithfully, especially as recorded in Vincent de Beauvais. It would be possible to show that the points were in fact part of the standard teaching, to be found also in Aquinas.[57] The emphasis in it all, from both the doctrinal and the literary point of view, rests on man's freedom to reject temptation. St. Thomas' *Summa* may prove rewarding reading because of the thesis about the purely external character of the evil spirit's action with regard to man.[58] This would account for the distinction the summoner's tempter makes between real bodies and the bodies he or his fellows may use (1. 1505–10). Elsewhere, too, the stress on the importance of man's consent is of course frequent: "The devil is no ordainer of vices, only their incentor,"[59] says one of many texts. For us it is the exempla that are of primary interest. There we note a tale from an anonymous fourteenth-century English collection, in which a devil tells a Jew that Christians can always escape him by confession.[60] A little similar to it, and more interesting, is the story in Jacques de Vitry about the devil preaching truth to enhance his hearers' guilt,[61] not altogether unlike the situation between our two protagonists.

It seems worthy of Chaucer's rich sense of paradox and irony to assign to the devil the role of lecturer on the secrets of hell. But it may have been suggested to him by some such saying as that of a bishop in an exemplum: "The devil is a great theologian."[62] This impression is not undermined by a contemptuous reference to human theology which, in *The Friar's Tale*, the tempter drops at one point. He is altogether very subtle and superior; compared with him, the self-revealing devil in Guillaume de Deguileville is clumsy, though interesting and instructive, for he gives another use of the same convention. In Guillaume Satan discusses his rights as a hunter in the "King's land" and describes the various kinds of nets he uses. Some of them are hung in the air, to catch even the winged victims. In this respect he compares himself to a spider:

> Jamais araigne tu ne vis
> Qui tant de retz ne de las fist
> Pour mouches prendre et arrester
> Ni si subtillement pener
> Comme ie mefforce et me peine
> De gagner creature humaine.

With this we should like to compare the summoner's straight-forward question: "What maketh yow to han al this labour" (1. 1473)?

The dismal spider in Guillaume admits that his intended victims escape him whenever they make an effort, and his nets are often torn. This could be one more parallel to the emphasis on man's consent in the remarks of the pseudo yeoman, but in Chaucer these have a dramatic function. They set off the blindness of the summoner. And we can say in a general way that the functional character of the devil's lecture raises it artistically very much above the mere "piece of erudition" for which some might take the excursus.

The next manifestation of the summoner's blindness and obstinacy—at the moment when he has just been reminded of the possibility of his escape!—is connected with the previously mentioned background of his tragic eagerness in evil: "I am a yeman, knowen is ful wide" (1. 1524), and so he must keep his word. Socially ambitious and economically acquisitive, he offers the devil a deal; they shall share what they get. At this moment Peraldus is whispering in our ear that "an avaricious man's iniquity is shown" in that "in the first place he sells himself to his enemies."[63]

This attitude, of which we have already seen many instances, will remain characteristic of the summoner to the end. "The first stupidity of the sinner is that in the way already mentioned he is hurrying to hell and by many labours and expenses prepares his hell like heaven." Thus Bromyard[64] shows considerable awareness of the dramatic potentialities behind scenes of temptation in the minds of popular preachers. The summoner's behavior is planned accordingly when he urges the devil to seize out of hand the horses that seem to be offered to him: once more he outdevils the devil, who is much more moderate. Later on, when he proceeds to call on the poor woman, he goes to the length of setting himself as a model to the evil spirit: "Taak heer ensample of me" (1. 1580). This may be another instance of the boasting of sin which Bromyard, instructively enough, associates with the oppressing of subjects: he discusses the so-called *gloria perniciosa,* pernicious boasting, which may consist of several points, "first in the committing of sins, such as the oppressing of the subjects. . . ." There follow comparisons applicable to people who are like lions catching their prey or like children playing with the silk shroud in which are wrapped the bodies of their dead parents: "Thus these, having a dead soul, take pride in external evils"—like madmen or people ignorant of the verdict that condemns them.[65]

After a dialogue with the poor woman whom the summoner is determined to rob, we reach the point when the widow, grown desperate, curses the extortionate rascal. The usual comment is to point to the obvious distinction which the devil, now extremely attentive, also makes between a curse that does not come from the heart and one that does—an emphasis especially suitable in the case of a priestly narrator. But why should the curse that comes from the heart be effective at all? The clue may be found in the relevant compendia and that in connection with the summoner's chief vice. Generally speaking, it is dangerous to curse people, says Bromyard, for the malediction may turn on the speaker. But God justly curses, among other kinds of people, "all those desirous of unjust gain . . . the avaricious . . . the tenacious in holding. . . ."[66] Peraldus is nearer our case: he explains "that the Lord shall greatly punish the robbers (*raptores*)," that is, "by imprecations and curses spoken at them by widows and children whom they despoil. For the scripture says that such imprecations are heard out."[67]

It is the last moment. The widow distinctly mentions repentance as a condition of withdrawing her curse, but it is in vain. In his *duritia cordis,* if we may borrow a remarkable comparison from another friar's treatise, the summoner is like a blood-sucking fly which it is impossible to drive away.[68] At the very moment when he holds out his hand, this hand is held:

> Note, too, that greed uses a mousetrap to catch the imprudent. . . . Of this mousetrap speaks Augustine, telling the avaricious man: The prey which you want to seize is in a mousetrap. You hold another and are yourself held by the devil. And such people can hardly be saved as it is very difficult to leave things unjustly possessed.[69]

The devil is now almost solemn: "Thou shalt with me to helle yet to-night" (1. 1636). Obviously, we have here a most striking case of *diabolus simius Dei,* extremely impressive from the literary point of view. The dramatic character of the tale is raised here, near its end, to the pitch of awfulness. This is brought about by Chaucer's excellent skill. But he follows the medieval tradition of parody with its use of parallels, ridiculous or unholy, to sublime motifs.[70]

The rapacious summoner has been taken soul and body to hell, which he has courted all the time. This is in accordance with the pattern of such cases: Bromyard refers to

> inordinate and greedy receivers of gifts (*Munerum inordinati and cupidi receptores*) whose penal place is deservedly hell. First because living from gifts and the raising of taxes they have no certain . . . order. These shall justly go where there is no order, Job. X.

Chaucer's Friar, in one brief line (again paraphrasing the Bible) states that the extortionate wretch went "Where as that somnours han hir heritage" (1. 1641).

VI.

As an additional point in favor of our main argument, it is worth adding that the stories surrounding the analogue to *The Friar's Tale* in Caesarius of Heisterbach also seem to throw some light on the subject matter prominent in the preacher's mind when dealing with the story of the devil and his overgreedy companion. The exempla preceding it emphasize the penetration and relative veracity as well as the limitations of the devil in contact with a human being (no. 14–16). But it is the succeeding story that appears more directly relevant, for there we find an account of how a merciless knight took some oats from a very poor widow and was struck by thunder on the spot for punishment. Some links between the exempla are undeniable in Caesarius, and these two are expressly coupled by himself as warnings for *pauperum exactores*. This supports the view that the Friar's Tale mainly exemplifies *avarice*.

VII.

To conclude: I first of all hope to have shown in some detail what we mean when we say that *The Friar's Tale* is an exemplum. It is important to know of what long underground root it is a flower and in what way the poet was aware of the "obligations" which this kind of tradition imposed on the narrator chosen to represent it.

The "obligations" in this particular case primarily concerned the features connected with the vice of *avaritia* and its typical effects. Among these it is blindness and obduration, vital for the construction of the tale, that come to the fore while dramatically provoking the fascinating and paradoxical reserve and irony on the part of the devil.

We also note how this element in the culture of his time could feed Chaucer's most celebrated qualities: his sense of drama, psychological acuteness, realism, and feeling for the comic.

If this is so, one feels authorized to say that we are in need of a new study of homiletic literature. It is, of course, far from unknown: many—though not all—of its texts have been well edited and many plots of the numerous exempla have been recorded. What demands consideration now is the role of this kind of writing as a matrix of creative literature and its value as social document.

FOOTNOTES

1. Archer Taylor, "The Devil and the Advocate," *PMLA* 36 (1921) 50ff., and the contribution by the same author to Bryan and Dempster, *Sources and Analogues of Chaucer's Canterbury Tales* (Chicago, 1941).
2. Taylor, "The Devil" 59.
3. C. E. Shain, "Pulpit Rhetoric in Three Canterbury Tales," *Modern Language Notes* 70 (1955) 235–245.
4. F. Tupper, "Chaucer and the Seven Deadly Sins," *PMLA* 29 (1914) 112–113.
5. Peraldus (Gulielmus), O. P., *Summa virtutum ac vitiorum* (Paris, 1519), but composed in mid-thirteenth century (now thought one of the sources of *The Parson's Tale*).

6. J. Bromyardus, *Summa Praedicantium*. I have used both the Venetian edition of 1586 and that of Nuremberg (1485).

7. Caesarius Heisterbacensis, *Libri Octo Miraculorum*, ed. A. Meister, *Römische Quartalschrift*, suppl. 13 (1901).

8. Cf. J. A. Herbert's *Catalogue of Romances in the British Museum*, vol. 3, and, among separate editions, *Le Speculum Laicorum*, ed. J. Th. Welter (Paris, 1914), which is especially interesting.

9. Guillaume de Deguileville, *Le Pèlerinage de Vie Humaine*, ed. J. J. Sturzinger (London, 1893). I also quote *Le Pèlerinage de l'homme nouvellement imprimé a Paris* (1511).

10. E.g., some of the ascetical writers printed in Migne, *Patrologia Latina* (*P.L.*), such as St. Bernard or Adam Premonstratensis.

11. Cf. e.g., Bromyardus (ed. 1485), *De prelatorum confederatione cum demonibus.*

12. Cf. Herbert, *Catalogue 3*, pp. 692, 490.

13. Bromyard (ed. 1485), s.v. *Ministratio,* articles 5 and 15, describes the situation he thinks is typical ("quod quotidiana docet experientia"), in which lords "mala intentione ministros instituunt: plus propriam quam communem intendentes utilitatem: qui et tales instituunt qui plus reportent non qui iustius regant."

14. Book II, Tractatus 4, *De Auaricia*, Part II, chap. 5, F° 61.

15. *Vices and Vertues,* Early English Text Society (1942) 34–35. (Cited hereafter as E.E.T.S.)

16. *Ludus Coventriae,* ed. K. S. Block, E.E.T.S., Extra Series 120 (1922) 127–128.

17. *Ministratio, loc. cit.* Expenses incurred in acquiring a post can be recovered from bribes provided by this particular clientele—"quod precium datum postmodum pro mercedibus soluant meretricum et latronum: quos pro muneribus peccare permittunt."

18. *De Auaricia*, Part II, chap. 2, F° 36: "Dicit enim mundus iste demonibus Math. xxvi. Quemcumque osculatus fuero ipse est tenete eum."

19. See B. Mus. MS. Tib. A vii f. 51.

20. Cf. e.g., St. Bernard's *In Festo S. Andreae Apost. Sermo.* See *P.L.* 183, col. 505, and *infra,* p. 112, nos. 8 and 9. The hunting devil in V. Mus. MS. Burney 361 is obviously after his victim's body and not only after his soul, so the case is different, but relevant. Cf. Herbert, *Catalogue 3*, p. 646.

21. 1511 ed., F° 74.

22. D. W. Robertson, Jr., "Why the Devil Wears Green" in *M.L.N.* 19 (1954) 470–472.

23. Cf. Oswald A. Erich, *Die Darstellung des Teufels in der christlichen Kunst* (Berlin, 1931) 88–89.

24. Petrus Berchorius in his *Reductorii Moralis . . . Libri Quatuordecim* (Venice, 1583) discusses the black color and its symbolism. There exists, he says, a blackness surrounding sin: "Talis niger color mortem infernalem significat, et ipsam affuturam praedicat et designat" (p. 586).

25. Ed. J. T. Welter, *Speculum* (Paris, 1914). Cf. chap. 11, "De Ballivis et eorum periculis" (pp. 17–18).

26. Same editor (Paris, 1926) 6.

27. A comparison of an oppressive mortal with the devil occurs in Peraldus,

Przemysław Mroczkowski

Part II, chap 2, F° 54: "Missi videntur a diabolo raptores ad faciendum talia opera in mundo qualia facit diabolus in inferno."

28. See the temptation of Christ in the York cycle where the devil says: "For olde acquaintance us betwene/I wolde now some more were sene."

29. There is a passage in St. Thomas Aquinas about the role of the lighter mood in temptation wherein it is interesting to compare with the "daliance" (1.1406) of the conversation between the devil and the summoner: ". . . angeli mali videntur aliqua facere quae sunt ex genere suo venialia peccata, provocando homines ad risum et ad alias huiusmodi levitates." In the *responsio* it is stated that this happens in order to lead humans to grave sins: ". . . omnia illa quae videntur esse venialia daemones procurant, ut homines ad sui familiaritatem attrahant, et sic deducant eum in peccatum mortale" (S. Th. I–II, q. 89, a. 4).

30. Cf. a remark in M. W. Bloomfield, *Seven Deadly Sins* (East Lansing, 1952): "The later Middle Ages became very 'class-conscious,' and we shall note with increasing frequency, in the treatment of the Sins, this habit of thinking in terms of classes. It even affected vision literature" (pp. 114, 397).

31. Cf. Herbert, *Catalogue* 3, p. 495.

32. In *Early S. E. Legendary*, E.E.T.S. 87 (1887) 256, there is a conversation between St. Dominic and the devil who appeared to him in a religious habit. In Calderon's *El Magico Prodigioso* the tempter confesses: "A este fin he venido Con aquesta apariencia, este vestido" (Madrid, 1931) 214. L. W. Cushman, in *The Devil and The Vice in the English Dramatic Literature before Shakespeare* (Halle, 1900) 43, notes that in the Noah play ". . . the devil is . . . adapted to his surroundings, that is, he is a sailor."

33. MS. Bodley, Rawl. C 84, "De modo temptandi" 32.

34. *Expositio in Psalmos.* Psalm 90, *P.L.* 152, col. 1126.

35. By St. Bernard. *P.L.* 184, col. 503–504.

36. B. Mus., MS. Egerton 1117, F° 184b, contains the story of an extortionate bailiff who hanged himself after his spoil had been taken from him by judicial verdict. A religious saw his soul in torments, two devils pouring liquid gold and silver into him.

37. Ed. 1586, s.v. *Amicitia,* A. 21, 26, art. 4.

38. *De Auaricia,* Part II, chap. 15 (*De duodecim stultitiis lusorum*). Later on in the body of the paragraph Peraldus introduces a remarkable quotation from Job 21: "Ducunt in bonis dies suos et in puncto ad inferna descendunt."

39. P. 283.

40. Book II, Tractatus 9, *De peccato lingue,* Part I, F° 208.

41. *P.L.* 197, col. 761.

42. Cf. Herbert, *Catalogue* 3, p. 62.

43. As reported by M. J. Rudwin, *Der Teufel in den deutschen geistlichen Spielen des Mittelalters und der Reformationszeit* (Göttingen, 1915) from the fourth *Erlauer Spiel.* It is true that Rudwin's general thesis underlines the essential friendliness of Lucifer toward his subjects, but there are many instances of his sternness. Dr. Plezia, the editor of *Legenda Aurea,* informs me that in chapter 43 of *De Sancta Juliana* a devil complains of what happens when they fail: their overlord *"facit nos graviter verberari."* Cf. also the complaint of the devils in *Vita Sancti Brendani* (*Early S. E. Legendary* 600–601).

44. *Summa,* ed. 1586, s.v., *Acquisitio,* chap. 12.

45. *De Auaricia,* Part II, chap. 2, F° 54.
46. P. 56.
47. P. 24.
48. *De Consideratione, P.L.* 182, col. 731.
49. Cf. Herbert, *Catalogue* 3, pp. 625–626.
50. Ed. 1485, *Index,* s.v. Peccator.
51. *Ibid.* s.v. Peccatum.
52. *Summa,* ed. 1586, s.v. Visus.
53. *Tabula exemplorum* 2; cf. p. 60 for a similar comparison.
54. Peraldus, *De Auaricia,* Part I, chap. 7, F° 41: "De insania auari diuitis."
55. *Vincent of Beauvais and the Green Yeoman's Lecture on Demonology* in *S.P.* 35 (1938) 1–9.
56. *Fiends as "Servant Unto Man" in the Friar's Tale* in *P.Q.* 21 (1942) 240–244.
57. Here are some of the more relevant places: S. Th. II–II, q. 172; II–II, q. 174, a. 5; III, q. 44, a. 2; II–II, q. 95, a. 4.
58. The texts referred to are S. Th. I–II, q. 80, a. 2–4. Cf. A. A. Parker, *The Theology of the Devil in the Drama of Calderon* (London, 1958).
59. *P.L.* 184, col. 1298/884.
60. Herbert, *Catalogue* 3, p. 525.
61. *Ibid.* 13.
62. *Tabula Exemplorum,* s.v. Sciencia.
63. *De Auaricia,* Part III, chap. 3, F° 34.
64. Ed. 1485, s.v. Peccator.
65. *Ibid.* s.v. Gloria (perniciosa).
66. *Ibid.* s.v. Maledictio.
67. *De Auaricia,* Part II, chap. 2, F° 55, 56.
68. Gilbertus Minoritz, *Summa Abstinentiae: De Duritia cordis* (MS. Bodl., 45).
69. Peraldus, *De Auaricia,* Part I, chap. 6, 7, F° 40.
70. P. Lehmann, *Die Parodie im Mittelalter* (Munich, 1922).

A BAROQUE CRUCIFIX

Stanisław Michalczuk

SEEKING AN EXPLANATION OF THE EXCEPTIONALLY RARE REPRESEN-
tation of Christ hanging on a palm tree in the Dominican church
in Lublin, I succeeded in finding four similar conceptions. A
comparison with contemporary liturgical, devotional, and theatrical texts permits us to treat them as a group that forms an undeveloped iconographical motif, characteristic of the religious art
of the Baroque Age.[1]

I. DESCRIPTION OF THE COLLECTED OBJECTS

1. The palm tree as a crucifix, in the Dominican church in
Lublin.

In the sacristy of the Dominican church in Lublin, renowned
for centuries because of the preservation of a relic of the Holy
Cross, there stands a wooden crucifix representing Christ nailed
to a slender palm. The Crucified has not died; nor does his body
bear any marks of the torment endured by him, except for the
wound in the right side and the crown of thorns. The face
expresses humility, the wide-open eyes look down, and the parted
lips show no sign of gasping. The stylistic features permit us to
date the sculpture as belonging to the second half of the seventeenth century.[2]

2. The engraving in the collections of Engravings in the Univ-
versity of Warsaw.

This engraving (about 12 by 9 cm.), of unknown origin, represents Blessed Juliana de Cornillon kneeling before an altar, worshipping the crucifix which stands between two burning candles.
The crucifix represents Christ nailed to a palm tree in a manner
identical with the carving at Lublin. The upper part of the com-

position is filled with a celestial scene—the adoration of the Trinity by all the saints and angels. This engraving perhaps comes from the seventeenth-eighteenth centuries.[3]

3. The engraving in the pictorial collections of the Ossoliński Library.

This engraving (12.8 by 8.2 cm.) is dated 1690 and represents St. Bruno bending over an open book with the text: *Memorare novissima tua et in aeternum non peccabis* (Eccl. 7:40). The book lies on a crozier and mitre, which he disdained when he refused the episcopate. The saint has his left hand placed on a skull, and in his right hand he holds a branch of palm with a likeness of Christ. It was done by an Antwerp engraver, Balthasar van Westerhout, according to a work of painter and engraver Johann Schumer, certainly a Hollander, born around 1670.[4]

4. The iconographic program of painting and sculpture in the ornamentation of the interior of St. Paul's church in Sandomierz.

The theme of the decoration in the nave church of St. Paul's was subordinated to one leading idea, which can be described as the victory of the cross. Without considering the much later scenes from the life of St. Paul painted beside the windows under the lunettes of the vaulting as well as the scenes of the orchestra of angels behind the music choir, there are the paintings filling the six frames on the vaulting (characteristic in the so-called Lublin Renaissance) and uniting in a harmonious meaning with the paintings that cover the multi-colored walls and the sculptured decoration of the rafter in the multi-colored vault. The crucifix on this rafter, with its painted figures of Adam and Eve, is the dominant element in the whole structure from the viewpoint of content and composition. Christ, somewhat less than life-sized, is nailed to a cross placed against the background of a spreading palm. The figures of the Mother of God and St. John are on the side. Against the background of a magnificent scene painted on the arch wall, two splendid trees are growing. Under the tree, on the gospel side, Adam is seated; under the other tree, on the epistle side, Eve is seated. At their feet two winged angels are adoring the crucifix. Above them two serpents are entwined about the trunks of the trees—above Adam one has the head of a woman, and above Eve one has the head of a devil. Beside the serpents are two shawls inscribed *Boni, Mali*. On the arch two angels hold a ribbon inscribed *Ascendam in Palman et apprehendam fructus eius* (Cant. 7), *Ne Comede—Morieris*. The first part of the text is the eighth verse of chapter 7 of the Canticle of Canticles; the

*The church of St. Paul, Sandomierz, ornamentation from the year
1710. Photo by S. Michalczuk.*

Crucifix, second half of the seventeenth century, Lublin, the Dominican church. Photo by S. Michalczuk.

St. Bruno. Engraving by B. van Westerhout, after a model by Johann Schumer (c.1690) in Zbiory Graficzne Biblioteki im. Ossolińskich in Wrocław. Microfilm from the Ossoliński library.

other words refer to the fruits of the tree of the knowledge of good and evil, under which the first parents are sitting. The content of the scenes on the vault can be read in chronological order, beginning with the scene placed in the choir on the gospel side. It represents a kneeling man and woman, to whom two angels show the Christ Child standing to one side and raising the cross. Before them sits death holding an apple in one hand, and in the other a document with the text *Momentaneum ad deletum* (meaning "Momentary and for destruction," or "Destined for destruction.") At death's feet stands a raven, the symbol of the devil. Before the man there lies an open book with the inscription *Durunt in bonis dies suos et in puncto ad inferorum . . . descendum . . . Rus me libere vi . . .,* etc. The second scene represents a man on his death-bed surrounded by priests and lay persons. Death stands above the dying man and touches him with an arrow, while it holds an hourglass above the heads of those gathered in the room. The final scene on that side of the nave is the Last Judgement. Christ sits as pantocrator; beside him are the Mother of God and St. John (or the man who is being judged). The center of the composition is occupied by Michael the Archangel holding scales, to which a small devil has attached himself. On the opposite wall, on the epistle side, there is a representation of heaven with a choir of angels singing and playing and with angels holding the inscription *Sanctus, Sanctus.* At the bottom of the scene are three figures kneeling in adoration. In the fifth arch stands a woman with a nimbus on her head, holding a golden circlet in her right hand, and in her left a stork. A rooster and salamander are at her feet. The last painting, much painted over, represents a woman (?) with a nimbus on her head; she is playing a harp (perhaps David or Cecilia).[5] These six scenes are completed by hierograms of Christ, the Mother of God, the inscription Jahwe, and the Eye of Providence, which are placed in the starlike rosettes, and by Cherubim and Angels painted in the smaller spaces of the stucco decoration who are holding the inscriptions *Alleluia, Alleluia,* and *Gloria in Excelsis Deo.*

The decoration originated with Jakób Orzechowski after the reconstruction of the church in 1710.[6]

5. The scene of the adoration of the cross on the vaulting of the church of St. Paul in Trier.

This church was decorated in 1740, or thereabout, with frescoes by Th. Scheffler. On one of the bays of the vaulting there is a scene of the adoration of the cross, which seems to grow from the crown of a spreading palm.[7]

II. AN INTERPRETATION: THE GENERAL PROBLEM

Replacing the cross with the palm tree, as cited in the three examples, is an exceptionally bold undertaking. To a great degree the Sandomierz and Trier solutions are compromises. All these examples, however, originated on the basis of the same scriptural texts, the works of the Church Fathers, and in dependence on the liturgical ritual as well as on the content of staged and published theatrical works of that time.

It is generally accepted that Christ was crucified on a cross known as the *crux immissa* or *capitata,* described generally as the Latin cross.[8] However, besides this type of cross and its variations, which one can describe as a cross made of beams, there are also in iconography other forms of crucifixion, for instance, on a live tree, bush, or lily. Hence, one can speak of a dead cross or a living cross.

The crucifixion of Christ on a living tree—the Tree of Life, for such is the meaning of the living cross—is the creation of Christian mysticism. It appears in literature and is illustrated in the plastic arts. The considerations of the mystics tended in two directions: the beams of the cross came to life, because they had been moistened with the blood of Christ, and sprouted roots and leaves—a thought expressed in the hymn *Pange Lingua*: "Relax thy limbs, O Tree, do not so stiffen their fibres, soften thy natural hardness, become soft to receive the members of the highest King. Thou alone wert worthy to raise the holy sacrifice . . . thou, who hast been dampened with the holy blood of the Lamb."[9] The second fruit of mystical considerations was the cross, the living tree, a medieval idea popularized by St. Bonaventure (1221–1274) in his treatise *Tractatus qui lignum vitae dicitur,* but its origins reach back to Christian archeology.[10] During the persecutions of the first Christians the cross was represented under the form of a tree—a sacred relic, the sign of redemption known only to the initiated.[11] The vivifying cross with Christ hung upon it appears in miniatures and in ivory carvings in the ninth and tenth centuries. Already as a tree, but still connected with the motif of the genealogical tree of Jesse, it appears in miniatures of the twelfth century among the circles from which St. Bonaventure came. It is in the fourteenth and fifteenth centuries that the cross as the Tree of Life appears most often. Later on it is rarely met in that form; a few examples are a tradition from the later Middle Ages.[12]

The Tree of Life was identified with the tree growing in paradise, described in the Old Testament, and it was considered a symbol of redemption and, subsequently, of Christ Himself—the source of life, the tree bearing fruit—[13] and "the leaves shall not fall from it nor shall its fruit cease; every month it shall bring new fruit, for its waters shall come from the sanctuary, and its fruit shall be nourishment and its foliage shall be healing" (Ezech. 47:12). This idea was reflected in ancient Christian art. Such a tree of paradise is the cross growing out of the acanthus bush against a background of braided vegetation, and from under it streams flow. It is done in mosaic in the apse of St. Clement's basilica in Rome (eleventh century), copied from a fifth-century composition that at one time decorated its lower church.[14]

We must recall the manner of representing the crucified Christ at that time. Down to the beginning of the eleventh century, faith in the divinity of Christ, in the memory of his resurrection, dictated that he be always represented with open eyes. This was the vision of the Triumphant Savior, often with a royal crown on his head. His body did not hang weakly on his outstretched arms, which in their level extension were to embrace all of humanity.[15]

In the ancient world the palm was the reward for victory; the symbol had the same meaning for pagans and for Jews.[16] Besides the cypress, it was synonymous with the eternally reborn Phoenix and like him it expressed immortality. These two meanings—victory and immortality—were united as well in the palm used in ecclesiastical art from the first Christian centuries.[17] The palm branch was the symbol of heaven and the emblem of martyrdom. We know of palm representations in the art of the catacombs, where Christ is portrayed as one of the variations of the Tree of Life.[18]

The palm is often mentioned in both the Old and New Testaments. Among other places, in the Canticle of Canticles the beloved is compared to a palm: "Thy figure is like the palm, and thy breasts like bunches of grapes" (Cant. 7:7). A further verse in this chapter contains the same words as those written on the ribbon above the crucifix at Sandomierz: "I shall ascend the palm and take its fruit." According to the Apocrypha, at the time of the flight to Egypt the palm tree bent down for Joseph, so that he could pick its dates for the Child. Palm branches celebrated the triumphant entry of Christ into Jerusalem (John 12:13).

In the art of the early Middle Ages, and particularly in Byzantine art, a type of cross developed known as the *crux gemmata*.[19] This was a continuation of the symbolic scenes that decorated the apses of the old Christian basilicas (St. Peter, Ss. Cosmas and Damian, St. Paul outside the walls), where beside Christ and the Apostles a palm was placed and sometimes the Phoenix sitting on one. The *crux gemmata* was also surrounded on both sides by two palm trees bending their crowns to it. They represented the trees of paradise: The Tree of Life and the Tree of the Knowledge of Good and Evil, as it were, adoring the sign of salvation.

III. THE SPECIAL PROBLEM

At present it is difficult to establish the immediate origin of the objects of our interest. They appeared in different evironments, and a lack of information makes an exact chronology impossible. Most of the information concerns the circles in which the crucifixion on the palm tree appeared in Poland. These are the Lublin Dominicans and the Sandomierz canons. Special attention must be given to two clerics and their activities: Paweł Ruszel, a Dominican from the priory at Lublin, and Jakób Orzechowski, a canon of Sandomierz.

Jakób Orzechowski,[20] who joined the Sandomierz chapter in 1706, was born after the death of Paweł Ruszel (1658),[21] author of the three-volume work, *Skarb nigdy nieprzebrany Kościoła świętego katolickiego Krzyż Pański . . . z doktorów świętych i historyków poważnych napisane przez . . . promotora drzewa krzyża ś. lubelskiego*. Both were characterized by great powers of the mind and a fruitful activity in important positions.

P. Ruszel was the first moderator of the *studium generale* established at the Dominican convent in Lublin in 1644, a scholar and professor, preacher and pastor, and a zealous propagator of the cult of the relic of the Holy Cross. In the first two books of his work he describes the history of the cross in connection with a description of the Lord's Passion. He presents very rich material, with many sketches, citations, and critical considerations; in the third book he describes the history of the relic preserved in Lublin and the miracles associated with it.

Particularly interesting are the author's comments about Christ on the cross and the dictatorial tone he uses in the words directed to the artists, whom he informs that Christ on the cross had his arms drawn out level: "And therefore worthy of reproach are those imperfect artists who draw Christ according to their own imagination, his hands nailed close to his head and extended toward heaven. . . . But someone will answer that *Pictoribus et Poetis omnia licent.* This may be so, that all is permitted them, but it is in *naturalibus conceptus* that they can imagine—the painter can paint an owl with a peacock's tail, and the poet can describe the Sirene imagined on the sea—but to disfigure the mysteries of the holy faith, *deprauando misteria fidei, quo ad suum conceptum,* is not permitted, *et si talis in hoc fuerit pertinax saperet haeresim.*"22

Chapter 33 of book I is devoted to Christ as King of the Jews: "Before his death, he entered Jerusalem on an ass. Then all the people from the city went out to meet and greet him as the King of Israel, and gave him royal honor carrying palms before him, which are the sign of a victor, and they cast their garments on the road before him as before a great monarch."23 The two following chapters proclaim the praise and triumph of the Crucified. Chapter 34 is entitled "Christ on the Cross Triumphed over the Enemy of the Human Race, the Prince of Hell."24

Ruszel expressly tries to create and to establish an iconographic motif for the time of the Church's triumph over the Reformation: "The triumph and reign of Christ on the cross was expressed by the Holy Spirit in the words of David, Psalm 96, 'Dicite in nationibus a ligno,' which words are not found in the Hebrew or the Greek text; however, according to St. Augustine, S. Symmachus, Theodoret, Tertullian, and others, this place in Scripture is to be read thus: 'Tell the nations that the Lord reigned from the tree.'" Appealing further to the Fathers, he pretends that this text was disfigured by the Jews, who "thought it to be an unbearable thing that God should reign hanging on a tree." He cites Jerome: "Christ was truly crucified in the flesh, but actually the devil was crucified there, for it was not a cross but a triumph."25 He then cites a series of descriptions of the cross from the other Church Fathers: Ambrose, Athanasius, Augustine, Chrysostom, "who call the cross the Lord's triumph, or the triumphal banner of Christ, the sword by which the devil was conquered, a Palm, and other titles which express his victory and triumph."26

True, the palm in the works of Ruszel is not identified with the cross to the degree that it could replace the cross in form as well as in conceptual content. However, the author believes that it shares in the crucifixion of Christ. Enumerating the opinions of the Fathers, he stresses "that the Lord's cross was made of four kinds of wood, that is, cypress, cedar, olive, and palm . . . the palm tree provided the transverse beam, to which the hands of Christ were nailed."[27]

The author twice compares Christ's victory on the tree of the cross with the fall of Adam by means of the Tree of the Knowledge of Good and Evil. He cites a thesis of St. Thomas and writes: "Just as Adam sinned by transgressing the divine commandment in daring to enjoy the fruit of the forbidden tree, and his sin then fell upon the whole human race, so it was proper that satisfaction be made to God the Father by a tree for that sin. The Holy Church sings about the Tree of Life: 'By the tree we were made slaves, and by the tree we were made free.' Christ, then, hung upon a tree, as it were, returned what Adam had taken from the tree, according to that which the Holy Spirit said about him in Psalm 68: 'Adam despised the commandment by taking the apple from the tree; but whatever Adam lost, Christ found on the cross. . . .' "[28]

In his work Ruszel cites the very same words from the Canticle of Canticles that are inscribed on the arch in the church at Sandomierz: *Ascendam in Palmam et apprehendam fructus eius.* He adds: "Adam, our first parent, took the forbidden fruit from the Tree, and it turned into bitterness for him; but Christ ascended the palm tree, which produces sweet fruit, so that he would take fruit from that tree with both hands, to remove that bitterness with which Adam had infected the whole human race."[29]

Jakób Orzechowski was the pastor of the church of St. Paul in Sandomierz; he changed its appearance fundamentally in 1710, when he enlarged the fifteenth-century building, extending the nave by one bay; installed a marble floor; erected a new altar; and procured many pictures and paintings. He also "painted the sanctuary." The dignities and functions offered him by the Sandomierz Chapter seem to testify to his readiness and ambitions, thus permitting us to assign to him some share at least in the choice of theme, if not in the elaboration of the iconographic program, that transformed the church.[30]

The statement of the ideological program for the internal decoration of the Sandomierz church was drawn from the same sources as theological and mystical considerations: the moralizing texts of the dramatic presentations staged in the religious colleges during the seventeenth and eighteenth centuries. In them we meet the same content, transmitted to the faithful in the same didactical concept. For instance, in the *Dialogue about the Tree of Life* (1609)[31] a sinner appears seeking the way to heaven in the tree. The "infernal powers" see this, and they seek to destroy the Tree of Life; but when they are unable to do this, they lead the sinner to the way of evil. The angel guardian comforts him, man wins the conflict, and "like a victor he enjoys the Tree of Life while angels sing to congratulate him on his victory."

Death sees its greatest enemy in the Tree of Life:

Nieprzyjaciół mój wielki to Drzewo Żywota.
[My great enemy is the Tree of Life.]

The *Dialogue* actually permits us to read the theme presented in plastic form in the church of St. Paul. Two people kneel there, face to face with death, which shows them the *vanitas* of the world. The raven-Satan stands there, but there are also angels who point to Christ with the cross on his shoulders. The second scene represents the moment that man leaves the earth—death. Then follows the judgment. Further, heaven is represented, but it is a reward only for those who accepted the reality of Adam's fall and Christ's victory. For before the eyes of the faithful there arise the two trees of paradise: the Tree of the Knowledge of Good and Evil with the inscription "Do not eat, for thou shalt die," and the Tree of Life, the palm, which the Lord ascended in order to pluck the fruit of eternal life. In a further development of the theme there is above the ambo the woman with a nimbus on her head, certainly symbolizing the Church. In her right hand she holds a golden circlet, perhaps the aureole of holiness—the attribute of virtue—and in her left a stork, the symbol of vigilance and religious exaltation. At her feet there stands a rooster—the symbol of vigilance, the fall and repentance of St. Peter—and a salamander (?), which is the emblem of purity. The victory of Christ is announced by angels who hold the inscription *Alleluia* and *Gloria in Excelsis Deo*. The word *Jahwe*, the Eye of Providence, and the hierograms of Jesus and Mary in a uniform manner complete the whole.

In the engraving of Juliana de Cornillon, the crucifixion on a palm tree is not without deeper meaning if we consider the role that she played in beginning and spreading the cult of the Blessed Sacrament. As a result of the revelations she had supposedly received from Christ, the feast of Corpus Christi was established in 1246 in the diocese of Liège; and Pope Urban IV then extended it to the Universal Church. Blessed Juliana is usually represented as worshipping the host exposed in a monstrance on the altar.[32] In the engraving the host is replaced by Christ, crucified on the palm tree, as Christ the Victor.

The engraving of St. Bruno also comes from Flanders, where the cult of Juliana de Cornillon had flourished. Lacking sufficient information, we cannot identify that country as the origin of this type of crucifix. The prominent mystical character of its complicated expression suggests rather that we see its origin in the religious culture of seventeenth-century Spain, whose influence on the life of the Church at that point was great.[33] Further research will undoubtedly expand and specify the area of this problem. At present it is even difficult to fix a chronological framework. In Polish literature this motif was expressed from the beginning of the seventeenth century, although at present we have not as yet found a text that would univocally describe what the Lublin crucifix represents. The paintings in Trier from 1740 are certainly later.

A search for mutual relations between those objects leads to a closer knowledge of their common climate and at the same time enriches our knowledge of post-Tridentine iconography, in which there is a return to the representation of the crucified Christ in the moment of triumph, and in which the victory of redemption on the cross is associated with the miraculous and victorious resurrection—*Deus regnans et triumphans a cruce*.[34]

The post-Tridentine return to dogma and mysticism, the quest for the victory of the Church through the victory of Christ, led the medieval conception—crucifixion on the Tree of Life—to a new form by associating both these iconographic motifs, the palm tree and Christ alive on the cross, so important to Christian art. Ideologically this created in an unusually consistent manner the type of Christ crucified on a palm tree—Christ victorious!

FOOTNOTES

1. The present work was presented in the doctoral seminar of W. Tomkiewicz, November 20, 1961.

2. Formerly, as we know from the visitation of 1888, the crucifix was in the upper corridor of the convent, at the stairs leading to the chapel of the Holy Cross. The visitation described the crucifix as "old."

3. Gabinet Rycin, U. W., no. T. 1086, II, 41.

A Baroque Crucifix

4. "Zbiory Graficzne Biblioteki im. Ossolińskich," Teczka no. i, 63, J. g. 20416. The engraving has the inscription *S. Bruno Cartusianorum Patriarcha,* and the date about 1690. Balthasar van Westerhout died in Prague in 1728, where he resided from 1683. In 1670 he was the student of Al. Goquier (Goutier) in Antwerp. See A. Wurzbach, *Niederländisches Künstlerlexikon* (Vienna, 1910) II, 855.

Johann Schumer, a painter and etcher, born about 1670, perhaps was also a Hollander. See E. Bénézit, *Dictionnaire des Peintres, Sculpteurs, Dessinateurs et Graveurs* (1954) VII, 661.

5. This painting seems to be entirely new, and hence we shall omit it in the remainder of our discussion.

6. J. Wiśniewski, *Katalog prałatów i kannoników sandomierskich od 1186–1926* (Radom, 1926) 225–226. The capitular chapters are included from 1581 to 1866.

7. H. Reiners, *Tausend Jahre Rheinischer Kunst* (Bonn, 1925) ill. 245.

8. G. Ricciotti, *Życie Jezusa Chrystusa* (Warsaw, 1956) 672–688; R. Hynek, *Święty całun. Męka Pańska w oczach nauki* (Poznań, 1937); L. Reau, *Iconographie de l'art Chrétien* (Paris, 1957) II, 483.

9. See also the *Office of the Holy Cross,* an old seventeenth-century printed work without title page, author, or date of publication, in the Library of the Catholic University of Lublin, XVII, 102–107, under the identification *Nabożeństwa różne 291–295.*

10. J. Timmers, *Symboliek en iconographie der Christlijke Kunst* (Roermond, 1947) 286; *Reallexikon zur deutsche Kunstgeschichte* (Stuttgart, 1948) II, 100.

11. F. Cabrol, *Dictionnaire d'archéologie chrétienne et de la liturgie* (Paris, 1907) I–1, 2706.

12. Timmers, *Symboliek* 288.

13. Paweł Ruszel, *Skarb nigdy nieprzebrany Kościoła świętego katolickiego Krzyż Pański* (Lublin, 1655) I, 135, where the author calls attention to this in the following words: "That tree planted in the middle of paradise, which is called the Tree of Life, was the figure of the Cross of Christ."

14. F. van der Meer and Ch. Mohrmann, *Atlas van de Oudchristelijke Werald* (Amsterdam, 1958) 145.

15. A. Grillmeier, *Der Logos am Kreuz* (Munich, 1956) and Reau, *Iconographie* 477.

16. Cabrol, *Dictionnaire* XIII–1, 904.

17. L. Cloquet, *Éléments d'iconographie chrétienne* (Lille, 1891) 356, 371.

18. *Ibid.* 372: on a goblet from the catacombs, the palm tree is represented as surrounded by the heads of the twelve apostles.

19. Z. Świechowski, "Drzewo Życia w monumentalnej rzeźbie romańskiej Polski," *Księga ku czci Władysława Podlachy* (Wrocław, 1957) 118.

20. Wiśniewski, *Katalog Prałatów* 225.

21. See A. Wadowski, *Kościoły lubelskie* (Cracow, 1907) 283–293; S. Baracz, *Rys dziejów zakonu kaznodziejskiego w Polsce* (Lwów, 1861) 242–244. Father Ruszel "was a religious of great holiness, a scholar, as well as the industrious author of several works." He taught in Lublin, Cracow, and Rome. From about 1640 he was the regent of the *studium formale* in Wilno. Shortly thereafter he returned to Lublin, obtained the degree of master, and served four years as the first regent, and later as pro-regent, of the *studium generale.* This

Stanisław Michalczuk

great master and teacher of youth died at the age of 65, in the year 1658. He was the author, among other works, of *Skarb nigdy nieprzebrany* (cited in note 13 above); a second edition appeared at Częstochowa (1723) and a third at Berdyczów (1767). Ruszel based his work on the book by Jakób Bosius, *Crux Triumphans et gloriosa . . . Libri Sex* (Antwerp, 1617). Bosius discusses extensively the words "Ascendam in palmam" in the *Canticle of Canticles*.

22. Ruszel, *Skarb* I, 29, 30.

23. *Ibid.* 96.

24. *Ibid.* 98.

25. *Ibid.* 98–100.

26. *Ibid.* 100; see also Św. Ambroży, *Mowy,* translated by Father Jan Czuj (Poznań, 1939) 235–257, in the discourse on the death of Theodosius, where he speaks of St. Helena seeking the cross of Golgotha: "On this place of conflict, where is the victory? I am seeking the sign of salvation, and I do not find it. I . . . in royal ornaments, and the cross of the Lord in the dust? I in gold, and the triumph of Christ in ruins? He is still hidden, and is the palm of eternal life hidden?"

27. Ruszel, *Skarb* (Częstochowa, 1725) I, 10, 22.

28. *Ibid.* 141, 142.

29. *Ibid.* 22.

30. Wiśniewski, *Katalog prałatów* 225–226: Jakób Orzechowski was elected *vice-custos* in 1708; in 1717 he received the first place in the stalls after Siwers; in 1725 he was entrusted in cooperation with Father Kalisz to put into order the chapter's library and to purchase new books in Gdańsk.

31. J. Lewański, *Dramaty staropolskie* (Warsaw, 1961) IV, 419–460. The dialogue about the Tree of Life was staged on June 22, 1609, in the Jesuit College in Kalisz.

32. K. Radoński, *Święci i błogosławieni Kościoła katolickiego* (Warsaw, 1947) 244; L. Reau, *Iconographie* III–2, 773.

33. This is especially true of Spanish religious literature, which was imbued with mysticism and which became popular in all Catholic countries, Poland as well. See St. Ciesielska-Borkowska, *Mistycyzm Hiszpański na gruncie polskim* (Cracow, 1939); W. Borowy, *O poezji polskiej w wieku XVIII* (Cracow, 1948); and the introduction to the works of St. John of the Cross by Father Otto de Angelis, in Św. Jan od Krzyża, *Dzieła* (Cracow, 1961) I, 52–56. St. John of the Cross in his spiritual *Canticle,* written in 1584, see *Dzieła* (Cracow, 1961) II, 152, expressly speaks of what we have emphasized in the work of Ruszel and of that which found its expression in plastic form in the church at Sandomierz, namely, the parallel between the fall of Adam and the redemption of Christ.

34. Among others, St. Francis de Sales (1567–1622)·expresses this idea when he describes Christ Crucified: "He suffers externally with great peace, his eyes, sweet and mild, gaze chiefly at the bosom of the Father. His lips are open and breathe in a peaceful and patient manner." See E. Mâle, *L'art religieux après le Concile de Trente* (Paris, 1932) 278. This type of the Crucified, spread especially by Guido Reni, is not without the crown of thorns but contrasts vividly with the crucifix based on the Gothic-German tradition appearing at the same time—Christ dying, or already dead, in terrible sufferings. See Geza de Francovitch, "L'Origine et la diffusion del Crocifisso gotico doloroso," *Kunstgeschichtliches Jahrbuch der Biblioteca Hertziana* (Leipzig, 1938) 145–261.

LUDWIG PASTOR AND THE

HISTORIOGRAPHY OF THE POPES

Mieczysław Żywczyński

THE YEAR 1964 MARKS THE ONE-HUNDRED-TENTH ANNIVERSARY OF the great historian, Ludwig Pastor. This circumstance calls for some consideration of Pastor's position in historiography and chiefly in the historiography of the papacy. It is in this field that Pastor rendered the greatest service.

I.

First of all, a few data from his life.[1] He was born January 31, 1854, in Aachen, but later his parents moved to Frankfort-am-Main, then the seat of the German Confederation—a city already known in the eighth century, and thereafter a free imperial city until 1866. For the first years of his life Pastor was a Protestant, until the death of his Protestant father; only then did his extremely pious mother begin to bring him up as a Catholic. Socially he belonged to the bourgeoisie. His father having been a wealthy merchant, the son was also destined to be one, but from the very beginning this occupation failed to attract him. He was more interested in history, old coins, and historical writings. The family tutor and the middle school undoubtedly contributed to this. His teacher in the *gymnasium* Pastor attended was Reverend Janssen, then an important, and later a renowned, historian. He exercised an enormous influence on Pastor—and the historian of the popes always remembered this. Janssen ultimately persuaded Pastor's mother to permit her son to devote himself to a learned career. He himself engaged in the study of the history of the German people from the fifteenth to the eighteenth centuries and the events that provoked the Reformation, Janssen encouraged his young student to study the renaissance of the Church in the sixteenth and seventeenth centuries—a subject that had been neglected in Catholic historiography, and that in Protestant historiography had been underestimated or imperfectly represented. On December 8, 1873, Janssen introduced his nineteen-year-old student to Ranke's *History of the Popes*.[2] This work made an enormous impression on Pastor, and even that early he decided to dedicate himself to this same theme, but conceived from a Catholic viewpoint. Janssen approved, though he knew his young charge lacked the "matura."

Rarely in the history of science does it occur that anyone quite so early determines the direction of his specialized studies—and even the subject of his work—and remains true to this subject for a lifetime, as Pastor did. He devoted nearly fifty-five years to the history of the papacy.

His first training in method was given him by Janssen, who with his help was preparing for the press his own history of the German people from the decline of the Middle Ages. Pastor then studied in Louvain, Bonn, Berlin, and Vienna. He had great professors: in Bonn, Moritz Ritter; in Berlin, Waitz, Droysen, and Treitschke. He also worked in the seminar of Ritter and Waitz. But none of them, except perhaps the first two, made a great impression on Pastor. Moritz Ritter, under whose direction he wrote his first work for a seminar, had been Ranke's last student; he possessed wide knowledge, as well as a thoroughly perfected method, but he was an Old Catholic and disliked Orthodox Catholics; and, as Pastor writes,[3] association with him was not easy.

Pastor was even less pleased with Droysen and Treitschke, with their narrow nationalism and their attacks on Catholicism. Professor Georg Waitz had a greater influence on him. A renowned student of the history of the German constitution, Waitz emphasized the complete use of sources—dry in thought, without imagination—and far from Ranke's breadth of historical horizons, even though he was his student, he was nonetheless a good teacher.[4] "My best works," he himself said, "are my students."[5] It seems that Pastor did not gain much at the University of Vienna. The well-known paleographer and student of diplomatics, Theodor Sickel, did not want to receive him in his seminar. In spite of this, Pastor established relations with distinguished Catholics, for instance, Karl Adolph Constantine von Hoefler, and in particular with Onno Klopp—a convert from Protestantism and an enormously fruitful historian who had engaged in effective polemics with the Protestant writers about the sixteenth and seventeenth centuries, as well as a determined opponent of the Prussians.[6] After Janssen, Klopp undoubtedly exercised the greatest influence on Pastor. As a zealous Catholic, even though a good scholar, he was not able to bring Pastor to the doctorate in Vienna at that time, but finally succeeded at Graz in 1878, under the direction of Professor John Weiss, who held similar views. Onno Klopp aided Pastor in reaching the Vatican sources, for he introduced him to the nuncio in Vienna, Jacobini, who recommended him in Rome. However, it was only with great difficulty, after months of effort, that Pastor in January 1879 was permitted access to the Vatican archive manuscripts, not in the archives proper, but in the library, and under the condition of showing his notes to the prefect of the library, who confiscated a number of his notes. The situation improved when the renowned historian, Cardinal Joseph Hergenröther, became the prefect of the archives. He returned the confiscated notes to the young scholar and allowed him to use the catalogue. Encouraged by this, Pastor presented to him a memorandum on the need of publishing sources from the Vatican Archives down to the sixteenth century. It was to bear the title *Corpus Catholicorum* and was to be the counterpart of the Protestant publication, *Corpus Reformatorum,* which had been appearing since 1827. The project was not carried out at this time,[7] but Pastor's memorandum contributed to the solution of a more important matter. A few years later (1883), Leo XIII made available in part the Vatican archives, which had been closed even to cardinals under pain of excommunication.[8]

In the year 1880 Pastor published a basic work about the efforts at church union during the reign of Charles V and the correspondence of the nuncio Contarini;[9] with other smaller works behind him, he wished to achieve his professional qualification, but this was not an easy matter. There could be no thought of a university career in Germany or in Vienna; so he qualified at a second-rate university in Innsbruck in February 1880. Only after eleven months—and that not without the intervention of Pastor's friends—did the Ministry of Education in Vienna confirm his *habilitation.* But even though he continued to do distinguished scholarly work, he could not even think of promotion. Efforts to get himself into the Czech university in Prague were without success. When he published the first volume of his history of the popes, his colleague, Professor Busson, said to him: "You can publish another dozen such volumes, but you will never be proposed for a professor, if you do not change your direction."[10] This "direction" was the ultramontane Catholicism of Pastor, as it was then called. Finally, only after the efforts of influential friends in Vienna, Pastor in 1888 became *professor extraordinarius* and then a year later *professor ordinarius* in Innsbruck. Efforts at having him transferred to another university also failed. In 1901 he became the director of the Austrian Historical Institute in Rome; in 1908 the emperor granted him hereditary nobility and in 1916 granted him the title of Baron.[11] After World War I he was named Austrian Ambassador at the Holy See. He died June 30, 1928.

As a professor he apparently lectured well, but he did not create any school. He had only two eminent students, Ignatius Philip Dengel, who also became his successor in the university chair and in the Austrian Historical Institute in Rome, and the Jesuit Emil Michael.

By conviction he was a sincere Catholic, nor did he hide this. But he was also alien to and unfavorable toward all the critical tendencies pervading German Catholicism at the turn of the nineteenth and twentieth centuries; he neither understood the need of social changes, nor saw the social questions either about him or in history. He was a thorough conservative, something that offended many Catholics. For instance, he withdrew from the editorial committee of the *Historisches Jahrbuch,* a periodical published by German Catholics, because cooperation with him proved difficult. He was offended by a quite correct review of a book by the Jesuit Michael.[12] It is clear from Pastor's diary how ill-disposed he was toward those who did not share his conservatism, namely, Hertling, Grauert, Ehrhard, Merkle, even though they were Catholics and eminent scholars.

Pastor played a mysterious role in Rome in 1907. It is not known exactly who persuaded Pius X to create the Catholic Institute for the Development of Sciences. This was meant as an institution to support science by the publication of learned works and the distribution of funds for their conduct. Cardinal Marian Rampolla was to be the head of it. The choice was really excellent, for the Cardinal was a respected scholar and pursued archeology actively, even while he was secretary of state for Leo XIII. At the Second International Congress of Archeologists in 1900, in spite of the burden of political work, he presented two lectures.[13] After his retirement from the Secretariat of State, he published a fundamental monograph on St. Melanie.[14] Pastor was to become the secretary-general of the Institute. And then quite unexpectedly Pius X withdrew his support from the enterprise. Undoubtedly, the fear of modernism played a part here, but, more exactly, no less than did certain intrigues of the Pope's usually successful advisers. Joseph Schmidlin, the author of a monograph about Pius X, states that Pastor played a special role in these intrigues.[15] It was not until 1936 that Pius XI created the Academy.

Pastor's role remains unclear in the matter of Schnitzer, who in his investigations into Savonarola arrived at conclusions differing from those of the author of the history of the popes. Schnitzer says that already in 1908 Pastor tried to have his work put on the Index, and that in 1926 he contributed to denying Schnitzer access to the Vatican archives. Actually Pastor denied both these charges, but Schnitzer repeated his charge and added that Pastor's friend, Bishop Aichner of Brixen, tried to have his works put on the Index.[16] This perhaps would not be convincing, for it would not follow from Aichner's efforts and his relationship with Pastor that he was acting under Pastor's influence; but Pastor's diary, published in 1950, states expressly that in his polemics with Schnitzer he was consulting with the prince-bishop of Brixen.[17] In this way Schnitzer's charge takes on the character of great probability.

Besides his history of the popes, Pastor published a series of scholarly works on the history of art, the history of the Church in the sixteenth century, as well as several monographs on prominent figures from the history of Germany and Austria in the nineteenth and twentieth centuries. Some of them are simply panegyrics.[18] But he won world renown with his massive, sixteen-volume *History of the Popes from the End of the Middle Ages,* published in the years 1886–1933. It embraced the history of the popes from the middle of the fifteenth century (only in a sketchy manner from the beginning of the fourteenth century) to the end of the eighteenth century, that is, 350 years.[19]

II.

In order to understand the importance of this work, it is necessary to consider Pastor's predecessors in this area, namely, the scholars who had tried before him to describe the whole of larger periods in the modern history of the popes. Obviously we cannot discuss here the authors of particular works or monographs, or even works on the general history of the Church.

If we omit the works of theologians about the primacy,[20] the first historian of the modern papacy was the custodian of the Vatican Library, Bartolomeo Sacchi, also called by the name of his birthplace, Platina.[21] The direction of the library and the task of writing the history of the popes was entrusted to him by Sixtus IV, even though Platina did not enjoy a favorable reputation as a good Catholic. His *Vitae Pontificum*, completed in 1474, included the pontificate of Paul II, that is, down to the year 1471. This was the first modern work in the history of the popes, based on Vatican sources, to which Platina had easy access. The work was written with clarity and talent. Platina attempted criticism here and there, but not enough to offend his patron or to spoil the smooth narrative. Only in one instance did he give way not merely to criticism, but to actual spite. He could not forgive his persecutor Paul II, and instead of a biography he presented a caricature. Platina's work was an enormous step forward from the annalistic historiography of the Middle Ages, but it was not strictly scholarly, for Platina was more concerned about a smooth narrative than about truth; he undervalued the importance of dates, and he showed only a superficial understanding of events. Nevertheless, he did achieve significant renown.

Platina's continuator was a learned Italian, the Augustinian Onofrio Panvini, famous in historiography not only because of a series of archeological works about Rome, a work about the cardinals, and his *Epitome Vitarum Romanorum Pontificum*, but above all by editing Platina's works, which he continued to the most recent times.[22] This continuation enjoyed significant esteem, and its author great recognition. For instance, it is emphasized that the learned Panvini would not even accept a bishopric.[23] In fact, however, Panvini was partisan in his writing and understood the history of the popes only in terms of external circumstances; and he could be bought. For instance, in the first edition of his life of Paul IV—written during the times of Pius IV, who did not like his predecessor—Panvini wrote of Paul IV rather negatively as hardly a normal human being (*haud satis mentis compos*); but in a later edition, written during the reign of Pius V, who took a positive attitude to Paul IV, Panvini makes him a distinguished pope. It is even worse with Pius IV, of whom Panvini wrote three times: first, rather indifferently, because he thought he was being paid too little; the second, with enormous

praise, because he had received money; and the third, rather negatively, since this was in the time of Pius V, who did not esteem his
namesake very highly.[24] Panvini retained the form he inherited
from Platina, just as the latter had received it from the humanists.
It is not a history, but a series of superficial panegyrics.

Similar in character were all the histories of the popes written
by the successors of Panvini in the seventeenth century: John
Anthony Petramellari; Alphonse Chacon, known as Ciaconius;
John Bordini; Andrew du Chesne; John Palazzi, and other lesser
lights.[25]

Down to the middle of the eighteenth century the humanistic
manner dominated in writing the history of the popes. Emphasis
was placed on literary form, much less on a criticism of the
sources; in this way one group repeated the facts from the other,
with generally little care of where the information first appeared.
It seemed that the eighteenth century would bring a change in
this matter, for in 1716 the first chair of history was established
at a Catholic university. At Freiburg in Baden the Jesuit Gregory
Kolb began to lecture on history, including the history of the
popes.[26] However, through the Jesuits' influence on the emperor,
history had to be taught in the scholastic method, which method,
with its apologetics and polemics directed against the Lutherans,
also characterized the work of Professor Kolb, *Series Romanorum
Pontificum*.[27] John Gandert produced a work completely similar.[28] This was a retreat in the historiography of the papacy to the
level on which it had stood in the Middle Ages. Even Platina and
his continuators provided more than the dry, sketchy works of
Kolb and Gandert, listing of popes and facts from their reigns.
French ecclesiastical historiography maintained a much higher
level but concerned itself only incidentally with the history of the
popes—within the framework of works devoted to other subjects.
Partly it was under the influence of Gallicanism. For instance,
the Jesuit Louis Maimbourg, the author of several larger works
on the history of the papacy, above all pointed out how the papacy
arbitrarily and improperly extended its authority.[29] In the long
run it was the Italians who were most fervently engaged in the history of the papacy, although their works continued in the manner
of the humanists and actually had no scientific value.

Nor did the works of the Protestant writers possess this scientific value. Just as the historical writings of Catholics, especially
in the sixteenth century, had an uncritical hagiographical character, so the Protestants in histories of the papacy applied an

excessively harsh criticism, and in the very institution of the papacy they saw something evil—the work of Satan and the enemy of the true Church. The first prominent work of Protestant historiography, *Chronica* of Sebastian Franck in 1531, devoted its entire third part (there were four) to the popes, and declared them all to have been intolerant. Franck's compilation did not have any scholarly value.[30]

Greater fame than Franck's was enjoyed in the sixteenth century by the Englishmen Robert Barnes and John Bale, who spent many years introducing into Protestant historiography a specific view of the papacy.[31] For the first of these Luther himself wrote an introduction and expressed his joy that the popes, who had until now been attacked *a priori,* were now being attacked *a posteriori,* that is, with the help of history.

It is also entirely understandable that the Enlightenment, taken generally, did not have any sympathy for the papacy. What is more interesting, this antipathy, in varying degrees, appears among Protestants and Catholics. The Protestants do not discuss the subject especially, but only incidentally when they show their contempt for the papacy. The former Protestant dislike of the papacy, which saw in the pope the servant of Antichrist, was now of a quite different nature. The popes of the past were perverse individuals, greedy for power, and the recent popes were rulers who guarded the remnants of power that was moving to its decline. They are not so much the servants of Satan, that is, as enemies of enlightenment and progress, as the opponents of modern culture. The Enlightenment also exercised an important influence on some Catholic historians of the Church. This is evident from the Austrian handbooks of the second half of the eighteenth century.[32] Like the Gallican historians, the Josephinistic historians too tried to show the abuses of papal power. Over and above this, the Catholic historiography of the Enlightenment was undoubtedly on a higher level than the humanistic historiography. It was able to rise above biographical presentation of history, it achieved a broader historical horizon, it won the respect of the majority of historians, and it showed a greater criticism of existing sources; but in the area of the modern history of the papacy, it did not advance scholarship. Consequently, edifying and pious works about the popes continued to appear, but these were little regarded in the scholarly world, or were tendentious in the service of the courts or governments, or in the opinion of the Enlightenment;

they inferred more than the sources permitted, especially the meager published sources.

According to current convictions, a basic change in treating the history of the popes came only with Romanticism; only under fear of presenting repetitious scenes of the French Revolution did the role of the papacy begin to be evaluated and its history studied. This motif appears, for instance, in the work of De Maistre, Hurter, and others. But this view is not correct. Already some writers of the Enlightenment broke with a view of the Middle Ages that had become traditional from the times of humanism; and in connection with this they tried to evaluate the role of the papacy adequately. This change occurred with the conviction of the philosophers about the constant progress of the human race, and in connection with their optimistic theodicy.[33] If the world, they thought, was directed to a goal, and if it moved constantly on the road of progress, the Middle Ages must also have had their meaning, and so also the papacy. This was understood most completely by the renowned John Gottfried Herder (1744–1803) in his *Ideen zur Philosophie der Geschichte*.[34] In spite of his small regard for the papacy as an institution, he did see that it performed three services: the defense of Europe against the Huns, the Saracens, and the Turks; its influence on the rise of government in the West; and its preservation of ancient culture.[35]

A further step in the rehabilitation of the Middle Ages and the papacy was made by an eighteenth-century scholar, long considered the greatest historian of Germany. Johann Müller, a native of Switzerland, became famous chiefly through his history of Switzerland, his general history, and a series of other works in which he apprehended the Middle Ages in a quite different manner—and, owing to this, he exercised a vast influence.[36] His book *Reisen der Päpste* (1782) possessed a fundamental significance. In it he praised the medieval papacy for its defense of the medieval order, the defense of the liberty of the Christian states; this was the first instance of its kind in Protestant literature. It was even then suspected that this professor from Kassel wanted to settle in Rome, and that his work was to obtain for him a residence on the Tiber.[37] It certainly did help him obtain a position in imperial Vienna. Whether this was so or not, Müller became an important person in this area of study, and his judgment of the papacy seemed at that time to have been a revelation.[38] Frederick Schlegel and Frederick Hurter, the Romantics and conservatives from the beginning of the nineteenth century, will appeal to this book, which was quite generally read at that time, and not to the pious lives—and they make this book their point of departure. Fifty years after its publication George Klatz, a Catholic priest, published it with emendations.[39]

During the Romantic period the history of the papacy became quite popular, even though the Romantics did not write a general history of the subject down to the time of Ranke. There were many extensive Catholic elaborations on the subject, though not one of them possessed any great significance. Quite unexpectedly a forty-year-old *professor extraordinarius* at the Berlin University, Leopold Ranke, achieved instant and immense renown with his *Die Römischen Päpste, ihre Kirche und ihr Staat im 16 und 17 Jahrhundert*.[40] The sensation created by this work was compared to that created at the same time by David Frederick Strauss's life of Jesus, although the latter wished to destroy traditional views while Ranke himself was not a destroyer. His significance depended on something else. He had written the first scientific history of the modern papacy, based on printed and manuscript sources. He had come to write it by degrees. It was to be a continuation of an intended work on a grand scale about the monarchies and peoples of Southern Europe. The first volume about the Ottomans and the Spanish monarchy in the sixteenth and seventeenth centuries had appeared in 1827, and its basis was the Venetian agents' reports in the state library in Berlin, to which Müller had first called attention.[41] In order to study the rest of these reports Ranke went to Venice; then studying other sources scattered in various Italian cities, he became interested in the history of Italy. Interest in the papacy was henceforth unavoidable. Even in the preface to the first edition of his work Ranke was somewhat at a loss to explain his writings about the popes in that their significance belongs only to the past, but in the following editions this statement is removed. At that time it was concluded that Ranke had changed his notion of the role of the papacy. This is only a misunderstanding. Ranke did not change his opinion, but the first edition appeared in Prussia during the reign of the dull, conservative anti-Catholic King Frederick William III. The professor from the University of Berlin had to reckon with this at least for the reason that he needed frequent and long absences for his scholarly work, the more so since he could not write the orthodox Lutheran antipapal pamphlet. Perhaps he did not foresee that in 1841 his work, the first among scholarly German historical literature, would be placed on the Catholic Index, and this in company with a German pamphlet.[42] The official Roman: *Annali della scienze religiose* from 1840 undoubtedly expressed the censors' view of Ranke's book, when it declared that the author had hoped to write a history of the papacy, but had presented a disorderly collection of facts—mostly incomplete, erroneous, and falsified—in which every page is permeated by the spirit of Protestant malice, which was the spirit of the whole book. One can doubt whether the censor made a basic examination of Ranke's work; undoubtedly he knew from "above" what the situation was. In any case, the evaluation that it was a *raccozzamento indigesto,* or *fatti guasti et falsati,* or even *malignita protestante*—was entirely incorrect. There is hardly need to mention the charge of calumny.

It is the general opinion that *Die Römischen Päpste* and the history of Germany during the Reformation are Ranke's best work.[43] He had, indeed, published a whole library; but in these works all the good qualities and weak points of the greatest German historian of the nineteenth century are evident. There is, above all, a vast basis in source material. Ranke did not repeat the data from the panegyrical biographical sketches of the popes, but the lion's share of the information he drew directly from sources, and these are mostly manuscript sources. He used these sources in a new way and applied a new method, the philological-critical method. He was not the creator of the method, for it began to be used in Germany at the new German university in Göttingen and went back to the traditions of the Dutch university in Leyden. Apparently, the first to use the method in history was Barthold Georg Niebuhr, and later it was used by Stenzel, Pertz, and Dahlmann. Ranke was also a prominent supporter of this method, and in the history of the modern papacy he was a pioneer.[44] Moreover, until then in the historiography of the papacy there was no such concept. These were not mere biographical sketches of the popes, wherein events they participated in were mentioned—as had been the fashion of older historiography—but was, in fact, a general history of the popes, a general history with particular consideration of the popes, as a result of which their role appeared clearly and visibly: the papacy was presented as a general historical factor. Finally, there was still another quality, namely, Ranke's enormous literary talent, a thing that is rare among German historians generally. The simple, easy, and uncomplicated style, the liveliness and colorfulness of the description, and the artistic presentation of events and people still absorb the attention of the reader. The tragedy of Adrian VI, the harshness of Paul IV, or the reforming zeal of Sixtus V[45] were never again presented so masterfully in simplicity and art.

Ranke's work was also characterized by many negative aspects, and every quality of his work was affected by them. The Berlin professor's basis in source material was in fact very narrow. His principal sources were the manuscripts of the Venetian ambassadorial reports from Rome, an important and very interesting source, but at the same time very one-sided. The Venetian agents inquired into everybody and into everything in Rome. When they could not get their information directly, they got it with the help of the one key that fits the majority of even hermetically sealed castles, namely, money. The Venetian intelligence was masterful, but one cannot use it as the principal source of one's knowledge of the papacy. The Venetians were interested in the persons and political sympathies of the popes and cardinals; they were interested in what had and could have an influence on the Roman Curia; they watched carefully the ambassadors and agents of foreign powers on the Tiber, their enmities, their intrigues, and their influence. However, they were not interested in the role of the papacy as a precisely religious factor; purely ecclesiastical interests were for them a matter of indifference, unless, of course, the pope began to concern himself suddenly with the church in the Most Serene Republic—a thing that the government disliked greatly. This source was, indeed, not the only source, but the principal one that Ranke used.

Independently of this, Ranke was not in a position to understand the papacy properly. Not that he falsified facts through Protestant malice, as the Roman censor declared, for this charge can be considered simple calumny. There is an entirely different reason. Ranke was a Protestant, and for him the papacy was the natural product of the development of things in Rome. In the Middle Ages the papacy possessed importance and had spiritual and political authority, which it was constantly trying to expand. In modern times it was crumbling more and more. It was only from this viewpoint that he considered the papacy; the political factor, above all, interested him. He understood the matter in this way not only because he was a Protestant, but even more because he was mostly, if not exclusively, interested in political history, taken quite broadly; but he considered only slightly the economic, cultural, and legal history.[46] Thus, for instance, he devoted very negligible consideration to the popes' attitude toward art and literature during the Renaissance and the Baroque Age. Hence, Ranke is not an objective writer—but hardly in the sense that he would consciously present a thing falsely. Indeed, if one speaks of a personal tendency, he is often reproached with excessive objectivism.[47] He was an honest writer, but it is necessary to remember the dialectic of the Protestant liberal historiography of the time, so as not to deceive one's self from this viewpoint.[48]

Ranke's work obtained vast popularity and left a permanent trace, for, after all, he founded a historical school, perhaps the greatest of those known in historiography. The majority of the most prominent German historians in the second half of the nineteenth century were Ranke's students. This could not be foreseen at the moment that his work appeared, but even then it made a great impression. Contemporary Catholic ecclesiastical historiography remained far behind the Protestant. The more important Catholic historians were but few, and they were not working on the history of the popes. One Catholic historian, Constantine von Höffler, undertook a casual polemic against Ranke, but he restricted himself to making more precise the Catholic view on the role of the Church and papacy in the Middle Ages.[49] Obviously we will not mention the small polemical and apolegetical works and articles in the Catholic press.

Then some twenty years after the appearance of Ranke's work came another, *Geschichte der Stadt Rom im Mittelalter*,[50] first one volume, and, in the course of years, further volumes, by a yet unknown writer from East Prussia, Ferdinand Gregorovius. Beginning the medieval history of Rome from the fifth century and ending it with the death of Clement VII in 1534, Gregorovius actually produced a history of the papacy, for after all it was the most important matter in the history of the Eternal City. Hence, the author, a perfect narrator and renowned raconteur, devoted most of his attention to it. He presented an extremely vivid and artistic picture, in which it did not matter what was more important and what was less important; at times even an exact use of sources or criticism of a malicious anecdote mattered, as long as it made the whole more colorful. He wrote in a more interesting manner than Ranke, for he was opening the scene on which the pope appeared in Rome. The residences, the palaces, the churches, the people and their habits, the art, the literature, the politics—it was all here. He used a series of sources for this, and although he used as his basis the publications of the great Italian scholar of the eighteenth century, Luigi Muratori, he himself also rummaged among manuscripts. Indeed, he did not gain great recognition in official scholarship,[51] but he did gain it with masses of readers, for he gave them something other than the pedantic official history—he gave them an aesthetic experience. Basically, it was not a history but a historical novel. The author presented a mass of detail and hence he is quoted sometimes even today, but he did not present any problems, and he had no understanding for economic and social problems.

In addition, he was an enemy of Catholicism and the papacy, whose early fall he predicted;[52] moreover, he was unfavorable to Christianity in general, and all this was reflected in his work. Nor is it strange that as soon as it was translated into Italian, the Roman Curia put it on the Index,[53] and the Jesuits began to plan the publication of a work which would be a counterweight to the work of Gregorovius. This task was undertaken by a Jesuit professor in Innsbruck, Hartman Grisar, but the plan was executed only partly and that very slowly.[54]

However, the work of Gregorovius did meet a counterpart from a Catholic historian. Eight years after the work of Gregorovius, there appeared *Geschichte der Stadt Rom,* by the eminent historian Alfred Reumont.[55] Gregorovius was greatly provoked by this work and referred to his rival's work as a compilation; his own work Gregorovius called an original work, based on sixteen years of work on the sources. This judgment was quite wrong. It is true that Reumont began his work on the history of Rome in 1863 and already in 1867 published the first volume, and that in three years he completed the whole thing; it is true also that in seven years he published the entire history of Rome down to the most recent times. But in fact he had been working on the subject for thirty years, for already in 1840–1841 he published a good description of the Papal States at the beginning of the nineteenth century.[56] He had behind him a monograph on Clement XIV plus a series of other works, and he had enormous material for the history of Italy, which he completed afterwards.

Reumont's work is chiefly a history of the popes, but from a scholarly viewpoint it is on an incomparably higher level than the work of Gregorovius. For he had a significantly broader and more scholarly conception. Reumont did not select curiosities and anecdotes, but rather described the legal, cultural, and even moral conditions in Rome; he gave a description of the total activity of the popes, ecclesiastical, political, and cultural; and he cited the sources and literature carefully, using them very critically. And although he was a Catholic very devoted to the Apostolic See, he wrote without taking sides, neither defending nor condemning. There is lacking a general historical background, but this is quite obviously deliberate, for the theme of the work was, after all, the history of Rome and not the history of the popes.

Although the work of Gregorovius went through several editions and even an abridgement was published, Reumont's work, in spite of its superiority over its predecessor's, made practically no impression and was very quickly almost entirely forgotten. And, in fact, this could not be otherwise—it is not a book for reading. It is written in such a dry style that it is not possible to read it without effort. Even his extremely favorable biographer, Herman Huffer, professor of law in Bonn, praised the book only by saying that amazement seizes one when one sees the vast collection of data, that only with difficulty would one find anyone else that had such an extensive knowledge of ancient, medieval, and modern times so as to be adequate to such a task.[57] The dry and sometimes careless style, the pedantic anxiety about exactness, and the extreme succinctness destined the book for oblivion, even though down to the times of Pastor it was the best Catholic work on the history of the modern papacy, and down to the times of Schmidlin one of the best on the nineteenth-century papacy.

When Reumont published his work, Catholic historiography already had several French works on this subject, but they had nothing to do with scholarship. It did, however, have the small but excellent work of Döllinger. This great church historian had until that time been interested in ancient history; but the appearance of Ranke's book on the Reformation caused him to publish a work on the same subject. It contained an immoderately severe criticism of Lutheranism. The history of the popes did not interest Döllinger directly; this subject became significant for him only in connection with political events in Italy, when the Roman Question began to engage the attention of politicians in Europe after 1848. His *Kirche und Kirchen, Papstthum und Kirchenstaat* originated in two public lectures. The first part described the relationship of the papacy to other Christian churches, and the second outlined the history of the papal state with particular attention to modern times from the end of the eighteenth century.[58] This second part, like many of the other works of Döllinger, has not become out of date even today, although when it was published it provoked great indignation in Catholic circles because of the author's view that the Papal States were not necessary for the pope. Besides this work, there also appeared several Catholic works on the history of the papacy, but only two publications of sources merit attention—the works by Roskovany and Theiner. Augustine Roskovany, an alumnus of the seminary in Budapest, seminary professor, and finally Bishop of Nitra, devoted his whole life to the publication of sources dealing with basic problems in the Church. On the subjects of mixed marriages, celibacy, the breviary, the papacy, the cult of the Blessed Virgin Mary, and the relations of Church and State he published about seventy volumes of sources and bibliography, usually translating texts already published but not easily available. The sixteen-volume *Romanus Pontifex* dealt with the papacy. Because the Bishop of Nitra added the literature to the text, his work has significant worth, although one cannot rely on him too much, since the editor was not always critical. He collected whatever came to hand. The situation is worse with the Silesian Augustine Theiner, the editor of a codex of documents for the history of the Papal States, for one cannot rely on the conscientiousness of this otherwise great scholar. Both these publications simply could not replace the works among which the most important position was Ranke's, and the most interesting was Gregorovius', along with a series of Catholic works that had a lower scholarly value; none of them could be compared with the renowned work of Ranke.[59]

Ranke also found an important continuator in the Protestant camp. Mandell Creighton, professor at Oxford and later an Anglican bishop, published his *A History of the Papacy during the Reformation* during the years 1882–1894.[60] Like Reumont, he had previously been interested in the history of Italy, but also in the Reformation. He was one of the creators, although not the most prominent, of the so-called Oxford school of history. This school tried to break with the utilitarianism dominant in English history and established as its goal research without presuppositions, objective and based on sources. Ranke was Creighton's model; Ranke's motto to write history "wie es eigentlich gewesen" exercised a fascination on that whole generation of historians. Creighton practiced this even more consistently than did Ranke. The goal of the professor from Oxford was to provide a better understanding of the Reformation by presenting the history of the papacy.[61] He began with the very beginning of the papacy's existence, but he described in detail only the times from the fourteenth century down to the year 1527. He had a narrower source base than did Ranke; besides published sources, he used some English archival materials, but he himself acknowledged that this material was not important. He, too, like his master, and even in a greater degree, saw in the papacy only a political factor, and saw in its activity only an effort at expanding its authority and winning leadership in Italy. The Reformation, he thought, brought about the decline of the papacy as an international factor. But Creighton surpassed Ranke in impartiality. This won him recognition even in Catholic circles. For instance, Pope Alexander VI is described as no better and no worse than the environment and the times in which he lived.[62] Creighton approached his investigation into persons and things with a natural *pietas*, as he said, and with sympathy; he tried to place himself in the situation of the persons described. This liberal, witty, at times malicious, often perverse professor who spoke disagreeably about his own nation, and later bishop, lived to see a second edition of his book, but by that time a new and dangerous rival had come on the scene.

III.

In 1886 there appeared the first volume of the *Geschichte der Päpste seit dem Ausgang des Mittelalters.* The subtitle promised that this would be something new, a revelation, and declared that the author had used the secret papal archives, which no one, with few exceptions, had used before. Pastor failed to recognize Ranke and he mentioned only Reumont with recognition. According to the title, this volume was to include only the first half of the fifteenth century, but Pastor promised that the work would be continued to the eighteenth century inclusive. So far as content is concerned, in the first volume Pastor cast a glance on the period from 1305, that is, from the time of the Avignon captivity. But this was not the usual general introduction, like Creighton's, for it had well over 200 pages, used printed material carefully, and in part contained manuscript sources, some of which were even published *in extenso.* The second volume of the work appeared in 1889 and covered only a period of twenty-six-years, that is, the pontificates of Pius II, Paul II, and Sixtus IV. After this every few years, and even for five years after his death, the following volumes appeared down to 1933. The last, the third part of Volume XVI, ended with the year 1799. With this Pastor kept his word as he had given it in 1886.

The first volume cited manuscript material from 109 archives

and libraries and contained 34 pages of bibliography; the following volumes were equally impressive in terms of sources. This
must have aroused general amazement, for even the first volume
had 76 reviews.[63] Julius von Pflugh-Hartung, an eminent historian also studying the history of the papacy, wrote that Pastor used
so vast an amount of material as had never been collected by anyone on this subject.[64] Essentially, the history of the modern popes
is based on amazingly vast source material. Pastor had used the
archives and libraries in 230 different locations; the bibliography
he cites includes thousands of items and has a value in itself as a
conscientious catalogue of what had been written about the papacy
until then.[65]

This was the external base and structure of the work. Its composition even at first glance looks uneven; this could be related
to the development of the author's intentions. At first he planned
to work only on the sixteenth and seventeenth centuries; then he
expanded his plan and decided to write the entire modern history of the papacy in six volumes. But then arose the problem of
where to begin. In Pastor's time modern history usually began in
1492, but this was not a key date in the history of the papacy, for
the reign of Alexander VI which began in that year was but a continuation of the work of his predecessors, and a definite change
occurred only in 1527, the year of the *sacco di Roma*. Pastor's
friend, an eminent dogmatician and prelate, John Heinrich,
advised him to write also on the Middle Ages. Another friend to
whom Pastor devoted a panegyrical biography later and a leader
of the Center Party, August Reichensperger, advised him to begin
with the end of the fifteenth century. Finally, and not too consistently, he made the beginning of the fourteenth century his point
of departure. Perhaps this decision was influenced most by a writer
considered one of the greatest masters of historiography in the
second half of the nineteenth century. Pastor was also under the
influence of the famous Swiss historian and student of Ranke,
Jacob Burckhardt, who placed the beginning of modern times,
the birth of modern man, in the Renaissance, that is, the fourteenth and fifteenth centuries, and saw the end of the Middle
Ages in that period.[66] Pastor's history of the popes then begins
with the Renaissance. Pastor retained this division even in later
editions, although in the meantime historiography had rejected
this concept, thanks especially to Burkhardt's student, Karl Neumann.[67] Pastor gave his work a title similar to the title of the
work by his master, Janssen. Both he in his subtitle to his history

of the German people, and Pastor in his subtitle to his history of the popes, used the same words: *Seit dem Ausgang des Mittelalters,* even though, according to Janssen, the Middle Ages ended in the middle of the fifteenth century, and Pastor began his first volume with an introduction from the beginning of the fourteenth century and began with his own narrative with the year 1417.

It was not only the title that Pastor took from Janssen, but he also adopted the external structure, although with important and quite proper changes. In both almost every sentence is supported with a citation from the sources or from the literature; in both almost one-third of the book is devoted to notes that are given in a similar manner. In Janssen, however, the major share of the book consists of citations from the sources or the literature given *in extenso* and intertwined with the comments of the author. One critic of this work reckoned that of the 1,900 pages in the first three volumes, as many as 1,400 come from another pen.[68] Janssen took this method of treatment from Döllinger,[69] without realizing that with the master that had a meaning, for this was determined by the goal of his work. Here the citation of negative judgments had been important, but with his disciple there was no justification for this. Perhaps under the influence of the malicious remarks of Max Lenz about this method, Pastor did not follow Janssen in this matter. However, beyond this, he remained his faithful student and retained his method and views in historiography, and especially the views of their common master, Onno Klopp.

In the literature, Pastor achieved greater recognition than Janssen, but not with everybody at once or with all in the same manner. Hundreds of reviewers were amazed at the mass of material collected by Pastor, but the content was variously evaluated. The infidel liberal, who, however, shared Pastor's social views, Jacob Burkhardt, pronounced the work a *Nachschlagwer.*[70] The Protestant student of the Reformation, Otto Clemen, wrote of the second part of the fourth volume: "We are indeed standing, at least if we consider this volume, before a *monumentum aere perennius.*"[71] More restrained at first was the official representative of German historiography, *Historische Zeitschrift*. But even in it, the same reviewer, a Protestant theologian and eminent Reformation scholar, Gustav Kaverau, who had given an extremely harsh evaluation of the second and third volumes of Pastor's work, already in the fourth volume and in the two parts of the fifth begins to see more positive qualities than negative ones.[72] Generally, the views resembled this last: they mentioned the negative and positive sides; among the latter was reckoned the immense source material and the bibliography.

Pastor heard the most praise in Rome on January 27, 1924, in the auditorium of the German College, where in the presence of some cardinals, superiors-general of religious orders, and the delegates of various learned institutions the speakers outdid themselves in his praise.[73] The luminary of medieval studies, the Jesuit Cardinal Francis Ehrle, called Pastor's history of the popes a work of Providence, and praised its vast source material, criticism, artistic structure, and impartiality.[74] But even before this Pius XI in a letter of January 8, 1924, had praised his knowledge as characterized *"cum peracuta judicii subtilitate incorruptoque veritatis studio."* The pope wrote that Pastor's history of the popes provides *"tabulas plenas veritatis, plenas artis."*[75] At a formal academic gathering in Vienna on January 22, 1924, in the presence of government and ecclesiastical dignitaries, the Vienna docent, Father John Hollenstein, pointed to Pastor as the model of Catholic historians.[76] This was even more expressly emphasized at a formal academic gathering in Rome on January 27, by a professor from Freiburg in Baden, Father Emil Göller.[77]

But it was not granted to Pastor to spend the last years of his life under the exclusive impression of praise from the Catholic camp. The encomia of 1924 were not the only reaction of Catholic scholars to Pastor's work. The first important clash was the appearance of the defenders of Savonarola, whom Pastor, they thought, had treated unfairly. But this concerned only one matter. More important was the entrance onto the scene of others who were leaders in Catholic historiography. One of the most important church historians of the time, renowned for his vast erudition and his perspicacity, Father Sebastian Merkle, a professor at the University of Würzburg, analyzed the scientific method of Pastor in the third volume of his history of the popes.[78] Merkle did not restrict himself to general matters, but step by step he pursued Pastor's sources. He showed Pastor's tendentiousness in citing and interpreting sources, his lack of knowledge in the history of theology and canon law, the superficiality of his judgments, and the contradictions. He even expressed a doubt as to whether Pastor himself wrote the work published under his name.

Another review was even more harsh. What Merkle had done for the third volume of Pastor's work, the eminent scholar and prelate Paul Maria Baumgarten did for the volumes from X to XIII. He not only showed Pastor's tendentiousness and ignorance of theology, but also his lack of criticism, his suppression and ignorance of sources.[79] Baumgarten arrived at the conclusion that the volumes discussed by him did not have much scientific value. The Jesuit Bernard Duhr rushed to the defense of Pastor's work, emphasizing quite properly the prejudices of the reviewers in their reviews, but he was not able to refute their essential objections.[80] However, it was not only they in the Catholic camp who questioned the value of the work of the Innsbruck professor, for at the same time the keen scholar Klemens Bauer evaluated the whole work rather negatively.[81] In this way even in the Catholic camp the star of Pastor, which had shone so brightly, faded somewhat, even though there were not lacking those to praise him, and his Innsbruck student Dengel would continue to repeat that the history of the popes was considered the prime work in modern historiography.[82]

Thus, Pastor's work did meet a varied evaluation in Catholic historiography—from the extreme praises of Göller and Dengel to the extreme condemnations of Merkle and Baumgarten. The Protestants gave less extreme evaluations, although there were not lacking among them scholars who understood these matters. The harshest criticism of Pastor was given by the Italian liberal philosopher and historian, Benedetto Croce, who denied that Pastor had any talent for historical thought and even denied him the name of historian.[83]

IV.

Thus Pastor, while not lacking marks of recognition, also received words of condemnation. Numerically, the first were more abundant; but the matter appears different if we consider the evaluations as to who expressed his opinion and what was said. The individual volumes were evaluated differently, and this for many reasons. One appears at once, and it is not possible to speak of Pastor's work without emphasizing this matter. This is the basic question posed by Merkle as early as 1928, namely, whether or not Pastor did write all that was published under his name as *Geschichte der Päpste?* After the Würzburg professor Baumgarten raised the same doubt, and wrote maliciously that until the collaborators of Pastor are made known, Pastor himself will have to bear the responsibility for the mistakes, the one-sidedness, the omissions, and the frivolity that are found in those parts of the work done by the collaborators.[84] Baumgarten also called attention to the differences of style in Pastor's work. Pastor's friends defended him against this charge rather weakly, but in 1932 this charge was repeated by a historian of culture, the successor of the great Lamprecht in Leipzig, Walter Goetz, who wrote of a "staff" of co-workers from the Jesuit order.[85] This statement provoked an immediate denial by Pastor's son.[86] He stated categorically that the "staff" of co-workers never existed, and he admitted only that students made notes for his father in the archives, that only recently did the Jesuit Carl Kneller collect material for his father, that certain gaps in the manuscripts were filled in by others but this is always mentioned in the text, and thus the co-workers are a pure mental fiction. In his reply Goetz expressed amazement that they had not considered the charges by Baumgarten.[87] Essentially, they had not been refuted, and then, in spite of young Pastor's denials, one of the co-workers revealed himself. Joseph Schmidlin, a professor at Munich, admitted that for many years he had worked with Pastor, and that he had gathered material for him for the period from Paul III to Pius VI.[88] A year later, in 1934, the matter was brought up again. A Franciscan, Leone Cicchitto, attacked with extreme harshness Pastor's volume on Clement XIV, and he even expressed the opinion that this volume was not written by Pastor, but by the Jesuits Kratz and Kneller.[89] The Jesuit Peter Leturia replied by explaining that only gaps in Pastor's manuscript had been completed by the Jesuits Kratz and Kneller and by Dr. Wur.[90] Cicchitto attacked this explanation as well, while Wilhelm Kratz and Peter Leturia replied by maintaining their original statement.[91] Indeed, they made many retreats with regard to the authorship of many paragraphs in Pastor's work, but they maintained their position in the matter of the volume on Clement XIV. They had a completely decisive argument on their side, namely, the manuscript of the author. But Father Cicchitto's polemics did establish that the principal paragraphs about the Jesuits in the last volumes of Pastor's work came from the Jesuits, and chiefly from Kneller, and that he also had responsibility for the earlier volumes. It must be emphasized that independently of the work of co-workers, Pastor assumed responsibility for the whole, and hence for its positive and negative qualities.

And the positive qualities are many. Some of them have been mentioned above. There is no doubt that Pastor's work is the first history of the modern papacy on a grand scale, that it is based on vast source material frequently unknown hitherto, and that Pastor cites the vast literature on the subject not just generally, but in the notes it is clear that he really knew it. It is impossible to count the number of things that Pastor was the first to write about among the historians of the papacy. It is, indeed, a pioneering work.

Pastor was not an artist with words, and did not possess such literary talent as did, for instance, Ranke, but he wrote in a simple clear language and gave a quite lively description.

These positive aspects of Pastor's do not exhaust the characteristics of his work. Above all, there is the basic question: What actually is this work? If we judge by the title, it is not a history of the papacy; but it is also clear from the content that it is not merely the biographies of the popes. Pastor himself and his friends pondered over the title of the work, and finally he took the advice of his friend, the dogmatician Heinrich. It is understandable that Pastor hesitated to write a history of the papacy, for he was not a theologian, and he would have had to give greater attention to the dogmatic side of the task. Pastor was a Catholic, he believed in the divine institution of the primacy, and in his work he often stressed the conviction that the institution and the actions of particular popes are not the same; but the failure to connect events and the artificial separation of the activities of the institution were reflected negatively in Pastor's work. It is as if the author supposed that the faith in the primacy and papal infallibility remained the same as in 1870—that from this viewpoint nothing had changed. The institution of the papacy was simply the same in the general consciousness, and only the popes were changing, as were their temporal interests and their policy. The scene is the same, and only new actors enter upon it. Therefore, Pastor was not in a position to understand those who at times found themselves in conflict with the pope, and he sees in them enemies of the papacy. A splendid example is the problem of Savonarola. Pastor evaluates his disobedience to Alexander VI according to the consciousness of the dogma which Catholics had after 1870, and he consciously omits the important matter that Savonarola did not reject the dogma, and that he opposed only the political policy of Alexander VI.[92] He disobeyed the command not to preach, but this matter looked quite different in the fifteenth century than in the nineteenth.

Pastor, then, as we have said, did not produce merely biographies of the popes. He did not imitate the example of Platina and his numerous followers. From this viewpoint, his work is a significant advance. He wished to present not only biographical sketches of his heroes, but to describe what they were doing in the Church and in the Papal States as well as their relationship to governments and to culture. In Pastor's work the line between the dogmatic institution and its historical expression is obliterated. For him not only the institution belongs to the essence of the Church—and his thought is completely understandable for a Catholic—but, amazingly enough, it seems that the Roman Curia, too, in its temporal policy belongs to the substance of the Church. There followed from this the simple conclusion that the history of the Roman Curia and the temporal history of the popes are the history of the Church. But Pastor himself must have been aware of the fact that many very important ecclesiastical matters were handled with a minimum of papal participation, at the peripheries of their influence, and beyond the reach of the activity of the Roman Curia and its cardinals. He escaped this difficulty in a mechanical manner; he simply included those parts of the history of the Church in his history of the popes. Thus, for instance, in the work about Gregory XIII we have chapters on the rebellion in The Netherlands and vast paragraphs on the Counter-Reformation in Germany;[93] in the work on Clement VIII paragraphs on the Counter-Reformation in Germany and in the Spanish Netherlands;[94] in the work on Paul V a vast chapter on the Reformation and Renaissance of the Church in France.[95] It was enough if Rome had an interest in a small matter, or even if Rome should have had an interest. Pastor would describe it extensively and usually rather extensively. And, hence, it is not simply a history of the popes, but rather a history of the Universal Church. But it is a strange history—strange in its structure, division, and concept. The lion's share of each volume deals not with the institution of the papacy—and this would be understandable —but with a weak human being. The background for him is the struggle of millions and the conflicts of whole nations about the faith, often for independence. This is not a history of the popes on the basis of universal history, nor is it a universal history with a special consideration of the role of the papacy, with reference to everything that was being done in the contemporary world and in which the pope played even a minimal role or even if he took no part in it at all, as long as it was something that ought not to have been a matter of indifference to the popes.

But this history of the Church by Pastor has still another strange peculiarity. It is divided into as many periods as there were popes.

With the death of each pope a period in that history ends, everything begins anew, and there is no thought of anything like continuity. Indeed, in the Church the pope plays an enormously
important role, and in modern times especially his personality
leaves a strong imprint on the whole (classical examples of this
are the pontificates of Pius IX, Leo XIII, and Pius X) but it was
not always so; besides this, the continuity of policy in many matters exists in spite of the changes of the most important people.
Omitting the doctrinal side of the question (for Pastor abstracted
from it), we must call attention to the continuity of the activity
by the legal institutions of the papacy, the various central administrative offices, and in modern times the congregations. Their
members are not changed with the popes, the laws which govern
them are rarely subject to reform, and often they are subject to
a free evolutionary process. It is they that, above all, guarantee
the continuity of papal policy, and even the popes must reckon
with their opinion. At times a powerful personality on the papal
throne introduces a series of changes and shows the Church the
way to new principles and new immediate goals; at times this is
suggested to the pope by his environment and its opinions, as was
the case with Paul III Farnese; then we can certainly speak of a
new period. But often a series of pontificates fit within one period,
characterized by the very same features. The schematic division
of the history of the popes according to their pontificates, as was
done by Pastor, is rather a vast historicized chronicle, which gives
a mass of more or less important details. But in the choice of
these details two other circumstances had great weight, besides
the ones mentioned above. The first is the very sources which
Pastor used. What was said above about the dependence of Ranke's
narrative on the type of sources he used, is also true to some
degree about Pastor. Very often his main sources are the official
instructions and reports of nuncios and other diplomatic agents,
and in these sources the political element predominates. Thus
Pastor writes mainly a political history of the popes, although he
tries to make out of this a history of the Church. Pastor's popes
are above all politicians. Although he never forgets about their
essential character, politics interests them as much as, and at times
more, than all other ecclesiastical and religious matters. Indeed,
he speaks of these matters, too, and in this regard he is superior
to Ranke and Creighton, but as a whole he writes chiefly the
political history. This from a Catholic viewpoint is a serious
defect, for it overshadows the essential role of the papacy.

Mieczysław Żywczyński

Connected with this is another matter of great significance. Pastor belonged to that generation of historians which studiously avoided all philosophy, as well as any connection of political events with economic and social processes, formulated generalizations with extreme care and by way of exception, and which usually restricted themselves to narrating events only from one area without connecting them with the general historical process or uniting them in a genetic manner. They wished to speak of historical processes but actually spoke of the fates of persons who occupied a higher place in society. On one permanent, unchanging scene new people appeared, and they told the events of their lives, more especially of those which were important to them. The masses appeared but rarely, and if they did appear it was in the manner of the Greek chorus, and they spoke *unisono* to explain the course of the action. History thus was a collection of the histories of prominent individuals, histories upalatable and often even unintelligible. This avoidance of philosophy owed much to the influence of Hegel, or rather the consequences of applying his system to history. Ranke himself feared this philosophy for many reasons besides the one above. Being a believing Protestant —and resenting Hegel because of his own jealousy of Hegel's influence, and being a representative of the bourgeoisie that was struggling for political rights—Ranke saw in history, above all, the struggle of individuals for political rights and the struggle of states in the very same character. Ranke's students were even more consistent than the master, for he had his own history of philosophy and he expressed it in his works. There is no philosophy in Pastor; there is no general conception of the historical scene; philosophy is replaced for him by theology in a very simplified form. Pastor's almost purely factual attitude toward the past at times caused his inability to explain certain processes that were of fundamental importance. For instance, he presented in a very vital manner the rebirth of the Church in the post-Tridentine period and the papacy's participation in it, but he did not try to explain why after this, even though the rebirth of the Church continued, there arose a series of average, weak popes who were preoccupied chiefly with their own families and the Papal States. In fact, what a small influence Paul V or Gregory XV had on the French Catholicism of De Berulle, Vincent de Paul, or Francis de Sales! And if, indeed, the Church had so brilliant a renaissance after Trent, why then was the Enlightenment most radical precisely in Catholic countries? Why did the Church, so splendidly strengthened, lose her leadership in the life of Europe in the seventeenth and eighteenth centuries and find herself in a grave internal crisis?[96] A factual narrative does not provide an adequate explanation. For the reader it must suffice that it was so, and he is most often given the explanation that the enemies of the Church raised their heads.

Only in the first volume does Pastor provide a general historical background, and in this way he tries to give an explanation of the history of the popes at the end of the fifteenth century and the beginning of the sixteenth. Pastor, as we have said, was under the influence of Burckhardt. For Burckhardt the beginning of modern times comes with the Renaissance; thence develops modern individualism. Burckhardt was a man without faith,[97] and his conception of the Renaissance was alien to the religious tradition. It was irreligious. Pastor accepted this statement, but he suggested the idea of two renaissances, a pagan and a Christian. It is from the first that the modern irreligious individualism had come;[98] the second cooperated with the Church. This idea pleased Burckhardt; after 1870 and the Paris Commune he began to fear a social revolution, did not hide his distaste for democracy, and even began to esteem more highly the social significance of the Church. In a letter to Pastor he expressed not only his recognition for his great work and for removing the prejudice in Germany against his book, but he also expressed his regret that although he had seen in the Renaissance a strong and great esteem for religion, he had not carefully handled that matter in his investigations; he also said that in his work on the subject he had not maintained the proper proportion.[99] But Burckhardt spoke of two currents, not of two simultaneous Renaissances. This last conception was artificial, unnatural, so that in later editions, certainly under the influence of Burckhardt's letter and the advice of friends—especially the historian and archeologist Kirsch—Pastor rejected it and introduced a new notion about the twofold character of the Renaissance as well as its twofold direction, antiChristian and Christian. The representatives of the first were Lorenzo Valla, Antonio Beccadelli, and Pogio Bracciolini.[100]

This concept for a long time passed for a permanent addition to historiography, and it was emphasized as one of Pastor's merits,[101] although at the moment it seems rather questionable. Pastor himself writes that Bracciolini never did become an unbeliever or a pagan, and that from a religious viewpoint Bracciolini was merely indifferent. Besides this, he and Beccadelli produced pornographic material, but if this were to be decisive in placing them within the anti-Christian current, it would be necessary to reckon Eneas Silvius Piccolomini in it as well. This leaves only Valla, and after him Machiavelli; hence it is difficult to speak of a whole anti-Christian tendency. And besides both these tendencies, it would be necessary to accept a third middle current, for, after all, there were such writers in the Renaissance who—using this standard—could be called mixed, for instance, Petrarch, Boccaccio, and later Erasmus of Rotterdam.

But even greater caution must be aroused by introducing the Renaissance only into the fields of literature and art, especially literature, and by explaining the Renaissance as a simple rebirth of interest in antiquity.[102] Pastor even simplified to an extreme degree the thesis of Burckhardt, and, what is worse, he maintained his view in the following editions down to the end, without considering the growing number of voices critical of the concept of the learned scholar from Basel. These voices were so numerous that today it is difficult to say exactly what remains of that concept in general. Basically, by treating the concept of the Renaissance too narrowly, Pastor failed to explain adequately that phenomenon which we call the "Renaissance Papacy," nor did he relate it convincingly to the period of the Renaissance. And hence, the only effort in Pastor's work at giving a general historical background against which the history of the popes would appear more clearly was done in an extremely simplified manner that did not explain very much. Consequently, we must say that the work of Pastor lacks a general historical concept; from this viewpoint he stands lower than Ranke, even though he controlled a much richer factual material than did Ranke.[103]

There is lacking, too, proportion in the description of the events of the past. The amount of space devoted to a matter or a person does not correspond to their importance. Things of great importance and things of small importance are treated on the same level; the completeness and extent of their description does not depend on their historical importance. The outline of the writing is always the same. At first there is an extensive description of the conclave, in which the intrigues seethe and criss-cross. Then there is a sketch of the life of the one elected pope, then his activity in internal ecclesiastical matters, then a description of events in the world and the pope's participation in them, a description of his death, a short judgment about him, and finally the history of art in Rome during his pontificate. The whole dialectic of the history of the popes is reduced to these outlines.

We said above that Pastor was chiefly a political historian. In this he was exactly like the majority of the contemporary historians, and he applied their method to the history of the popes. A sign of this, among other things, is his complete neglect of economic matters, the almost complete omission of the financial matters of the Roman Curia. We learn, for instance, that some popes gave thousands for art, and that others gave very little. The reader must conclude that this depended only on the will of the popes, on their greater or lesser interest in art. In relations with government, pecuniary matters do not play any role; and supposedly the papal temporal politics were influenced by his sense of dignity, by sympathy, and family interests or the interests of the Papal States, and at times even by patriotism, for instance, Julius II and Paul IV, but almost never were they influenced by financial matters! True, such a project involved enormous difficulties and demanded enormous labor that surpassed the strength of one man, but at least it was possible to call attention in general to these matters; it is difficult not to be surprised at their complete omission. Nor can it be said that Pastor was doing what the generality of historians were doing—what in fact Ranke had done—for Pastor had other models, which he neglected. Even Janssen called attention to the economic aspect of the Reformation.[104] Reumont devoted several pages to this matter in his history of the popes. And not he alone. Even before Pastor research had begun into papal finances, though it was exclusively in the ancient and medieval period. A number of works had been published about the Apostolic Camera, on its expenses and income, on the payments from particular countries,[105] and statements about the influence of the Curia's fiscalism on ecclesiastical matters in particular countries during the Middle Ages had already entered the textbooks. Even Pastor mentions this fiscalism when he speaks of the origin of the Reformation, for it would be difficult not to mention it, especially after the publication of the book by Aloysius Schulte about the Fuggers and ecclesiastical financial economy.[106] Outside of this, these matters do not exist for Pastor, and if he mentions them it is only when there is mention of a crisis in the Papal States, and even these crises are not adequately explained. And in fact it was precisely these matters that played a significant role in the history of the post-Tridentine papacy. For the papacy developed vast activity in the wars against Protestantism and against the Turks; it granted important subsidies to France, Bavaria, and the German Catholic League during the Thirty

Years' War, to the emperor, and to Poland (to the latter especially during the times of Batory and Sobieski); it developed a vital artistic activity to maintain Rome as the spiritual center of the world. All this involved enormous expenses, which the papacy tried to cover with income from the Catholic world, and above all with the income from the Papal States. But this did not suffice, for the disproportion grew between the income and the expenses. The popes were not thrifty managers, and their nepotism played a negative part in this, all of which had to contribute to the weakening of the political power of the papacy in the seventeenth and eighteenth centuries. Hence these are not matters of secondary importance, but, on the contrary, in the history of the popes they are fundamental.[107]

V.

But everything that has been said so far does not exhaust the important features of Pastor's work. There remains the important matter of his impartiality. Various views have been expressed on this subject, whether immoderate praise or unusually harsh judgments. Indeed, this is not a simple matter. Even if we omit the fact that the humanist-researcher is always dependent on his view of reality, whether consciously or unconsciously, we must remember the specific ideology of Pastor. He belonged to that branch of the Catholic bourgeoisie which still had a great sympathy for feudalism. The title of nobility and baron impressed him greatly. He was thus a conservative and saw in the papacy not only a religious institution but also an important conservative social factor, a factor of the "social order." He constantly emphasized this role. Nor was he indifferent to the regard of some Italian ecclesiastical dignitaries, generally conservative, who had been educated in schools where church history stood on a very low level. On the other hand, he had to reckon with the vast development of studies, especially of Protestants unfavorable to the popes. He had to reckon with the fact that his sources would be examined later, and that certain matters had already been accepted in scholarship and there was no way to question them.

He evaluated persons of the past according to moral standards, but this evaluation was conditioned by his general views. He was not consciously an apologist, and he certainly delivered some harsh judgments. It is worth, for instance, considering what he wrote about the Reformation in Germany or about Leo X.[108] He tried to present calmly and impartially the events of St. Bartholomew and rejected the legends connected with it.[109] With great courage he presented the attitude of Gregory XIII to the English Queen Elizabeth,[110] and he wrote in the same way about Paul IV[111] and Pius V.[112] Pastor's judgment of Alexander VI is decidedly negative, even though he had many predecessors who tried to defend this pope. Modern efforts at rescuing the reputation of Alexander VI were considered by Pastor a perversion of the truth, and he felt that they must be rejected.[113] He himself added a series of facts impugning this pope. The volume about Alexander VI came out during the reign of Leo XIII in 1895, and some dignitaries of the Curia were not too pleased with it.[114] As late as 1920 the conservative Cardinal Cajetan de Lai, so influential during the reign of Pius X, said that he could not forgive Pastor what he had written about Alexander VI, for "first of all charity and then truth in history." If this were so, said Pastor, history would have to cease to exist.[115] The historian of the popes did not know that there were voices in Rome wanting to place the volume on the Index; this was, for instance, the counsel of Cardinal Thomas Boggiani. These judgments were undoubtedly too harsh. Pastor's monograph can be considered tendentious, but certainly not against that pope. The documents on which the professor from Innsbruck based his work inclined him even to harsher judgment, and he should rather have been praised by Cardinal Boggiani.

It must be said that Pastor differed in impartiality from many of his colleagues who were of the same branch of conservative Catholicism. He differed in this that he touched sensitive matters, that he did not remain silent about them, even though the most disagreeable matters he placed in the footnotes or he limited himself to indicating the sources on the subject, so that often the reader does not know just what was intended.[116] However, in spite of this, Pastor's hold is not always convincing. We shall state a few examples. For instance, in the chapter about Alexander's ecclesiastical activity, Pastor writes of the line of demarcation drawn by that pope in 1493 between the areas the Spanish had a right to take and the areas the Portuguese had a right to take. This was a peaceful solution, he writes—and it contributed to the development of missions—and hence this is a reason to praise the pope. Only blind tendentiousness and ignorance can lead to any other judgment.[117] And yet how to explain the expression of the Borgia pope: we grant. Pastor easily answers that obviously the pope granted only that which had been acquired in a just manner. But he himself must have asked if seizure by force makes a just title, for then he explains, in addition, that Alexander did not wish to limit the freedom of the pagans, since the expression "we grant" was used elsewhere with the additional phrase about the voluntary submission of the natives to the Portuguese. Such an explanation of papal acts in 1493 cannot be convincing. They can be explained by contemporary views, but it is difficult to accept the fact that Alexander VI seriously believed in the voluntary submission of the Indians to the conquerors. It can and must be considered that Alexander did not depart from the legal views that were then current, but it is difficult to make of him a naïve or narrowminded person. And certainly the reader must make the same judgment when he reads a little further on in Pastor that Alexander supported the Portuguese undertaking in Africa as crusades for spreading the faith. Alexander perhaps believed that the Portuguese were going to Africa in order to convert the Negroes and perhaps he really thought that the crusades were undertakings in the service of supernatural ideas, but it is hard not to be amazed at a modern historian who also thinks so, who forgets that the Portuguese went to Africa principally for economic purposes, among them, to seize slaves, whom they did not at all plan to return.

Pastor also gave a very unjust evaluation of Savonarola. When his presentation met with opposition, he wrote another irritable work about Savonarola, in which he repeated his former charges. Then, however, a series of scholars supported Dominican opinion, and among them was one of the most eminent representatives of a tendency in historiography different from that of Pastor, Father Sebastian Merkle. His arguments against Pastor were devastating. The historian of the popes did not emerge triumphant from this contest. Moreover, in spite of evidence in the sources, Pastor presented Alexander's death erroneously.[118] Again in the very same source Pastor managed to read only what was convenient for him. Merkle gave drastic examples of this, for instance, Pastor's selectiveness in the report of the master of ceremonies of Julius II, Paris de Grassis, by choosing paragraphs that were favorable to the Della Rovere pope and omitting paragraphs saying something other.[119] The German scholar showed how tendentiously Pastor presented Goethe's attitude toward Rome and the papacy.[120]

One could cite a whole series of examples of Pastor's partiality from all his volumes. This tendentiousness led to truly amazing judgments, for instance, the donation of Alexander VI and in the matter of the conflict between the Molinists and the Thomists at the end of the sixteenth century, which the author so presented that the reader can have no doubts about the connection between the Dominican views and the Lutheran and Calvinist views, nor can he have any doubts about the obstinacy of the Dominican order or the reasonableness of the Spanish Jesuits.[121] This second matter is connected with a problem of a more general nature. Pastor was a friend of two Jesuits, and he was under their strong influence. It is difficult here to speak of the influence of the order, for it produced some very eminent church historians, nor did it encourage only the conservative and apologetical tendency in the historiography of the Church. Many Jesuit historians, for instance Delahaye, managed to overthrow generally accepted conceptions and followed in the footsteps of their predecessors, the Bollandists, who in the seventeenth century for decades waged a war against legends, even with the Spanish Inquisition. Although then the order did not engage in supporting only one tendency in the writing of history, this cannot be said of the two members of the order who were Pastor's friends, Kneller and Kratz. These two were Pastor's chief advisers in theological matters, and they continued to publish the history of the popes after Pastor's death. This influence is evident in Pastor's presentation of the struggle between the Molinists and the Dominicans. Not being a theologian and indicating that he does not wish to give an exhaustive explanation of the subject, the author devoted 81 pages to this matter, and he informed himself on the matter chiefly through the Jesuit author Astrain.[122] He willingly and extensively cited the objections made against the Dominicans by the Jesuits, even though they did not touch the essence of the conflict, but in a marvelous manner he did not know or cite what the supporters of Banez said about the Jesuits. When at a certain moment Pope Clement VIII began to incline to the side of the Thomists, Pastor did not fail to point out that Clement was no theologian and that he did not understand very much about the scholastic subtleties.[123] There are no grounds to question this statement, but it can be freely pointed out that Pastor was not consistent in such explanations. For instance, in the seventies of the seventeenth century there arose a conflict between Pope Innocent XI and the Spanish government about the diplomatic immunity of the quarter where the Spanish Ambassador Di Carpio lived, and the Spanish government refused to retreat. Then in 1680 an earthquake occurred in Malaga that killed many men, women, and children; Innocent XI saw in this a divine punishment for Spain's abuse of diplomatic immunity in Rome.[124] In writing of this Pastor did not add that Innocent XI was a poor theologian, but in fact he presented the matter as though he himself shared that view.

Most obvious and least fortunate was the influence of his advisers on the last volumes of the history, especially on the seventeenth and eighteenth centuries. If we set aside the inexactness where the Jesuits are concerned, is it not amazing that the matter of the suppression of the Jesuits gets 88 pages, and the history of the Church in Poland and in Russia is given only 10 pages?[125] The entire history of the Church in Poland during the time of Stanisław August Poniatowski and the whole policy of Catherine II toward the Latin Church and the Uniate Church seem less important than the matter of one religious order, and were treated very generally, while the problem of the legality of the Jesuits' existence in Russia after 1773 is given in the greatest detail.

But even more amazing in the history of the popes by Pastor is the volume devoted to Pope Clement XIV.[126] In this book the whole history of the Church at that time (except for the problem of the Jesuits), the Partition of Poland so important for the whole Church, the anticurialism in Germany, the missions, and art are treated in some 80 pages, while over 300 are devoted to the suppression of the Jesuits. This is not the only reason the author, or the authors—always so restrained in their judgments of the popes, putting opposite views in the footnotes and trying to weaken them—abandon their basic attitude only with regard to this one pope. The Jesuit Kratz, supplementing Pastor, praises Ganganelli occasionally, but then he cites several reports of his pride, his ambition for the tiara, his hypocrisy, his intrigues, his deceitfulness, so that nobody believed Ganganelli.[127] At the end of the book the author adds that the more sources one consults about this pope, the harsher the judgment of him becomes. And the author cites sources, with which he agrees, that this pope was a weak spirit—an average spirit that did not grow up to the position he occupied—that pride led him into compromising steps, that at the end he suffered torments of conscience and fear, and that pride and fear made him ridiculous and the slave of others.[128] No pope had been judged so harshly—not even Innocent VIII or Alexander VI. In this volume nothing is omitted that is disadvantageous to this pope.[129] Leopold Ranke wrote with greater respect for this unfortunate man, as did the Protestant professor from Leipzig, Albert Hauck.[130] The author wrote about the adviser of that pope, the Franciscan Bontempi, that after the death of the pope he was secularized; tormented by conscience and fear he died outside of Rome in Monte Porzio.[131]

However, this monograph provoked a lively discussion.[132] As we have said, it was begun by the Franciscan Leone Cicchitto, who defended the pope from his religious order. The defenders of Pastor's book replied, and lively polemics began. Many people were drawn into it, and it even reached the columns of the daily press. Cicchitto had no reason to deny Pastor's authorship of the volume about Clement XIV, but he undoubtedly illuminated the methods of that scholar and the type of scholarly service rendered him by his friends. The Franciscan stated that Pastor did not use all the sources; he had not, for instance, used the Franciscan archive in the church *degli Dodici Apostoli,* from which he would have learned that Bontempi did not abandon the Franciscan habit, that he died peacefully in the Franciscan convent. He also declared that Pastor was tendentious. New reports were discovered about Clement XIV. The Passionist Irenaeus of St. John showed what great respect St. Paul of the Cross had for Ganganelli.[133] The Franciscan, Abate, gave a new interpretation to a letter of St. Alphonsus about Ganganelli—this letter was also known to Pastor—but it was wrongly interpreted by him to the disadvantage of the pope.[134]

This whole discussion occurred after the death of Pastor. Even after his death he continued to receive new proofs of recognition. On December 1, 1930, in the presence of Pius XI, a bronze bust of Pastor was solemnly placed in the Vatican Library in the gallery of Urban VIII, and a shelf of his works placed beside a shelf of the works of Giovanni Rossi.[135] The scholarly heritage of the founder of modern Christian archeology was now beside the heritage of the creator of the first great and fundamental history of the popes. The first was a pioneer in his field and created a whole school. Pastor was also a pioneer, but from other viewpoints. He was not a pioneer in the same sense that Rossi was, for he had important predecessors. He used the same method as others, even though it did not always fit the matter being described. He did not equal other Catholic church historians in impartiality; he was simply quite often tendentious. He did not have the breadth of thought that Ranke had or that Pastor's contemporary, the Catholic historian Ehrhard had; however, he did not often represent the

Mieczysław Żywczyński

German point of view in history, which was then so characteristic of contemporary German historiography. He was never such a nationalist as were his north German colleagues. His origin from the Rhineland, the influence of Janssen and Höffler—especially that of Onno Klopp—and his long residence in Austria worked on him positively, even though he was obviously not a cosmopolitan. He did not disguise his German sympathies. Furthermore, there is lacking in his work a theological concept and a philosophical depth. His work is not so much a synthesis of the history of the popes, but rather a series of monographs and essays connected chronologically; and it is difficult to consider him a model researcher. In the history of the development of method he did not make any advance at all. He was, however, a pioneer by reason of his vast labor, by bringing to light a whole series of new sources, new facts, and new problems. In spite of all the defects, this work, completed in the space of some twenty years, remains and must remain a point of departure for all subsequent research, even though this is so not by reason of its conception but by reason of the material on which it is based.

FOOTNOTES

1. "Pastor, Ludwig von," *Deutschlands, Österreichs, Ungarns und der Schweiz Gelehrte, Künstler und Schriftsteller* (Hanover, 1911) 3rd ed. 414; "Ludwig Freiherr Pastor," *Die Geschichtswissenschaft in Selbstdarstellungen* (Leipzig, 1926) II, 169–198; Pastor Ludwig Freiherr, *Tagebücher, Briefe, Erinnerungen* (Heidelberg, 1950); I. Ph. Dengel, "Ludwig Freiherr v. Pastor," *Historisches Jahrbuch* 49 (1929) 1–32; see also Dengel, "Pastor," *Deutsches Biographisches Jahrbuch* 10 (1931) 2–7, 219, and "Pastor," *Lexikon für Theologie und Kirche* (Freiburg, 1935) 1018–1020; E. Göller, "Ludwig von Pastor, der Geschichtsschreiber der Päpste," *Der Katholische Gedanke* (1929) II, 137–155; K. Loffler, "Ludwig von Pastor," *Hochland* (1921) IX, 529–544; *Ludwig von Pastor, Denkschrift an den 70. Geburtstag zum 40. Jahrestag des erstmaligen Erscheinens der Geschichte der Päpste herausgegeben von seinen Freunden, als Manuskript gedrukt* (Freiburg, 1926); M. Schermann, "Ludwig von Pastor, Ein Gedenkwort zum siebzigsten Geburtstag," *Charakterbilder Katholischer Reformatoren* (Freiburg, 1924) 139–160; H. Srbik, "Ludwig von Pastor," *Neue Östereichische Biographie* (Vienna, 1931) VII, Part I, 201–206; A. Pelzer, "L'historien Louis von Pastor d'après ses journaux, sa correspondence et ses souvenirs," *Revue d'histoire ecclésiastique* 56 (1951) 192–201; E. Raitz von Frentz, "Ludwig von Pastor als Historiker und Geschichtszeuge," *Schweizer Rundschau* (1951) N.F. 345–353; F. Cognasso, "Pastor," *Enciclopedia Cattolica* (1952) IX, 925–928; J. Brodrick, "Pastor and his History," *The Month* 7 (1953) 41–47. I am omitting all the mere panegyrics.

2. Leopold von Ranke, *Die Römischen Päpste, ihre Kirche und ihr Staat im*

Ludwig Pastor and the Historiography of the Popes

16. und 17. Jahrhundert (1834–1839) 3 vols. Expanded to include the eighteenth and nineteenth centuries in the editions from 1878, it was entitled *Die Römischen Päpste in den letzten vier Jahrhunderten.* I have used the 10th ed. (Leipzig, 1900). On the first impression this work made on Pastor see his *Tagebücher* 33.

3. "Pastor," *Die Geschichtswissenschaft* 4; *Tagebücher* 69. For M. Ritter, see W. Goetz, "Moritz Ritter," *Historische Zeitschrift* 131, (1925) 472–495.

4. See E. Fueter, *Geschichte der neueren Historiographie* (Munich, 1936) 487–488; K. Tymieniecki, "Charaktrystyka naukowej działalności Stanisława Smołki (1854–1924)," *Życie i myśl* 1 (1950) 483–485. Pastor attacked Waitz for his tendentiousness with regard to Catholics. See Pastor, "Georg Waitz als Preussischer Geschichtsmonopolist," *Katholik* 55 (1875) 435.

5. Göller, "Ludwig von Pastor" 145.

6. J. Uttenweiler, "Onno Klopp," *Lexikon für Theologie und Kirche* (1934) VI, 48–49; E. Laskowski, "Die Entwicklung Onno Klopps. Ein Beitrag zum Problem Persönlichkeit und Geschichtsauffassung," *Historisches Jahrbuch* 56 (1936) 481–498; I do not know the work of W. v. Klopp, *Onno Klopp, Leben und Wirken* (Munich, 1950), edited by F. Schnabel. Onno Klopp also influenced Janssen; see G. Beyerhaus, "Ein Mitarbeiter an Janssens Geschichte des deutschen Volkes," *Historisches Jahrbuch* 132 (1925) 465–471. For Pastor's relationship to Klopp, see W. Klopp, "Die Beziehungen Ludwig Pastors zu Onno Klopp," *Jahrbuch der Österr. Leo-Gesellschaft* (1934) 18–64.

7. This was renewed in 1915 by the professor of church history in Münster, Joseph Greving, although the first volume was published in 1909. This was continued by his successor in the chair at Bonn, Albert Ehrhard, as the editor of *Gesellschaft zur Herausgabe des Corpus Catholicorum;* the actual publisher was Wilhelm Neuss and others. Before the war 21 volumes were published.

8. This is what Pastor said to the secretary of state, Cardinal Nina.

9. *Die kirchlichen Reunionsbestrebungen während der Regierung Karls V* (Freiburg, 1879); *Die Korrespondenz des Kardinals Contarini während seiner deutschen Legation 1541* (Münster, 1880).

10. Pastor, *Autobiography* 12; *Tagebücher* 184–185.

11. Freiherr von Campersfelden. Pastor did not use this name, but the title "von" and "Freiherr" he used in his correspondence.

12. W. Goetz, "Ludwig Pastor," *Frankfurter Zeitung,* October 12, 1928; also *Historisches Zeitschrift* 145 (1932) 559.

13. *Di un catalogo cimiteriale romano* and *Di una biografia di Santa Melania giuniore.* Rampolla did not give these lectures but he published them in the form of a letter to the president of the Congress, Louis Duchesne. These are careful descriptions of manuscripts which Rampolla had found. See *Revue d'histoire ecclésiastique* 1 (1900) 808–809; G.P. Sinopoli da Giunta, *Kardinal Mariana Rampolla del Tindaro* (Hildesheim, 1929) 271.

14. *Santa Melania Giuniore senatrice Romana, documenti contemporanei e note* (Rome, 1905). For Rampolla as a scholar and as a writer, see G. P. Sinopoli da Giunta, *Kardinal Mariana Rampolla* 263, 270.

15. J. Schmidlin, *Päpstgeschichte der neuesten Zeit* (Munich, 1936) III, 154.

16. J. Schnitzer, *Der Tod Alexanders VI* (Munich, 1929) 810.

17. Pastor, *Tagebücher* 18–19.

18. For instance, *Conrad von Hetzendorf, ein Lebensbild* (Freiburg, 1916); *Generaloberst Victor Dankl* (Freiburg, 1916). A complete bibliography of

Mieczysław Żywczyński

Pastor's work is given by W. Wuhr in an appendix to Pastor's *Tagebücher* 911–918.

19. *Geschichte der Päpste seit dem Ausgang des Mittelalters mit Benutzung des Päpstlichen Geheim-Archives und vieler anderer Archive, bearbeitet von* . . . was published by Herder in Freiburg in 1886 (vol. I); vol. XVI, Part III, in 1933. This will be cited hereafter as *GP*. It has been translated into Italian, French, Spanish, English, and Dutch. The most valuable translation was the Italian because of the addition of valuable source material by A. Mercati.

20. The texts of the authors from the ninth to the seventeenth centuries were published by J. T. Rocaberti, *Bibliotheca Maxima Pontificia* (Rome, 1695–1699) 21 vols. A bibliography of the later works is given by A. Roskovany, *Romanus Pontifex tamquam Primas Ecclesiae et princeps civilis* (Nitra, 1867–1879) 14 vols.; vol. XV is the index. H. Hurter, *Nomenclator litterarius theologiae Catholicae* (Innsbruck, 1903–1913), 3rd ed., 6 vols.

21. He was born in 1421 and died in 1481. See Gregorovius, *Geschichte der Stadt Rom im Mittelalter* (Dresden, 1926) II, 925–926; F. X. Wegele, *Geschichte der deutschen Historiographie* (Munich, 1885) 35; Pastor, *GP* (1904) II, *passim;* E. Fueter, *Geschichte der neueren Historiographie* (Munich, 1936) 3rd ed. 47; G. Paparelli, "Platina Bartolomeo," *Enciclopedia Cattolica* (1952) IX, 1602–1603.

22. Panvini was born in 1530 and died in 1568. See W. Humpfner, "Panvini," *Lexikon für Theologie und Kirche* (1935) VII, 923–924, for a good article on him.

23. F. Bonnard, "Panvinio," *Dictionnaire de la Théologie Catholique* (1932) XI, Part II, 1875.

24. Pastor, *GP* (1913) VI, 693. Attention was called to this by S. Merkle, the editor of *Concilii Tridentini Diariorum Pars II* (Freiburg, 1911).

25. See Hurter, *Nomenclator* (1907) III, and *Lexikon für Theologie* und *Kirche* under that name. For Palazzi see H. Reusch, *Der Index der verbotenen Bücher* (Bonn) II, 137.

26. E. C. Scherer, *Geschichte und Kirchengeschichte an den deutschen Universitäten* (Freiburg, 1927), 290–291.

27. *Ibid.* 292, 504.

28. *Series Romanorum Pontificum per saecula digesta* (Prague, 1755–1756), 2 vols.

29. Especially *Traité historique de l'établissement et des prérogatives de l'église de Rome et des ses évêques* (1684). See H. Reusch, *Beiträge zur Geschichte des Jesuitenordens* (Munich, 1894) 71–73; see also Reusch, *Der Index* II, 583–586; E. Fueter, *Geschichte* 267; G. Wolf, *Quellenkunde der deutschen Reformationsgeschichte* (Gotha, 1915) I, 9; J. J. Carreyre, "Maimbourg," *Dictionnaire de Théologie Catholique* (1927) IX-II, 1656–1661.

30. W. Dilthey, *Weltanschauung und Analyse des Menschen seit Renaissance und Reformation* (Berlin, 1929), Gesammelte Schriften II, 80; H. Oncken, "Sebastian Franck als Geschichtsschreiber," *Historisch-politische Aufsätze und Reden* (1914) Part I, 273–319; G. Wolf, *Quellenkunde der deutschen Reformationsgeschichte* I, 48–481; F. Schnabel, *Deutschlands Geschichtliche Quellen und Darstellungen in der Neuzeit* (Leipzig, 1931) Part I, 114–121; E. Fueter, *Geschichte* 188–189; W. Nigg, *Geschichte des religiösen*

Ludwig Pastor and the Historiography of the Popes

Liberalismus (Zurich, 1937) 52; W. E. Peuckert, *Sebastian Franck, ein deutscher Sucher* (Munich, 1943).

31. Robert Barnes (1495–1540) brought his *Vitae Romanorum Pontificum* down to Alexander III (Basel, 1535). Even the Protestant writer R. Buddensieg, "Barnes," *Realencyklopedie für Protestantische Theologie und Kirche* (Leipzig, 1897) II, 414–415, sees in this work a "masslose Leidenschaftigkeit." Hereafter I cite this work as *RE*. For Barnes and Bale see E. Feuter, *Geschichte* 247–249.

32. K. Zinke, *Zustände und Strömungen in der Katholischen Kirchengeschichtsschreibung des Aufklärungs-Zeitalters im deutschen Sprachgebeit* (Bernau, 1933) 32. For the ecclesiastical historiography of the Enlightenment generally, see K. Völker, *Die Kirchengeschichtsschreibung der Aufklärung* (Tübingen, 1921) 61–62, for the views of that historiography about the papacy.

33. R. Stadelmann, "Grundformen der Mittelalterauffassung von Herder bis Ranke," *Deutsche Vierteljahrschrift für Literaturwissenschaft und Geistesgeschichte* 9 (1931) 76–77.

34. In the years 1784–1781. The last edition was entitled *Zur Philosophie der Geschichte* (Berlin, 1952). See also R. Haym, "Herder," *Allg. Deutsche Biographie* (Leipzig, 1880) XII, 83; R. Stadelmann, "Jacob Burckhardt und das Mittelalter," *Historische Zeitschrift* 142 (1930) 460–461; see also Stadelmann, *Grundformen* 82; F. Meinecke, *Die Entstehung des Historismus* (Munich, 1936) II, 416; K. Breysig, *Die Meister der Entwickelnden Geschichtsforschung* (Wrocław, 1936) 192; E. Fueter, *Geschichte* 407; J. W. Thompson and B. J. Holm, *A History of Historical Writing* (New York, 1942) 134; W. Harich, "Herder und die bürgerliche Geisteswissenschaft," in the introduction to the Berlin edition in 1952, pp. 7–82.

35. *Zur Philosophie* II, 529–530.

36. E. Fueter, *Geschichte* 403. Likewise, Thompson, *A History* 140: "He was undoubtedly the most widely read historian of his time." Besides this, for Müller, see F. Schnabel in *Lexicon für Theologie und Kirche* VII, 359–360; K. Henking, *Die Schweizerische Geschichtsschreibung im 19. Jahrhundert* (Zurich, 1938) 19–21.

37. F. Schnabel, *Deutsche Geschichte im neunzehnten Jahrhundert* (Freiburg 1937) I, 275. *Reisen der Päpste* in Müller's Sämmtliche Werke (Stuttgart, 1833) XXV, 13–45. Müller describes seven journeys of the popes: the first, the journey of Pope Leo to the Huns, the seventh, the journey of Innocent IV to Lyons in 1244; on the meaning of the papacy see pp. 43–44.

38. E. Göller, "L. v. Pastor," *Denkschrift* (1926) 29. On Müller's suspicion, see Wegele, "J. Müller," *Allgemeine Deutsche Biographie* (1885) XXII, 596.

39. R. Stadelmann, *Grundformen* 83.

40. Ranke, *Die Römischen Päpste* (Berlin, 1834–1839) 3 vols. Later Ranke completed the work down to 1870.

41. A. Dove, "Ranke," *Allgemeine Deutsche Biographie* (Leipzig, 1888) XXVII, 252.

42. H. Reusch, *Der Index* II–II, 1044.

43. A. Dove, "Ranke" 252, considers the *History of the Popes* as "unstreitig sein grösstes Werk." A. Harnack, *Geschichte der Königlichen Preussischen Akademie der Wissenschaften zu Berlin* (Berlin, 1901) 675, says that the *History of the Popes* with the work on the Reformation is Ranke's "Das vollendetste Werk." J. W. Thompson, *A History* 179, writes that the *History of the*

Mieczysław Żywczyński

Popes "is certainly his best known, and perhaps his best work." This judgment is supported by G. P. Gooch, *History and Historians in the Nineteenth Century* (London, 1928) 85.

44. G. Below, *Die Deutsche Geschichtsschreibung von den Befreiungskriegen bis zu unseren Tagen* (Munich, 1924) 22–23; F. Schnabel, *Deutsche Geschichte* I, 214, 439, and III, 32; J. W. Thompson, *A History* 124–225; G. P. Gooch, *History* 79.

45. Ranke, *Die Römischen Päpste* I, 59, 183, 285.

46. G. Below, *Die Deutsche* 25; A. Harnack, *Geschichte* 673–674; M. Lenz, *Kleine historische Schriften* (1913) 9.

47. Harnack, *Geschichte* 674.

48. O. Diether, *Leopold von Ranke as Politiker* (Leipzig, 1911); M. Lenz, "Ranke," *Kleine Schriften* (Munich, 1913) 1–13; K. Borries, *Die Romantiker und die Geschichte* (Berlin, 1925) 213–214; G. Ritter, "Die Neue Ranke-Ausgabe," *Historische Zeitschrift* 139 (1928) 105; H. Srbik, "Zu Leopold von Rankes Universalismus und Nationalbewusstsein," *Mitteilungen des Institut für Österreichische Geschichtsforschung* 52 (1939) 355–384; L. Dehio, "Ranke und der deutsche Imperialismus," *Historische Zeitschrift* 170 (1950) 307–328; F. Fischer, "Der deutsche Protestantismus und die Politik im 19. Jahrhundert," *Historische Zeitschrift* 171 (1951) 478.

49. Konstantin von Höffler, *Die Deutschen Päpste* (1839) 2 vols. See T. Borodajkewycz, *Deutscher Geist und Katholizismus im 19. Jahrhundert dargestellt am Entwicklungsgang Constantins von Höffler* (Salzburg, 1935) 120. Höffler's other works deal with the Middle Ages, as does his *Die Deutschen Päpste*.

50. F. Gregorovius, *Geschichte der Stadt Rom im Mittelalter* (Stuttgart, 1859–1872) 8 vols. I used the edition in 2 vols. (Dresden, 1926) with an introduction and valuable notes by F. Schillmann. The latest edition of vol. I in Tübingen (1953) was unavailable. Gregorovius was born of the Polish family Grzegorzewski (something that they did not deny), on January 19, 1821, in Neidenburg; he died January 1, 1891, in Munich. On the publication of his letters, see Dahlmann-Waitz, *Quellenkunde der deutschen Geschichte* (Leipzig, 1931) 9th ed., no. 1512. See also F. X. Kraus, "Ferdinand Gregorovius," *Essays* (Berlin, 1901), Series II, 137–147; J. Hönig, *Ferdinand Gregorovius der Geschichtsschreiber der Stadt Rom* (Stuttgart, 1921); H. Holldack, "Victor Hehn und Ferdinand Gregorovius, ein Beitrag zur Geschichte der deutschen Italienaauffassung," *Historische Zeitschrift* 204 (1936) 285–310; C. Schneider, "Gregorovius als Ostpreusse," *Altpreussische Forschungen* (1942) XIX, 79–97; C. Traselli, "Gregorovius," *Enciclopedia Cattolica* (1951) VI, 1160–1162. I do not know the evaluation given by H. Srbik, *Geist und Geschichte* (Munich, 1950); Gregorovius also shed light on the history of Rome in his *Römische Tagebücher* (Stuttgart, 1893), 2nd ed., and partly also in his *Wanderjahre in Italien* (Dresden, 1925).

51. See, for instance, E. Fueter, *Geschichte* 600, but there were other judgments as well, such as by the medievalist and methodologist Ernst Bernheim, *Lehrbuch der historischen Methode und der Geschichtsphilosophie* (Leipzig, 1908) 795, who considers Gregorovius a worthy model.

52. This is clear especially from his letters and from *Römische Tagebücher;* see F. X. Kraus, "Ferdinand Gregorovius" 144–145; J. Hönig, *Ferdinand*

Ludwig Pastor and the Historiography of the Popes

Gregorovius 131; H. Holldach, "Victor Hehn" 301–302; C. Schneider, "Gregorovius" 88–89.

53. In 1874, when its reading was forbidden "in originali germanico et in quocumque alio idiomate." See Reusch, *Der Index* II, 1045.

54. H. Grisar, *Geschichte Roms und der Päpste im Mittelalter mit besonderer Berücksichtigung von Kultur und Kunst* (Freiburg, 1901); vol. I includes the period from the end of the fourth century to the end of the sixth century; no other volumes appeared.

55. Alfred von Reumont, *Geschichte der Stadt Rom* (Berlin, 1867–1870) 3 vols. For Reumont see Zeck, *Kirchenlexikon* (1897) X, 1118–1119; H. Hüffer, *Allgemeine deutsche Biographie* (1889) XXVIII, 284–294; see also Hüffer, *Alfred von Reumont* (Cologne, 1904); H. Hurter, *Nomenclator* (Innsbruck, 1913) V-II, 1643–1644; J. Beckmann, *Lexikon für Theologie und Kirche* (1936) VIII, 852.

56. *Römische Briefe* (Leipzig, 1840–1841) 4 vols.

57. H. Hüffer, *Allgemeine deutsche Biographie* XXVIII, 291; see also his book *Alfred von Reumont* 157.

58. *Kirche und Kirchen, Päpstthum und Kirchenstaat* (Munich, 1861).The literature on Döllinger is vast, but I do not cite it because the significance of his book is only incidental for us. However, see the malicious pamphlet of E. Michael, *Ignaz Döllinger, eine Charakteristik* (Innsbruck, 1892) 10–11; J. J. Friedrich, *Ignaz Döllinger, Sein Leben auf Grund seines schriftlichen Nachlasses* (Munich, 1901) III, 184–185, 234, 237–238; J. E. Jorg, "Döllinger," *Historisch-politische Blätter* 109, (1890) 246; H. Herter, *Nomenclator* V-II, 1621. See also Döllinger's letter to Anna Gramich dated September 7, 1862; H. Schors, ed., *Ignaz Döllingers Briefe an eine junge Freundin* (Kempten, 1914) 146–147; see also the letter of December 22, 1861, *ibid.* 107–109.

59. J. F. Schulte, in *Die Geschichte der Quellen und Literatur des Canonischen Rechtes* (Stuttgart, 1880) III-¹, 778, speaks of it as a "geradezu komisches Buch, in dem alles figuriert, bei dem der Päpst betheiligt war." See also C. Schneider, *Kirchenlexikon* (1897) X, 1292–1293; H. Herter, *Nomenclator* 1751; Augustine Theiner, *Codex Diplomaticus dominii temporalis S. Sedis* (Rome, 1861–1862) 3 vols. We are concerned with vol. III, which includes the documents from 1389–1793. This is quite an arbitrary selection and does not give a complete picture.

60. Mandell Creighton, *A History of the Papacy During the Reformation* (London, 1882–1894) 3 vols. I have used the new edition with the changed title, *A History of the Papacy from the Great Schism to the Sack of Rome* (London, 1907) 6 vols. On Creighton, see Wollschläger, *Religion in Geschichte und Gegenwart* (Tübingen, 1909) I, 1912; Th. Kolde, *Realencyklopedie* (1913) XXIII, 323–329; G. Wolf, *Quellenkunde* II–II (Gotha, 1922) 214; J. W. Thompson, *A History* 572–574; G. P. Gooch, *History* 374–378.

61. The introduction to vol. I, in 1882.

62. Creighton, *A History* V, 50.

63. I. Ph. Dengel, *Historisches Jahrbuch* 49 (1929) 23.

64. Julius von Pflugk-Hartung, *Literarischer Bericht* (1886) II, 39.

65. Dengel, *Historisches* 29.

66. Mainly in his work *Die Kultur der Renaissance in Italien*.

67. This includes three pieces by K. Neumann, "Byzantinische Kultur und Renaissance," *Historische Zeitschrift* 91 (1903) 215; see also Neumann, "Ende

Mieczysław Żywczyński

des Mittelalters. Legende von der Ablösung des Mittelalters durch die Renaissance," *Viertel-Jahrschrift für Literaturwissenschaft* 12 (1934) and "Ranke und Burckhardt und die Geltung des Begriffes 'Renaissance' insbesondere für Deutschland," *Historische Zeitschrift* 150 (1934) 485.

68. M. Lenz, "Janssens Geschichte des deutschen Volkes," *Kleine historische Schriften* (Munich, 1913) 25. Lenz published this evaluation in 1883.

69. From Döllinger's *Die Reformation, ihre innere Entwicklung und ihre Wirkungen* (Regensburg, 1846–1848) 3 vols.

70. In a letter to Pastor, May 12, 1889. See J. Burckhardt, *Briefe* (Leipzig, 1941), 524–525.

71. *Archiv für Reformationsgeschichte* 3 (1908).

72. *Historische Zeitschrift* 56 (1891) 505–513; *ibid.* 80 (1898) 299–305; *ibid.* 105 (1910) 361–370.

73. L. v. Pastor, *Denkschrift* (1926); *Tagebücher* 786.

74. *Denkschrift* 16–19.

75. *Ibid.* 15–16.

76. *Ibid.* 11; *Tagebücher* 789.

77. *Denkschrift* 29.

78. *Deutsche Literaturzeitung*, N. F. 5 (1928) 1199–1214.

79. *Zeitschrift für Kirchengeschichte* 46 (1928) 232–244; 48 (1929) 416–442.

80. Bernard Duhr, "Pastors Papstgeschichte, ein providentielles Lebenswerk," *Stimmen der Zeit* 116 (1929) 413. Even Pius XI was annoyed with Baumgarten; see *Tagebücher* 889.

81. Klemens Bauer, "Ludwig von Pastor, ein Profil," *Hochland* 26 (1928–1929) 578–588.

82. Dengel, *Deutsches biographisches Jahrbuch* X, 216, and in *Lexikon für Theologie und Kirche* (1935) VII. A similar view is expressed by the Jesuit J. Brodrick, "Pastor and his History," *The Month* 193 (1952) 41–47. So also J. W. Thompson, *A History* 546–549, and E. Raitz von Frentz "Ludwig von Pastor" 345. Worthy of attention are the reservations by Prof. F. Cognasso, in the Vatican *Enciclopedia Cattolica* (1952) IX, 927–928.

83. Benedetto Croce, *Scritti di storia letteraria e politica* (Bari, 1939) 232–233: Pastor selected and arranged material for apologetical purposes; he lacked completely any historical sense; he did not understand spiritual tendencies at all—that is, their meaning. The harshest evaluation of Pastor among the German historians was given by Walter Goetz, "Ludwig Pastor," *Frankfurter Zeitung* (October 12, 1928) where he considered Pastor a simple apologist who twisted truth for ecclesiastical purposes and who gave a false picture of the history of the papacy; see also his "Ludwig Pastor," *Historische Zeitschrift* 145 (1932) 550–563. A rather weak attack on the article in the *Frankfurter Zeitung* was made by F. X. Seppelt, "Um Ludwig von Pastors Papstgeschichte," *Schönere Zukunft* 36 (June 8, 1930) 862.

84. *Zeitschrift für Kirchengeschichte* 48 (1929) 417.

85. *Historische Zeitschrift* 145 (1932) 560.

86. *Ibid.*, 146 (1932) 513.

87. *Ibid.* 146 (1932) 514–515.

88. In his autobiography edited by E. Stange, *Die Religionswissenschaft der Gegenwart in Selbstdarstellungen* (Leipzig, 1927) 173. The younger Pastor did not know this. *Zeitschrift für Missionswissenschaft und Religionswissenschaft* 19 (1929) 182; *Papstgeschichte der neuesten Zeit* (Munich, 1933) I. vii.

Ludwig Pastor and the Historiography of the Popes

In 1930 I heard in Rome that the secretary of the Austrian Historical Institute, Dr. Pogatscher, also collected material for Pastor. These were not students, as the younger Pastor had written.

89. Leone Cicchito, *Il Pontefice Clemente XIV nel vol. XVI p. 2-a 'Storia dei Papi' di Ludovico von Pastor* (Rome, 1934).

90. *Civiltá Cattolica*, November 3, 1934.

91. Cicchito, "Ancora intorno al Clemente XIV del barone von Pastor," *Miscellanea Franciscana* 34 (1934); P. Leturia, "Quaenam Dr. Ludovicus von Pastor in Historia suppressionis Societatis Jesu conscribenda de penu suo protulerit," *Archivum Historicum Societatis Jesu* 3 (1934); G. Kratz and P. Leturia, *Intorno al Clemente XIV del Barone von Pastor* (Rome, 1935). The second part of the volume was written by Leturia.

92. *GP* III–I, 158, 476; see also Pastor, *Zur Beurteilung Savonarolas* (Freiburg, 1898). The other discussion is described by J. Schnitzer, *Savonarola. Ein Kulturbild aus der Zeit der Renaissance* (Munich, 1924) II, 282. See also F. Vernet, "Savonarola," *Dictionnaire Apologétique de la Foi Catholique* (Paris, 1922) IV, 1214–1228; S. Merkle, "Der Streit um Savonarola," *Hochland* 25 (1928) 462–485, and his *Deutsche Literaturzeitung*, N.F. 5 (1928) 1193; H. Jedin, *Geschichte des Konzils von Trient* (Freiburg, 1951) I, 30–31, 113; Ch. Journet, "Alexander VI et Savonarole," *Nova et Vetera* 27 (1952) 127–138.

93. *GP* IX, 1925.

94. *Ibid.* XI, 1927.

95. *Ibid.* XII, 1927.

96. H. Luebe, *Archiv für Kulturgeschichte* 23 (1933) 132–133.

97. C. Neumann, *Jacob Burckhardt* (Munich, 1927) 27–28, 65; P.W. Krüger *Das Dekadenzproblem bei Jacob Burckhardt* (Basel, 1930); W. Nigg, *Geschichte des religiösen Liberalismus* (Zurich, 1937), 312–313; A. Martin, *Die Religion in Jacob Burckhardts Leben und Denken* (Munich, 1943).

98. This is a visible influence of the dualistic view of history that already appeared with St. Augustine (even though he is not its creator); it also occurs with the medievalists who speak of two sides in the Middle Ages.

99. In the letter of May 12, 1889, cited above. For the social views of Burckhardt, see Neumann, *Jacob Burckhardt* 16, 18, 70–71; Krüger, *Das Dekadenzproblem,* and O. A. Wajnsztiejn, *Istorigrafija sriednich wiekow* (Moscow, 1940) 222–232.

100. *GP* (1931) X, xiii: "Die antichristliche Richtung und christliche Richtung."

101. E. Göller, "Ludwig von Pastor," *Der Katholische Gedanke* 2 (1929) 152.

102. *GP* I (1931) 3.

103. This judgment was already stated by C. Bauer in *Hochland* 26 (1928–1929) 588.

104. For instance in III (1870) 280.

105. This was described by C. Bauer, "Die Epochen der Papstfinanz," *Historische Zeitschrift* 138 (1928).

106. Aloysius Schulte, *Die Fugger in Rom (1495–1525). Mit Studien zur Geschichte des kirchlichen Finanzwesens jener Zeit* (Leipzig, 1904) 2 vols.

107. C. Bauer, "Die Epochen" 492–493.

108. *GP* IV-I (1906) 419, 487, 604–605. J. Schmidlin, *Historisches Jahrbuch* 28 (1907) 371–372, judges Leo X even more harshly.

109. *GP* IX (1925) 352 (but see also the amazing interpretation that Rome

Mieczysław Żywczyński

did not rejoice because of the massacres but only because of the effects of the massacres).

110. *Ibid.* IX (1925) 365.

111. *Ibid.* IX (1925) 321.

112. *Ibid.* VI (1913). However, see the reservations of W. Friedensburg, *Historische Vierteljahrschrift* 17 (1914) 426.

113. *GP* VII (1920).

114. *Ibid.* III-I (1926) 596.

115. *Tagebücher* 695–696.

116. For instance, in describing Sixtus IV or Julius II.

117. *GP* III-I (1926) 620. See G. Kawerau, *Historische Zeitschrift* 130 (1898) 299.

118. *GP* III-I (1926) 588. See J. Schnitzer, *Peter Delfin General des Camaldulenserorderns (1444–1525)* (Munich, 1926) and *Der Tod Alexanders VI. Eine Quellenkritische Untersuchung* (Munich, 1929). This author (*Der Tod*, p. 121) puts the question whether finally "die Fabel vom Fiebertode Alexanders VI" will disappear from historical literature, and he answers pessimistically: "Ich glaube es nicht." His pessimism was correct, but only partially; see F.X. Seppelt, *Geschichte des Papsttums* (Leipzig, 1941) IV, 379.

119. *GP* III-II (1938) 870; S. Merkle, *Deutsche Literaturzeitung* 5 (1928) 1211–1212. At times Pastor underestimates a source that is not flattering to the popes, as he did with the diary of Stephen Infessura; see S. Infessura, *Römisches Tagebuch* (Jena, 1913); introduction by H. Hefele, xxix-xxx.

120. P. Meinhold, "Goethes Begegnung mit dem Katholizismus in Italien" *Saeculum* 2 (1951) 973.

121. *GP* XI (1927) 513, 527, 534. See also P. M. Baumgarten, "Kritische Bemerkungen auf elften, zwölften, und dreizehnten Band von Pastors Papstgeschichte," *Zeitschrift für Kirchengeschichte* 48 (1929) 419.

122. *GP* XI (1927) 517, note 1.

123. *Ibid.* XI (1927) 588.

124. *Ibid.* XIV-II (1930) 911–913. See Croce, *Scritti* (Bari, 1932) XXXII, 233. The matter of this diplomatic circle was not insignificant; see D. B. Lewin, *Diplomaticzeskij immunitiet* (Moscow, 1949) 59–60, 65.

125. *GP* XVI-III (1932) 150–238 (on the Jesuit matter); 119–129 (on the Church in Poland).

126. *Ibid.* XVI-II (1932).

127. *Ibid.* XVI-II (1932) 64–71.

128. *Ibid.* XVI-II (1932) 396–398.

129. In bringing this up, I do not intend to question the correctness of the views of Pastor and his co-workers. If we wished to question this, it would be necessary, first of all, to examine the sources for the history of Clement XIV. But here we are concerned with something else, namely, the manner of writing about this pope departs so much from that used in writing of other popes.

130. Ranke, *Die Römischen Päpste* (Leipzig, 1900) III, 138–142; G. Voigt, A. Hauck, "Clemens XIV" *RE* (1898) III, 153–155. Among the Catholic writers see the calm judgment of F. X. Seppelt, *Geschichte des Papsttums* (Leipzig, 1936) V, 478, and especially 488.

131. *GP* XVI-II (1932) 391.

132. See the works cited above, as well as O. Montenovesi, "Un Pontificato

da riabilitare: Il Papa Clemente XIV, e il volume a lui dedicato da L. von Pastor," *Archivi* 8 (1941).

133. Irenaeus of St. John, "Clemente XIV e S. Paolo della Croce," *Miscellanea Franciscana* 34 (1934) 98–121.

134. Abate, "Clemente e S. Alfonso," *Miscellanea Franciscana* 34 (1934).

135. A. Pelzer, "L'historien Louis Pastor," *Revue d'histoire ecclésiastique* 46 (1951) 201.

CATHOLICISM AND LITERATURE

Stefan Sawicki

I.

FOR SEVERAL YEARS THERE HAS EXISTED WITHIN THE LEARNED SOCIETY of the Catholic University of Lublin the Commission for Research on Catholic Literature. The need arose for a deeper study of the character, the problematic, and extent of such research. The Commission was called upon to undertake the direction of these matters.

Let us begin with the term "Catholic literature," even though terminology is obviously not the most important matter. This term—sometimes replaced by terms close in meaning—was already known in prewar criticism and journalism. It became common in modern times in connection with a phenomenon in the second half of the nineteenth century—an effort to determine the Catholic elements in Western European literature. This phenomenon is vital even today and embraces such writers as Claudel, Chesterton, Mauriac, Sigrid Undset, and Gertrud von LeFort. It was a matter of identifying in literature new and numerous facts which called for attention actually in its express relationship with Catholicism, with the Church. The term "Catholic literature" seemed to be the most practical; it pointed to what was certainly most important for the creators, as well as for the readers, in identifying the literary phenomena by that title. This term was particularly common in French criticism. Nor was it rare in Poland during the interwar period, especially in the 1930's. One meets it in the prewar annuals of Catholic periodicals, for instance, *Verbum* in Warsaw and *Kultura* in Poznań. However, it was only after the last war that the term and the very problem of Catholic literature became significant among us. This was related to the particular atmosphere of the postwar years, the special social sensitivity in ideological, philosophical, and religious matters. Nearly all writers and critics close to Catholicism somehow considered it their duty to raise their voices publicly on subjects dealing with Catholic literature. Even today one recalls some of the most important statements by Konrad Górski, Jerzy Zawiejski, and Antoni Golubiew.[2]

These works frequently dealt with Catholic literature as an undoubted, existing fact and studied the related problems: its role in contemporary culture, its central problem of sin and grace, Catholic realism, its present problem of pessimism and exhibitionism, its various defects and falsities, and its professional difficulties, involved above all in the task of a literary exposition of the supernatural. Besides the affirmation of the phenomenon, there appeared continued doubts about the term itself and the problem of distinguishing literary phenomena. Some of these doubts suggested the complete abandonment of the concept "Catholic literature." "Everyone knows that there is no Catholic novel; there exist only novels written by Catholics."[3] The meaning of this statement, with which Woźniakowski agrees, can naturally be extended to literary forms other than the novel.

Those who would not abandon the term try to define precisely what determines us to call a certain work "Catholic." In this there are three possible criteria: that of the author, that of the reader, and the "immanent" criterion in the work itself. The first criterion is very uncertain and frequently erroneous. The fundamental difficulty is the confirmation of the author's Catholicism. Its weakness can be illustrated by Werfel's *Song of Bernadette,* which is reckoned as part of Catholic literature, even though it was written by a man outside the Church. The second criterion, that of the reader, is equally fallacious. On the one hand, it is difficult to limit the Catholic reader's interest to works that we would like to describe as Catholic, and on the other hand it is difficult to write Catholic books only for Catholics. Hence, there remains the third criterion, which is usually sought in the theme or the problematic of the work. However, if the problem is considered, it is difficult to rely on theme as a criterion. In his article, "The Responsibility of the Catholic Writer,"[4] B. Marshall clearly and accurately defines the freedom of the Catholic writer and also of Catholic literature in the matter of theme: "The Catholic writer can write about a murder in Baluchistan or about chorus girls in the Folies-Bergères, under the condition that he sees the meaning of the world beyond them. Only the supernatural background has meaning, and not whether the persons portrayed on this background are contemplative natures or bespattered ones." Hence, the criterion of Catholicity: the problematic and the tendency suggesting its solution, viewing people and things under the aspect of the supernatural.

Stefania Skwarczyńska, wishing to transfer the term "Catholic literature" to the science of literature, analyzed exhaustively these three criteria of a work's Catholicism as established by criticism. I am thinking of the article "Literatura katolicka jako termin w nauce o literaturze" [Catholic Literature as a Term in Literary Criticism], published in *Znak* in 1950.[5] In it Skwarczyńska refers to the immanent criterion and tries to define it exactly. "We propose to call Catholic literature all those works whose content follows from the Catholic theory of reality." The final formulation speaks of the "contents" of a work. The entire study shows that the author was simply concerned with the *world* presented in the literary work, with the dependence of its structure and internal relationships on the Catholic theory of reality as its foundation.

Skwarczyńska's article exposed several misunderstandings that have arisen about the problem of Catholic literature and tried to solve them in the only possible framework. However, it did not remove all difficulties in the use of that term in literary research. There remained a whole series of doubts. First of all, there are doubts because of the difficulties involved in interpreting the concrete and existential language of a literary work into an "essential" language, the language of concepts, in which one must effect the definition of the Catholicity of literature. Is such a translation possible, and to what degree is it possible? How can one realize it in practice? These are great difficulties for a methodically conscious design. Semantic methods in literary research try partially to remove them, but it is a long way to the solution of the problem.[6] There are further doubts about the change of the general term "Catholic literature" into some sort of generic or specific description. The "Catholic novel" does not awaken unfavorable reactions, but the "Catholic lyric" does not ring true, and it seems to jar our linguistic sensibility. We would choose another description: religious lyric. Naturally, it is possible to approach these difficulties and to take the position: the most important thing is whether a Catholic lyric exists or whether it does not exist; and if it exists, what do linguistic habits matter? They are to be undone. For if the problem of the Catholic lyric's existence is not entirely obvious, one can treat the linguistic difficulties objectively. If certain definitions disturb us, can it be that this has its grounds in the reality indicated by it? It is possible that the term "Catholic" is more adequate with regard to a novel than to a lyric, since in a lyric the problematic and ideological matters play a significantly lesser role, and the broad aspect of the reality described gives place to personal emotions, which are significant for all mankind. Finally, other doubts arise when the term "Catholic literature" is treated as a "classifying" term. Consequently, one would have to accept the existence, indeed the possibility of the existence of Protestant, Orthodox, Moslem, and Buddhist literature. Having made such a division, we would soon find that we had actually divided religions or ideologies, that we had created in essence an ideological network to which we transferred literary phenomena in a manner external to them. Besides, an ideological classification of literature is not an exhaustive classification. Many more literary phenomena remain unclassified than in a division into literary genera and species.

The various difficulties described above arise constantly whenever we try to use the term "Catholic literature" in contemporary scholarship. In pointing to these difficulties I have not solved the problem itself, nor is a solution the purpose of these considerations. It seems that the term can be useful in criticism, and even more in Catholic journalism. It can perhaps remain in the discipline of literature, but only in the sense proposed by Skwarczyńska as a descriptive term, analogical to the description "psychological novel," which does not require any further divisions and does not imply existence (I am using a term purposely clear) of a "physiological" novel. But, I repeat, I am not solving the problem; I am merely indicating the doubts and difficulties that have not been overcome thus far.

In discussing the problem of classification based on the term "Catholic literature," it appeared clearly that the description "Catholic" with regard to literature—independently of whether we accept it or not—was ultimately a genetic description, a description "from without." It explains the value of a work by its relationship to the "Catholic theory of reality," as though that theory were a factor in characterizing its structure. If this is so, then the phenomena usually described by the name "Catholic literature" are only a part, a very significant and characteristic part, of all those literary phenomena of which one could say that they have the "Catholic system" of reference. In understanding the "externality" of the description "Catholic" with regard to literature, there is no sufficient justification to confine Catholicism to a particular theory of reality. It would be more proper to expand the area of relations studied by embracing under the term "Catholicism" all those phenomena immediately connected with the Church, for instance, the liturgy and Sacred Scripture. On the part of the work itself, such an expansion of the concept of "Catholicism" would be justified, as we have already said, by the fact that what we describe as "Catholic literature" does not exhaust many of the relations between literary phenomena and Catholicism. All this inclines some to a more general discourse about the Catholic elements in literature. These elements are able to create a "Catholic literature" (the problematic, the motivation), but they can also appear in literary works in a more or less fragmentary function.

Hence, is it possible to retain the expression "Catholic" elements in literature if it includes that which is called Catholic literature and the other phenomena accepted as Catholicism? But even this term leaves doubts. The thought arises: Why precisely Catholic elements, for instance, why are we not interested in Protestant elements? For in a literary work they can play quite a similar role. It is easy to prove this by investigating the manner of introducing and portraying supernatural reality in literature. For Catholic as well as Protestant elements can expand the world in a literary work about the supernatural world and can actually fulfill the same artistic function in the work. Moreover, do we always recognize the Catholic elements in a work? If we study biblical motifs, for example, can we be certain that they are the Catholic elements in the work? Let us suppose this in German or English literature, where the influences cross: Catholicism and Protestantism, the Catholic Church and the Anglican Church.

The difficulties last mentioned disappear if we transfer the whole problem to another level, that of the history of Catholicism. Then we say that we are studying the history of Catholicism in the area of literature, namely, its historical features and its creative cultural forces, manifested by literature. These investigations can proceed in two directions: from Catholicism to literature; and the reverse, from literature to Catholicism. In the first case, literature is illustrative material for the "life of the Church," a limited area of man's creativity. In the second case, it becomes a historical source, on the basis of which (preserving methodological safeguards) we arrive at the historical features of Catholicism and its cultural vitality. A typical example of this method is A. Jesionowski's *Motywy religijne w współczesnej powieści polskiej* [*Reli-*

gious Motifs in the Contemporary Polish Novel].[7] However, it seems that this second direction is a methodical one. The direction of the actual historical process—which is the one that interests us at the moment—is one: from Catholicism to literature, and that direction will always be the ultimate goal of historical reconstruction, without regard to methodological process and without regard to the composition of scientific works, where at times the proportion of problems depends not on the ultimate purpose of the investigations, but on their nearest subject.

The investigations of Catholic elements in literature as the influence of Catholicism on literature has still other good aspects. In the first place, there are Catholic elements in literature that are very important from the literary viewpoint: they organize the structure of the work, give a new color to various aesthetic elements, and create new elements. But there are also those elements not actually necessary in literary investigations. They all naturally fulfill some single localized function in the work if the work is a worthwhile one; such a function can be fulfilled even by various linguistic fragments, i.e., "as I love God," "O Jesus," and so on, but they usually do not create any of the qualities the literary researcher seeks; relatively these qualities work together with non-Catholic aspects, for instance, to give an emotional coloring to particular expressions. In a word, these elements hold little significance for the literary researcher and usually are not considered in literary works. These same elements can be very essential for the historian of Catholicism—sometimes as an individual phenomenon, and sometimes as a significantly frequent one. After all, neither the episodic function within the limits of literary works nor the small artistic value of these works can determine whether in practice their literary study is to remain at a minimum. At the same time their study in order to fix the features of Catholicism in a definite epoch seems to be unquestioned. In the second place, the study of the Catholic elements in literature as the influence of Catholicism on literature would also permit in these studies the consideration—besides certain difficulties of method—of biblical themes (but only those which entered into literature through Catholicism) and of those works whose orthodoxy is suspect for various reasons, but whose inspiration is undoubtedly Catholic (Mauriac, Green), and even of those that arose in opposition to Catholicism, and for which Catholicism served as a "negative inspiration."

Finally, then, the considerations made so far incline one toward integrating the studies of "Catholic literature" and "Catholic elements" in literature with the history of Catholicism, broadly understood. Everything that is related to Catholicism and is presently in literature can interest the historian of Catholicism. A significant part will also be essential for literary studies; it will show the number and variety of ways by which Catholicism enters into literature. And, naturally, the uncovering of these ways will also be an unveiling of the structure of the work and the role of the Catholic elements in it. We expressly enter into the borderland between the history of Catholicism and the history of literature, a borderland that results from the character of the subject of study and—what is more important—from the two-sided usefulness of these studies.

One more explanation. Research into the phenomena and problems that occur within the framework of the relationship of Catholicism and literature can be integrated into historical studies only when treated as a distinct field of interested studies. Particular phenomena and problems can also be treated within the framework of the discipline of literature: in this or that concrete work, in this literary species, in the creative work of a particular author —in a word, where they are of literary importance. But, actually, they are then studied from the viewpoint of their single literary importance, and not from the viewpoint of their relationship with Catholicism. Besides this, such studies will always be scattered among the learned statements within a given discipline, and not mutually related, and thus they would not create a distinct field of learned interest. It is possible to integrate and connect the particular research problems dealing with the relationship of Catholicism and literature only on the level of the history of Catholicism.

II.

Let us now consider the various kinds of influence Catholicism has on literature and on the traces of that influence which can be found in literary works. Catholicism influences literature through various "aspects." It enters into literature through the elements of its liturgy, through Holy Scripture, through the works of the Fathers. There are those who think that the Bible in a limited time changed the whole character of European literature.[8] An example of how deeply the writings of the Fathers of the Church penetrated into the literary world is the somewhat out-dated work

Stefan Sawicki

of Zofia Niemojewska, *Dziady Drezdeńskie jako dramat Chrześci-jański.*[9] Naturally, it is necessary to define more precisely what we understand by the word Catholicism, namely, whether we mean only that which the Church has stated in an undoubted, official manner or also those phenomena that have grown closely associated with Catholicism, but do not possess an unchanging and binding character. The difficulties in defining the limits of Catholicism for use in these studies are not slight. It is worth stating, however, that the difficulties possess chiefly a theoretical character; in the concrete historical instance, it is much easier to free one's self from them.

Let us now examine from a literary viewpoint the traces of Catholicism's influence. They can be found in many elements or aspects of a literary work. At times, this influence—direct or indirect—has a genetic character and does not make the work itself "Catholic." For instance, there is the hypothesis that explains the rhythmic character of asyllabic medieval verse through the unmeasured ecclesiastical music of the age.[10] Dłuska speaks of the influence of litany composition in the process of forming Polish tonic verse.[11] There is the well-known influence of liturgical tropes and sequences on the development of verse (stophes) in Europe during the Middle Ages: French *lais et descorts,* German *Lieche,* and the majority of the verse forms of love lyrics.[12] The influence of Catholic traditions has here an external character and does not touch the work itself. This externality of origin had touched not only the formalized elements of work like verse, but also its problematic. It is often thus in the poetry of Norwid, whose harsh attitude toward the world is conditioned precisely by his Catholicism. If this writer "judges people so sharply, it is precisely because it is they and they only who by their conscious aversion from divinity build evil in the world."[13]

That external influence can also be considered in the field of metaphor, which, for instance, in the Middle Ages is frequently built on the model of biblical metaphorical structures. But much more often we here have to do—in the metaphor or the comparison—simply with Catholic elements as secondary motifs, which are a formative factor influencing other related meanings. And this is often so even in nonreligious themes. For instance, Mickiewicz uses religious motifs in his works, among other things, for coloring women's charms poetically. In *Pan Tadeusz,* for Tadeusz Sophia's hair at their first meeting shone "jak korona na świętych obrazku" [like a crown on a picture of the saints]. And Jacek

Soplica ends with the epithet "anielski" the series of poetic descriptions of Ewa; and wishing to express the power of her influence, of her charm, achieved an exceptional comparison:

> Jak gdybym Sanctissimum ujrzał.
> [As though I had seen the Most Holy Sacrament.]
> *(Pan Tadeusz* X, 572)

We here have to do with a comparison that passes into style, which, besides allusion, plays an important role in the problem occupying our interest. This stylization reaches the limit of rhythm and syntax, and is dependent on the Bible as a stylistic model. It is usually dependent on a wealth of various types of parallelisms: syntactical and compositional. It suffices here to indicate the *Księgi narodu i pielgrzymstwa polskiego* [*Books of the Polish Nation and Pilgrimage*] in which Mickiewicz—in the opinion of the majority of scholars—by using biblical style attempts to transfer the problematic of patriotism into a religious atmosphere.[14] In the little known novel of F. Bernatowicz, *Reginka z Sieciechowa* (1834), the biblical style—discreetly suggested for the most part with the aid of syntax—is related to the idea of the narrator, who is a sacristan, poor in spirit and penetrated with the Bible. In Sienkiewicz's narrative *Wspomnienie z Maripozy* [Reminiscences from Mariposa] old Putrament, living in the California forests and wishing to retain contact with his native language, for decades reads the Bible in the translation by Wujek, and he himself ends by speaking in a biblical style.

In this last instance, besides syntax, the vocabulary sparingly used by Mickiewicz in *Księgi* plays an important role in the technique of stylization, which, however, is not merely a stylistic, linguistic phenomenon, for it touches as well the world portrayed in the work. In Scene IX of Wyspiański's *Legion,* Mickiewicz and his disciples (legionnaires) for purposes of suggestion and surprise are stylized as Christ and His Apostles and the quibblers as the enemies of Christ in the gospels. In a poetic epilogue from the pen of T. Makowiecki—*W Soplicowie po latach*—Sophia is expressly but discreetly stylized as the Mother of God of Ostrobrama.[15] The functions of this type of stylization can naturally be varied.

Motifs with a Catholic character can serve as more than a metaphorical element; they can also appear as independent thematic wholes. Hence, the biblical and liturgical motifs and those of the Mother of God, Christ, God, angels, saints, and priests. The

Stefan Sawicki

author of the book *Matka Boska w poezji polskiej* [*The Mother of God in Polish Poetry*] tried to indicate the problematic in the various and often interesting forms of this type of motif and the various possibilities in their functional use.[16] The problem of motifs is naturally only a part of the broader problem of the theme in a literary work.

Particularly important for our interests in the problematic of the Catholic quality that appears so powerfully in the contemporary novel portraying man in two fundamental relationships to sin and to grace, as well as his actions within supernatural perspectives. This is very strongly connected with the problem of the speaking subject (the narrator) and with the question of motivation. I think of that subject as of someone who is responsible for every word spoken by him in the work, as of someone who through the work reveals his convictions, his thoughts about man and the world. In the area of supernatural motivation, which is the interpretative principle of the events portrayed in the literary work, it is worthwhile to call attention to the technique of silence. Motivational silence suggests the mystery of causal connections, removes the essential agent from the field of vision; the context is so built that it suggests the idea of the agent's supernatural character. The problem of motivation also involves the technique of presenting the supernatural world and the methods of suggesting its reality. These are important and interesting matters, which only now are being dealt with scientifically. In the medieval mystery-plays Satan appeared as Satan, without any disguise, in a form determined by a long tradition of representation. The world of the angels was similarly portrayed. Today the presentation of these figures is much more indirect and discreet. Their supernatural character is often suggested. A further step in the development of artistic discretion is the removal of supernatural beings from the scene; their presence is suggested with the help of light, a voice, the reaction of those who see or hear it.

These have been efforts within the framework of the literary work. At times it is necessary to go beyond the work in the strict sense of the term and to seek the traces of Catholicism in the titles, in the mottoes, where they give the actual tendency of interpretation for the whole, where they generalize the message of the work.

In looking at the traces of Catholicism's influence on literature, we spoke frequently of the various functions of elements introduced by Catholicism into concrete literary works. These functions can naturally be very different; nor can they be counted.[17]

It is, however, worthwhile to call particular attention to two functional possibilities of religious elements in literature. First of all, there is the manner in which these elements mould the qualities whereby the literary work is to influence the reader. Thus, happiness, which can be the chief quality of a literary work or of a whole group of works, quickly takes on dimensions of exceptional broadening, deepening, and ennobling if it is a happiness with a religious motivation that takes on supernatural perspectives, or appears as a fundamental tone in the literary work whose dimensions were inspired by a Catholic view of the world. There is simply a qualitative change. Such happiness, present in Mickiewicz's verse *Rozmowa wieczorna* [*Evening Conversation*], is called by Borowy a happiness—so unusually and ineffably great and intense that in the work it is inexpressible and hence unexpressed: "Unspoken! we can use the expression here without exaggeration; for after all the most powerful accord of feelings consists in that which is beyond words, and is only their consequence."[18] Simplicity, too, takes on another character when it is deepened by a Franciscan's glance at life, for instance in the *Flowers of St. Francis*. Sublimity acquires a new, solemn, and nobly dignified hue. The rock of tragedy is changed when it is based on conflict within the framework of the highest values. An example of such a tragedy, which appears often in literature, is the tragedy of Judas. Unethical conduct, accompanied by the conviction of justice beyond the grave, enhances the tragedy of Konrad Wallenrod. Comedy takes on a particular coloring when it is portrayed, for example, in the novels of Marshall and the works of Guareschi, on a basis of religious motifs; when laughter came as a greater surprise because it somewhat approaches perverse self-will, and somewhat good-natured irony.

In all these cases, the elements introduced into literature by Catholicism produced changes in certain qualities and determined their variety. The influence of Catholicism on literature also created new qualities. This new quality can be of biblical or apocryphal character: the litany-like quality of some work, which, however, is not a litany; the quality of a mystery of some lyric verse; the morality-like character of some novel; and finally, to give an example of another kind, the mystical character of the works of St. John of the Cross, other writers of the seventeenth century, and even the poetry of K. Benisławski.[19]

Besides the problem of quality—we might call them esthetical qualities—it is necessary to consider particularly the various types of composition and literary species which either genetically or functionally and structurally are related to Catholicism. Thus, in the realm of lyric poetry we have the litany, prayer, psalms, and religious hymns—with particular consideration of the hymns for Mass (Feliński, J. D. Minasowicz), so common in the preromantic period. In epic poetry, there are above all the apocrypha, supplements to the gospels so popular in the Middle Ages. Then there are the tales so renowned in our own tradition (it suffices to mention Mickiewicz and Norwid). In drama, there are the liturgical offices, the mysteries, and the morality-plays. An especially rich inheritance came from the Middle Ages and the Spanish literature of the sixteenth-seventeenth centuries; but we also know of later developments that modified these literary types in the romantic period, as well as in contemporary literature, and that quite frequently.

III.

We have thus presented briefly some ideas on investigation of elements introduced into literature by Catholicism. They do not exhaust the possible relations between Catholicism and literature, even in terms of the direction from Catholicism to literature about which we have mostly spoken until now and within whose framework the problematic of these investigations would approach most closely the problematic of historical-literary studies.[20] There still exists the problem of the external influence of Catholicism on the development of literature: on the one hand, the matter of the Church's patronage in the area of literature, the creation of an immediate or mediate social environment for a special type of literary creation (e.g. hymns) and for translation (e.g. psalms); on the other hand, the very delicate matter of ecclesiastical censorship, which was able not so much to limit the development of literature as to pressure the readers about certain concrete works (although the reaction to the Index was indeed the opposite!). Then, finally, there is the matter of all that which influenced literary life of particular epochs, and which might be called the cultural policy of the Church in the field of literature. To this type of phenomena we must reckon the more or less official statements of the Church on literary subjects, for instance, statements by the popes. If Pius XII had written or said as much about literature as he said about films, we could freely consider a special comprehensive essay on that subject. Research in all these matters would in some way be a fragment of research into Church history, but it would also naturally interest the students of literature.

The opposite direction—from literature to Catholicism—brings new investigative perspectives. On the one hand, the literary nature of certain source texts of Catholicism could be investigated, especially the Bible and the epistles of St. Paul. This is not purely a stylistic matter. The consideration of particular types and literary species in Scripture is presently the methodological basis for the interpretation of the text.[21] On the other hand, there is investigation of the social influence on the religion of certain epochs; this was initiated by *Znak* in 1951 in its inquiry into the subject of the influence of reading on the moral and religious foundations of contemporary man.[22] In the first instance we would be in the field of literary investigations, and in the second we would have to use the methods of sociology.

IV.

This essay at defining the research problematic that comes from the relationship of Church and literature is surely not adequate. It will certainly be necessary to modify it in many points and perhaps even to change it. But these modifications and changes must now be made on the basis of particular investigations and the basis of evidence discovered in them. And these investigations must be undertaken independently of whether the problematic is entirely clear or not. Western science understands this well enough; its works in this field (and it is difficult to say whether they have been methodically defined), as well as works not always on a corresponding level, are recently increasing significantly. In a short time it will be necessary to count them not in tens but in hundreds. These are works on a variety of subjects: they deal with the present times as well as with the remote past; with writers who are still living as well as with Dante, Shakespeare, or Calderon; with works in which the Catholic problematic is the dominant theme; and with works remote from the Church, in which the echoes of Christian thought appear, but only sporadically and by way of exception. Among these works we find productions possessing eminently the character of a synthesis, as well as books devoted to a single subject.[23] We find monographs on the creations of particular authors who pass for Catholics; on elucubrations of

Stefan Sawicki

particular problems, such as man, love, tragedy, grace, religious
feeling (echoes of the renowned book of Henri Bremond, *Histoire
litteraire du sentiment religieux* . . .); and on the problems of
evil and guilt. We find the history of religious motifs: the Mother
of God, Christ, St. Francis, a saint, a priest, Satan—in particular
epochs, literary types, and so forth. Numerous works are devoted
to literary species: religious lyric, the various types of religious
drama, the Catholic novel, and the biblical epic.

Let us repeat once more that these tasks must be undertaken,
independently of any "methodological defects," and this in order
to evaluate the cultural creativity of the Church and discover in
what degree the literary appearance of particular epochs was
formed by religious Catholic elements. They are also studies that
will deal with a border area, that demand in various degrees a
knowledge of the problematic of the history of Catholicism and
the history of literature; the history of literature and biblical
studies; sociology and the history of literature—studies especially
necessary at a time when science is becoming highly specialized,
and the branches thereof are losing bond with one another.

FOOTNOTES

1. See the title of the collective work edited by Forst Battaglia, which J.
Birkenmajer translated: *Udział twórczości katolickiej dzisiejszej literaturze
świata* (Cracow, 1936).
2. K. Górski, "Rola pisarza katolickiego w dobie współczesnej," *Tygodnik
Powszechny* 37 (1946); "Między lurecją i kadenismem," *Tygodnik Powszechny*
39 (1951); "W Obronie powieści katolickiej," *Tygodnik Powszechny* 49 (1951);
J. Zawiejski, "Zagadnienie literatury katolickiej," *Tygodnik Powszechny* 23
(1947); A. Golubiew, "Z rozważań nad problemami literatury katolickiej,"
Znak 5 (1947) 520–540.
3. This is the article by J. Woźniakowski, "O lichej powieści katolickiej,"
Tygodnik Powszechny 4 (1950). It is worth mentioning that Graham Greene
takes a position similar to that of the author mentioned by Woźniakowski.
4. *Dziś i Jutro* 49 (1949).
5. Stefania Skwarczyńska, "Literatura katolicka jako termin w nauce o
literaturze," *Znak* 24 (1950) 222–233.
6. This is confirmed by J. Warszawski, "Katolickość dzieł Mickiewicza,"
Sacrum Poloniae Millenium (Rome, 1956) III, 433–632.
This definition is used quite often in scholarly practice. M. Jasińska, "Prob-
lematyka badań nad liryką religijną," *Sprawozdanie . . . Towarzystwa Nauko-
wego KUL* 8 (1957) 57–59, tries to make the term's meaning more precise.
7. (Poznań, 1939.) The following quotation is characteristic of the tendencies of this work: "If on the one hand we state that the Catholic novel is only
in its beginnings, that we do not have a novel as yet in the grand style in

which the problematic of religion plays an important role, this does not mean that there is a lack of secondary religious motifs in our novel-writing on the basis of which the reader can make quite an adequate picture of the religious life in Poland, of the religious character of the people and intelligentsia, of the meaning and role of the clergy and the Church" . . . (p. 9.)

8. See Z. Kubiak, "Poezja Biblii, "*Znak* 68–69 (1960) 180–181.

9. Zofia Niemojewska, *Dziady Drezdeńskie jako dramat Chrześcijański* (Warsaw, 1920).

10. K. Budzik, "Polskie systemy wersyfikacyjne," *Przegląd Humanistyczny* 4 (1958) 45–74.

11. M. Dłuska, *Studia z historii i teorii wersyfikacji polskiej* (Cracow, 1950) II, 217–224.

12. J. Worończak, "Tropy i sekwencje w literaturze polskiej do połowy XVI wieku," *Pamiętnik Literacki* 43 (1952) 1–2, p. 345.

13. B. Wosiek, "Norwid poeta katolicki," *Homo Dei* 6 (1958) 855.

14. Such an interpretation of the basic function of biblical stylization in the *Księgi* does not exclude, it seems, certain connections with the tradition of Polish parody and biblical travesty to which W. Kubacki calls attention in his "O stylu biblijnym 'Ksiąg Narodu i pielgrzymstwa polskiego,' " *Żeglarz i pielgrzym* (Warsaw, 1954) 206–274.

15. In the text of the "epilogue" printed in the *Zeszyty Wrocławskie* 3 (1952) 129–143, the fragment containing this is omitted.

16. M. Jasińska, Z. Jastrzębski, T. Klak, S. Nieznanowski, A. Paluchowski, S. Sawicki, "Matka Boska w poezji polskiej," in *Szkice o dziejach motywu* (Lublin, 1959).

17. I. Sławińska, "Ci git l'artise religieux," *Znak* 73–74 (1960) 911–920, calls attention to the various functions of religious elements in Norwid's work.

18. W. Borowy, "O Wierszach religijnych Mickiewicza," *Znak* 21 (1949) 543.

19. W. Borowy, "Benisławska," *O Poezji polskiej wieku XVIII* (Cracow, 1948) 200–220; A. Paluchowski, "Matka Boska w poezji czasów Stanisławowskich i okresu romantyzmu," *Matka Boska w poezji polskiej* (Lublin, 1959) I, 62–115; for Benisławska pp. 71–76.

20. Here we are dealing with the direction of the relationship itself, and not with the direction of the investigations of which we spoke earlier.

21. After a half-century of evidence in this field, Pius XII in his *Divino Afflante Spiritu* (1943) emphasized the importance of literary forms in exegesis.

22. Ksawery Pruszyński quite properly evaluates this influence as very significant. See his "Jan Dobraczyński czyli trudności katolickiego pisarza," *Odrodzenie* 26 (1947): "Obviously the Church needs bishops and priests; she needs lambs as well as many other things; but in our times the Church also needs writers. Mauriac, Bernanos, Daniel Rops, Claudel, Peguy, and whoever else adorns France—these people expanded the shrinking boundaries of Catholicism better than any encyclical, not to speak of pastoral letters."

23. For instance, Charles Moeller, *Litterature du siècle XX et christianisme* (Paris, 1953–1957) 3 vols.; Randall Steward, *American Literature and Christian Doctrine* (Baton Rouge, 1958); A. Wilder, *Theology and Modern Literature* (Cambridge, 1958).

THE ROLE OF WOMEN

IN PASTORAL WORK

Leokadia Małunowicz

BECAUSE THIS IS A VAST AND MANY-SIDED SUBJECT, IT HAS PROVED
necessary to suggest only certain problems without giving particular solutions. We shall try to present an overall view of women in
pastoral work in Poland and the difficulties this creates for the
clergy—a view outlining current thinking and conclusions: results
of private interviews and group discussions along with observations made in the course of many years in various localities.

The replies sent from eighteen dioceses (Białystok, Częstochowa,
Drohiczyn, Katowice, Kielce, Cracow, Łomża, Łódź, Poznań, Płock,
Przemyśl, Sandomierz, Siedlce, Tarnów, Warmia, Warsaw, Włocławek, Wrocław) are only partially concerned with the participation of women in pastoral work, for certainly—and I emphasize
this—there exists a whole series of problems and undertakings not
noted at all. Numbers reveal something, but not the whole picture.
It is, above all, in pastoral work that we must apply the principle
"Quality before quantity." From the viewpoint of the actual and
practical character of the problem, there was very little to be found
in either Polish or other books and articles which I was able to
consult.

At the beginning it might be well to state certain propositions
serving as point of departure for further considerations— such that
serve as the bases of a kind.

1. In the thought of Christ and the Church, the woman is
equally a worker in the Lord's vineyard, responsible for her own
salvation and the salvation of others. We can cite the words of Pius
XII (in an address to the members of the International Union of
Catholic Women's Leagues, April 14, 1939): "In all human

works—as well as in the human-divine work of salvation—God gave woman as a companion and helpmate to man: but that cooperation of the woman seems to us more necessary today than at any other time."

2. The psycho-physical qualities of the woman define certain areas of activity as most especially suited to the woman. The limits between the activity of man and woman are obviously not strict; except for the physical fact of motherhood, there is no activity that could not be performed by a man. In speaking of women's participation in pastoral work, it is necessary to keep in mind the type and frequency of certain phenomena.

We are suggesting the thesis that even when there is a sufficient number of priests, certain sectors of pastoral work can be entrusted to a woman, such as nursing, care of infants and children, and the like.

3. The dechristianization of the contemporary world demands that the Church mobilize the laity for a more active cooperation in the renewal of all things in Christ. Two factors play a role here: the lack of priests (even though the situation is different in certain dioceses) and the unfavorable or even hostile attitude of many people and centers toward the clergy. In Poland this happens more often in the urban rather than rural environment. Among the many statements of Pius XII, I cite only one—the allocution to the pastors and Lenten preachers in Rome, 1954. The Pope states that an enormous mass of people do not live for God. The priest has no means of approaching them, and the only means of influencing them are supernatural means. "It follows naturally from this, my beloved sons, that you must create help for yourselves, good helpers that will increase your energies and your powers, helpers ready to substitute for you where you cannot reach. Hence the great importance of the lay apostolate, which, as you know from your own experience, can become a great force for good." True, the pope does not mention woman especially, but undoubtedly appeals to them as well as to the clergy.

4. The parish is the proper field of activity for the faithful. In reviewing the work of women in pastoral work we shall begin with catechetical work, then pass to charitable activity, and finally the activity of parish workers. We shall pause for a moment and ponder the reasons behind the limited amount of activity among women in the apostolate, and then touch upon the problem of the choice and education of women for work in the care of souls.

In conclusion, we shall summarize the considerations and make practical suggestions.

I. WOMEN AND CATECHETICAL WORK

1. Professional catechists. We can make the questionnaire our point of departure. On the basis of the eighteen replies, this is the numerical picture of conditions among teachers of religion: lay women catechists, 700; men catechists, 200; religious women, 661; priest catechists (including 16 students in the diocese of Wrocław), 3,596.

This division of the catechetical forces is conditioned not only by external circumstances, but chiefly by the psychic structure of women. From the purely psychological viewpoint it indicates that small children should receive instruction from women teachers. The maternal instinct, together with an intuitive delicacy, makes it easier for a woman to enter into closer contact with children up to the age of ten, or thereabout. This was the thought of a recent statement by the ordinary of the diocese of Częstochowa, January 5, 1957. Bishop Goliński emphasized an important circumstance: women catechists can conduct instruction with greater responsibility and diligence than priests, who are often called from religious instruction by the other obligations of pastoral work. It is recommended in larger rural parishes that women catechists live near the school (sometimes the parish priest must travel many kilometers to reach a school located at the extremities of the parish). In the diocese of Częstochowa there is a great need for women catechists.

Often the authority of the priest-catechist hampers the openness of the child. Thus, children, prepared for their first confession by the catechist, wish to make their first confession to her. For the child to feel comfortable with the priest, a close cooperation is needed between catechist and child. Hence, it is clear that women catechists require professional training. Well-prepared women catechists can teach in the higher grades of the elementary schools and in the middle schools, especially in a woman's school, for girls in reaching puberty will more readily discuss moral problems with a woman than with a priest. In some areas parents and children take a negative attitude to women catechists (an old woman teaching religion!); this became known late in 1956 when religion was restored to the schools, with women catechists appearing instead of priests. That these are prejudices is clear from the fact that, for instance in Silesia, where the lay teacher for many years past had a canonical mission and taught religion, this opposition did not appear among the urban population. It will be the clergy's task to overcome the parents' and children's psychological resentment of the women catechists and to convince them of the error in thinking that the priest by virtue of his ordination teaches religion better than any one else. Indeed, not every priest has teaching ability, and the women catechists generally have special talents in this field.

2. Besides women professionally engaged in catechetical work, the persons who participate in the Church's magisterium other than the teacher's capacity can render great service to the Church. In the first place, it is necessary to mention the mother. The pastor will engage all his zeal and thought to instruct his women parishioners about the obligation and responsibilities which fall upon the mother in forming the religious conscience of the child. A certain Silesian priest had a very fine idea when in the advanced courses of new and old material (dogmatic, moral, and sacramental theology) he dealt with the subject matter from the viewpoint of marriage and motherhood. Extremely useful are the special courses which train parents, and especially mothers, in the religious teaching of the child; here the psychologist and the educator must take part. For instance, in the diocese of Tarnów—according to the questionnaire— "besides the priest, the burden of religious instruction falls on the mothers." The mothers are prepared for this over a period of years. They are given printed material for instruction. Sisters, trained in pastoral care, conducted a course in the diocese for mothers to prepare them for religious instruction in the family (e.g., teaching of preschool children, preparation for Holy Communion). In order to instruct the mothers it is easy to exploit the period of preparation for First Holy Communion, because at that time the parents experience a greater interest in religious matters.

The pedagogical and didactic training of mothers is not enough; it is more important to attract women to religious education and to facilitate a continuing program for them: to awaken a sense of the great responsibility the mother bears for the child and for its fate not only in the temporal but in the eternal sense. The diocese of Cracow (I do not know if it is the only one in Poland) began to use correspondence courses to complete the religious education of mothers for their preparation in teaching children. In many rural areas women gather in special locations for one day, and in a number of lectures they receive general, methodological, and practical suggestions as to material, which they are to master in the immediate future; and the next meeting determines whether the participants mastered the relevant material, and the work moves on to the next chapter (e.g., first the Old Testament and then the New).

In the task of teaching religion it is also possible to utilize girls from the elementary school. They can help the women catechists (either with a whole group or with slower children), especially in the preparation for First Holy Communion. Often, if properly trained, they can assume some of the catechetical instruction of younger children in the home.

3. Beyond the systematic teaching of religion to children and school youth, it is also indispensable to provide religious training for advanced youths and adults in the problems of Catholic faith and morals, for the extent of religious knowledge in Poland is quite low on all social levels. Here, too, the women—without regard to family, profession, degree of education, and age—have a great field of activity. Through individual conversations, discussions, the propaganda of the press, and of Catholic books, the woman can influence her proximate and remote environment; thanks to her special psychological and physical features, the woman can often reach individuals whom a wall of hostility separates from the clergy. Future women apostles must have sound preparation. For this reason, in many dioceses various courses are conducted for women—conducted mostly by women, lay women as well as religious. Somehow the problems of marriage and family belong to the special competence of women.

In the problems of marriage, the words of wives and mothers are most effective, for often village women are scandalized when "maidens" discuss problems connected with the physiological side of marriage. Premarriage courses, for instance, were conducted in the dioceses of Tarnów (1950–1954), Warsaw, Poznań, Łódź, Cracow. Usually Mohammed goes to the mountain, and the women lecturers travel widely to engage in discussions and lectures. For instance, in the diocese of Kielce ten groups of two to three women lecturers after a six-day course go to the individual parishes on Sunday. But the general number of these appearances and the relative proportion of lay and religious women cannot be fixed exactly because of the lack of statistical material. The participation of religious women was certainly great; for instance, the convent of Sacre Coeur in Zbylitowska Góra sent lecturers to 108 parishes. At present Jasna Góra has undertaken to organize various courses for women.

We have described only a few typical examples. The reality of the women's apostolate is much richer in content and form if we consider the spreading of Christ's truth. There are certainly many possibilities open for us. Perhaps we shall undertake to effect—with certain modifications—the striking thought of Father Błaszyński of a century ago: creating "a feminine army" of zealous catechists; they drove the fundamental truths of the Catholic Faith so deeply into the minds of the mountaineers that the catechetical formulas of Father Błaszyński, transmitted from generation to generation, can still be found among the mountaineers of Sidzina.

II. CHARITABLE ACTIVITY

Charitable activity is the field that especially befits women. Here we are not dealing with the gesture of a Lady Bountiful wiping away the tears of a beggar by giving him alms, but with the practical organized conduct of all acts of mercy. Although canon law and synodal decrees do not oblige the pastor to "fatherly care of the poor," the very logic of charity, whose official servant the priest is, obliges him to practice such charity. The first essential condition for the parish to begin living the life of the Mystical Body is the awakening among the faithful of an active charity embracing every need and every suffering. Parochial charitable activity—and hence activity in the name of and with the consent of the pastor, and not individually practiced works of charity—forms the widest and most distinctive mark of pastoral care. Thus, the data in the questionnaire have only a directive value. Nevertheless, it should be required that charitable activity in all dioceses be centrally directed to increase its effectiveness and to coordinate all the efforts of particular cells. It would be well if women would enter into these plans of charitable pastoral work, for the greater burden of this work rests on women. For instance, in the diocese of Łódź 201 women and only 10 men are engaged in this work.

What types of charitable work should women undertake above all? In the first place, there is the protection of the family, especially, the family with many children. In speaking to a group of lay Catholics, the Cardinal Primate strongly emphasized this obligation and called for its realization. It is not enough to teach about the spectre of sin; it is necessary to help wives and mothers carry the burden of life, which is often beyond their strength. We must welcome with joy such organizations (for instance in Łódź), which provide for women free gynecological medical care from doctors who recognize Catholic ethics. The cooperation of women doctors of various specialties and with a positive attitude toward the teachings of the Church is greatly needed and produces important results, as is evidenced by the experience of Warsaw. In the marriage counseling centers (which exist in Włocławek, Kalisz, and Cracow) the cooperation of men is not excluded, but a woman is much more practical as physician and psychologist. We must also mention Cracow where courses are offered to young mothers and fathers, and this experience has been excellent.

In the concrete reality of everyday life we must enter into the "family rescue service," especially in families with many children and in which mothers are alone. Obviously, in most cases material assistance is necessary, whether permanent, limited, or temporary. Not only the women who are gainfully employed outside the home, but also those who are with their husbands and are engaged in domestic work are not in a position to fulfill the most elementary religious obligations; the development of their internal life is hampered by constant work and lack of free time. Not only illness or some misfortune but the daily burden of either gainful or domestic employment produces a situation where the woman simply cannot go on. The pastor will persuade the less burdened woman to perform acts of charity, though small in effect (washing, cooking, supervision of the children) but significant in their social aspects; they save the lives of the unborn (since in many cases for the woman to agree to a child requires heroism on her part), and they prevent the dissolution of family life. It is possible to draw into this activity even young girls. It is a good idea to organize neighborhood self-help, where possible. That this is a social necessity is clear from the alarming facts on all sides. The call for help comes especially from mothers who are alone (widows, unwed, abandoned), who must work for a living, and who have no one with whom to leave the children. Let us also remember that every mother does have a right to some type of recreation and rest. I place a little more emphasis on the above aspect, because I fear that men are not always aware of the woman's role and her psychology.

We now pass to the second task that awaits the woman in pastoral work: care of children and women who are alone. This is an important task especially in urban centers because of the immigration of the village population. In many cases this will involve experiences of a moral nature, with the realization of intense spiritual works of mercy. A girl, separated from her natural environment (the family or the village) feels strange in her new surroundings; frequently she is faced with conditions that lead to demoralization, and hence it is understandable that her life remains entirely without intellectual content. She tries to fill the gap with erotic experiences and banal recreations. If she encounters some good experience, hears the words of truly pastoral instruction, or if an enlightening book falls into her hands, then mental activity will very likely be aroused in her. This can be the beginning of reflection on the meaning of life, however naïve, and possibly of a new sense of values. The soil of the soul is then conditioned for a return to religious practices, which in turn makes way for a richer union with God.

In the urban parishes the problem of prostitution has been increasing steadily. Even if the Council of Ministers approves the proposed project and effective action against prostitution, there still remains a great deal to be done in the framework of Christian charity. Emphasis must be placed on the removal of the sources of evil and on the creation of facilities for the rehabilitation of individuals who are willing to cooperate. This type of pastoral work in Poland will require women helpers to be well informed about the problem of prostitution in Poland.

Care of the sick is a vast task. As is clear from the questionnaire and the information gathered in the country, there is a great deal to be done in this sphere. The parish must above all concern itself with the chronically ill who do not have care or material means. So far as we know, the Department of Health does not provide care for the chronically ill; in Cracow, there is but one nursing home, sponsored by the school of nursing. Elsewhere the conditions are pitiable. Only the health centers (rural) and the clinics (urban) have professional nurses who give injections, and surgical nurses are restricted to surgery. As a consequence, many of the chronically ill are subjected to a miserable state. Hence, there is a great demand for qualified nurses. Depending on the condition of the patient and the domestic situation, the help will vary in quality and number. One nurse can handle at most seven-eight sick persons. I repeat, seven-eight persons. Thus, if every parish would employ but one nurse, this would give help to only seven-eight persons; and any parish would certainly have more sick members than that who require permanent care by others. At the same time (would that the information were not correct), it is possible to count on one's fingers the number of parishes that have the professional means to care for the sick. We can mention one in Cracow, where two nurses have been working for the past several months. That is the proverbial drop in the ocean, for only twenty-four chronically sick persons receive aid. The nurses receive about 1,000 złotys a month, insurance, and working equipment. It is obvious that professionally trained help needs the assistance of able persons who do not have such training. Caring for the sick also involves a series of basic activities: bathing, cooking, washing, and so forth. It is indeed a tribute to Cracow that some months ago the university youth organized to give assistance in so-called home care. The volunteers for the most part are the women students in the school of medicine who are in nurses' training. Their service is valuable, for it is most important to stimulate the interest of the immediate environment or community in the situation of the sick, as well as to teach the sick person the elementary principles of nursing care. The Church likewise teaches that the immediate and personal care of the sick is one of the greatest works of charity. Perhaps it is not necessary to prove that every person in contact with a sick person must consider his or her spiritual welfare, *sub specie aeternitatis;* this must also be done by the woman taking part in the pastoral care of the sick.

The care of the old and the physically or mentally retarded has its own specific character. These individuals pose difficult problems for those around them and besides are economically dependent. For this reason religious women are recruited to work in this field—no one will do it even for money. We quote the statement of Z. Średniawska from an article "Subtelna Zmowa": "Care for the elderly and the sick is neither easy nor attractive. It is a task that requires dedication, self-denial, and tact. . . . In a word: the care must be comforting and not merely nursing. Hence, it is not accidental that in the majority of cases of this type in Poland, the care and nursing personnel consists of religious women. This kind of work requires something more than monthly pay."[1]

Work with this group demands great sacrifice and true charity, and it is without the joy that comes from work among children and youth. It is not possible to enumerate all the forms of assistance. We can only emphasize that persons willing to do this work must be distinguished by great tact and great patience, gifted with a balanced personality, and have a period of psychic rest since they cannot sustain a longer period of work; they must know the current social legislation in order to direct the individuals to the proper institutions; and they need an elementary knowledge of psychology relevant to those under their care. It seems that this field of pastoral work in Poland is slow in developing. Several of the questionnaires state that they do not have any form of care for the elderly. Again we must repeat that it is possible to draw school youth into this work. Even materially independent elderly persons feel strongly the need of human love and kindness, and we must remember that since they are nearing passage "to the beyond," the greater the need to care for their souls.

III. WOMEN AUXILIARIES IN PAROCHIAL WORK

With this we close our reflections on charitable activity, in order to consider women as auxiliaries in parochial work. The term parochial auxiliary also appears in the narrow sense of a woman taking part in charitable pastoral care. Hence, certain misunderstandings resulted in the questionnaire and elsewhere. I shall use it in the broader sense: a parochial auxiliary (another title, parochial sister, e.g., in the diocese of Częstochowa) is a woman who in the name of the pastor and with his permission and under his direction carries out pastoral care in catechetics, charitable activity (in the widest sense), and in other ecclesiastical needs. Her sphere of activity is exactly like that of the pastor, except for strictly priestly functions. Obviously, not all possibilities can be realized in a particular parish; this depends on local needs and the psycho-physical and material circumstances of each auxiliary. Let us turn to the questionnaire. In the twelve dioceses which have women parochial auxiliaries, the following areas of activity are most often mentioned: (eight times) service in the church, catechetics, health and material care, work with children and youth, library work; (seven times) assistance in the office; (six times) ecclesiastical music; and finally (three times) the organization of festivities and pilgrimages. These data are only suggestive and fragmentary and do not reflect the whole picture of women auxiliaries' work in Poland. It is not possible to establish the absolute number in the particular dioceses or the percentage of parishes that have women auxiliaries. The diocese of Tarnów is an exception; there all the parishes (334) use the services of parochial auxiliaries; in four dioceses the number of parochial auxiliaries is very small (a slight percentage). The suggestion is well founded that the idea of women parochial auxiliaries in Poland is one for tomorrow, and not for today, even though as far back as twenty years ago there were voices raised (e.g., Father Adam Kuleszo) emphasizing their need. "We need organizational forces, professionally trained, entirely and indivisibly devoted to the service of the parish. We need individuals free of all other tasks to accept one great task—total dedication to the service of one's neighbor. This is the precise vocation of the parochial auxiliaries. They will go to all the corners of the parish and bring aid, spiritual and moral, to the parishioners; they will take upon themselves the burden of silent work, whose goal will be the creation of a closer bond between the parish church, as the center of religious life, and the parishioners." The first condition for a bond between the pastor and the parishioners is a detailed knowledge of their spiritual and material needs, acquired not only by way of the confessional but through immediate contact. The simplest mathematical calculations suffice to show that even priests in small parishes do not find time to make at least a half-hour visit biannually to each family. Unable to carry out this obligation, the pastor will use the parochial auxiliary. In German literature the parochial auxiliary's principal task is the home visit (*Hausebesuch*). Very closely tied to this is the use of the file card, which is of great help in parochial visits. The best memory, the quickest perception, and even perfect alertness on the part of the pastor will not replace the use of the file card. The pastor will never discover means of action in this or that case, if he does not glance at the file card and recall all the circumstances connected with the particular problem he is to solve. Following the German example, western Poland has used the parochial file-card system a long time in many places; but it is unknown in central and eastern Poland. Only the priest can establish the system, but the maintenance of the system in a current state can be entrusted to the parochial auxiliary, who will give (and is obliged to give) a guarantee of professional discretion.

Even with the greatest self-sacrifice, the parochial auxiliary will not be adequate in all the tasks, even in a small parish, but in the closest understanding with the pastor she must bring into cooperation as many parishioners as possible. In most centers it will be her task to direct activity, organize the cooperation of others, supervise the realization of the pastor's directives; she shall function partly as the intelligence and as the shepherdess. She herself will engage in work for which she has special talent or for which she is especially responsible.

The parish must be divided into smaller units, for which one person shall assume the responsibility. In some instances where pastoral care is already developed, the auxiliaries can be divided into certain groups, to be headed by one responsible person; for instance, in one Warsaw parish (about 18,000) the charitable activity is directed by one responsible head with the aid of twenty-four persons.

I would like to call attention to a certain area, which is not immediately connected with pastoral work in the current understanding of the term, but which today has a vast significance—a task that must be undertaken by the parochial auxiliary with her mind, heart, and activity. The purpose is to develop the spiritual aspects of man, in order to prepare the corresponding bases for charity. In youth work there is a burning need to teach good recreation. I quote from a youth questionnaire recently sent out by me. Very often the answers revealed that youth does not know how to entertain itself and how to rest, that it must be taught these things. Practically all the participants were of the opinion that recreation is necessary; the educational value of recreation was also emphasized, and certain concrete conclusions were suggested. In a significant degree hooliganism results from the inability to use leisure. There is a great deal of truth in the slogan *"Kraft durch Freude."* For instance, whoever attracts youth to recreation in the Catholic spirit does more than the one who organizes antialcoholic discussions or discussions appealing for a greater respect toward the Polish woman. It is not formal talk, but rather the awakening of artistic interests, travel, sports, and the attraction to good reading that are the effective means in the introductory phase of pastoral care. Not every priest is adapted for such work; at times lay persons possess greater talent and disposition for it. It is the task of the woman parochial auxiliary to win the cooperation of such persons if she herself is not able to work in that area.

In discussing the various and time-consuming tasks of the parochial woman auxiliary, we demand from her that she devote herself entirely to her work. In our economic conditions this means that she must receive some compensation; this does not militate against her disinterestedness (otherwise we would have to agree that all clerics do not work disinterestedly, for they live at the expense of the faithful). On the basis of the questionnaire, it is difficult to fix the average compensation of the parochial auxiliary. In a certain parish of the Cracow diocese the auxiliary receives a dwelling, light, fuel, and 1,000 złotys; for further church work (e.g., repairing the church linens) she receives breakfast or lunch. In Warsaw (1955) a parochial sister (that is, in charity work) earned 600–800 złotys and insurance; and in case of other work, breakfast or dinner.

The moral attitude of the auxiliary will determine whether people will be offended by the fact that she receives money for charitable work. Persons devoting only part of their time to work in the parish will obviously have financial resources. We have examined the participation of women in parochial work. It is obvious that every pastor needs such help. Why is it, therefore, that only a small percentage of parishes use the help of women? We often hear the answer: the lack of women willing to undertake the work. This is not true, for there is a vast potential of good will and altruism among the Polish women. The *devotus femineus sexus* is awaiting the call: *Cur otiosae statis?* Why do all the pastors not issue this invitation? I will answer briefly: because they do not want to. Why do they not want to? This is a long and somewhat sensitive matter. Certainly, many factors operate here. We shall try to isolate some of them, and this in a theoretical manner. The replies which I received from clerics as well as lay people suggest the following reflections. Let us proceed from the simple statement: where nothing is being done, there is no need of a helper. In how many cases does the priest confine his pastoral obligations to the purely sacramental aspect (Mass, the prescribed devotions, preaching, the dispensation of the sacraments)! It is no wonder that such a "dental method"—for the dentist serves only those who come to his chair—does not provide the priest with a knowledge of the spiritual and material needs of his sheep. If the priest is interested in comfort and material things, the parish will certainly be dead, and an empty ritualism will dominate it. This can kill charitable initiative begun from below.

For example, a parish with 20,000 members in a city of some tens of thousands is served by several priests. A qualified catechist (graduate of the Catholic University of Lublin) applied for catechetical work; she agreed to accept 200 złotys for twenty hours a week. A contract was signed in September, and it was broken in June because (*risum teneatis amici*) the parish could not stand such an expense. Consequently, a significant number of children and youth were deprived of religious instruction. In several other instances a trained catechist asked the pastor for permission to teach—without compensation—religion to preschool children, and she met with the reply that the children will be able to learn their religion in school. In some cases it is pride that hinders the priest, for an auxiliary because of her zealous work can win greater popularity. In others, either consciously or subconsciously, there is the fear of being subjected to a critic—even though a silent one—of one's own conduct, for the auxiliary is well acquainted with church affairs and is dedicated to the work of the Lord. It is much more comfortable for such a priest not to have a witness to his passivity. Then, too, many priests hesitate to bring women into church matters for fear of undue interference; they fear that such helpers have a tendency to gad about and to impose their will on the pastor. It is true, of course, that parishioners resent women in control in the church and in the rectory. Beyond this, priests who are thoroughly convinced that every woman is a *fomentum mali,* a *janua diaboli,* wish to avoid all contact with women, as did St. Aloysius Gonzaga—and yet it is impossible not to meet with one's female fellow worker. Often one encounters the view, as I did in a certain lecture written by a priest for priests, that with woman there is a great danger of exaltation in relation to the priest, that woman serves an idea through the person, and that the woman sanctifies herself and saves herself in the first place through the priest. Always he must think of himself as worthy of being such an object of veneration by the chambermaid! However, these misconceptions as well as other obstacles can be removed if the priest is sincere, zealous, and judicious in his role as pastor, and if he assumes a positive attitude to the merits of auxiliary work.

A regard for the success of the parish apostolate does not permit the rule of an absolute monarch; it is necessary to leave sufficient room to the initiative of responsible persons wherever possible.

Now we must consider whether a religious or a lay person is better suited for parochial work. The obvious answer is that it depends on the person. The most important condition for effectiveness in the work is the degree of dedication and the personality of the auxiliary, but certain secondary factors can facilitate or hinder the work in a concrete situation. There are several factors that argue for the use of religious.

1. They already possess a certain inclination toward the interior life, and have the advantage of a general religious education. They can begin work at once.

2. With many people, especially in the rural environment, the nun's habit carries a great deal of prestige. The nun is treated like a superior being. First there is the priest, then nun, then a big gap between, and finally the ordinary lay person. In charitable activity nuns meet with a greater confidence in respect to professional ability.

3. The religious provide for a greater continuity of effort, for by reason of the rule they work together; for instance, if the auxiliary becomes ill, the congregation names someone to take her place.

However, we cannot omit the following reservations.

1. A nun working in a parish is not an independent person, for she is subject to both the pastor and her superior. In theory the religious authorities are to give complete autonomy; but in practice they frequently interfere in parochial matters. In speaking of charitable activity, Canon Kliszko said: "In naming a nun for charitable activity, the congregation actually treats that work as its own outpost. The congregation treats work in parishes as a means of maintenance and not as a work of the heart. Working independently, the congregations do not integrate themselves into the general diocesan plan of activity. . . ."

2. In the urban environment the religious habit is often an obstacle in pastoral work. There are certain prejudices, not only against priests but also against nuns. There is usually doubt as to the personal convictions of a nun should she express herself on religious questions ("She says this because she has to"). Often people feel that the nun is merely treating them like an object on which she exercises her love of neighbor, that they are only the fuel for her good deeds. In charitable work this is an especially sensitive and delicate matter.

3. Certain orders, whose members are engaged in parochial activity only secondarily (in Poland, so far as I know, the Sisters of Bethany, founded by Cardinal Hlond in the 1930's, have as their prime objective the task of helping the pastor), do not possess sufficiently flexible rules; in greater or lesser degree the rules restrict the freedom of movement. This may not be as harmful in catechetical work, but the effect is certainly negative in charitable activity. The restrictions of the rule make it difficult to establish contacts with lay people on a person-to-person level.

4. The alienation of the nun from her working environment is not a rare phenomenon. Her segregation from the lay world, even in active orders, reveals itself in that she does not find even a common language (conceptual and verbal) with lay people. She becomes psychically estranged, and it is difficult for her to sense their problems and the conditions of their life. This is damaging to all phases of pastoral work. For instance, the nun catechist is frequently separated from life, and children easily suspect this—especially older boys: "Sister doesn't know what it's all about." Also, as a result of a long tradition in a given congregation as to the method of charitable work, the nun will find it more difficult to adapt to the modern concept of charitable pastoral work, and in charitable work it is more important in most cases to find a common ground than to provide actual material help. In giving family aid her status can be a hindrance, for example, the incongruity in seeing a nun wash clothes or scrub a floor on her hands and knees.

5. People are more readily scandalized by the weaknesses and imperfections of persons who obviously belong to the "state of perfection"; that which is easily tolerated in a lay person would soon disqualify the religious in their eyes. Furthermore, when persons meet a kind act from the religious, they are inclined to treat this as an obligation; and yet, this same act done by a lay person takes on a greater meaning, for they see in it something unusual, something beyond the call of duty. In terms of awakening faith in man, faith in the Christian ideal, the testimony of charity performed voluntarily by a lay person can have a greater eloquence.

6. The demands made by the religious orders are quite high. The individual nun might perhaps agree on a smaller compensation, but it is the religious authorities that decide, and they consider the material needs of the whole order.

7. A nun often has difficulties negotiating with various offices and institutions, and in charitable activity, of course, it is often necessary to deal with them. We might add that since October (1956), the superiors are recalling workers from many parishes to place them in other positions.

These reflections have shown us the advantages and disadvantages of religious and lay auxiliaries; it is like the negative and positive of the same photograph. What argues best for the lay auxiliary is her state of life in the world, thanks to which she can better understand people and communicate with those among whom she works—she is one of them. It seems that the best solution will be provided by the lay institutes, whose system of formation, religious and moral, is no less strong in essence, though different in form, from that in the orders, but provides at the same time a conditioning for work in the world.

As to whom the pastor selects and invites to this cooperation will depend on many circumstances—mostly on his personal views. Priests should keep in mind the suggestions of Pius XII on the cooperation of lay persons with the priest (1954), which are quite relevant. He gave the following directives.

1. It is necessary to find zealous souls that wish to work for God; to know their potentialities and talents.

2. Great emphasis must be placed on the formation of these auxiliary forces. "Nor is the time lost that is used in the preparation and training of these workers."

3. It is necessary to use them in various fields of activity. Do not suppress their initiative.

The realization of the program outlined by the Holy Father demands personal holiness from the priest and great apostolic effort, but the zealous pastor will find here as well the *merces copiosa*. Experience shows that charity—and all apostolic work is charity—after the sacramental life is the second means for a moral rebirth. Canon Michael Kliszko, Director of the Charitable Pastoral Work in the Archdiocese of Warsaw, is the zealous propagator of this idea among us. Charitable work causes the core of egotism and egocentrism to crumble within us; it awakens us to a need of deepening our own interior life, especially a sense of responsibility for the soul of our neighbor and our own life. It also improves the psycho-physical personality of the woman, as is confirmed by gynecologists and neurologists. This has great importance if the woman is alone, for the practice of charity preserves her from bitterness, from eccentricity, and spiritual atrophy. The sense of not being needed, which is a torment of people who are alone, disappears. Even on the natural level a woman tends to free herself from the sense of not being needed—as is shown by the initiative of Hildegarde Schmidt, who not long ago founded a club in Hanover for older persons who do not know how to utilize their time. The members visit the sick; as "adopted grandmothers," they substitute for parents who go out in the evening and leave the children alone. Especially young couples are turning more and more to this club.

A woman living alone can be a valuable auxiliary, for she tends to see in her apostolic work the goal of her life. Again we appeal to a statement of Pius XII (address to A.C.I., October 21, 1945): "The common good makes demands on the women who have time and who can give themselves more completely to social matters. Is not this a special calling for those women . . . to whom some basic views dictated their calling, and who thanks to some events are destined to be alone, though unintentionally and unwillingly, and could lead to an egotistical and purposeless existence. It is clear that their mission is indeed varied and absorbs the strength which married women cannot dispose of . . . nor can nuns who are bound by their rule." A priest has properly remarked that it is a bit too late to transform a woman who is alone, when a certain interior deformation has already set in. Young girls should be hearing from their priests that besides physical motherhood there is spiritual motherhood, no less joyful and rewarding.

Now we pass to the following point. It is worthwhile considering one problem in the choice of auxiliaries, namely, their age. Should they be older women, as St. Paul recommended in speaking of widows, or young girls, or mature women? Again an important caution: it is not possible to give a general, absolute rule, but only to indicate typical cases. On the one hand, certain factors favor the choice of young people for this work: psychic flexibility, greater possibility of training the person, and adaptability to new methods of work. On the other hand, there is lack of experience and lack of know-how, especially in certain areas of work. Older women have a deeper knowledge of life and in general a greater sense of responsibility for the tasks they have undertaken, but find it more difficult to free themselves of their own ideas and methods—and this, in the rapid tempo of transformation in our circumstances, can be a negative factor in cooperative pastoral care.

Briefly we shall enumerate the qualities which every auxiliary in pastoral work must have: integrity, gentleness, courtesy, tact, understanding, equanimity, prudence, and discretion. Valuable, too, is a sense of organization and social awareness that expresses itself in a deep conviction that the whole work is undertaken within the framework of the Church and is not an individual effort.

A special task, and no less important, is the professional training of women for pastoral work, as good will and zeal do not suffice. Thus far this fact is being realized chiefly in the area of catechists. From the questionnaire we learn that of the eighteen dioceses, nine have a permanent educational program. In some, besides courses during vacation, there are monthly, and even weekly, conferences. Commendable is the effort of the diocese of Katowice, where "from 1946 there have been conducted systematic, graded catechetical courses, and the professional and spiritual training of the catechists is directed by a school official of the diocesan chancery. A permanent catechetical staff (eight auxiliaries) is engaged in preparing catechetical help."

Besides raising the didactic-pedagogical qualifications of the catechists, their spiritual formation must be considered. Only three dioceses reported that they do not provide any spiritual care for the catechists. Generally there are meetings (several times a year), and in some dioceses annual days of recollection. In the diocese of Katowice the catechists are obliged to make a closed retreat annually, and every two months a day of recollection. About 500 catechists took part in the latter. It would be desirable if all the dioceses employed such energy.

Quite striking is the lack of understanding for that fact that charitable activity (*sensu lato*) also requires professional workers. Already in 1939 Bishop Pękala wrote: "In order that *Caritas* [National Catholic Charitable Organization] should continue to be on a footing of equality in the modern conditions of culture, it must be based on scientific foundations. Hence the pastor will make every effort that his helpers in *Caritas* receive special schooling." However, since the war there is no indication that any of the responding dioceses either maintain or foresee a permanent center for training charitable workers. In eight dioceses their spiritual formation is carried on through retreats, days of recollection, and special devotions. There is certainly enough evidence that the pastoral auxiliaries are not only in demand, but that they work well. We mention here the example of Canon Kliszko and Zofia Czacka, who are trying to organize charitable activity in Warsaw by way of modern methods, that is, by developing the interior lives of auxiliaries as well as training them professionally. In 1953–1957 there were five educational centers on various levels. Łódź accepted the same method of cooperation.

In Warsaw and Łódź the Officials of the Charitable Pastoral Work Commission organized vacation courses for their parochial assistants (and candidates as well). The diocese of Cracow introduced an educational program for midwives and lay nurses.

In the matter of professional parochial auxiliaries, we in Poland are not as yet formally training them, even though abroad special schools or institutes have long existed for them. The diocese of Wrocław with its Catholic Scientific Institute (a two-year program) and the Department of Catholic Culture of the Catholic Institute (a four-year program) provides an exception.

In ending our discussion, we must conclude that in Poland the use of women auxiliaries in parochial work is hardly perceptible. Women are more active in teaching religion than in the field of charity. But in many of the dioceses there is no organized charitable activity, and where it exists, only a small percentage of the parishes are engaged in it (and this is mostly in urban parishes). The idea of women parochial auxiliaries is only in its initial stage of development.

Hence, we can raise the following *desiderata*: 1. the introduction of a parochial auxiliary into every parish, which will direct the groups of women and girls engaged in various fields of pastoral activity; 2. the organization of diocesan or interdiocesan educational programs for parochial auxiliaries; 3. the preparation of a two-year study program for the parochial auxiliaries; and 4. the employment of publicity media to indicate the present participation of women in pastoral work in Poland.

FOOTNOTES

1. Z. Średniawska, "Subtelna Zmowa," *Tygodnik Powszechny*, January 12, 1958.

CARITAS AND POSTWAR

RECONSTRUCTION

Józef Majka

I. THE SOCIAL AND ECONOMIC CONDITIONS IN POLAND AFTER THE WAR

IT IS IMPOSSIBLE TO PRESENT IN A FEW PAGES THE LOSSES SUFFERED by Poland in the Second World War. We shall try to sketch only an outline of the situation that required immediate help and extraordinary efforts on the part of the nation.

The war effected enormous losses in population. We are not referring here to the loss of population suffered by the shift of borders and transfer of population. The extermination policy of the occupying power reduced the prewar population by 17.4 per cent, of which 27.7 per cent, or 1,690,000, were responsible for families. We must add that this number included 50 per cent of all the physicians and dentists as well as 25 per cent of all the teachers and priests—personnel that from the social viewpoint was extremely valuable. The age levels of the population were also affected. Before the war 45 per cent of the Poles were under 18 years of age, but later this fell to 34 per cent. From this it is clear that death caused great losses among children and young people, thereby arresting much of the natural growth. Moreover, the increased mortality among children and the young was destined to continue after the war because of the economic, housing, and health conditions. Immediately after the war the situation was so acute that one fourth of the population needed help in their material conditions or special social location (repatriation). Among the adults 700,000 were completely unsuited for work, and so destitute that they were totally dependent upon the state, or upon the respective social organizations.

Poland also suffered enormous economic losses and thus found it difficult to achieve economic independence. Over 65 per cent of all industrial establishments had been destroyed—42.5 in the ancient territories and 22.5 in the restored territories. There was no less destruction in agriculture[1] whose reconstruction was hindered by the exchange of territories, the activities of the UPA, floods in the years 1946 and 1947,[2] and finally settlement problems in the restored territories along with adjustment difficulties under new conditions of work.[3] An important element in this devastation was the destruction of farm implements and cattle.[4]

Destruction also touched centers of craftsmanship.[5] A circumstance which made it difficult to achieve independence in this area was that the Germans made every effort to destroy the leading individuals of Polish society, and those who happened to escape this fate were in the emigration. Hence, the lack of experts and individuals qualified to organize economic life. Let us add that the war had a negative effect on the economic morality of society —a situation that could hardly help increase the productiveness of labor and bring about a stabilization of the social and economic order.

The war also had an adverse effect on the housing situation. Even though the general indication of the density of dwellings improved from 2.02 persons for each room in 1931[6] to 1.7 in 1946, the situation appeared unchanged, largely because of the transfer of people to the restored territories where the condition and number of dwellings was significantly more advantageous. The housing problem in the older territories was indeed catastrophic, as indicated by the fact that during the war we lost dwellings for 4.5 million people.

Like catastrophes marked the area of providing food for the population. It is generally accepted that the optimum of food per person is 2,400 calories per day;[7] in 1946 we were far from that, when the average was 1,600 calories. There did exist a difference between the city (1,245 calories) and the village (2,131 calories). From this we arrive at the conclusion that 11 million nonrural people of Poland were literally hungry, for their nourishment came to barely half of the required amount. This crucial period was especially harmful to the health of growing children, as illustrated by the fact that in the years 1946–1947 2.5 million youngsters under the age of 18 needed food sustenance. Other areas, of course, such as clothing and footwear, were equally critical. This is quite understandable if one considers economic exploitation in times of war, the lack of raw materials, and the usual low level of postwar production.

Among other consequences the sanitation problem,[8] if we face the facts, was not up to par even before the war. As late as 1936 we were still second highest, next to France, in terms of mortality rate.[9] But during the war and after the war the situation became decidedly worse, especially with regard to children. Evidence is the fact that 30 per cent of Polish children were underweight and had not achieved their proper growth for their age. While the percentage of mortality among children was 13.6 in 1937, it had risen to 20 by 1945—and among the repatriated families to 40–50. Poland had more crippled and blind children than any country in Europe. Let us add one-half million war invalids.

An expression of the hygienic conditions and the lack of resistence was reflected in the prevalence of contagious diseases to a greater degree than that of any other country.[10] This postwar crisis, from the health viewpoint, was chiefly indicated by tuberculosis and venereal diseases. After the war Poland had ten times as many cases of tuberculosis than England or the United States, and the consequent death rate was fifteen times greater than in those two countries. Data from 1944 illustrate this situation: in Warsaw 500 people died of tuberculosis for every 100,000 population, while in New York the rate was only 48, and in Copenhagen only 40.[11] A serious danger was also posed by cases of venereal disease, which were spreading with alarming rapidity.[12]

The lack of physicians and nursing personnel intensified the danger. Even prior to the war the number of physicians was inadequate (3.7 for 10,000 population), and this condition grew worse after the war (2.7 for every 10,000 population). This can be compared with conditions that we note in other countries (e.g., Denmark, 7.7 per 10,000 population). The situation of hospitals was even more appalling. After the war Poland needed 66,000 hospital beds and sanatorium beds for tuberculosis cases, and there were barely 4,000. In other areas of medical care the situation was no better.[13]

These few facts illustrate the critical condition of the population and its dire need of aid. This assistance could only come and did come from without; it came not only in official form (UNRRA) but also from philanthropic agencies (voluntary agencies). But it was necessary to mobilize the whole nation, which in the face of such danger had to find a solution, even at the price of great sacrifices. The state alone could not give this aid, for it was just being organized; and, strangely enough, the needs were so great and demanded such sacrifices that public authority could not demand them from the citizens and could not produce them by force. Hence, the state called for the cooperation of every social organization and opened wide possibilities for philanthropic activity.

II. THE FORMS AND AREA OF DOMESTIC PHILANTHROPIC ORGANIZATIONS

Already before the war a significant supplement to governmental social welfare (whose budget was relatively low, 2.6 per cent of the national income) came from the activity of various philanthropic organizations and the income of foundations. The number of these organizations and foundations in 1939 was over 1,511. During the occupation the whole of social welfare matters was taken over by the Rada Główna Opiekuńcza (Chief Welfare Council); only the Polish Red Cross and *Caritas* managed to survive here and there and to preserve a certain independence of action.

After the war the state saw the extent of the need and designated significant sums of money for aid. The budget from the period June 1 to December 31, 1946, assigned 18.8 per cent of all the budgeted expenditures for education and social welfare and placed the fund at the disposal of these three departments: Labor and Social Welfare (2.7), Health (3), and Education (13.1).

Besides this, social factors were called into cooperation to solve the growing difficulties. The Central Committee of Social Welfare, created for this reason, did not, however, centralize all activity after the example of RGO, for numerous organizations and foundations began to undertake activity outside the Committee. But their number was significantly smaller than before the war: only about 550 had survived. Taking into consideration those of most importance, we can thus classify and characterize them:

1. The first group contained semi-official organizations, endowed by the state with special privileges as being institutions of greater public utility. The Polish Red Cross and the Central Committee of Social Welfare especially belong here, the latter having been dissolved in 1949.

2. The second group included philanthropic organizations with a religious character. We must mention here above all the official charitable organization of the Catholic Church in Poland, *Caritas,*

which, besides conducting its own social and charitable activity, coordinated the activity of all the religious organizations, societies, fraternities, and foundations in charitable work. Other Christian Churches and the Central Jewish Committee also conducted charitable activity.

3. We can count as the third group the charitable organizations associated with some political party, which besides charitable activity engaged also in political educational work. Here we must mention the Workers' Society of Children's Friends (RTPD), related to the workers' parties (PPR and PPS), the Peasant Society of Children's Friends (ChTPD), whose existence was brief and rather insipid. In 1949 the two organizations were combined under the name Society of Children's Friends (TPD) and devoted themselves chiefly to political educational work.

4. Some organizations provided assistance only to a strictly defined group and to their own members (the Union of War Invalids of the Polish Republic, the Union of Former Political Prisoners, etc.), or to some specifically defined group (the Society of Orphanages, the Society of Scholarships, and Society of Friends of Youth in Higher Education, etc.).

5. Nor should we fail to mention here the youth organizations that conducted charitable activity: the Polish Scouts, the Red Cross Youth, etc.

6. There was a whole series of organizations that conducted charitable activity as a supplementary function, while their basic principles were quite different. We can cite here the Social and Civil League of Women, the trade unions, the Union of Peasant Self-Sufficiency, and others.

What type of activity did these organizations engage in? Mainly two categories: the acquiring of means and the provision of help for those in need. The means at the disposal of the above mentioned organizations came from various sources: collections from members, spontaneous offerings, collections of various kinds, income from property (foundations), income from enterprises, gifts from abroad, government and independent endowments. From this it is clear that not all the means at the disposal of these organizations originated in charity in the strict sense of the word, that is, disinterested free-will offerings from the population. Approximately half of these means the organizations acquired from other sources. However, they were combined on behalf of these organizations and disposed of for charitable purposes.

The type of assistance given the population by these organizations was determined in great measure by the urgency of their needs. In the first place it was important that human life be saved, and this involved provision of warm food, protection against the cold, provision of basic medical care, and the organization of prophylaxis. Hence, the first form of action stemmed from grants— and this in such a way that the greatest number of persons would satisfy their needs from a minimum of means. This involved procurement of kitchens, seeking gifts of clothing, and providing general medical and sanitary attention. The second type of aid was in the form of institutional care for those needing such aid (abandoned children, cripples, the aged, etc.).

This does not mean that effort was lacking in helping these to become independent and in gradually removing them from the relief rolls.[14] It was impossible to continue a status where one fourth of the people had to have social aid. Hence, these charitable organizations had this in mind and endeavored to help the population achieve economic independence. As early as 1945 *Caritas* tackled the agricultural problem in the Cracow and Rzeszów provinces by providing seed collected in areas that had suffered less. Efforts were made to find employment for those being aided; tools were provided; trade schools were organized, and so forth. This activity, however, developed essentially in the second phase of assistance, that is, from 1947 on, after the basic needs were satisfied to some degree.

These charitable organizations were chiefly concerned about the children, whose health and welfare were being threatened the most. Here help was given individually, for instance, to families with many children, and collectively by means of schools, nurseries, and other educational institutions. Many organizations conducted schools and maintained nurseries in which education was provided along with sustenance. During vacation months they conducted camps and day-camps, either without charge or for a very low fee. Another vital project on behalf of the youth was the establishment and maintenance of numerous reading rooms. Also, specialized care was available for all children under three years of age, a program conducted on a very large scale by most of the institutions.

After the children it was the repatriates who needed most assistance, for they were deprived of all means of support, not economically stabilized, seeking new housing, and desiring integration into the new communities. They needed extensive and diversified aid—ranging all the way from food provision to professional guidance. Hence food centers, shelters for mothers and children, night-lodging, information and counseling centers, etc., were organized to help them.

A special problem was involved in medical care, sanitary and preventive, and rehabilitation for the crippled and invalids. This meant mass action to discover illness (X-rays) and to protect against disease (innoculation), as well as individual and special action (free individual medical care, educational and rehabilitation centers).

The final, but not the least important, field of work was social educational activity: education as well as concern about raising the moral level of society. To mention only a few, there was the fight against beggary, prostitution, and alcoholism. Then there was family counseling and saving the lives of the unborn. Finally, charitable activity by its very existence—by appealing to self-sacrifice and by advocating brotherhood and respect for one's fellow human being, generosity toward others, and kindness to children—played an educational and unifying role. It created an atmosphere of mutual closeness and cooperation.

What were the dimensions of this activity? To fix them is not easy for two reasons: there are difficulties in getting complete information; and much in this charitable activity is an *imponderable* that is not comprehended in economic dimensions and cannot be defined in numbers. However, let us try to describe a reasonably close picture of the reality.

Above all, the most elementary aid—provision of food for the population—in the years 1946–1947 rested almost exclusively on the shoulders of the charitable organizations—to the extent of 90 per cent: of the 1,300 people's kitchens in existence, they conducted 1,225.[15] A second great operation was in the area of summer activities (camps and day-camps), which in the postwar years involved the following number of children: 1945, 175,000; 1946, 750,000; 1947, 785,000; 1948, 932,000; 1949, 1,072,000.[16] In the first two years this operation depended exclusively on the organizations' own funds; in 1947 they provided half of the financing; but in the subsequent years their participation gradually decreased.

Very important, too, was the share of the charitable organizations in conducting nurseries: in 1945–1946, of the general total of 2,287 nurseries, they maintained 691; in 1947, of 3,738, they maintained 1,115 (of these *Caritas* conducted 972 with 57,000 children, and 133 belonged to the Central Committee of Social Welfare with 9,600 children). From this it follows that the growth of nurseries maintained by charitable organizations was more or less proportional to the public nurseries and those maintained by labor institutions.

Very essential was the charitable organizations' investment in the care of mothers and children. Among the 232 welfare centers, 100 were under the control of labor organizations controlled by the Ministry of Industry; the rest, that is 123, belonged to only two organizations, *Caritas* and the Central Committee of Social Welfare. Even more important was the participation of the charitable organizations in the complete care of children, conducted by means of children's homes. Before the war, in 1937, there were in Poland 754 such homes (with boarding schools and dormitories); after the war, in 1947, there were 700 of them. Before the war, they were conducted by social organizations, foundations, and religious orders; after the war, 303 of them were under the supervision of *Caritas*, 70 belonged to other organizations or were independent, and only some of them belonged to the government.

Besides the giving of alms to adults, institutional care was also provided. This involved especially homes for the aged and lodgings. Significantly, in 1947, more than half of these shelters belonged to social organizations, foundations, religious orders, and denominational groups.[17] Charitable organizations also maintained 49 shelters and lodgings, of which 44 belonged to the Central Committee of Social Welfare, and 5 to *Caritas*.

It is very difficult to grasp the financial extent of charitable activity, because not everything can be expressed in figures. However, we shall give some indications illustrating the scope of this activity. The extent of funds that can be collected by an appeal to social generosity is clear from the results of the Winter Aid drives in the years 1945–1946:[18]

Sources	1945–1946	1946–1947	1947–1948
Total	195,997,000	719,928,000	877,663,000
Donations	162,589,000	518,539,000	809,541,000

Let us add that one organization, *Caritas*, in the course of one week (Charity Week) in 1947 collected about 80,000,000 złotys, and in 1948 over 103,000,000.[19] Let us call attention to the fact that while the Ministry of Labor and Social Welfare in 1947 provided over 4 billion złotys for social action,[20] the contributions from *Caritas* at that same time amounted to 2 billion złotys.[21]

It is clear from this that charitable activity responded to the existing needs by mobilizing a great number of people and means, that it was able to provide varied and many-sided action, that it was flexible in its activity by demonstrating adjustment to existing needs. Let us add that it was a continuous operation, developing and inexpensive, because it mobilized the people to idealistic and often disinterested work. Therefore, the administrative costs of this activity were particularly low. Consequently, the government authorities as well as autonomous authorities supported the activity of the charitable institutions, used them, and subsidized them in solving a whole series of social problems.

Footnotes

1. See *Agriculture and Food in Poland, UNRRA European Regional Office, Operational Papers,* no. 39 (London, 1947).
2. The flood in 1946 involved chiefly the land around Bydgoszcz; in 1947 the counties of Sochaczew and Węgrów. As a result of military operations, the Gdańsk lowlands were also flooded.
3. See J. Majka, "Rola człowieka w rolnictwie," *Znak* 10 (1958) 515.
4. See *Agriculture and Food in Poland* 9.
5. Their number fell from 191,746 in 1938 to 133,212 in 1946. See *Mały Rocznik Statystyczny 1939,* p. 106, and *Rocznik Statystyczny 1947,* p. 80.
6. Prof. S. M. Grzybowski reckons the lack of housing grew by 50 per cent between 1933 and 1939, that is, from 1,000,000 to 1,500,000. It would follow that the situation in 1939 was worse than in 1931. See S. M. Grzybowski, *Wstęp do nauki polityki społecznej* (Cracow, 1949) 145.
7. See J. Tremoilieres, "Sous-alimentation et santé publique," *Économie et Humanisme* 6 (1947) 172. According to the opinion of the Food committee of the FAO, the average level of nourishment of the whole society cannot drop below 2,200 calories per person per day without an adverse effect on public health.
8. J. Tremoilieres declares that public health is in great measure a function of nourishment.
9. See *Health Conditions in Poland, UNRRA, European Regional Office, Operational Analysis Papers* (London, 1947) no. 31, 4.
10. *Ibid.* 20.
11. *Ibid.* 26.
12. *Ibid.* 30.
13. *Ibid.* 27.
14. See J. Majka, "Usamodzielnienie," *Caritas* 3 (1947) 36.
15. This is illustrated by the following:

Owners of kitchens	Number of kitchens	Number of means in 1,000
Total	1,300	71,195
State	11	361
Autonomous	64	7,155
Charitable institutions	1,225	63,719

Source: *Rocznik Statystyczny 1948,* p. 176. See *Social Services in Poland,*

UNRRA Mission to Poland (Warsaw, 1947).

16. See *Foreign Voluntary Aid to Poland 1945–1949, an Account of the Work of the Foreign Voluntary Agencies* (Warsaw, 1949).

17. Of the 493 institutions to care for adults, 171 were autonomous, 43 belonged to the state, 95 to social organizations, 46 to foundations, 94 to religious orders, and 39 to denomination groups. See *Rocznik Statystyczny 1948*, p. 175.

18. *Rocznik Statystyczny 1948*, p. 177.

19. See *Sprawozdanie z działalności Caritas, 1947* (Cracow, 1948). See also "Wyniki cyfrowe VI Tygodnia Miłosierdzia w r. 1948," *Caritas* 5 (1949) 52.

20. An itemized statement of the expense by the Ministry of Labor and Social Welfare for social action in 1947 reports the following (in millions of złotys): maternal and child care 1,665.4; care of adults 1,608.4; care for victims of natural disasters 22.6; care for victims of accidents 28.8; care for war victims 43.7; medical care 57.9; aid to voluntary welfare institutions 451.2; miscellaneous 129.3; total 4,007.3. (Source: *Rocznik Statystyczny 1948*, p. 174.)

21. The following represents the expenditures of *Caritas* for social action in 1947 (in millions of złotys): assistance 128.2; flood relief 18.0; caritas kitchens 244.0; work places for those on welfare 14.8; nurseries 134.6; reading rooms 24.9; welfare institutions 951.9; summer activity 411.2; total 1,927.8. (Source: *Sprawozdanie z działalności Caritas za rok 1947*.)

VITAE OF CONTRIBUTORS

Father Marian Rechowicz was born September 4, 1910, in the Tarnopol province (now in the Soviet Union). He completed the middle school and his seminary training in Lwów (at present in the Soviet Union). After his ordination in 1933, he obtained his master's degree in theology at the John Casimir University of Lwów, and in 1939 his doctorate. He won his *habilitation* at the Jagellonian University in 1948. Since 1950 he has been lecturing at the Catholic University of Lublin, and in 1956–1957 he was named *professor extraordinarius*. He holds an honorary doctorate from the Catholic University of Lille. In 1956 he was named rector of the Catholic University of Lublin, an office which he held until 1965. He is a specialist in church history, namely, the Polish medieval period, and has published many works on this subject, among them a study of St. John Kanty and Benedict Hesse.

Mieczysław Gogacz, docent, was born in 1926. He received his master of arts degree at the Catholic University of Lublin in 1952 and his doctorate in 1954. He won his *habilitation* in 1960. His field is the history of medieval and contemporary philosophy. He has written extensively on those subjects.

Father Wincenty Granat was born April 1, 1900, in the Kielce province. He completed the middle school and his seminary training in Sandomierz, where he was ordained in 1924. He studied in Rome in 1923–1928 and obtained doctorates in theology and philosophy. In 1952 he began to lecture at the Catholic University of Lublin. He obtained the rank of a docent in 1956 and was named *professor extraordinarius* in 1960. His specialty is dogmatic theology. He is the author of many works, among them the ten-volume *Catholic Dogmatics*. In 1965 he was named rector of the Catholic University of Lublin.

Father Józef Pastuszka was born in 1897 in the Kielce province.

He pursued his theological and philosophical studies at the seminary in Sandomierz and furthered them in St. Petersburg (Leningrad) and in Austria. He received his doctorate in 1920. In 1930 he won his *habilitation* at the Jagellonian University in Cracow. Since 1934 he has been a professor at the Catholic University of Lublin. He was named *professor ordinarius* in 1935. He has fulfilled many functions at the university, including that of rector in 1951, and has authored many works in theology and psychology.

Father Mieczysław Krąpiec was born May 25, 1925. He was ordained in 1945 and in 1948 received his doctorate. From 1946 he lectured in philosophy at the Philosophical-Theological Institute of the Dominicans in Cracow. Since 1951 he has been lecturing at the Catholic University of Lublin. He received the title of docent in 1956 and was named *professor extraordinarius* in 1961.

Zdzisław Papierkowski was born March 29, 1903, in the province of Lwów (now in the Soviet Union). He completed his legal studies in Lwów and pursued advanced studies in Austria, Germany, and France. He received his doctorate in 1927, the rank of a docent in 1933, and was named *professor extraordinarius* in 1937, and *professor ordinarius* in 1946. His specialty is criminal law. He has been lecturing at the Catholic University since 1931. After the dissolution of the department of law and socio-economic studies, he lectured on contemporary Polish law and criminal psychology, the history of the state, and the laws of the modern Slavic states. He has produced many works in the field of criminal law and fulfilled many functions at the Catholic University of Lublin, among them that of prorector in the years 1945–1949, and again from 1957 to the present.

Jerzy Kłoczowski was born in 1924 in the Warsaw province. He completed his historical studies at Poznań University in 1948 and obtained his doctorate in 1950. Since 1950 he has been engaged at the Catholic University of Lublin at the chair of medieval history. He won his *habilitation* in 1956. He was honored as *professor extraordinarius* in 1956, and has been teaching Polish medieval history. His numerous published works are chiefly in that field. He is director of the chair of medieval history and the Institute of Historical Geography of the Church in Poland.

Aleksander Kossowski was born in 1886. He studied in the historical and philological department of the University of St. Petersburg. In the years 1918–1924 he lectured at the University of Persk (USSR), and then returned to Poland; in 1926 he was summoned to the Catholic University of Lublin. In 1938 he was named *professor extraordinarius*, and from 1954 he was a *professor ordinarius*. He was an eminent specialist in the history of church union in Poland and the history of the Reformation. He fulfilled a variety of functions in the administration of the University. He died in 1965 and left a heritage of many scholarly publications.

Jan Turowski, docent, was born in 1917 in the Lublin Province. He completed middle school in Lublin in 1936 and his studies at the Catholic University of Lublin in the years 1936–1939, 1944–1945. He received his doctorate in sociology in 1947 and the rank of docent in 1957, being named *professor extraordinarius* by the approval of the Senate in 1965. He is the director of the department of sociology at the Catholic University of Lublin. He specializes in the sociology of the village, the family, and the city, and has published a number of works in these areas.

Jerzy Ozdowski, docent, was born in 1925 in the province of Poznań. He completed his studies at the University of Poznań—doctorate and *habilitation*. He specializes in the economic sciences, predominantly in the study of services. He teaches at the Higher School of Economics in Poznań, as well as lectures at the Catholic University of Lublin on the history of social economic doctrines. He has authored works in the field of economic problems.

Father Józef Majka, docent, was born in 1918 in the province of Rzeszów. He completed his advanced studies at the Jagellonian University in Cracow and at the Catholic University of Lublin; he holds three master-of-arts degrees: theology, social economic studies, and philosophy. He received his doctorate in 1952. From 1949–1950 he has been working at the Catholic University of Lublin, where he earned his *habilitation* in 1958. His specialty is social politics, social philosophy, and the sociology of religion. His scientific works have included monographs and journal articles.

Stefan Kunowski was born in 1909. He completed his studies in *Polonistica* at the Catholic University of Lublin in 1934. From

1937 he has been engaged in scholarly work at the Catholic University and in 1945 received his doctorate, in 1957 the title of docent. His field is education and he has published pertinent scholarly works.

Przemysław Mroczkowski, docent, was born in 1915. He completed his philological studies at the Jagellonian University (French and English philology). He received his doctorate in 1947 and thereafter continued his scholarly work at the Catholic University of Lublin. He received his *habilitation* in 1951. In 1961 the Academic Senate of the Catholic University of Lublin proposed naming him *professor extraordinarius*. In 1962 he left the Catholic University to continue his work at the Jagellonian University.

Stanisław Michalczuk was born in 1933 in Kowel (at present in the Soviet Union). He completed his historical studies at the Catholic University of Lublin in the years 1951–1956 with the degree of master of arts. He has been engaged at the Catholic University in scientific work and attached to the chair of the history of art since 1957. He obtained his doctorate in 1963 and has published in the field of ecclesiastical art.

Father Mieczysław Żywczyński was born January 13, 1901, in Warsaw. In 1921 he obtained the equivalent of a Bachelor of Arts degree, and then completed his studies in the seminary of Płock, 1921–1926. In 1926 he was ordained a priest. From 1926 to 1930 he studied in the department of humanities, University of Warsaw, and from 1929–1930 was engaged in scholarly work in the *Główny Archiw Akt Dawnych* in Warsaw. The Polish Academy of Arts provided a scholarship for him to Rome in 1930. In 1931 he taught history and philosophy in the *gymnasium* in Płock, served as librarian of the Płock diocesan library, and as the vice-director of the diocesan archives. In 1933 he received his doctorate. From 1935 to 1937 he conducted research in the archives of Italy, Switzerland, and Austria. In 1939 he was removed by the Germans from his living quarters in Płock and had suffered the loss of his library and all his manuscripts. The years 1940–1941 he spent in a village in Łowicz and 1941–1942 in a village in Kielce. In 1942 he came to Warsaw incognito and taught history. From 1944–1945, after the uprising, he taught history in the *gymnasium* at Kielce and in disguised university courses. In 1945 he became deputy professor at the Catholic University of Lublin, in 1946 was named docent, and in 1954 was named *professor extraordinarius.*

Stefan Sawicki was born in 1927 in the Polesie province (at present in the Soviet Union). He completed his studies in *Polonistica* at the Catholic University of Lublin and the Jagellonian University. Since 1951 he has been engaged at the Catholic University of Lublin at the chair of Polish history. He received his doctorate in 1960. His published works deal specifically with the theory of the methodology in literature and Catholicism and literature. He is in the process of acquiring his *habilitation.*

Leokadia Małunowicz, docent, was born in 1910 in Baku in the Caucasus. She completed her studies in classical philology at the Stefan Batory University in Wilno in 1936. In 1947 she received her doctorate. She has been engaged at the Catholic University of Lublin since 1956. As docent, she is the director of the chair of classical philology and has published scholarly works in that field.